Making Russia and Turkey Great Again?

Making Russia and Turkey Great Again?

Putin and Erdoğan in Search of Lost Empires and Autocratic Power

Norman A. Graham
Folke Lindahl
Timur Kocaoglu

LEXINGTON BOOKS
Lanham • Boulder • New York • London

Published by Lexington Books
An imprint of The Rowman & Littlefield Publishing Group, Inc.
4501 Forbes Boulevard, Suite 200, Lanham, Maryland 20706
www.rowman.com

6 Tinworth Street, London SE11 5AL, United Kingdom

British Library Cataloguing in Publication Information Available

Library of Congress Cataloging-in-Publication Data

Names: Graham, Norman A., author. | Lindahl, Folke, author. | Kocaoğlu, Timur,
    1947– author.
Title: Making Russia and Turkey great again? : Putin and Erdogan in search of lost
    empires and autocratic power / Norman A. Graham, Folke Lindahl, Timur Kocaoglu.
Description: Lanham : Lexington Books, [2021] | Includes bibliographical references
    and index. | Summary: "This book discusses the rise of Putin in Russia and Erdogan
    in Turkey to authoritarian power in the context of the global debate over the fragility
    of democracy and the persistence of authoritarianism"—Provided by publisher.
Identifiers: LCCN 2020056233 (print) | LCCN 2020056234 (ebook) |
    ISBN 9781793610225 (cloth) | ISBN 9781793610249 (pbk)
    ISBN 9781793610232 (epub)
Subjects: LCSH: Authoritarianism—Russia (Federation) | Authoritarianism—Turkey. |
    Democracy—Russia (Federation) | Democracy—Turkey. | Power (Social sciences)—
    Russia (Federation) | Power (Social sciences)—Turkey. | Politics and government—
    Russia (Federation) | Politics and government—Turkey. | Putin, Vladimir
    Vladimirovich, 1952-. | Erdoğan, Recep Tayyip.
Classification: LCC JN6695 .G6947 2021 (print) | LCC JN6695 (ebook) |
    DDC 320.947—dc23
LC record available at https://lccn.loc.gov/2020056233
LC ebook record available at https://lccn.loc.gov/2020056234

Contents

List of Tables

Acknowledgments

This volume was the product of an intense set of conversations among the authors over many years of teaching, debating, and learning together under the auspices of the Center for European, Russian and Eurasian Studies (CERES) and James Madison College of Public Affairs at Michigan State University. As such, we would first like to acknowledge the supportive environment provided by Dean Sherman W. Garnett at the College and Dean Steven D. Hanson of International Studies and Programs at MSU. This goes beyond welcome financial support for research travel and gainful employment to include encouragement to develop our academic and research ties in Turkey and the Former Soviet Union. We were able to take advantage of numerous opportunities to try our ideas out on a wide range of scholars and officials at various Russian and Turkish universities and research institutions, while leading intensive study abroad programs for our students and associated faculty. We were able to witness the fragility of democracy and persistence, indeed growth of authoritarianism first hand. Russian, Turkish, and Eurasian scholars who were helpful to us are too numerous and perhaps too vulnerable to list here. You know who you are, and we are very thankful for your generous commitments of time and expertise.

Over the course of the last five years, as our ideas began to take shape, we benefitted greatly from CERES and Madison College students who kept us on our toes in a series of capstone senior seminars for our majors in International Relations and Political Theory and Constitutional Democracy which were directly focused on the future of democratic and authoritarian rule in Europe and Eurasia. More specifically, we would like to acknowledge the dedicated research assistance provided by Evan Anderson, Eric Gerson, Ryan Lumsden, Alyssa Meyer, James Millar, Cody Schulz, Alan Shulman, and Allie Virginski.

A large group of MSU faculty and visiting scholars have been important to us: inspiring this project, informing our inquiry, or commenting on early drafts. These would include George Bird, Emine Evered, Kyle Evered, Charles H. Fairbanks, Jr., Sergey Fedunyak, Eric Freedman, Axel Hadenius, Andras Lanczi, Ghia Nodia, Anthony Olcott, Martha Brill Olcott, Matt Pauly, Eric Petrie, Steven G. Pueppke, Jiaguo Qi, Simei Qing, Linda Racioppi, Michael G. Schechter, Lawrence Scott Sheets, Lilia Shevtsova, Volodymyr Tarabara, Matt Zierler, and M. Richard Zinman. We would also like to thank Mary Firdawsi for her skilled and industrious support in document preparation and formatting, as well as for her help in keeping the activities and operation of CERES running smoothly. As may be evident from some of the contents of this volume, we owe a collective debt to our inspiring teachers of Russian and Eurasian Studies during the time Graham and Kocaoglu spent at Columbia University, especially Edward Allworth, Zbigniew Brzezinski, and Marshall D. Shulman.

We cannot say enough about the patience and support we enjoyed from our families. Dr. Anna Kirkwood Graham, Carolyn Donna Kirkwood Graham, Nora Karin Kirkwood Graham, Oumatie Marajh, and Stefan Mitra Lindahl also accompanied us on numerous study ventures to Europe and Eurasia and provided interesting observations about political and economic conditions.

Editorial support and peer review comments provided by Lexington were very important to our revision process. Alison Keefner and Joseph Parry were thoroughly professional and responsive during these unusual times of pandemic and periodic lockdown.

Chapter 1

The "Waves of Democratization" versus the Persistence of Authoritarianism in Eurasia

It is not an exaggeration to suggest that the political reality with regard to democratization in various regions and countries in the world in the past thirty years has been on a roller coaster with rapid movements up and down and sharp, unpredictable turns. This is also reflected in the scholarly debate regarding the democratization process and its consolidation. It is as if the wave metaphor introduced by Samuel Huntington is an understatement.[1] If the *Journal of Democracy* is a bellwether for political scientists and policy makers on the issue, one can follow the trajectory for thirty years and identify most of these twists and turns—from the euphoria surrounding the collapse of communism and the relatively rapid democratization process in former communist countries in Eastern Europe to the more recent (the past five to ten years) focus on the question of whether democracy is in decline in many parts of the world, including the West.[2]

Other pessimistic themes have now become central for the journal; for example, "The Authoritarian Resurgence,"[3] "Authoritarianism Goes Global,"[4] "The Authoritarian Threat,"[5] "The Danger of Deconsolidation,"[6] and so on. All these trends reflect social and political events and developments taking place on virtually all continents and across multiple regions, albeit in very different forms depending on cultural and historical traditions and circumstances. There is also a noticeable rise of populism—right-wing, left-wing, or neither—and nationalism, by definition, country-specific. Taken together, these rather disturbing and largely unanticipated political and social tendencies certainly justify and make it urgent to analyze and enhance our understanding of *the fragility of democracy and the persistence of authoritarianism*. The urgency is particularly acute in the Eurasian cases of Russia and Turkey, for reasons that should be apparent to anybody who has followed both recent events and past historical patterns in these two countries.

1

Before we turn to Russia and Turkey specifically, we should make some general observations and historical remarks regarding the tension or conflict between democracy and authoritarianism. If one takes the *longue duree* on this issue, it is undeniable that authoritarianism has often been transformed into democracy—sometimes violently and through revolution; sometimes through slow reforms and long-term social and political changes. One could even make the claim that all current democracies have evolved from one form or another of authoritarianism. Before they had even taken one single step in the direction of democracy, European countries, for example, were feudal orders: hierarchical, brutal, and authoritarian. It took centuries for these orders to slowly change in the direction of democratic regimes; it took even longer for them to become well-functioning, stable democracies. For the vast majority of countries in Europe, consolidated democracy is a twentieth-century phenomenon. As John Dunn recently reminded us: "But even in Britain, as throughout the European continent, until almost the end of the nineteenth century, democracy, under the name, remained the political goal of small groups of extreme dissidents, or movements which sought to challenge the existing order frontally and fundamentally."[7]

The embryo and beginning growth of social democracy in Europe can be observed in the decades before World War I, but then two world wars, a depression, and two forms of totalitarianism disrupt and destroy the democratic evolution for thirty years in most of Western Europe and for about seventy years in East and Central Europe. This alone should give us pause regarding an overly confident faith in the inevitability of democratic consolidation, only in a handful of European countries and the former British colonies of America, Canada. Australia and New Zealand have the development of democracy being *relatively* smooth and long-term, if by long-term we mean at least a century or two rather than decades. (Still, we have to remember and reflect on the impact and legacy of slavery and the Civil War in America. Hardly a mere bump in the road.) If we move beyond these countries and beyond Europe, to take a more global perspective, the "fact" of democracy is of course even more recent and much more fragile—but of whatever depth and quality, these democracies, too, emerged from authoritarian and imperial pasts.

However, until very recently, when we discuss the history and development of the modern democratic and egalitarian sentiment, and the long evolution toward modern democratic regimes, we usually see signs of the rise of democracy and increased equality at least for the past two or three hundred years. We have, as it were, developed a meta-narrative in a "progressive" mode that spans centuries, and we continue to add new chapters to this story. Virtually all "democratization" literature in the social sciences in recent decades can be situated within this teleological perspective, albeit within a wide variety of timeframes. Nevertheless, no matter what time span, democracy *has* historically evolved out of authoritarian forms of rule, but not in the orderly fashion that the deterministic narrative seems to imply. Hence, we need to keep this in mind when we address both the fragility of democracy and the persistence of authoritarianism, but without falling into the "progressive" perspective. This was a dominant and hopeful position among both academics and journalists in the West after the fall of communism in Russia and Eastern Europe, and certainly at the beginning of Putin's rule. In Turkey, the period of democratization between 1950 and the first years of Erdoğan's rule were equally positive and infused by a positive determinism among Western observers. It is this optimistic progressivism that has changed to a more nuanced and critical perspective in recent years. This change has also resurrected the critical literature regarding both authoritarianism and totalitarianism that was written after World War II and is now permeating current evaluations of both Russia and Turkey. We will return to these thorny issues throughout the treatments of both countries, especially in the conclusion.

If contemporary political scientists tend to view democratization in terms of decades and "waves"—with more or less predictable setbacks[8]—Alexis de Tocqueville took the ultimate of long-term views. In the very introduction to *Democracy in America*, he made the following gigantic and universal claim regarding the inevitability of the growth of equality and democracy, if not in all societies, certainly in the societies of the Christian world. Quoting the relevant passage:

> If you examine what is happening in France every fifty years from the eleventh century on, at the end of each of these periods you cannot fail to perceive that a double revolution has operated on the state of society. The noble has fallen on the social ladder, and the commoner has risen; the one descends, the other climbs. Each half century brings them nearer, and soon they are going to touch.
>
> The gradual development of equality of conditions is therefore a providential fact, and it has the principal characteristics of one: it is universal, it is enduring, each day it escapes human power; all events, like all men, serve its development.[9]

Not only is this a long-term perspective, it also has to be one of the most sweeping examples of so-called unintended consequences in the history of political theory. Without venturing into an attempt to interpret the meaning of "providential fact,"[10] Tocqueville's statement will represent one side of the framework for the investigation of Russia and Turkey in this book; it will remind us of the necessity of reflecting on the underlying long-term historical continuities and the deeper patterns (however fuzzy) buried underneath the more visible short-term political and social movements of history.

In addition, Tocqueville explicitly argues both descriptively and prescriptively that, given the inevitability of this evolution, there is little or no purpose in attempting to oppose the process. "To wish to stop democracy would then appear to be to struggle against God himself, and it would only remain for nations to accommodate themselves to the social state that Providence imposes on them."[11] This does not mean, however, that Tocqueville is a historical determinist or fatalist.[12] On the contrary, he calls for "a new political science" suitable for "a world altogether new." Unfortunately, he saw few indications in France that those in power had actually acquired this new skill. Instead the leaders had looked the other way, refused to recognize the movements of events, and had "proceeded haphazardly" without trying to intervene and steer the rapidly changing political process. "Never have heads of state thought at all to prepare for it in advance; it is made despite them or without their knowing it."[13] The political will or the appropriate leadership was lacking. (This introduces the important problem of the role of political leadership, or statesmanship—a decisive dimension of both the Russian and Turkish situation.)

What then does Tocqueville mean by his "new political science"? How can human beings intervene in a process that for him appears as a "providential fact"? He answers these questions in a vague but much quoted sentence: "To instruct democracy, if possible to reanimate its beliefs, to purify its mores, to regulate its movements, to substitute little by little the science of affairs for its inexperience, and knowledge of its true interests for its blind instincts; to adapt its government to time and place; to modify it according to circumstances and men: such is the first duty imposed on those who direct society in our day."[14] Hardly a political science as we understand it, today, but one that allows for both political action and political understanding. There is also an explicit commitment to a qualitative evaluation of democracy in Tocqueville's formulation: we can judge a democracy better or worse. This normative element—if that is what we should call it—is central to Tocqueville's political science. It is, among other things, a prudent advice to his fellow aristocrats, not to lament the passing of aristocracy but to accept the democratic transition as a "fact" that can only be modified "according to circumstances and men." There is room for politics and social change, in other words, but only within democratic parameters, and there is no guarantee for success.[15] This position, especially the last point, will also be a premise for the investigation at hand.

Good or bad, the inevitability of democracy is a given, at least for most of the West; its quality, virtue, and substance are not. (Where to draw the line between an unsuccessful democracy and down-right autocratic rule remains an open question, especially in the cases of contemporary Russia and Turkey.) Our conclusion will elaborate this issue. In his own works, Tocqueville provides us with two almost opposite poles of democracy: a negative one in the form of France and a more positive one in the case of America. In France, democracy blossomed originally (as a result of the French Revolution) under a despotic regime that replaced the feudal authoritarian order in the name of equality and the common good. It was a top-down approach to democratization that replaced one central authoritarian regime by an even more centralized government: "it sought to increase the power and jurisdiction of the central authority."[16] The pertinent element in Tocqueville's analysis of France is the remarkable continuity between the pre- and post-revolutionary conditions: "Under the old regime, as nowadays, there was in France no township, borough, village, or hamlet, however small, no hospital, factory, convent, or college which had a right to manage its own affairs as it thought fit or to administer its possessions without interference. Then, as today, the central power held all Frenchmen in tutelage. The term 'paternal government' had not yet been invented, but the reality already existed."[17] Although the ideology and rhetoric of the Revolution emphasized both liberty and equality, Tocqueville shows how historical preconditions and prejudices pushed all political actors and classes away from liberty and in the direction of equality under a centralized, authoritarian government—before, during, and after the Revolution. In the midst of a tremendous break with the past, several crucial features—most importantly, for our purpose, centralization, top-down reforms, leadership, and authoritarianism—remain constant. Not even the Revolution itself attempted to change these aspects: "the reason why the principle of the centralization of power did not perish in the Revolution is that this very centralization was at once the Revolution's starting-off point and one of its guiding principles."[18] On this ground alone, we can see a long-term tendency in the French democratization process that makes for an illiberal democratic component at the center of its national politics.[19] (There is a striking similarity with Turkey's evolution toward democracy; the illiberal and authoritarian features are a constant from the late Ottoman Empire and the Tanzimat reforms in the nineteenth century, to Atatürk's nationalism and Erdoğan's contemporary authoritarianism. A similar historical continuity can be said to exist in Russia from pre-revolutionary times, throughout the Soviet period, and Putin's Russia today.)

This illiberal dimension has critical consequences for both the democratic and the liberal elements of society. The highly centralized system prevents, or at the very least, discourages the emergence of a robust civil society. The necessary "intermediary bodies" between the state and the individual fail to materialize, and this failure further accentuates the power of the already dominant "paternal" government. The strongly anti-clerical stand of the French Revolution added another element that weakened the mores of the people and strengthened the hand of the central government. Self-government in the democratic equation loses out to a top-down authoritarian government, endorsed perhaps by a majority of the people, but without proper liberties and duties for the citizens—rule *for* the people (even in the name *of* the people), but not *by* the people. Hence, a vicious circle permeates the French democratic evolution that threatens and debases good government: a tradition of centralized government undermines political initiatives on the local level; civil society, with its intermediary bodies, remains weak and underdeveloped which necessitates more central government intervention, and thereby makes local initiatives unnecessary, etc. In combination with poor and of course ambitious and power-driven leadership at the top of the government, this is a political pattern that is demonstrated today by both Russia under Putin and Turkey under Erdoğan.

As the history of nineteenth- and twentieth-century France shows, this is an historical trend difficult to break, but not impossible. Today, in spite of all current political problems, there is consensus that France has turned itself into a consolidated liberal democracy, even if its liberal component remains fragile and contested.[20] Top-down, centralized features persist, but most of the calamities identified by Tocqueville have been cured or substantially weakened, and France has taken its place as a leading "democratic" nation in the European Union. Whatever the strengths and weaknesses of French democracy, its authoritarian past has slowly but surely transformed into something of a modern liberal democracy. Again, we see how authoritarianism, if not fosters, certainly precedes but also influences democracy. And it is an interesting and telling example that liberalism does not have to be a prerequisite for democracy: France was notably and undoubtedly an illiberal democracy before it became a (sort of) liberal democracy. This, too, will be important when we turn to Russia and Turkey in following chapters.

If France represents one pole—the top-down, authoritarian path—in Tocqueville's analysis of democratization, the United States illustrates the more positive one. The latter is characterized by a bottom-up approach to government, a participatory and public-spirited local population, and the presence of religious mores supportive of democracy. This familiar perspective begins with the juxtaposition of the top-down approach in Europe with the bottom-up of America: "In most European nations, political existence began in the higher regions of society and was communicated little by little and always in an incomplete manner to the various parts of the whole. In America, on the contrary, one can say that the township had been organized before the county, the county before the state, the state before the Union."[21] The main consequence of these local origins is the broad participatory activities that are necessary and encouraged on the grass-root levels throughout both colonial and post-colonial America; in short, the conditions were conducive for both the creation of the civil and political associations that make up civil society, and the appropriate mores—the habits of the heart and mind—essential for the development of a well-functioning liberal democracy.

The positive role of civil society in a democracy is now all-too familiar in the social science literature, and does not need further elaboration here, although we will of course return to the issue below in the analysis of democratization in Russia and Turkey. What is often not discussed at length is another element of American society that Tocqueville makes central for the strengthening of the virtuous circle of democracy: public education. "But it is by the prescriptions relative to public education that, from the beginning, one sees revealed in the full light of day the original character of American civilization."[22] Tocqueville immediately makes the observation that in all the preambles to the ordinances that create public schools in the townships, there are religious references and that, "in America, it is the observance of divine laws that guides man to freedom."[23] He then connects, again in a well-known manner, "the *spirit of religion* and the *spirit of freedom*."[24] Both are necessary, and each one creates a boundary and a balance for the other. "Religion sees in civil freedom a noble exercise of the faculties of man; in the political world, a field left by the Creator for the efforts of intelligence. Free and powerful in its sphere, satisfied with the place that is reserved for it, it knows that its empire is all the better established when it reigns by its own strengths alone and dominates over hearts without support."[25] In a different context, but still in Volume I, Tocqueville addresses the question of truth in religion but sidesteps it by making it secondary for his purpose: "If it serves man very much as an individual that his religion be true, this is not so for society. Society has nothing to fear nor to hope from the other life; and what is most important to it is not so much that all citizens profess the true religion but that they profess a religion."[26] It is an open question, but an important one, to what degree this argument applies to Putin's Russia and Erdoğan's Turkey. In the latter case, it is more obvious perhaps than in the former, although both leaders certainly make use of religion to strengthen their own powers.

This quick outline of a few of Tocqueville's central arguments regarding the relationship between democracy, local independence (decentralized governments), widespread public education, civil society, religious mores, and political freedom are included here to illustrate the virtuous circle that can exist to further and elevate a democracy. One can take this a step further and suggest there are also important relationships between this degree of democracy and broad-based economic prosperity as well.

Admittedly, America is the outlier, and the exceptional case, since its unique historical circumstances that play the central role in Tocqueville's long-term scenario are impossible to duplicate. The American model has nevertheless provided somewhat of an ideal type for the contemporary discussion of democratization and together with the French case set up the two poles between which one can move in the analysis of cases like Russia and Turkey.

It will be the theological-political problem that will loom large in the discussion of Turkey.[27] Russia's experiment(s) with democracy share some commonalities with the case of Turkey, but there are also some distinctions.

Lest there be no misunderstanding: neither model is a deterministic one—Tocqueville presents argument for corrections and possibilities in the French case; he worries, especially in Volume II of *Democracy in America,* about the future and prospect for American democracy. Virtuous circles can easily turn vicious; vicious circles can, over a long period, be reversed. There are no guarantees in either case. Contrary to much mainstream academic opinion, the life and health of liberal democracy is precarious under the best of circumstances. (In this sense, Tocqueville's dichotomy might be overstated.) This is why we speak of "The Fragility of Democracy"—particularly in political systems like those that have formed in Russia and Turkey, with a long tradition of authoritarianism and a supply of strong personal leaders. There can be tyranny in the midst of apparent democracy.

The argument in the chapters that follow is that the fragility of democracy is clear in the post-Cold War cases of Russia and Turkey. Putin and Erdoğan began their rule as the result of fair electoral success and built a popular following after some important policy initiatives to reclaim or restore order and extend benefit. In each case, there was a struggle with culture and tradition—perhaps the persistence of authoritarianism (and its acceptance), as well as difficult economic and political challenges. Both leaders have ambition to restore their countries to international prominence—indeed recover lost empire to some extent, while at the same time ensuring that domestic challenges to their growing political power were negated. Both have been largely successful in the latter, at least in the short to medium term but have been less successful in the former; thus far there have been serious limitations in building international power and regional stability. Both have contributed to increased instability in their neighborhoods and have stimulated some responses from real and potential adversaries that might be regarded as reckless, perhaps with unintended consequences for their own security postures. Putin and Erdoğan also face substantial challenges in building dynamic economies and broad-based prosperity. They risk stagnation at best and catastrophic collapse at worst.

Putin and Erdoğan have had opportunities to remake their political economies to meet the needs of their broad populations, as well as to contribute to regional order; but both squandered them in favor of personal wealth and power gain and the desire to control their own personal political security. Regional order was in fact disrupted substantially or at least threatened at times by both Putin and Erdoğan, during a larger global pattern of disruption and weakened international norms and institutions. Authoritarianism is persistent and on the rise in much of Europe and Eurasia. The promising trend toward democratization that had developed in the wake of the collapse of the Soviet Union has been dashed in Russia and in some of the other post-Soviet successor states, while the progress toward liberal democracy made by successive regimes in Turkey after Atatürk has been substantially curtailed by Erdoğan. The fragility of incipient democracies is evident, and many would argue that many mature democracies are threatened now to a degree largely unanticipated in the late twentieth century.

We argue that this is in large part due to the machinations of Presidents Putin and Erdoğan —each driving for centralized power, wealth, and personal security, following a long established pattern of emerging dictators. Long-term cultural patterns and influences have been important and in many respects have enabled both Putin and Erdoğan to gain substantial support for their presidencies. Nationalism is clearly important to their relative popularity and has been manipulated skillfully by each, though to different degrees and extent.

Finally, one must add the impact of the naiveté and incompetence in key Western democratic governments and opinion outlets, which at times served to fan the flames of Russian and Turkish nationalism and misread the true intentions of Putin and Erdoğan. Part of this was wishful thinking—hoping to welcome a fully democratic Russia and Turkey into the Western liberal fold—urging Russia to liberalize its political and economic system and to embrace globalization and its attendant international institutions: the World Bank, IMF, WTO, and even NATO. At the same time, Western leaders, too readily perhaps, accepted the prospect of Erdoğan leading Turkey to a closer relationship with the European Union, as a perceived moderate Muslim leader who could also make Turkey a key bridge between the West and the Muslim countries of the greater Middle East. Both leaders had alternative priorities and plans in mind. The regional and indeed global order is threatened by this misreading and the subsequent failure of policy and action.

The reader will note that we have placed a question mark (?) after the main title of this volume: *Making Russia and Turkey Great Again?* One could easily place a question mark on the thousands of "MAGA" hats worn by the enthusiasts that President Trump has attracted to his political rallies from 2016. In the case of both Russia and Turkey, we would argue that the jury is clearly still out on the question. Both Putin and Erdoğan have succeeded in making their countries relevant to many of the main challenges faced by states and citizens of the world, as disrupted and depressed as they may now be. This volume will provide important background to this question and endeavor to note and analyze some of the key elements of the prospects for a return to greatness. We have become convinced that both countries have a long way to go in this journey, and we have serious doubts that either president is up to the task. Indeed, we are skeptical that they can see beyond their own personal interests, ambition, and drive for power to do what would be required. Our plan of presentation for this set of arguments is as follows:

Chapter 2 describes the rise of the Soviet Union, with its periods of totalitarian rule, the bankrupting of the economy under Brezhnev, and the political and economic collapse after the reform failures of Mikhail Gorbachev. Considerable attention is devoted to the concept of totalitarianism and how it may or may not apply to successive Soviet political regimes—and beyond. The growing dysfunctionality of the Soviet system, especially economically— unmistakable structural weakness, in the face of the technological revolution underway in the West and East Asia—made the need for serious reform strikingly apparent. Gorbachev's approach in response clearly failed and indeed unleashed forces that would doom his rule and in fact lead to the disintegration of the Union.

Chapter 3 discusses the chaotic 1990s under President Boris Yeltsin. His "radical" reforms were rather less successful than those of several neighboring East and Central European transition countries, in part due to design flaws and inconsistency, but also due to fierce opposition in the democratically elected Duma, which included a complex mix of former communists, who sought a return to state socialism in some form and nationalists who sought to reclaim international prominence and an independent foreign policy. Yeltsin's foreign policy was decidedly pro-Western at times. Unfortunately, key Western leaders tended to ignore Yeltsin's increasingly precarious political position as the economic dislocation of ineffective transition was apparent. They declined to provide substantial financial assistance at key points and ignored the distinctive political economic challenges at work, as they advised adherence essentially to the Washington Consensus strategy for economic liberalization. The 1998 financial crisis, in part brought on or at least worsened by misguided IMF policies, stemmed the modest progress toward economic transition; the economic power of the oligarchs that had profited from the corrupt privatization of rich state assets, left Yeltsin's state with little to invest or expend. Yeltsin resigned and left the reins of government to Vladimir Putin.

Chapter 4 analyzes the rise of Vladimir Putin, and his systematic consolidation of autocratic power. Initially, he was welcomed as a stabilizing savior who moved to recover the tradition of a strong state and claw back economic power from the oligarchs. Putin profited from high oil and gas prices in his early economic recovery policies, and his efforts to centralize and strengthen the state were adopted readily by the Duma. Re-elected easily in subsequent elections, even while economic stagnation began to emerge, he established a patronal political system fortified by legislation and constitutional changes that seem to ensure his centralized rule for the foreseeable future.

The chapter proceeds to analyze the elements of Putin's apparent failure to produce a dynamic, globally competitive economy beyond its natural resource exports, not to mention his inability or lack of desire to achieve broad-based prosperity for the Russian citizenry; systemic and debilitating corruption prevails. The chapter concludes with a discussion of Putin's search for lost empire in his increasingly aggressive actions to redress Western slights and reassert Russian power. Putin is highly successful in channeling Russian nationalism and challenging Western political and economic liberalism in thought and deed. But his actions had unintended consequences in some cases. Russian security and international standing have not been enhanced.

Chapter 5 describes the establishment and development of the Turkish Republic by Mustafa Kemal Atatürk. It shows the intellectual and political background for Atatürk's convictions as he became the Founder and popular hero of the Turkish Republic. We also discuss his ability to connect a strong Turkish nationalism with modernization and radical reforms, heavily influenced by Western ideas. He ruled a one-party state with authoritarian and sometimes brutal methods but still established a lasting and popular foundation for the next few decades after his death in 1938. Establishing a secular state was a clear part of his program, especially for urban elites. We argue that he underestimated the challenges involved in this, as became clear with the rise of Recep Tayyip Erdoğan, given his large support among rural Turks who continued to hold Islam close to their hearts.

Chapter 6 analyzes the subsequent efforts at modernization and democratization, and also the growing centralization of autocratic power by Erdoğan. It includes a brief discussion of Ismet İnönü, who took over power after Atatürk's death. İnönü introduced a multiparty system that lasted for half a century, with temporary interruptions by military coups. It appeared that democratization had taken hold, and this was reinforced by some degree of economic liberalization. Throughout this period, a gradual re-Islamization took place undermining Atatürk's vision of a secularized Turkey. The chapter ends with an analysis of Erdoğan's rule from 2002 until this day. The authoritarian tendency during his regime was reinforced substantially by the failed coup of 2016.

What emerges finally as we return to these themes in the conclusion is a clear picture of two authoritarian leaders who have stable situations in the medium term but who are far from securing the long-term stability and prosperity for which their compatriots yearn. Whether this yearning is shared by Putin and Erdoğan, along with personal power and wealth motivations, is yet to be seen. What drives them to authoritarian rule? We review some of the recent literature on "Why Dictators Emerge" to this end. Authoritarian leaders who have the broad national interests of their populations front and center seem to be quite rare. Putin and Erdoğan thus far cannot be counted among that modest number. Indeed, both seem to fall prey to what may be called the "Dictator's Dilemma": To achieve a successful modern state, a leader must modernize and diversify the economy and encourage innovation. Measureable performance is important. But diversification and innovation introduces new ideas and new centers of power into the country. Modern communication systems and media provide great opportunity for idea exchange and collaborative entrepreneurial activity, but there is also the danger of subversive communication—subversive to the dictator. It is hard for any emerging dictator to resist the reflex to try to control the media—seeking to eliminate the vestiges of a free press and to block or take down unfriendly websites and platforms of social media. Similarly, the temptation to ensure electoral success by eliminating centers of opposition is hard to resist, even if they may have valuable ideas and qualities for the pursuit of national prosperity.[28]

Is there no other future for Russia and Turkey? If not, then it seems that there is little prospect for broad-based prosperity for Russians or Turks. We conclude with some commentary on the implications of authoritarian rule in Russia and Turkey for the prospect of continued disruption of the post–World War II order. Memories of the chaos and conflict that followed World War I, especially with the disruption of the Great Depression, have faded it seems. The return to nationalist and protectionist strategies are evident in both Russia and Turkey, as the leaderships seek to gain independence and status. The prospect for regional and perhaps global conflict appears stronger than at any time since World War II, as economies weaken from the impact of trade wars and the COVID-19 pandemic.

NOTES

1. Samuel P. Huntington, *The Third Wave: Democratization in the Late Twentieth Century* (Norman: University of Oklahoma Press, 1991).

2. *Journal of Democracy*, 26, no. 1 (January 2015).

3. Ibid., 26, no. 2 (April 2015).

4. Ibid., 26, no. 3–4 (July and October 2015).

5. Ibid., 27, no. 1 (January 2016).

6. Ibid., 27, no. 3 (July 2016).

7. John Dunn, *Democracy: A History* (New York: Atlantic Monthly Press, 2005), p. 153.

8. Huntington, *The Third Wave*.

9. Alexis de Tocqueville, *Democracy in America*, trans. and ed. Harvey Mansfield and Delba Winthrop (Chicago and London: The University of Chicago Press, 2000), pp. 5–6. There is another, equally famous, *longue duree* argument in Tocqueville that

should be mentioned: his claim that the conditions surrounding the origins of a nation are decisive for later social and political developments. Tocqueville makes the analogy between the growth of a human being and the birth and aging of a nation: "The man is so to speak a whole in the swaddling clothes of his cradle." And: "Something analogous takes place in nations. Peoples always feel [the effects of] their origins. The circumstances that accompanied their birth and served to develop them influence the entire course of the rest of their lives." Ibid., 28.

10. Mansfield and Winthrop's definition of "providential fact" can serve well for the purpose here: "A providential fact is a trend of contingencies too constant not to have been planned, yet not within the planning capacity of human beings, not even a full generation of them." Harvey C. Mansfield, Jr. and Delba Winthrop, "Tocqueville's New Political Science," in Cheryl B. Welch, ed., *The Cambridge Companion to Tocqueville* (Cambridge and New York: Cambridge University Press, 2006), p. 102.

11. Tocqueville, *Democracy in America*, p. 7. For a fascinating and even longer perspective than Tocqueville's, see Larry Siedentop, *Inventing the Individual: The Origins of Western Liberalism* (Cambridge: The Belknap Press of Harvard University Press, 2014). For Siedentop, the coming of equality and the recognition of the individual—linked to Christianity—is a matter of millennia; not centuries. His book, in other words, is a call for patience and humility.

12. "The providential fact leaves us between the extremes of determinism and arbitrariness (which amount to the same)." Mansfield and Winthrop, "Tocqueville's New Political Science," in Welch, ed. *The Cambridge Companion*, p. 102.

13. Tocqueville, *Democracy in America*, p. 7.

14. Ibid.

15. As Mansfield and Winthrop formulate this argument: "Aristocracy and democracy are successive eras in history, not constant possibilities for human beings to choose between or to mix, as Aristotle argued." And: "The object of political science is politics as divided into democracy and aristocracy, but this generality is wrapped in the particular fact that providence has made our age a democratic revolution." Mansfield and Winthrop, "Tocqueville's New Political Science," in Welch ed., *The Cambridge Companion*, pp. 100, 102.

16. Alexis de Tocqueville, *The Old Regime and the French Revolution*, trans. Stuart Gilbert (New York: Doubleday; Anchor Books, 1955), p. 19.

17. Ibid., p. 51.

18. Ibid., p. 60.

19. For a recent discussion of the relationship between democracy and liberalism that also informs my own understanding of the issue, see Marc F. Plattner, *Democracy Without Borders? Global Challenges to Liberal Democracy* (Lanham, MD: Rowman & Littlefield Publishers, 2008), esp. Chapters 4–5.

20. For an assessment on contemporary French politics, from a social democratic perspective, see Timothy B. Smith, *France in Crisis: Welfare, Inequality and Globalization since 1980* (Cambridge and New York: Cambridge University Press, 2004). For a different, and more positive take on French civil society, see Pierre Rosanvallon, *The Demands of Liberty: Civil Society in France since the Revolution*, trans. Arthur Goldhammer (Cambridge and London: Harvard University Press, 2007).

21. Tocqueville, *Democracy in America*, p. 40.

22. Ibid., p. 41.

23. Ibid., p. 42.

24. Ibid., p. 43 (italics in the original).

25. Ibid.

26. Ibid., p. 278.

27. For a definition of this problem, different from Tocqueville, but still in his spirit, see Pierre Manent, *An Intellectual History of Liberalism*, trans. Rebecca Balinski (Princeton: Princeton University Press, 1994), pp. 3–9.

28. See: Ronald Wintrobe, *The Political Economy of Dictatorship* (UK: Cambridge University Press, 1998), especially chapter 2; Torrey Taussig, "The Autocrat's Succession Dilemma," *The American Interest*, March 14, 2018; and Xin Sun, "Autocrats' Dilemma: The Dual Impacts of Village Elections on Public Opinion in China," *China Journal*, 71 (January, 2014).

Part I

FROM THE SOVIET UNION TO THE RUSSIAN FEDERATION

Chapter 2

Authoritarianism and Totalitarianism in the Soviet Union

Is there an irresistible tendency toward authoritarianism in Russia that is somehow related to political culture and history?

At least two key questions flow from this:

1) Is this a universal strategy applied readily by most authoritarian leaders at some point? (If so, does it usually work in the long term?)
2) If it is at least common in Russia and Eurasia, does it reflect long-standing imperatives and constraints in the region or is there something stable that is inhibiting democracy and encouraging authoritarianism (again) in Russia?

There are several recent and interesting interpretations of Soviet and Russian political history that begin to shed light on these questions. William Zimmerman argued in *Ruling Russia* that in the 1930s, the USSR was totalitarian but gradually evolved into a "normal" authoritarian system.[1] After the collapse of this system in 1991, the Russian Federation then evolved from a competitive authoritarian to again a normal authoritarian system under Putin. What he terms the selectorate —that chooses the decision makers—is a constant feature but one that has evolved across different regimes since the end of tsarist rule. The selectorate was limited in the period after the revolution and contracted further during Joseph Stalin's dictatorship, only to expand somewhat after his death. Zimmerman also assessed Russia's political prospects in future elections. He predicted that while a return to totalitarianism in the coming decade is unlikely, so too is democracy.

Zimmerman noted that Western and Russian scholars with access to the Soviet archives on the years 1937 and 1938

> . . . documented the features of Stalinist totalitarianism—the atomization and hyper-mobilization of society, the depths of the terror, and the absence of intra-elite norms. Over time these attributes of Stalinist totalitarianism gradually softened (the threat remained), the society become less mobilized, and modest but significant intra-elite norms emerged. Gradually, the mobilization system evolved into a more conventional (read "full" or "normal") authoritarianism, hence the need to distinguish two Soviet systems.[2]

One can argue that the second conventional authoritarian system was less successful in building a prosperous society—without the mobilization and the task of heavy industrialization (mission accomplished) where such mobilization could pay real dividends—along with the successful mobilization system during World War II. Zimmerman argued that there is no consensus on how to characterize the post-communist Russian political systems, citing several competing conceptions.[3]

After 1996, he pointed to the evolution to a "normal police state" with the 2008 selection of Dmitry Medvedev to replace Putin [temporarily] as an "election-type event." Levitsky and Way argue that of thirty-five states coded as competitive authoritarian in 1990–95, Russia and Belarus were the two that were coded as "full authoritarian" in 2008.[4]

Zimmerman concluded his analysis with an assessment of the transition from Medvedev as president back to Putin as president in the 2012 elections. In his words:

> This "castling" did not sit well with a sizeable fraction of the Russian populace. Initially they were stalled by a variant of the first mover problem and did little by way of public demonstration until November when Putin was whistled (booed) at a boxing event in Moscow.[5]

As we shall see in chapter 4, there was some strengthening of political opposition versus Putin, particularly in the December, 2011 Duma elections, but he prevailed in the presidential elections the following March with ease. Moreover, the period that followed was characterized by systematic repression of the opposition and the media. Zimmerman concluded that Russia was best described as competitive authoritarianism, and he doubted that it would either change to Stalinist style totalitarianism or return to incipient democratization.[6] The more recent situation would lead us to agree on the latter, but not rule out the former.[7]

THE CONCEPT OF TOTALITARIANISM AND ITS APPLICATION TO THE USSR AND BEYOND

Totalitarianism is a concept used to describe political systems in which a state regulates nearly every aspect of public and private life. Totalitarian regimes or movements maintain themselves in political power by means of:

- an all-embracing ideology and propaganda disseminated through the state-controlled mass media;
- a single party that controls the state, personality cults, control over the economy, regulation and restriction of free discussion and criticism;
- the use of mass surveillance;
- a monopoly on control of weapons; and
- the widespread use of terror tactics.

What Then is the Difference between Authoritarian and Totalitarian States?

Most scholars seem to agree that totalitarianism seeks to mobilize entire populations in support of a coherent ideology and is intolerant of activities which are not directed toward the goals of the state, entailing repression or state control of business, labor unions, churches, or political parties.[8]

The concept of totalitarianism was criticized severely in the 1960s and 1970s.[9] This seemed to coincide with what Zimmerman described as the Soviet Union's transition to a normal authoritarian state after the death of Stalin. But the story is more complicated than that, as analysts began to question the evolution of the Cold War and interpret Soviet politics and society through a less ideological lens.[10] This was complicated by the debate among European intellectuals over what Raymond Aron termed the danger of tyranny by a "secular religion" and his clever flipping of a famous Marxist quote in his proposition that Marxism was *The Opium of the Intellectuals*. Aron concluded his path-breaking critique of intellectuals besotted with Marxist/Communist ideology, despite the Stalinist totalitarian example, with the following passage:

> The secular religions dissolve into politico-economic opinions as soon as one abandons the dogma. Yet the man who no longer expects miraculous changes either from a revolution or an economic plan is not obliged to resign himself to the unjustifiable. It is because he likes individual human beings, participates in living communities, and respects the truth, that he refuses to surrender his soul to an abstract ideal of humanity, a tyrannical party, and an absurd scholasticism.[11]

Aron's student, Francois Furet, subsequently depicted the dangers of fascination with ideology in *The Passing of an Illusion*.[12] Gradually, Furet and Aron shifted much of the intellectual climate in France, indeed Europe, away from ideological commitment to the promises of Marxist theory.

Most striking in this effort was Furet's characterization of the willingness of the French left to give Stalin a pass for totalitarian excess, apparently because the goals of his professed social project were laudable. A former Marxist himself, who had changed his perspective after the brutal Soviet repression of the Hungarian revolt against the Communist yoke in 1956, he traced the rise and fall of Communism and its "twin," Fascism, in twentieth-century Europe. He described the two regimes in rich detail:

> Bolshevism and National Socialism shared a religion of power, the most openly professed in the world. To conquer and retain power, any means were good, not only against enemies but against friends as well, even assassination—a common practice for both parties, regimes, and dictators. Nevertheless, even this precious power originated in a superior logic—the end it was intended to fulfill, that of fulfilling history, hidden in the tumult of conflict, revealed by ideology. Terror, no longer reserved for real or imagined reprisals against the enemy, became a daily practice of government. The purpose was to impose universal fear, the key to realizing the future, whose secret was the exclusive possession of the Supreme leader, followed by the Party. The fact that Communism and Fascism assigned contradictory roles to history and reason—the emancipation of the proletariat versus the domination of the Aryan race—mattered little. Though not insignificant on a philosophical level, that distinction detracts nothing from the similarity of the nature and workings of the two political systems.[13]

Referring to the impact of the collapse of the Soviet Union in 1991, Furet noted in conclusion:

> But the end of the Soviet world in no way alters the democratic call for another society, and for that very reason we have every reason to believe that the massive failure of Communism will continue to enjoy attenuating circumstances in world opinion, and perhaps even renewed admiration. The Communist idea will not rise again in the form in which it died. The proletarian revolution, Marxist–Leninist science, the ideological election of a party, a territory, or an empire have undoubtedly come to an end along with the Soviet Union.[14]

Furet subsequently engaged in an interesting debate, through correspondence, with German historian, Ernst Nolte, on the similarities and distinctions between Nazism and Communism. Was Nazism/fascism a response to Bolshevism (as Nolte posits) or were they both manifestations of a critical response to liberal democracy and bourgeois individualism?[15] Furet comments on the impact of the collapse of the Soviet Union on the debate with:

> The more capitalism triumphs, the more it is despised. With the Soviet Union it has lost one of its foils, which had made it the showcase of freedom. It has been deprived of its best argument—anticommunism . . . . It no longer has to justify another society, because no other society exists anymore. It can be content to criticize democratic society as nondemocratic, that is, incapable of answering the expectations it created and the promises it made. It is now rooted only in the oldest dream of modern democracy, which consists of separating democracy and capitalism, to keep one and drive out the other, when together they form a single history.[16]

Furet extends his discussion of democracy and totalitarianism, with interesting reflections on *The Passing of an Illusion,* in his last book *Lies, Passions & Illusions: The Democratic Imagination in the Twentieth Century.* This began as a dialogue with philosopher Paul Ricoeur but was disrupted by Furet's untimely death in July of 1997. His reflection on the Soviet collapse is thought provoking: "When opened just a crack to liberty, [by Gorbachev] 'real' socialism collapsed like a house of cards, incapable of competition with capitalist civilization . . . . Soviet Communism perished through its incapacity to fulfill its ambitions for a better society."[17] Furet goes on, though, to express concern about the "surrender to nationalist craziness, to the arrogance of national superiority."[18] He writes: "I am a European because it is the least bad way of being true to the national idea in a very depressed landscape, where Europe is no longer what it was."[19]

Universalism remains an illusion, however. Furet speaks with some eloquence to put this in historical perspective:

> Universalism never provides a framework for action. We see this very clearly today with respect to humanitarianism and human rights. Less than ever do these ideas provide a framework for politics; inevitably they bring to mind the words of Pascal: "He who would act the angel, acts the beast." In reality political action in the nineteenth and twentieth centuries has occurred through the interests and passions of classes and nations. I would say that this was already true during the French Revolution. All the French Revolutionaries spoke of universality. All of them. And they conquered Europe in the name of a "great nation."[20]

This theme of nationalism is persistent in both the Russian and Turkish cases to this day, as we will return to throughout the book. Whether it expresses itself in Russian "Eurasianism" or Turkish "Neo-Ottomanism" it is still nationalism that infuses the politics in both countries. Universalism and/or human rights are not on the agenda.

The "lies" element of Furet's title in this book is perhaps best summarized in the following passage:

> The Communists' most reprehensible behavior was in lying about the Soviet regime. We can reproach the Communists much less for what they did—after all, in a country like France, they were mostly on the side of the angels—than for what they said, or, inversely, what they did not say. They never stopped lying. This lie, which today seems so huge, so obvious, was shared and believed to such an extent only because it was not a deliberate deception. In the twentieth century, the lie encountered the passion for democratic universalism of which the Soviet Union was supposed to be the historical legend; that is why it had to be fanatically protected from contamination by forces opposed to violence and dictatorship.[21]

This is later amplified with his criticism of the European left's animus toward capitalism:

> To add some "materialistic" weight to the contrast, the Communists attempted to anchor it in economics, casting Fascism as the product of financial capitalism's final phase: henceforth the only real anti-Fascist was necessarily anticapitalist and therefore Communist. This thesis is absurd, but the fact that it was so widespread in the twentieth century and so often held for true (which remains the case in certain quarters in spite of the now available evidence against it) shows that it draws in strength more from political passion than from intellectual coherence. Once again, we return to Orwell's judgment: the twentieth century Left was anti-Fascist but not antitotalitarian—an excellent summary of the predominant role played by the Communist idea.[22]

This double standard remains remarkably persistent to this day. Violence, repression, and dictatorship are overlooked if it is perceived as "a good cause"—even by radical pacifists. If it can be formulated in terms of "necessity" or "progress," it is acceptable or at least excusable. (Just to give one example: Maduro's Venezuela: millions of people starving, millions of people fleeing, and opposition jailed, repressed, or exiled—all in the name of the Bolivarian communist/socialist Revolution. The apologists for this dictatorship are plentiful.)

Of course it can be argued that this debate has a much longer tradition, with roots in the French Revolution, according to prominent political theorists like J. L. Talmon. For example, in his classic work on *The Origins of Totalitarian Democracy* (1951), he introduced his concern about totalitarian democracy or *Political Messianism* which along with liberal democracy constituted the key streams of political contention up to the present. In his words,

> The totalitarian democratic school, on the other hand, is based upon the assumption of a sole and exclusive truth in politics. It may be called political Messianism in the sense that it postulates a preordained, harmonious and perfect scheme of things, to which men are irresistibly driven, and at which they are bound to arrive. It recognizes ultimately only one plane of existence, the political. It widens the scope of politics to embrace the whole of human existence.[23]

Talmon continued his writing on the emergence of *Political Messianism* with a book of the same title, first published in 1960, which moved from the French revolutionary roots to *The Romantic Phase* through 1848. While detailing the impact of the industrial revolution and streams of eighteenth and nineteenth-century political thought, he stressed:

> It was Karl Marx's deepest conviction that the total concentration of all assets, which the Industrial Revolution was making imperative, and the growing discomfiture of the shrinking minority of monopolists overwhelmed by the recurrent crises of overproduction and besieged by the cohorts of awakened proletarians—imminent, was bound to result in the total liberation of man by the almost automatic transformation of self-alienation into self-recovery.[24]

> As an aspiration to total change brought about by a universal revolution, Political Messianism is a manifestation of the dichotomy that runs through the whole of European history: the permanent tension, breaking out now and again into sharp conflict, between some abstract, universalist, proselytizing creed, and the intractable resistance of forces which may appear to have no other justification than that they are just there. The whole struggle between political Messianism and the objective obstacles, as well as the rivalry between it and the other ideologies, such as those of the Right, Liberalism of various shades (including liberal democracy), and nationalism, may be presented as the conflict between Unity and diversity.[25]

It should be pointed out that contemporary liberal democracy also contains elements of universalism—and even a disguised form of Political Messianism—in its emphasis on human rights as being universal. As we will argue in the conclusion, this poses a dilemma for the West, especially the European Union, but also for North America. Universal human rights as Political Messianism does not sit well with most nations and regions, especially in our current situation. As Talmon formulated it:

The real victor of Political Messianism was neither the conservative Right nor liberalism, neither capitalism nor democracy, but nationalism, which in the early days of a common struggle against the same enemy, dynastic absolutism, appeared as an integral part of Political Messianism . . . . The evolution of nationalism from a universalist ideology into the dogma of the absolute primacy of the dictates of national survival and greatness emphasizes once more the victory of traditional diversity over the trend towards universal innovation and abstract unity. The real strength of nationalism was however in its ability to offer a substitute to the Messianic universalist solution of the dilemma of individual self-expression and social cohesion.[26]

Hannah Arendt in her masterpiece on *The Origins of Totalitarianism*, originally published in 1951, traced the rise of totalitarianism to the anti-Semitism movements in Europe in the 1800s in a comprehensive analysis of Nazi Germany and Stalinist Russia, but some of her most intriguing writing is on the role played by ideology. In her words,

It is the monstrous, yet seemingly unanswerable claim of totalitarian rule that, far from being "lawless," it goes to the sources of authority from which positive laws received their ultimate legitimation, that far from being arbitrary it is more obedient to these suprahuman forces than any government ever was before, and that far from wielding its power in the interest of one man, it is quite prepared to sacrifice everybody's vital immediate interests to the execution of what it assumes to be the law of History or the law of Nature. Its defiance of positive laws claims to be a higher form of legitimacy which, since it is inspired by the sources themselves, can do away with petty legality. Totalitarian lawfulness pretends to have found a way to establish the rule of justice on earth—something which the legality of positive law admittedly could never attain.[27]

Ideologies—isms which to the satisfaction of their adherents can explain everything and every occurrence by deducing it from a single premise—are a very recent phenomenon and, for many decades, played a negligible role in political life. Only with the wisdom of hindsight can we discover in them certain elements which have made them so disturbingly useful for totalitarian rule. Not before Hitler and Stalin were the great political potentialities of the ideologies discovered.

. . . The ideology treats the course of events as though it followed the same "law" as the logical exposition of its "idea." Ideologies pretend to know the mysteries of the whole historical process—the secrets of the past, the intricacies of the present, the uncertainties of the future—because of the logic inherent in their respective ideas.[28]

It is the certainty which is exhibited by leaders and functionaries in an ideologically driven society that is perhaps most disturbing. The "big lie" or indeed multiple lesser lies are proffered so readily without embarrassment and sometimes with no apparent correspondence to empirical reality. Graham remembers vividly his own first experience of this in the USSR while serving as a UN staff assistant on a "training" trip to Moscow, Leningrad, Tbilisi, and Tashkent in 1979 to demonstrate the wonders of Soviet central economic planning to visiting delegates from the planning agencies of several Asian and African countries. The primitive technology and practices on display in the various collective farms and factories visited were touted as economic miracles of efficiency and productivity in accompanying lectures and ideological shaded explanations, while the reality evident to the group's eyes was so obviously different.

Pierre Manent, who also regards Raymond Aron as his mentor, has offered an important set of related perspectives more recently. For example, in a series of interviews with Benedicte Delorme-Montini, he explained what it means to be *Seeing Things Politically* in France and Europe, with respect to Communism, Totalitarianism and the new Europe. He noted:

> . . . that France was decisively affected in its very heart by the establishment of a very powerful communist conviction . . . . At bottom, with the exception of Aron, who rowed against the current largely alone, a coherent and rigorous critique of communism was hard to find in France . . . . What happened in the years in question (late 70s and early 80s) was, it seems to me, the rise and spread of a more general awareness, which brought our generation together, of totalitarianism as an extraordinarily meaningful political phenomenon whose radical character had to be assessed. This was an awareness that, in communism and totalitarianism, some of the most fundamental problems of modern politics came to view.[29]

Svetlana Alexievich paints a vivid picture of the degree to which Communism still has a hold on some of those who grew up in the Soviet system in *Second Hand Time: The Last of the Soviets.* Drawing from extensive interviews, she tells the stories of many Russians who unashamedly prefer the Soviet system to what they have experienced under Yeltsin and since.[30] Westerners find it hard to understand why more freedom is not always the obvious first choice for every human. Utopian society to which we are irresistibly driven and guided by ideology clearly has its attractions.

The question remains, however: Does the concept of totalitarianism have any analytical utility for explanation? Is it relevant today (anywhere)? Is there a coherent ideology evident that goes far in justifying such brutal repression and sacrifice? If development and prosperity are goals, is there evidence that the potential benefit is widely spread to the mass population?

We would argue that the concept of totalitarianism has some limited utility (not necessarily enduring) in at least two respects: First, it was designed to differentiate this system from other traditional authoritarian systems; and second, Zbigniew Brzezinski argued that the concept tells us something about the particular phase in political development an authoritarian regime may find itself, particularly in terms of the relationship between the political system and society.[31] Adapting and updating his lectures on the subject at Columbia University in the 1970s, one might posit the following stages of the Soviet system and post-Soviet Politics in these terms:

1) 1902–1912 Years in which political movement took shape seeking radical restructuring of society (not just to seize power)
2) 1917–1920 Lenin: Seizure of power phase
3) 1921–1928 Lenin to Stalin
    Civil War and consolidation of power; marks beginning of the Soviet state; NEP as a strategic retreat from socialism due to economic chaos and famine threat
4a) 1929–1938 Stalin: The political system penetrates and mobilizes society—phase of social Revolution; famine especially in Ukraine and Kazakhstan flowing from collectivization of agriculture, repression of kulaks, and requisition of produce to feed the cities;[32] priority to heavy industrialization, purges of military leadership and political opponents (real and imagined); Stalin exiles Trotsky, eliminates Kirov, and all others who could be a challenge, including his former ally Bukharin; strident charges of betrayal, with demands for confessions; Kamenev, Zinoviev and fourteen others put on public trial; gives offer that cannot refuse: confess to save retribution against family.[33] Stalin eliminates all that could challenge him including half of the military leadership; forced relocation of ethnic populations, establishment of the gulag, public show trials. Revised estimates based on archives opened after the collapse of the Soviet Union, including the Yale Annals of Communism project, suggest the total of deaths from state repression during this period was as much as 20 million.[34]
4b) 1939–1945 Stalin: War—different problems, slowdown in political consolidation and industrialization (a kind of divergence); mobilization for defeat of Hitler, but also imprisonment of perceived traitors without much evidence.[35]
5) 1945–1956 Stalin to Khrushchev: The political system grows more conservative, but a strong system of social control remains; 20th Party Congress in 1956, condemning abuses of Stalinism and his personality cult; rise of the Cold War.
6) 1957–1964 Khrushchev: Beginnings of new separateness of society from the political system, change in values; some recognition of development of a bureaucratic system, what Milovan Djilas called "The New Class":

"Having achieved industrialization, the new class can now do nothing more than strengthen its brute force and pillage the people. It ceases to create. The spiritual heritage is overtaken by darkness."[36]

Confrontation with the United States during the Cuban Missile Crisis, which together with a stagnating economy and persistently weak agriculture production levels, essentially spelled the end of the Khrushchev administration.

7) 1964–1985 Brezhnev, Andropov, Chernenko: Military Rise/Economic Decline; Social conservatism by a privileged bureaucratic "class," as Djilas had warned, was emerging.

8) 1985–1991 Gorbachev: Glasnost and Perestroika—reform and beginning of the end; triumphs (including Nobel Peace Prize) and failure.[37]

9) 1991–2000 Yeltsin: The collapse of the USSR; chaotic and partial experimentation with democracy and economic liberalization. Rise of the oligarchs. Svetlana Alexievich chronicles the demise of communism in this period through the eyes of everyday Russians, along with their accounts of memories of oppression, terror, famine, massacres but also pride and belief in "utopia."[38] In *The Man Without a Face: The Unlikely Rise of Vladimir Putin*, Masha Gessen details tribulations of Yeltsin in his struggles to pursue democratization and market capitalism in the face of enormous political resistance, corruption, and instability.

10) 2000–2020 Putin–Medvedev–Putin: Reclamation of the State's assets from the oligarchs; promise for rule of law but renewed Authoritarianism; potential for totalitarianism?

The term totalitarianism applies largely to phases 4 & 5 of the Soviet Period, at least according to Zbigniew Brzezinski. Lithuanian theorist and activist, Aleksandras Shtromas, engaged with Professor Richard Lowenthal on this question, arguing that a totalitarian regime extended well beyond the Khrushchev era. Subsequent Soviet rulers were "not essentially different from their predecessors." And it does not matter if they are "idealistic believers in a higher and better order of things" or are acting in basic policies "in order to survive, do everything they can to perpetuate the single ideology and teleology of the power they have inherited."[39]

But what about Turkmenistan or North Korea (and maybe Putin's Russia now—or in the near future)? Is the Russian Federation (and other successor states to the USSR) heading in that direction? What about Turkey?

Brzezinski helped to clarify the ingredients of totalitarianism in *Ideology and Power in Soviet Politics*:

Totalitarianism, being a dictatorship, characteristically includes the coercive qualities noted in such varied dictatorial systems. But unlike most dictatorships of the past and present, the totalitarian movements wielding power do not aim to freeze society in the status quo; on the contrary, their aim is to institutional- ize a revolution that mounts in scope, and frequently in intensity, as the regime stabilizes itself in power. The purpose of this revolution is to pulverize all existing social units in order to replace the old pluralism with a homogeneous unanimity patterned on the blueprints of the totalitarian ideology. The power of the totalitarian regime is derived not from a precarious balance of existing forces (e.g., church, landed gentry, officer corps), but from the revolutionary dynamism of its zealous supporters, who disarm opposition and mobilize the masses both by force and by an appeal to a better future. This appeal is nor- mally framed in the official ideology, or action program, of the movement. In time, of course, the dynamism decreases, but by then the system is buttressed by complex networks of control that pervade the entire society and mobilize its energies through sheer penetration. An institutionalized revolution, patterned on the totalitarian ideology, thus makes totalitarianism essentially a forward- oriented phenomenon.[40]

Alfred G. Meyer dissented somewhat from this perspective and spoke about the development of a bureaucratic Soviet state, especially after the death of Stalin. While granting that it was less conservative than other types of authoritarian regimes, it deserved evaluation in terms of its success or failure in meeting the goals and aspirations of 1917.[41]

STATE SOCIALISM AND THE ECONOMY: WHAT LED TO THE COLLAPSE OF THE USSR?

In 1972, Soviet historian Roy A. Medvedev published his path-breaking analysis, *On Socialist Democracy*, which diagnosed the failings of the Soviet political system, with its cumbersome centralized bureaucratic structures; he called for a vigorous gradual democratization— implementing rights and privileges already stipulated in the Soviet Constitution. A severe critic of Stalinism in *Let History Judge*, Medvedev (who was expelled from the Communist Party when it was published in the West) had not given up his commitment to socialism.[42] But the economy clearly needed reform and democratization. The specific failings of the Soviet system under Khrushchev and Brezhnev included:

- inflexibility of the centrally planned economy—only responds to predeter- mined signals in a rigid way;
- inability to make efficient use of state investments;
- lack of incentives for productivity and needed innovation;

- substantial drops in needed production while unneeded products (but not food) filled warehouses;
- inefficient bureaucratic decision-making that by the 1970s was seen as out of step with the requirements of industrial and societal change, in contrast to effectiveness for marshalling and applying resources to large-scale project goals of heavy industrialization under Stalin;
- development of privileged elites—not so much a "new class" as Djilas termed it, but clearly individuals in control of decisions and resources that were unresponsive to the requirements of a modern industrial economy.[43]

Much has been written on the failings of the Soviet economy and reform efforts after the impressive success of heavy industrialization and rapid growth from 1928 to 1940; three successive five year plans were accompanied by annual economic growth rates reported at more than 5 percent.[44] Growth rates after World War II moderated somewhat as industrialization and urbanization continued. Stagnation in the collectivized agricultural sector was persistent, frustrating Khrushchev's limited reform and decentralization efforts. Still, one should keep Medvedev's appraisal of the inherent weaknesses of the Soviet state socialist bureaucracy in mind.

Indeed, we can add to the list that he offers. By the 1970s, basic inefficiencies and disincentives were evident in the state-owned, centrally planned economy that hampered productivity, innovation, and effective allocation of scarce resources. There was little or no incentive to manufacture quality products. Consumer goods were woefully uncompetitive with products manufactured in the West, and even in comparison with those available in several Eastern European countries, especially East Germany. The emphasis on "fulfilling the plan" focused on quantity of production, not quality or innovation in design. Plant managers were punished for missing production quotas and not rewarded for developing new designs and varieties, especially if this meant reduced numbers produced, even temporarily.[45] The depth of the economic crisis only became broadly apparent later, as the 1990 U.S. intelligence estimate indicated, noting the Soviet economic growth had averaged more than 4.8 percent for each 5 year increment from 1951 to 1970, but declined to less than 2 percent for the 5 year increment from 1976 to 1985. The CIA study pointed to some positive impact both of perestroika (decentralization, consumer-orientation, and incentives for innovation) and glasnost (more data became available). Indeed, the overall growth rate in 1986–1987 suggested a modest recovery to 2.7 percent.[46]

Relying upon formerly secret archives, Paul Gregory's impressive study of the Soviet administrative-command system, especially under Stalin, stressed key reasons for failure: "poor planning, unreliable supplies, the preferential treatment of indigenous enterprises, the lack of knowledge of planners, etc.;

but it also focuses on the basic principal-agent conflict between planners and producers, which created a sixty-year reform stalemate."[47] He further noted: "Collectivization ruined agriculture's long-run chances; the imposition of force in the countryside did not transfer net resources from agriculture to industry. Superindustrialization created a massive industrial capital stock that was either poorly selected or misused, and high investment rates generated only a temporary spurt in economic growth, followed by protracted decline and stagnation."[48]

Marshall I. Goldman, professor of economics at Wellesley College and a long-time associate of Harvard's Russian Research Center is perhaps the most distinguished and perceptive analyst of the Soviet economy. Writing in 1968, he provided an excellent systematic assessment of thirteen myths (and the reality) of the Soviet economic structure and performance. "Myths" he dissects include:

3) Upon coming to power, the Bolsheviks adopted a Marxist blueprint for action which they have been following ever since.
4) Russia needed the Bolshevik Revolution to spark the economic growth necessary to make it the world's second largest industrial power.
10) The Soviet Union is becoming capitalist, and in a few years, there will be no differences between the Soviet and American economic systems.
12) When it comes to foreign trade, it is impossible to compete on equal terms with the Russians. Because all foreign trade activities are monopolized in the hands of the state, it is impossible for private traders in a foreign country to command the resources and coordinate themselves as well as a state Ministry of Foreign Trade.[49]

In this sweeping survey, Goldman stressed that since Marx did not really provide a clear blueprint for how to pursue communism, it is hard to describe Soviet efforts purely in pursuit of his ideology. Indeed, there were important aspects of the policies and challenges of the Soviet economy that also characterize the pursuit of economic development more broadly in the developing world, though with certain disadvantages.

Moreover, Goldman noted that the key challenges included the fact that there was a "dual society" in operation—a modern and productive sector and a primitive and backward sector. His view in the late 1960s was that the modern sector was gaining.[50] But he concluded, in part,

> With the growing rush of technology comes a need for more interchange of materials and knowledge. Thus, if they want to compete, the Russians find it necessary to become more involved with the world. Only in this way can they share in the improvements in technology and production that are taking place at such a rapid rate.[51]

This was prescient. The failure to reform the basic characteristics of the "autarkic" and absurdly centralized and bureaucratic Soviet economy became more and more problematic as the global economic environment changed dramatically in the 1970s and 1980s.[52] It is also interesting to examine the extent to which challenges faced by the Soviets during this period were apparent beyond Soviet borders. Marc Trachtenberg explored this question in some detail. While providing excellent insight on this by synthesizing a wide range of CIA estimates and Soviet and Western academic assessments, he also stressed the seriousness of the challenge faced by the Soviets by the time Gorbachev came to power. This derived in part from the complexity of the Soviet economy as well as the inherent difficulty involved in dismantling the command economy—beyond the necessary but difficult ideological backtracking. Brezhnev and his colleagues were well aware of the weaknesses in the system but could not bring themselves to act on them decisively.[53]

There is no space in this volume for a thorough treatment of the political and economic elements leading to the collapse of the USSR. Fortunately, there is no shortage of serious treatments of the complexities involved, from a variety of perspectives and disciplines.[54]

The actual collapse (and especially the degree or depth of economic weakness underpinning it) came as a shock to most Western analysts—even those privy to classified intelligence. It is not easy to build a consensus on the range of factors involved, particularly on their relative weight as determinants, but it is reasonable to summarize some common themes that seem important to most assessments: First, as touched on above, there were the evident characteristics of the centrally planned, command economy. Poorly informed centralized decisions were made for millions of minute product prices by GOSPLAN in Moscow (studiously avoiding insights that "market demands" might provide). This system worked well during the remarkable Soviet efforts to marshal resources in this command economy for high priority projects requiring substantial manpower and construction—for example, heavy industrialization effort, armament production for World War II, damming the Volga, the Soviet space program, ICBM production numbers.[55] But there was little scope for individual drive and innovation—little or no reward, indeed disincentives at times, in normal consumer product manufacturing. Consequently, an enormous and growing technological gap opened up with the West, clear to all by the 1980s, especially with the onset of the microelectronic revolution.[56] Incentives were in the wrong direction, emphasizing, for example, production quantities—meeting the plan—over quality and variety; Grigory Yavlinsky argued, after observing the Soviet mining industry, that production quantities were also poor. The workers were not working, because there was no incentive to work hard.

The Soviet system demonstrated a striking inability to manufacture competitive consumer products for export or even satisfactory domestic consumption. The authoritarian Soviet system, with nearly complete state ownership of property—left no room for entrepreneurial innovation and competitive commercial drive; no evidence of the state "whithering away" in this respect, indeed there was no real plan for reducing the role of the oppressive state machinery. There was a continuing focus instead on raw material exports (esp. oil and gas) to earn hard currency for necessary imports. This made the energy supply relationship evolving with Germany and Europe a high priority.

Increased efforts at arms sales for commercial gain, not just security assistance to allies and proxies in the developing world, were prioritized (especially simple but rugged arms, for example, AK 47s!); this was complemented by substantial effort to acquire higher technology weapon systems and related devices from the United States and Europe through espionage when purchase was denied. Reverse engineering of Western products remained an important strategy, but it became less and less viable in the context of increasingly rapid technological change, especially in the Western and East Asian microelectronic industries.

Not surprisingly, the substantial black and/or grey markets thrived in a persistent environment of consumer good shortages. This in turn weakened ideological motivation/commitment since participation in the informal economy, by high level party members and their special access to scarce supplies and foreign luxury goods, revealed that a double standard was operative.

Economic policy making, indeed governance generally, lacked transparency and legitimacy; there was little or no real popular input on priorities. Secretary Brezhnev's massive spending priority to strategic defense to catch up with the United States largely went unchallenged; indeed, its true extent was an intriguing mystery even to Western intelligence agencies well into the 1980s. Robert Strayer (1998), for example, placed much emphasis on Brezhnev's drive to catch up with the United States after the embarrassment of the Cuban Missile Crisis, as a causal factor in the Soviet collapse.[57] Others, while emphasizing that spending on strategic nuclear weaponry did essentially bankrupt the Soviet economy, noted that the nail in the coffin was the Soviet willingness to believe that President Reagan's Strategic Defense Initiative in 1983 might actually make much of Brezhnev's spending for naught—leading to a whole new round of arms race competition (and expenditure) potentially. (See also, Yergin and Stanislaw's PBS Series "The Commanding Heights" in which they report on the revelations of Oleg Gordievsky, a KGB defector to the United Kingdom, who stressed that the Soviets were already committing at least one-third of total economic resources to the military in the 1980s. The British could hardly believe the expenditure could be that high.)[58]

Soviet dependence on oil and gas income—with the corollary failure to diversify the industrial base—was key. Soviet and sympathetic conspiracy theorists drew attention to this dependence with recurring reports that the United States and Saudi Arabia had colluded to push oil prices down, thus depressing Soviet income. The effort reportedly was to punish the Soviets for the 1979 invasion of Afghanistan; the facts of the situation are hard to unravel, but it is clear that oil prices were low through much of the 1980s. The lack of export income in return made it hard for the Soviets to purchase needed grain from the West; the Soviet collective farm agricultural system continued to fail to perform adequately.[59] The U.S.–Saudi collusion argument resurfaced in 2014 as a reported strategy to punish Russia for the annexation of Crimea.

The fact that serious reform was needed seems not to have been in dispute to most analysts. Writing in 1983, Marshall Goldman noted:

> A few years ago, Soviet citizens used to console themselves with the thought that it may have been bad in the past, but conditions had improved and would be even better in the future. Now there is a sense that economic life may actually have been better in the past and that the future may be even worse.[60]

Mikhail Gorbachev clearly recognized that serious reforms were needed. It is possible that a different approach might have saved the Soviet Union in some measure. But his chosen reform efforts were too little and too late and unleashed (destructive) forces that could not be countered.[61]

One is mindful of the picture of the run-up to the French Revolution painted by Alexis de Tocqueville in *The Old Regime and the French Revolution*. Tocqueville captured the consciousness raising that occurred as the plight of the poor was described and modest reforms were introduced. An explosion of pent-up frustration ensued:

> Louis XV did as much to weaken the monarchy and to speed up the Revolution by his innovations as by his personal defects, by his energy as by his indo-lence. . . . Some of the reforms he personally put through made overhasty, ill-considered changes in ancient and respected usages which in certain cases violated vested rights. They prepared the ground for the Revolution not so much because they removed obstacles in its way but far more because they taught the nation how to set about it.[62]

Gorbachev's reforms included an attack on Party (CPSU) procedures and elite personnel (the Nomenklatura) without condemning communist ideology and the associated utopian dream; he encountered resistance in the Party hierarchy which maintained a strong interest in the privileges they held in the status quo.

He called for Glasnost and Perestroika (openness and restructuring). The former helped to "let the cat out of the bag," creating new awareness of what was wrong with the system and allowing serious opposition to blossom and the rise of alternative perspectives instead of unified national focus on substantial restructuring. It legitimized dissent while adding to delegitimization of the state socialist system.

Aside from marginalizing some aspects of the role of the CPSU, key elements were some decentralization of economic planning and decision-making and the Law on Cooperatives, which permitted some private ownership and entrepreneurial activity.[63] Beyond these modest reforms, Gorbachev sought to reduce the pressure on the economy through arms control agreements with the U.S. President Reagan's Strategic Defense Initiative and his interest in following through on the nuclear weapons modernization efforts begun by President Carter. These steps had raised the importance of curtailing the expensive arms race that Brezhnev had helped to fuel.[64]

The reform effort by Gorbachev did unambiguously fail to revive the Soviet economy. Committed British Socialist Tony Benn famously argued that it was now possible to actually get Communism right! The August 1991 coup attempt, which in effect brought down Gorbachev while it repudiated bungled efforts by the hardline members of the CPSU to turn back the clock, also removed Benn's dream from contention. The coup attempt lasted only two days, but the Gorbachev reforms, including a negotiated new union treaty that decentralized power to the republics, were discredited. Anatoly M. Khazanov pointed to the ethnic and nationalist forces at work that made the Commonwealth of Independent States option largely meaningless.[65] The Soviet Union voluntarily disintegrated, and the fifteen successor states, including Russia embarked on a tortuous dual transition of political and economic transformation.[66]

The tortuous path followed for essentially the next decade by President Yeltsin failed to produce a vibrant economy with broad-based prosperity, and essentially set the stage for a return to authoritarianism under President Putin. Are there parallels between Stalin and Putin? Russia under Putin seems to be missing a coherent ideology beyond nationalism, though the arguments on the need to pursue Eurasianism by Alexandr Dugin[67] and a range of Putin's close associates and historical authorities may be providing an ideologically tinged foundation for the requisites of desirable, unfettered state action. Putin's recent policies, however, do seem to "freeze" the status quo for most Russians except for a very narrow and very wealthy elite of Putin loyalists. Mikhail Gorbachev, in *The New Russia*, explains the rise of Putin and what he is up to but also argues for democracy and modernization, in the context of global poverty, climate change, and the global water crisis. He contends Russia has become over-centralized; it needs pluralism and social democracy. Moreover, the world needs a new development model (neither the Washington Consensus, nor the centralized state control of the Soviet Union).[68] We shall explore these issues carefully in chapters 3 and 4.

NOTES

1. William Zimmerman, *Ruling Russia: Authoritarianism From the Revolution to Putin* (NJ: Princeton University Press, 2014, 2016).
2. Ibid., p. 7.
3. Ibid.
4. Ibid., p. 8.
5. Ibid., p. 300.
6. Ibid., pp. 306–310.
7. Zimmerman's 2016 paperback edition of his book updates this somewhat in an afterward.
8. See: Friedrich, Carl J. and Zbigniew K. Brzezinski, *Totalitarian Dictatorship and Autocracy*. Second edition revised by Friedrich, 1965 (NY: Praeger, 1956, 1965); and Hannah Arendt, *The Origins of Totalitarianism* (NY: Harcourt, Inc., 1951, 1985).
9. Examples would include the three distinctive evaluations offered in Carl J. Friedrich, M. Curtis and B. Barber, *Totalitarianism in Perspective: Three Views* (New York: Praeger, 1969); and the collection of interesting essays on *Change in Communist Systems*, ed. Chalmers Johnson (Palo Alto, CA: Stanford University Press, 1970).
10. See, for example, Marshall Shulman, *Stalin's Foreign Policy Reappraised*, 1963; and *Beyond the Cold War*, 1966.
11. Raymond Aron, *The Opium of the Intellectuals* (New Brunswick, NJ: Transaction Publishers, 1957, 2004), pp. 323–324.
12. Francois Furet, *The Passing of an Illusion: The Idea of Communism in the Twentieth Century* (Chicago, IL: The University of Chicago Press, 1999).
13. Ibid., p. 191.
14. Ibid., pp. 502–503.
15. Francois Furet and Ernst Nolte, *Fascism and Communism* (Lincoln, NE: University of Nebraska Press, 2001), see especially pp. 9–20.
16. Ibid., p. 90.
17. Francois Furet, *Lies, Passions & Illusions: The Idea of Communism in the Twentieth Century* (Chicago, IL: University of Chicago Press, 2014), p. 10.
18. Ibid., pp. 18–21.
19. Ibid., p. 21.
20. Ibid., pp. 28–29.
21. Ibid., p. 48.
22. Ibid., p. 52.
23. J. L. Talmon, *The Origins of Totalitarian Democracy* (NY: Praeger, 1951), pp. 1–2.

24. J. L. Talmon, *Political Messianism: The Romantic Phase* (NY: Praeger, 1960), pp. 507–508.

25. Ibid., pp. 509–510.

26. Ibid., p. 513.

27. Hannah Arendt, *The Origins of Totalitarianism*, pp. 461–462.

28. Ibid., pp. 468–469.

29. Pierre Manent, *Seeing Things Politically: Interviews with Benedicte Delorme-Montini* (South Bend, IN: St. Augustine's Press, 2015), pp. 76–79.

30. Svetlana Alexievich, *Second Hand Time: The Last of the Soviets* (NY: Random House, 2016).

31. See: Zbigniew Brzezinski, *The Grand Failure: The Birth and Death of Communism in the Twentieth Century* (NY: Scribner, 1989; London: Macdonald, 1990); and Friedrich and Brzezinski, *Totalitarian Dictatorship and Autocracy*.

32. See: Anne Applebaum, *Red Famine: Stalin's War on Ukraine* (NY: Doubleday, 2017); Sheila Fitzpatrick, *Stalin's Peasants: Resistance & Survival in the Russian Village After Collectivization* (NY: Oxford University Press, 1994); and R.W. Davies and Stephen G. Wheatcroft, *The Years of Hunger: Soviet Agriculture, 1931–1933* (London: Palgrave/Macmillan, 2009).

33. There is an enormous literature on this period of Stalin's rise to power and dominance. See, for example, Stephen Kotkin, *Stalin: Waiting for Hitler, 1929–1941* (NY: Penguin Press, 2017); and the classic by Adam B. Ulam, *Stalin: The Man and His Era* (NY: The Viking Press, 1973). An excellent summary of this period and the development of Stalin's "cult of personality" is presented by Frank Dikotter in chapter 3 of *How to Be a Dictator: The Cult of Personality in the Twentieth Century* (London: Bloomsbury, 2019).

34. See: Conquest, 1990, pp. 484–489; see also Medvedev, 1980 and 1989; and for insight into the life of Soviet citizens during this phase, see Siegelbaum and Sokolov (2000) and Fitzpatrick (1999).

35. See: Marius Broekmeyer, *Stalin, the Russians, and Their War 1941–1945* (Madison, WI: University of Wisconsin Press, 2004); Solzhenitsyn, 1963 and 1973. See also Mark Harrison, *Accounting for War: Soviet Production, Employment, and the Defence Burden, 1940–1945* (UK: Cambridge University Press, 1996). See also: Aleksandr Solzhenitsyn, *The Gulag Archipelago, 1918–1956* (NY: Harper, 1973); and Aleksandr Solzhenitsyn, *One Day in the Life of Ivan Denisovich* (NY: Dutton, 1963).

36. Milovan Djilas, *The New Class: An Analysis of the Communist System* (NY: Praeger, 1957), p. 69; see also Alfred G. Meyer, *The Soviet Political System: An Interpretation* (NY: Random House, 1965).

37. See: Robert G. Kaiser, *Why Gorbachev Happened: His Triumph and Failure* (NY: Simon and Schuster, 1991); Mikhail Gorbachev, *The August Coup: The Truth and the Lessons* (NY: Harper Collins, 1991); and Stephen F. Cohen and Katrina Vanden Heuvel, *Voices of Glasnost: Interviews with Gorbachev's Reformers* (NY: W.W. Norton, 1989).

38. Alexievich, *Second Hand Time*. See also: Vladimir Solovyov and Elena Klepikova, *Boris Yeltsin: A Political Biography* (NY: G.P. Putnam's Sons, 1992);

and Lilia Shevtsova, *Lost in Transition: The Yeltsin and Putin Legacies* (Washington, DC: The Carnegie Endowment for International Peace, 2007).

39. Aleksandras Shtromas, *Totalitarianism and the Prospects for World Order: Closing the Door on the Twentieth Century*, eds. Robert Faulkner and Daniel J. Mahoney (Lanham, MD: Lexington Press, 2003), p. 132.

40. Zbigniew Brzezinski, *Ideology and Power in Soviet Politics* (NY: Praeger, Rev. ed., 1967), p. 42.

41. Meyer, *The Soviet Political System*, pp. 467–476 and 480.

42. Roy A. Medvedev, *On Socialist Democracy* (NY: Alfred A. Knopf, 1975), see pp. 310–332 in particular.

43. Ibid., pp. 242–273.

44. See Paul R. Gregory, *The Political Economy of Stalinism: Evidence from the Soviet Secret Archives* (Cambridge, UK: Cambridge University Press, 2004), and George R. Feiwel, *The Soviet Quest for Economic Efficiency: Issues, Controversies, and Reforms* (NY: Frederick A. Praeger, Publishers, 1967).

45. See Chapter 5—Managerial Motivation in Industry, in Abram Bergson, *The Economics of Soviet Planning* (Westport, CT: Greenwood Press/Yale University, 1964).

46. Central Intelligence Agency, *Measures of Soviet Gross National Product in 1982 Prices*. For the Joint Economic Committee, U.S. Congress (Washington, DC: USGPO), pp. 51–52 and 58.

47. Gregory, p. i.

48. Ibid., p. 20.

49. Marshall I. Goldman, *The Soviet Economy: Myth and Reality* (Englewood Cliffs, NJ: Prentice-Hall, 1968).

50. Ibid., p. 165.

51. Ibid., p. 166.

52. See also the concise analysis of the rise and fall of the Soviet economy offered by Mark Harrison, "The Soviet Economy, 1927–1991: Its Life and Afterlife," *The Independent Review*, 22, no. 2 (2017), pp. 199–206.

53. Marc Trachtenberg, "Assessing Soviet Economic Performance During the Cold War: A Failure of Intelligence?" *Texas National Security Review*, 1, no. 2 (March 2018), pp. 94–98.

54. For example, see: Anders Aslund, *Gorbachev's Struggle for Economic Reform, 1985–1988* (Ithaca, NY: Cornell University Press, 1989); Anders Aslund, *Building Capitalism: The Transformation of the Former Soviet Bloc* (UK: Cambridge University Press, 2002); Anders Aslund, *How Capitalism Was Built: The Transformation of Central and Eastern Europe, Russia and Central Asia* (UK: Cambridge University Press, 2007), pp. 11–42; Archie Brown, *The Rise and Fall of Communism* (London: Vintage Books, 2009); Zbigniew Brzezinski, *The Grand Failure: The Birth and Death of Communism in the Twentieth Century* (NY: Scribner, 1989. London: Macdonald, 1990; Dallin, 1992); Yegor Gaidar, *Collapse of an Empire: Lessons for Modern Russia* (Washington, DC: The Brookings Institution, 2007); Marshall Goldman, *The Soviet Economy: Myth and Reality* (NY: Prentice-Hall, 1968), esp. Chapter 8; Marshall Goldman, *USSR in Crisis: The Failure of an Economic System*

(NY: W.W. Norton, 1983); Bernard Gwertzman, and Michael T. Kaufman, ed., *The Collapse of Communism* (NY: Times Books/Random House, 1990); A. Hewett, ed., *Reforming the Soviet Economy: Equality versus Efficiency* (Washington, DC: The Brookings Institution, 1988); Stephen Kotkin, *Armageddon Averted: The Soviet Collapse, 1970–2000* (NY: Oxford University Press, 2008); Marie Lavigne, "Problems Facing the Soviet Economy," in Alexander Dallin and Condoleezza Rice, eds., *The Gorbachev Era* (Palo Alto, CA: Stanford Alumni Assoc., 1986), pp. 43–59; Marie Lavigne, Marie. *The Economics of Transition: From Socialist Economy to Market Economy.* Second edition (NY: St. Martin's Press, 1999); Konstantin Simis, *USSR: The Corrupt Society—The Secret World of Soviet Capitalism* (NY: Simon and Schuster, 1982); Joseph E. Stiglitz, *Whither Socialism?* (Cambridge, MA: MIT Press, 1994), pp. 197–205; Robert Strayer, *Why Did the Soviet Union Collapse? Understanding Historical Change* (Armonk, NY: M.E. Sharpe, 1998); Stephen White, *Communism and Its Collapse* (London: Routledge, 1990); and Stephen White, *Gorbachev in Power* (Cambridge, UK: Cambridge University Press, 2001).

55. See: Jack Verona, "The Soviet March Toward Technological Superiority," *Defense*, 80 (March 1980), pp. 2–4; Bruce Parrott, *Politics and Technology in the Soviet Union* (Cambridge, MA: MIT Press, 1983); and William J. Perry and Cynthia A. Roberts, "Winning Through Sophistication: How to Meet the Soviet Military Challenge," *Technology Review* (July 1982), pp. 27–35.

56. See, for example: Phillip J. Klass, "Soviet Microcircuits Found Trailing U.S." *Aviation Week and Space Technology*, December 8, 1980, pp. 64–67; and David M. Russell, "Is there a Soviet Computer Challenge?" *Defense Electronics*, March 1984, pp. 79–84.

57. Robert Strayer, *Why Did the Soviet Union Collapse?*

58. See: Daniel Yergin and Joseph Stanislaw, *The Commanding Heights: The Battle for the World Economy* (NY: Simon & Schuster, 2002), Chapter 10; and Oleg Gordievsky, *Next Stop Execution: The Autobiography of Oleg Gordievsky* (London: Macmillan, 1985, 2018).

59. See: Yegor Gaidar, *Collapse of an Empire: Lessons for Modern Russia* (Washington, DC: The Brookings Institution Press, 2007), pp. 115–161.

60. Marshall Goldman, *USSR in Crisis: The Failure of an Economic System* (NY: W.W. Norton, 1983), p. 182.

61. See: Anders Aslund, *Gorbachev's Struggle for Economic Reform: The Soviet Reform Process, 1985–88* (Ithaca, NY: Cornell University Press, 1989); Andrei Melville and Gail W. Lapidus, eds., *The Glasnost Papers: Voices on Reform from Moscow* (Boulder, CO: Westview Press, 1990); and Archie Brown, *The Gorbachev Factor* (Oxford, UK: Oxford University Press, 1996).

62. Alexis de Tocqueville, *The Old Regime and the French Revolution* (Garden City, NY: Doubleday, 1955), p. 188.

63. See: Aslund, *Gorbachev's Struggle for Economic Reform*, 1989; and Stephen F. Cohen and Katrina Vanden Huevel, *Voices of Glasnost: Interviews with Gorbachev's Reformers* (NY: W.W. Norton, 1989), for detailed descriptions and analysis.

64. Gorbachev offers his own account of his goals and initiatives, in *Perestroika: New Thinking for Our Country and the World* (NY: Harper & Row, 1987).

65. Anatoly M. Khazanov, *After the USSR: Ethnicity, Nationalism, and Politics in the Commonwealth of Independent States* (Madison, WI: University of Wisconsin Press, 1995).

66. Brown, *The Gorbachev Factor*. See also Mikhail Gorbachev's own account of the period leading up to the Coup, and its defeat and impacts in *The August Coup: The Truth and the Lessons* (NY: Harper Collins, 1991).

67. See, for example, Alexander Dugin, *Eurasian Mission: An Introduction to Neo-Eurasianism* (London: Arktos); Dugin, *Putin vs. Putin: Vladimir Putin Viewed from the Right* (London: Arktos, 2014); Dugin, *The War of the World-Island: The Geopolitics of Contemporary Russia* (London: Arktos, 2015); Dugin, Alexander, *The Foundations of Geopolitics*. Russian edition (Moscow: Arktogia, 1997).

68. Mikhail Gorbachev, *The New Russia* (Cambridge, UK: The Polity Press, 2016).

Chapter 3

Yeltsin in Search of a Viable Russian Federation

Boris Yeltsin emerged from the attempted coup in August 1991 as the dominant political actor in the USSR. He stood up to the Communist hard-line plotters bravely—scrambling atop a tank to speak and rallied opposition against their attempts to roll back the perestroika reforms initiated by Gorbachev. He had been elected as president of the Russian Soviet Federative Socialist Republic on June 12, 1991 despite opposition from Soviet president Gorbachev who favored Nikolai Ryzhkov, in a free and competitive election. While Yeltsin initially supported Gorbachev's reforms, he came to the view that they did not go far enough. Accordingly, a serious rivalry developed between the two politicians.[1] Gorbachev had become the first truly elected chief executive—president—of the Soviet Union, but he ran unopposed on the ballot. A substantial portion of the electorate voted no.

Yeltsin's "radical" reforms were rather less successful than the economic and political transitions in the post-Soviet Baltic republics of Latvia, Lithuania, and Estonia, which subsequently earned membership in both the European Union and NATO. The Republic of Georgia is often seen as a successful reform effort as well, but most of the rest of the successor republics are generally regarded as stalled/incomplete transitions to democracy and market economies or clear failures that have not reverted to state socialism for the most part but are flawed economies and authoritarian states.

Former members of COMECON and the Warsaw Treaty Organization in Eastern Europe also may be "graded" in terms of their success at transition. Poland likely gets the best marks by most analysts. Hungary, the Czech Republic, Slovakia, Bulgaria, Romania, Slovenia, and finally Croatia all were successful enough in their efforts to obtain EU and NATO membership. But most found some disappointment in what membership meant to their economic development and prosperity. In part, this is due to limitations in the reform effort, but the timing of membership unfortunately also coincided with the global financial crisis and the debt challenges that constrained EU development spending and threatened the stability of the Eurozone.

On the political side, democratization seemed promising in 1991, as Yeltsin won a convincing free and fair presidential vote with significant competition. He managed 58.6 percent of the final vote tally; Nikolai Ryzhkoy representing the Communist Party was second with only 17.2 percent, and Vladimir Zhirinovsky of the inappropriately named Liberal Democratic Party tallied only 8 percent of the vote.[2] As noted earlier, Yeltsin had emerged as the hero of the attempted coup by Communist hardliners in August 19–21, 1991.[3] In the words of early biographers, Solovyov and Klepikova:

> We know who the hero of August was—Boris Yeltsin. His triumph over the conspirators exceeded even his election victory and endowed his reign with an extra dose of legitimacy. Henceforth his real inauguration date would be the 19th of August, when he made his speech from the tank, instead of the official July the 10th. The country had voted for a President and a knight in armor had shown up in addition.[4]

Nonetheless, Yeltsin faced extremely difficult economic and political challenges, given the state of the Russian economy and the centers of power remaining in the political and economic machinery. He set about to develop a market economy, ensuring economic freedom and financial stability, while removing the CPSU as a legal entity and property holder. He recognized the independence declarations of the Baltic republics and presided over the dissolution of the USSR and formal resignation of Gorbachev on December 25, 1991.

Yeltsin's prime ministers were many and varied before he settled on Vladimir Putin near the end of his tumultuous reign. The Russian version of "shock therapy" was directed largely by Yegar Gaidar, who became Yeltsin's acting prime minister from June to December 1992. An economist who had become committed to free markets and free trade for some time, Gaidar was influenced in part by Harvard's Jeffrey Sachs and Swedish economist Anders Åslund.[5] The resulting plan:

> . . . was modeled after Poland's successful shock-therapy reforms of January 1990. The aim: to liberalize the economy by stabilizing its precarious finances and privatizing state property. The first stage would involve freeing most retail and wholesale prices, which the state had controlled since the 1920s; drastically slashing government spending; and shrinking the money supply by soaking up the vast pools of ruble that flooded the country.[6]

Critics focused on the implementation shortcomings, especially in damping down inflation. Rose Brady, however, noted quite perceptively that Yeltsin had made a serious mistake in pushing his plan through the Congress of People's Deputies:

> He pledged that after a rough, six-month transition, Russians would begin to see their lives improve. That prognosis turned out to be wrong. Economic reform would prove to be a far harsher and far longer process than Yeltsin and the reformers envisioned.[7]

Indeed, by late 1992, the pain was broadly felt, from a sharply devalued ruble and rampant inflation; the patience of the Congress of People's Deputies was gone, confronting Yeltsin with an order to stop executing economic decrees without parliamentary approval. Gaidar resigned and was replaced by Viktor Chernomyrdin.[8] This executive personnel change was not the answer to Russia's challenges. Indeed, a period of political conflict and economic decline set in with little hope on the horizon.

Writing in 1994, Jeffrey Sachs captured the period effectively from his viewpoint as a highly regarded outside adviser who, unfortunately, was often ignored or at least whose recommendations for comprehensive and swift reforms were only partially implemented. While critical of Russian political maneuvering, he also pointed to the unwillingness of Western governments to seize the opportunity to support Russian restructuring with adequate levels of financial aid and investment:

> Russian stabilization has been a continuing story of missed chances, by the Russians and the West. As the saying goes, Russia and the West have never missed an opportunity to miss an opportunity. The good news is that Russia has so far avoided hyperinflation. The bad news is that the climate of Russian public opinion vis-à-vis market reforms has continued to deteriorate; most reformers have left the government; political extremism and criminality seem to be on the rise; relations are cooling with the West; there are signs of increasing militarization of Russian politics; and inflation remains high and unstable. In short, Russia remains adrift, and still vulnerable to political upheaval.[9]

Yeltsin's struggles with weak political institutions in the face of economic crisis were a major feature of the 1990s. The inability of Russia's Central Bank to contain inflation and stabilize the Ruble was serious and continuing, and the political opposition to Yeltsin in the Congress of People's Deputies and its Supreme Soviet for control of economic policy erupted into a constitutional crisis in September and October of 1993. As noted above, this included rejection of Yeltsin's nomination of Gaidar for full prime minister and Yeltsin's decision to suspend the Supreme Soviet and rule by decree until a new constitution could be approved by a national referendum. The Supreme Soviet in turn moved to try to remove him from the presidency, naming Vice President Alexander Rutskoy as acting president. The confrontation spiraled into a military attack on the White House (parliamentary building) ordered by Yeltsin, when deputies and protestors occupied offices and the Ostankino television centre. This shocked many observers, domestic and foreign alike, who found this particular use of force quite unsettling; frustration at the Supreme Soviet's efforts to countermand Yeltsin's reform efforts during increasingly dire economic times, however, provided him with some sympathy. Masha Gessen describes the atmosphere succinctly:

> On September 21, 1993, Yeltsin issued a decree dissolving the Supreme Soviet and calling for the election of a proper legislative body. The Supreme Soviet refused to disband, barricading itself inside the White House—the very same building where Yeltsin's people had set up camp during the coup two years earlier. This time troops did open fire and shelled the White House, forcing Supreme Soviet members out on October 4.
>
> Leading democratic politicians, including former dissidents, supported what became known as "the execution of the Supreme Soviet," so exasperated were they with seeing the president stonewalled.[10]

The new constitution was approved subsequently by a national referendum on December 12, 1993; it modernized and provided more clarity on institutions, giving the president less ambiguous executive power. The U.S. Agency for International Development apparently played some role in the Constitution's design; it also seemed to have influence from DeGaulle's constitution for the 5th Republic of France, in its effort to create institutions that were both "legitimate and capable of action."[11] The Constitution provided for a bicameral legislature—the Federal Assembly, consisting of the Council of the Federation and the State Duma, with 450 deputies. The Constitution specified a long list of citizen rights and clearly established presidential decree power among other normal executive responsibilities of the head of state in a presidential system of government; the president also had the power to dissolve the Duma.[12]

Nonetheless, the subsequent reform efforts by the more powerful president did not seem to bear any measureable improvement in the living conditions for the average Russian citizens. Aid from the West was uncertain and modest—certainly no new Marshall Plan, for fear that it would just be wasted without real reform agreement/commitment broadly in the Russian Government—and little hope for more effective implementation. The Western governments, especially the United States worried about the growing strength of the Communists (led by Gennady Zyuganov) and the nationalists (led by Vladimir Zhirinovsky) in the legislature, especially after the 1995 parliamentary election.[13]

Returning briefly to cross-national comparisons on transition success, it is important to note the extent to which most former state socialist countries in East and Central Europe managed the dual transition to a vibrant competitive democracy and broad-based prosperous market economy much better than did Yeltsin's Russian Federation. A rough and simple way to do this is to use the "scorecards," based on expert surveys published by Freedom House on democratization and the European Bank for Reconstruction and Development on economic transition. The Freedom House ratings for progress in providing political rights and civil liberties indicate that all the major East and Central European transition states showed substantial improvement in the 1990s. But the Russian Federation did not.[14] Moreover, table 3.1 rates and ranks these countries on progress in economic liberalization. Again, Russia does not compare favorably with most East and Central European transition countries. One can safely argue that Russia enjoyed less direct support from the West, in comparison with East and Central European countries who sought to "return to Europe" and join the European Union. The massive size and complexity of the Russian economy was daunting to committed reformers as well, but of course Russia was blessed with substantial marketable natural resources, a well-developed, though in some cases aging, transportation and manufacturing infrastructure, and a well-educated population.

Why does this matter? There is no shortage of experts warning of and addressing the dual transition challenges. Claus Offe stressed that "Only

Table 3.1   Progress in Economic Reform Central and Eastern Europe and Russian Federation

	Privatization		Macro-Economic Reform		Micro-Economic Reform		Rank
	1998	*2002*	*1998*	*2002*	*1998*	*2002*	*2001*
Bulgaria	4.0	3.0	4.0	3.0	4.25	3.75	11
Czech Rep.	2.0	1.75	2.0	2.25	2.0	2.25	4
Hungary	1.5	1.5	1.75	2.5	1.75	2.0	1
Poland	2.25	2.25	1.75	2.0	1.75	1.5	3
Romania	4.5	3.75	4.5	3.75	4.5	4.25	8
Slovakia	3.25	2.0	3.75	2.5	3.75	2.5	9
Slovenia	2.5	2.5	2.0	2.0	2.0	2.0	6
Russian Fed.	3.0	3.5	4.25	3.75	4.25	4.5	16

Source: Freedom House Annual Ratings 2003 and European Bank for Reconstruction and Development 2001.

Key: Ratings are based on the normal Freedom House system where essentially 1=maximum "progress" and 7=no progress; the rank summarizes the reform progress reported by the EBRD on a range of specific measures of economic liberalization in 2001 for 27 transition countries.

a developed market economy produces the social structural conditions for stable democracy and makes it possible to form compromises within the framework of what is perceived as a positive-sum."[15] Phillipe Schmitter warned that disillusionment flows from the economic performance of neo-democracies—tempting disaffected actors to revive old authoritarian themes or invent new ones. Even if there is no revival of authoritarianism, the danger of failing to consolidate acceptable rules for political competition and cooperation is serious.[16]

Not unrelated to the challenges of dual transition are the questions of how rapid and complete should economic reform of a state socialist economy proceed. Anders Åslund was clearly the most consistent proponent of "big bang" or "shock therapy" in this respect, both originally, as he wrote about and advised transition countries and more recently, as he assessed their relative success stories. He credits the radical and comprehensive deregulation/liberalization strategies employed in Central Europe, Estonia, and Lithuania with success in achieving "real" market economies and less pervasive corruption, especially from rent seekers. He suggests that external competition should limit rents, and liberalizing reform becomes more difficult beyond the initial "jump." Political support for reform clearly tends to wane after the early period of euphoria toward system change.[17]

David L. Bartlett is in some ways the most interesting with his detailed analysis of transition Hungary. Bartlett pointed to Hungary as a clear dual transition success story, in that state agencies were insulated from the opponents of economic reforms by democracy and the creation of democratic institutions; political reform can, in fact, promote economic reform.[18]

Russia had changed, however. There was evidence by this time of an entrepreneurial spirit—indeed perhaps excessively so by formerly devoted *nomenklatura* now firmly in control of what had been state assets. Those taking advantage of the new environment included black marketeers and corrupt or uncommitted "Communists" from the past. Chrystia Freeland captures the climate of the "casino capitalism" of the 1990s that evolved, as she describes the rise of the oligarchs and the Russian financial collapse in August 1998 in vivid, entertaining, and yet sobering detail. Her presentation of economic indicators for the period helped to document the extent of the economic dislocation. Rose Brady compiled trends in Russian poverty from a variety of Russian sources, noting that the percentage of the total Russian population below subsistence level was about 32 percent in 1992 and declined with some oscillation to 21 percent in 1997.[19]

Independent surveys and estimates by the World Bank and the United Nations Development Program (UNDP) put the percentage of population in absolute poverty in Russia at 18.8 percent and the percentage of population below the national poverty line in 1994 at 30.9 percent. The Gini Index of income inequality for Russia reported by UNDP in the late 1990s was 45.6—a higher level of inequality than any other post-Soviet state.[20] Jeni Klugman and Sheila Marnie examined the rise in poverty and inequality in the 1990s in some detail, stressing that "poverty in Russia is not a phenomenon which arrived with transition, but the economic reforms have been associated with steep rises in the levels and severity of poverty, and changes in the profile of poverty."[21]

The World Bank also reported that per capita purchasing power parity in Russia was $6,186 in 1996 and $7,820 by 2002. This compared unfavorably with the levels of PPP in the Czech Republic, Hungary, and Poland for the same period, at $12,197, $9,832, and $7,543, respectively, in 1996. But the Russian per capita level was higher than all other USSR successor states, save Belarus ($6,318), Estonia ($7,563), and Lithuania ($6,283) for that year. The World Bank also reported that growth in the Gross Domestic Product in Russia from 1990 to 1995 was negative, at -7 percent and was only at .8 percent for the period 1995–2000—again, much less impressive than the growth rates enjoyed by most Eastern European and former Soviet economies for the same periods, especially 1995–2000.[22]

In *How Capitalism Was Built* (2007), Anders Åslund took the opportunity to reflect on the 1990s in what was in effect a sequel to his impressive assessment of post-communist transition economics—*Building Capitalism* (2002). This reflection argued, among other things, that the oligarchs were important to Russian economic growth and that "The Russian financial crash turned out to be the catharsis Russia needed to accomplish a full-fledged market economy with a critical mass of markets, macroeconomic stability, and private enterprises."[23]

As the realities of governing in a bitterly divided political system with limited progress on the economic front, the June 1996 elections were sharply contested. Yeltsin was able to prevail finally over Communist Party candidate Gennady Zyuganov in the second round runoff in July, as depicted in table 3.2.

Table 3.2   1996 Presidential Election Results, Russian Federation

First Round		
Boris Yeltsin, Independent	26,665,495	35.8%
Gennady Zyuganov, Communist Party	24,211,686	32.5%
Alexander Lebed, Congress of Russian Commun.	10,974,736	14.7%
Grigory Yavlinsky, Yabloko	5,550,752	7.4%
Vladimir Zhirinovsky, Liberal Democratic Party	4,311,479	5.8%
Second Round		
Boris Yeltsin, Independent	40,203,948	54.4%*
Gennady Zyuganov, Communist Party	30,102,288	40.7%

Source: Central Election Commission of the RF.

The Communists had grown to be a substantial force in Russian politics again by 1996, clearly the largest party in the Duma with 157 seats after the December 1995 parliamentary elections. The coalition of left-leaning parties was far stronger than the weakening pro-government coalition previously centered on Our Home—Russia which only managed fifty-five seats. Zhirinovsky's nationalist and misleadingly named "Liberal Democratic Party" earned fifty-one seats. A strong "Red-Brown" coalition thus confronted the government.

The worsening economic conditions and ineffectual reforms put the Yeltsin government under serious pressure. Re-election had appeared doubtful until key oligarchs realized that a victory by Gennady Zyuganov, standard bearer of the Communist Party, would likely diminish their wealth and hold on economic power gained through the questionable voucher privatization process. Boris Berezovsky of Channel One TV, Vladimir Gusinsky of NTV and *Sevodna* (his daily newspaper), and Mikhail Khodorkovsky of Menatep Bank and Yukos Oil led this effort, along with Pyotr Aven, Mikhail Fridman, Vladimir Potanin, and Alexander Smolensky. The younger "oligarchs" had largely taken over from managers left from the state socialist regime and were both more dynamic and less inclusive in their pursuit of prosperity. By this time they had substantial financial resources to contribute to the Yeltsin campaign, likely making a sham of the campaign finance limits.[24]

The Clinton Administration clearly supported Yeltsin's re-election. Indeed, plans to support NATO enlargement were put on hold for fear that this would sour U.S.–Russian relations and hurt Yeltsin's prospects. Western politicians worried that a victory by Zyuganov would clearly disrupt the progress made, as problematic as it was, on privatization and market capitalism.[25]

FOREIGN AND SECURITY POLICY UNDER YELTSIN

Boris Yeltsin's presidency obviously coincided with the initial euphoric years after the "end of the Cold War." As such, much of his early policy continued the reduction of tensions with the West begun under Gorbachev, while domestic and new "near abroad" distractions from the neighboring successor states to the FSU, tended to overwhelm the attention space of Yeltsin and his ministers and deputies. Andrei P. Tsygankov captures this sentiment effectively, as he describes "the worldview of the westernizers" who were in charge early on and intent on joining Western institutions and dispositions.[26] Tsygankov traces the transformation of this inclination, as it confronted the political realities after the early euphoria:

Westernizers gave little consideration to the country's past experience and, by offering it the "solution" of becoming a part of the West, they denied it the very legitimacy of a search for its own post-Soviet identity . . . . Such was the irony of the radically pro-Western course that it could produce only non-Western, at times even anti-Western, economic and political outcomes.[27]

An early challenge on the near abroad/CIS (Commonwealth of Independent States) side was whether there could or should be a ruble zone joined by some of the newly "independent" states. This would be costly to the Russian Federation as the presumed central banker and currency value defender of the zone, but it would also remove important degrees of sovereignty for each of the potential transition successor states to the FSU. Economist Robert Mundell's famous "Trilemma" would apply here just as it does for the weaker members of the Eurozone struggling with external debt, like Greece. These governments gave up the prospect of adjusting the values of national currencies or interest rates as partial strategies. Austerity often then becomes the only option. From the Russian point of view, the case against national currencies was to seek to maintain trade links between the CIS members.[28]

Initially, the fifteen successor republics "inherited" a common, unconvertible currency, the Soviet ruble; this proved unworkable because of the impact on trade postures, despite being pushed on them by financial advisors from the European Community and the IMF. Belarus maintained an interest in monetary unity the longest; indeed the economic relationship between Belarus and Russia more generally grew tighter than between those of any other CIS states. This had not been without tension, however, especially after Alexander Lukashenko succeeded Vyacheslaw Kebich as president.[29]

Kazakhstan explored its external trade prospects, given its oil and natural gas reserves, but also was careful not to break firmly with Russia. The real innovation among FSU successor states, however, was the independent moves by President Heydar Aliyev in Azerbaijan and President Nursultan Nazerbaev in Kazakhstan to establish cooperation with the West and China, to establish production partnerships and external shipping networks for their oil and gas reserves. The Baku–Tbilisi–Ceyhan (BTC) pipeline to the Eastern Mediterranean Turkish terminal gave Azerbaijan a path to reach European markets without Russian control. Similarly, the Kazakh pipelines to China also provided independent export opportunities beyond Russian control. These initiatives were significant in providing considerable prospect for economic independence of key successor republics. But more important, perhaps, was the extent to which they reflect both the clever maneuvering of the two CIS presidents, and the lack of interest, or at least attention, by the Yeltsin government. President Clinton was effective in making the BTC pipeline a reality working closely with Georgia and Turkey. Putin would seek to recoup influence in the Caspian Basin but would not easily gain back the degree of control that he wished.[30] President Nazarbaev reportedly proved to be the impetus for development of the Eurasian Economic Union, which President Putin later embraced as a means for recapturing FSU economic integration.

The primary security challenge faced by President Yeltsin was of course the pressure for secession by ethnic and religious communities, evident most strikingly in Chechnya. Although national self-determination inclinations here date well back to the Russian Empire, Chechen independence from the Russian Federation was first declared September 6, 1991. Armed conflict was most serious between December 1994 and August 1996. The Russians largely prevailed initially, given superior manpower and weaponry, particularly in the large-scale destruction of Grozny. But extended guerrilla warfare, especially in the surrounding rural mountains, frustrated Russian forces; Chechen success in retaking Grozny and demoralizing the Russian forces led Yeltsin to declare a ceasefire in 1996. Estimates of the total casualties on both sides during the First Chechen War are shocking: 3,000–17,000 Chechen soldiers killed and 14,000 Russian soldiers killed; estimates of Chechen civilians killed range as high as 80,000, but the Russians estimate less than half that many.[31]

Carlotta Gall and Thomas de Waal argue that the real tragedy was that the war could have been avoided if the Chechens could have struck a deal for special status similar to that enjoyed by Tatarstan early on. The incompatibility of claims of "territorial integrity" vs. "independence," as opposed to negotiating over some degree of self-determination left little room for compromise.[32] A second Chechen War began in 1999 and lasted into 2000. Cynics saw it largely as an effort to raise the status of Vladimir Putin in Yeltsin's waning days of rule. The impact was similarly destructive to Chechnya, and some would say to the whole Russian Federation.[33]

Yeltsin's relations with the United States and European NATO members declined in part because of Russian actions in Chechnya, but more seriously by the challenges of instability and atrocities growing out of the breakup of Yugoslavia. In response to the Bosnian war, 1992–1995, and the Kosovo War, 1998–1999, European "humanitarian" intervention and later NATO military operations were mounted against the forces of Slobodan Milosevic, president of Serbia. The massacre of Bosnians at Srebenica by Serbian forces under the direction of Radovan Karadzic and General Ratko Mladic was particularly heinous. The efforts by Milosevic to repress the separatist Albanian Muslims in Kosovo led to his prosecution for war crimes at the International Criminal Tribunal for the Former Yugoslavia (ICTY) in the Hague. The NATO bombing of Serbian forces, including installations in Belgrade, seemed somewhat appropriate to much of the international community, given widespread concern about ethnic cleansing and potential genocide. But the attacks on fellow "Slavs" were hard for Russians to accept, particularly since there was no authorizing resolution by the UN Security Council. Russia and China worked together to make sure one was not adopted.[34]

WHAT WENT WRONG WITH "TRANSITION" IN YELTSIN'S RUSSIA?

This question is also complex and requires a detailed examination beyond the scope of this volume to do it justice, but again we are fortunate, in that it has received detailed analysis by a variety of respected economists and political scientists.[35] A summary of the key points may nonetheless be useful to help us understand the situation of Russia and its economic and political relations with the West.

Western aid and advice—especially advice—was forthcoming to support the transition. The simple guidance of the "Washington Consensus" developed as conditionality for loans and grants to developing countries by the IMF and World Bank, heavily influenced by the economic liberalism perspective of U.S. and UK theorists and politicians, provided the general core of the advice:

- Privatization—selling state enterprises to the private sector
- Eliminating price supports (state subsidies) and controls—submit to market forces
- Reducing government deficits—cut state subsidies and social welfare expenditures, providing the discipline of the market
- Encouraging free trade
- Attracting foreign capital for needed investment and technology transfer through liberalization of controls
- Establishing convertibility of currencies—devaluing to world market value
    (The Ruble fell to < .2 cents by 1993 (from the nominal exchange rate fixed by the Soviet government as late as 1979 1\$ =1 Ruble)
- Decentralization of economic decision-making

Advice differed on what to do first (tactical sequencing) and how rapid or gradual the process should be. Proponents of "shock therapy" said that it was best to institute the new system as quickly and completely as possible—to avoid rent-seeking behavior, corruption, and loss of political support.[36] Poland largely followed this strategy, at the advice of Jeffrey Sachs. Most other countries followed a gradualist, incremental approach, assuming they were really committed to market reforms at all. For Russia, the common label was "shock but no therapy." Marshall Goldman spoke of the "the reform that never was."[37] In point of fact, there was a plan, or more properly, there were plans, as Gregory Yavlinsky and his colleagues detailed in *500 Days;* there was just no real implementation, or at best faulty efforts.[38]

There was no better test for this challenge than the weak democratic political system emerging in the Russian Federation. The factors contributing to the enormous challenge included: ethnic and regional tension, deadlock between President Yeltsin and the Duma over anything beyond half measures, the rise of oligarchs manipulating the privatization process to seize state enterprises with assets (especially natural resources), extremist political movements (right and left), weak institutions, and limited rule of law—dissuading substantial foreign investment, growing external debt, modest foreign assistance (no new Marshall Plan), growing poverty as pensions and the social safety net disappeared, and declining life expectancy.[39]

Russian (and Western) conspiracy theorists had a field day. Some argued, for example, that the Western-inspired race to dismantle state-controlled economies was not so much motivated by a sincere effort to translate and transmit economic liberalism (since there were true believers in the perspective) to the Eastern European and post-Soviet context. Instead, they argued, it was to destroy any opportunity for the rise of social democracy in Eastern Europe, on the one hand,[40] or more insidiously to create a system of tycoon capitalism for the privileged few, on the other.[41] There were also suspicions that military planners were aggressively supporting this dismantling of the state machinery and welfare state system to make sure that the USSR could not be reconstituted in any way that would serve as an ideological inspiration or a political-military competitor.[42]

The privatization campaign, largely masterminded by Yegor Gaidar, pushed ahead and had important impact in several key sectors of the post-Soviet economy. One sector that was largely ignored in the 1990s was agriculture. Indeed, while producer autonomy was encouraged in other sectors as part of the effort to construct a market economy, this was not pushed in the management of agriculture in the 1990s. As Leonard and Serova attest:

> . . . the government of the Russian Federation, while granting private ownership
> in the reorganization of farms, reaffirmed a collectivist principle in agriculture
> and did not promote thoroughgoing restructuring. Re-chartering of large farms
> confirmed their dominance in the agricultural sector mainly in a new form, that
> is, joint stock associations and co-operatives, although roughly 30 per cent of
> the total number of farms refused to be privatized and retained their status as
> state farms.[43]

The lack of autonomy and incentives to individual farmers (to benefit from possible increased production) led to stagnation. This was in great contrast to Deng Xiaoping's initial reforms in China in the late 1970s. Indeed, Leonard and Serova note that agricultural "output steadily dropped in Russia in the 1990s."[44]

Privatization opportunities in other sectors opened the way for insider deals and corruption. Some of this began and grew out of the perestroika reforms under Gorbachev which permitted cooperatives and entrepreneurial import business to satisfy a clear demand for Western products including personal computers and related electronic devices. Long-standing black and grey market activity got a boost and quasi-legitimacy and a more lucrative response from pent-up consumer demand.[45] Much of the popular discontent evident during the 1990s derived from the enormous wealth accumulated by "oligarchs" some of whom benefited from government voucher privatization (loans for shares) schemes and became fabulously wealthy. This process often seemed to be at the expense of the state budget, while much of the rest of the Russian population languished and then saw their living standards tumble. Indeed, David Satter argued: "The reforms were dominated by three processes: hyperinflation, privatization, and criminalization. Their interaction led to economic collapse, mass poverty, and the effective privatization of the Russian state."[46] The gap worsened dramatically when the economy essentially collapsed in 1998.

The big winners in the struggle to control Russia's immense natural resources after the end-of-state socialism included Mikhail Khodorkovsky, who became rich combining Siberian oil fields under Yukos Oil, until he ran afoul of President Putin's efforts to claw back state control of natural resource income and limit the political influence of the oligarchs more generally. Khodorkovsky subsequently lost control of Yukos and served ten years in prison on charges of embezzlement and money laundering. He then went into exile in London, while maintaining a critical posture toward Putin.[47]

Other important "oligarchs" acquiring wealth and influence during the Yeltsin regime were Pyotr Aven (head of Alfa-Bank and LetterOne investments), Boris Berezovsky (a prominent Soviet mathematician who established AvtoVAZ automobiles and software, and developed media–Channel 1), Mikhail Fridman, (co-founder of Alfa-Bank and LetterOne, including L1 Energy with a focus on North Sea oil and telecommunications), Vladimir Gusinsky (media–especially NTV television and *Sevodnya* newspaper), Vitaly Malkin (Banking, established Rossiysky Kredit, with Bidzina Ivanishvili of Georgia), Vladimir Potanin (United Export Import Bank and Folletina Trading; Norilsk Nickel/nonferrous metals), Alexander Smolensky (banking and currency speculation), and Vladimir Vinogradov (Inkombank–bankrupt essentially after 1998 financial crisis).[48] Berezovsky,

Fridman, Gusinsky, Khodorkovsky, Potanin, Smolensky, and Vinogradov together comprised the Seven Bankers—*Semibankirschina*—who had been instrumental in saving Yeltsin's electoral prospects in 1996.[49] This sample is incomplete, of course; private ownership of Russian assets was much more extensive, but these were the corporate actors who most sought to wield power and maximize their personal wealth, often depositing very large sums in foreign bank accounts.

Toward the end of the Yeltsin administration, the capitalist economy in Russia appeared broken. There was no reliable rule of law, and little of the broad-based prosperity that was promised from entry into the globalized economy was evident. Conspicuous *Kleptocrats* and crony capitalism dominated. Political power seemed less wielded by the state than by a less formal web of oligarchs.

> . . . oligarchic capitalism was entrenched. Two researchers in Moscow, Peter Boone and Denis Rodionov, prepared a study of Russia's sixty-four largest companies in August 2002—all firms in which the government no longer had a controlling stake. They found that 85 percent of the sales of these companies were controlled by just eight large financial-industrial groups.
>
> The bigger companies thrived, but one consequence of the age of the oligarchs was that small- and medium-size enterprises were stunted and did not expand. A huge obstacle for these firms was lack of access to capital. The banking system was still largely dysfunctional, a legacy of the 1990s. It was hard for entrepreneurs to get loans to start new businesses, while the oligarchs had plenty of capital and could easily finance their own needs.[50]

Indeed, some analysts argue that along with "financing their own needs," these oligarchs provided needed investment that the state could not or would not muster and that foreign sources were increasingly reluctant to offer. Sergei Guriev and Andrei Rachinsky provide a systematic and nuanced assessment of this issue, noting widespread concern about the rise in oligarchic political power but finding that there have been some productivity and marketing strengths evident in their operations.[51]

Nobel Prize laureate and former chief economist at the World Bank, Joseph E. Stiglitz, argued that the Washington Consensus was less flawed in conception than poorly managed—often in support of corporate interests and against the real interests of recipient countries, including Russia (especially on currency valuation and the liberalization of capital flow controls). Focusing on specific management errors on the part of the World Bank and IMF, among other external actors in a chapter on "Who Lost Russia," Stiglitz provided persuasive arguments to the effect that the diagnosis and remedies offered for Russia's very large debt load and overvalued Ruble in 1998 were disastrous.[52]

Speaking as an "insider," while at the World Bank, Stiglitz noted that:

While those in Russia must bear much of the blame for what has happened, the Western advisers, especially from the United States and the IMF, who marched in so quickly to preach the gospel of the market economy, must also take some blame. At the very least, they provided support to those who led Russia and many of the other economies down the paths they followed, arguing for a new religion—market fundamentalism—as a substitute for the old one—Marxism—which had proved so deficient.[53]

Stiglitz got very specific on what advice was problematic, particularly as it played out in the 1998 financial crisis:

The country was deeply in debt, and the higher interest rates that the East Asia crisis had provoked created an enormous additional strain. This rickety tower collapsed when oil prices fell. Due to recessions and depressions in Southeast Asia, which IMF policies had exacerbated, oil demand not only failed to expand as expected but actually contracted. The resulting imbalance between demand and supply of oil turned into a dramatic fall in crude oil prices (down over 40 percent in the first six months of 1998 compared to the average prices in 1997). Oil is both a major export commodity and a source of government tax revenue for Russia, and the drop in prices had a predictably devastating effect. At the World Bank, we became aware of the problem early in 1998, when prices looked ready to fall even below Russia's cost of extraction plus transportation. Given the exchange rates at the time, Russia's oil industry could cease being profitable. A devaluation would then be inevitable.[54]

Stiglitz criticized the policies then pushed by the IMF. There was pressure to avoid devaluation, betting that the currency markets were wrong about the value. This risked that the Russians would have to pay back the IMF loans at a higher dollar level if devaluation did occur. He noted: "By inducing greater foreign borrowing, by making Russia's position once it devalued so much less tenable, the IMF was partly culpable for the eventual suspension of payments by Russia on its debts."[55]

Massive restructuring of a dysfunctional system no matter the sequencing of tactical reform measures or the speed of implementation means a collapse of production, unemployment, and dislocation. As Lee Kuan Yew recognized in post-independence Singapore, serious economic reform is difficult for a democracy, especially an immature one facing contentious "parties."[56]

The depth of the economic decline and social dislocation to which the Russian Federation fell was hard to believe for most not experiencing it. On the surface, Russia appeared to have everything required to prosper under a new liberal economic order: a well-educated population, enormous reserves of natural resources—particularly oil and gas—an extensive transportation network with related infrastructure in place, and the prospect for access to markets well beyond its former key trade partners in Eastern Europe.

The World Bank reported in 1995 and 2005 substantial poverty and weakness in health and social services. Life expectancy declined significantly after the collapse of the Soviet Union, while income inequality grew dramatically.[57] There existed a very wealthy elite, perhaps only .3–1.5 percent of the population.[58]

Initial progress to address these challenges was terminated essentially with the 1998 Russian financial crisis and subsequent policy to decrease social and health service spending in order to consolidate the financial recovery. Indeed, in 2000, four out of ten Russians were reported to live in poverty. The World Bank pointed to growing consumption inequality, higher than much of the rest of the CIS and Eastern European transition countries, and stressed the rise of infectious diseases and continued weakness in health services.[59]

The challenge of "dual transition" (to democracy and a market economy) was not fully met under Yeltsin; progress was modest at best. Certainly, there was no near-term prospect for democratic consolidation. Yeltsin had managed to be re-elected in 1996 with the help of key oligarchs and Western governments.

Larry Diamond classified Russia in the late 1990s as a "non-liberal electoral democracy," based on 1997 Freedom House data and assessments. One would not be so generous in 2020, as elections have become less competitive in the hands of President Putin, and the overall FH rating has slipped from Partly Free to Not Free after 2010.

In an earlier work, Diamond argued:

> . . . the consolidation of democracy is not civil society but political institutionalization. Consolidation is the process by which democracy becomes so broadly and profoundly legitimate among its citizens that it is very unlikely to break down. It involves behavioral and institutional changes that normalize democratic politics and narrow its uncertainty . . . .
>
> Robust political institutions are needed to accomplish economic reform under democratic conditions. Strong, well-structured executives buttressed by experts at least somewhat insulated from the day-to-day pressures of politics, make possible the implementation of painful and disruptive reform measures.[60]

According to this definition, few of the post-Soviet republics could be termed consolidated democracies, and certainly the Russian Federation would not qualify.

Anders Åslund argued in a 2007 book on *Russia's Capitalist Revolution* that "Market Reform Succeeded and Democracy Failed."[61] He stressed that key changes were made in price and trade liberalization in January 1992 and were not reversed. Inflation and currency instability plagued Russia all during the 1990s, as noted above, but swift small-scale privatization worked well, and the controversial voucher privatization succeeded in transferring most state enterprises to the private sector. This was the key, according to Åslund: "Public enterprises breed corruption, monopolies, and subsidies, and if they dominate a country, neither democracy nor market economy can be maintained."[62] He further argued that democracy failed ultimately because so little was done to build it.[63]

At minimum, it appears that there is little evidence that there was real progress under Yeltsin "in the institutional aspects of marketization . . . the ways in which democratization enhances the market-promoting elements of the state's role in transitional socialist economies." David Bartlett argued this was the positive of "dual transition" in Hungary and several other East European transition economies.[64]

As we shall see in the next chapter, there are growing doubts as to how well market reform ultimately succeeded, as Putin began his own restructuring. Indeed, Åslund raises some of these doubts in his most recent analysis of Russia's "Crony Capitalist" economy.[65]

NOTES

1. Vladimir Solovyov and Elena Klepikova, *Boris Yeltsin: A Political Biography* (NY: G. P Putnum's Sons, 1992), part three. See also Yeltsin's own account of the period leading up to his rise to the Presidency of Russia in *Against the Grain: An Autobiography* (NY: Summit Books, 1990).

2. Central Election Commission of the Russian Federation, 1991.

3. See: Boris Yeltsin, et al., *PutschL The Diary—Three Days That Collapsed the Empire, August 19–21, 1991* (Oakville, ON: Mosaic Press, 1992).

4. Solovyov and Klepikova, *Boris Yeltsin*, p. 267.

5. Lynn D. Nelson and Irina Y. Kuzes, *Property to the People: The Struggle for Radical Economic Reform in Russia* (Armonk, NY: M.E. Sharpe, Inc., 1994), pp. 35–56.

6. Rose Brady, *Kapitalizm: Russia's Struggle to Free Its Economy* (New Haven, CT: Yale University Press, 1999), p. 10.

7. Ibid., p. 11.

8. Ibid., pp. 42–43.

9. Jeffrey D. Sachs, "Why Russia Has Failed to Stabilize," in Anders Åslund, ed., *Russian Economic Reform at Risk* (London: Pinter, 1995), p. 53.

10. Masha Gessen, *The Man Without a Face: The Unlikely Rise of Vladimir Putin* (NY: Penguin Riverhead Books, 2012), p. 126.

11. Leon Aron, *Yeltsin: A Revolutionary Life* (NY: St. Martin's Press, 2000), pp. 709–717.

12. The full Constitution is readily available at: http://www.constitution.ru/.

13. Michael McFaul, *From Cold War to Hot Peace: An American Ambassador in Putin's Russia* (Boston, MA: Houghlin Mifflin Harcourt, 2018), Chapter 2.

14. Freedom House Annual Surveys, rating degree of political rights and civil liberties depict all of Central of Eastern Europe as closed to the highest score (1), while the Russian Federation languishes at 4–5 in 1999–2000.

15. Claus Offe, "Capitalism by Democratic Design? Democratic Theory Facing the Triple Transition in East Central Europe," *Social Research*, 58, no. 4 (1991), p. 881.

16. Phillippe Schmitter, "Dangers and Dilemmas of Democracy," in Larry Diamond and Marc F. Plattner, eds., *The Global Resurgence of Democracy*, Second edition (Baltimore, MD: Johns Hopkins University Press, 1996), pp. 91–92.

17. Anders Åslund, *Building Capitalism: The Transformation of the Former Soviet Bloc* (Cambridge, UK: Cambridge University Press, 2002), pp. 194–196.

18. David L. Barlett, *The Political Economy of Dual Transformations: Market Reform and Democratization in Hungary* (Ann Arbor: The University of Michigan Press, 1997), p. 3.

19. Rose Brady, *Kapitalizm: Russia's Struggle to Free Its Economy* (See also: Chrystia Freeland, *Sale of the Century: Russia's Wild Ride from Communism to Capitalism* (NY: Crown Business/Random House, 2000)).

20. World Bank, *World Development Report, 2000–2004*; United Nations Development Programme, *Human Development Report, 2003*.

21. Jeni Klugman and Sheila Marnie, "Poverty," in Brigitte Granville and Peter Oppenheimer, eds., *Russia's Post-Communist Economy* (NY: Oxford University Press, 2001), p. 445.

22. World Bank, *World Development Report, 2000–2004*.

23. Anders Åslund, *How Capitalism was Built: The Transformation of Central and Eastern Europe, Russia, and Central Asia* (Cambridge, UK: Cambridge University Press, 2007), p. 8. See also Chapter 10.

24. Ibid., pp. 259–272. See also: Anders Åslund, *Russia's Capitalist Revolution: Why Market Reform Succeeded and Democracy Failed* (Washington, DC: Peterson Institute for International Economics, 2007), pp. 164–173.

25. McFaul, *From Cold War to Hot Peace*, pp. 41–49.

26. Andrei P. Tsygankov, *Russia's Foreign Policy: Change and Continuity in National Identity*. Fourth edition (Lanham, MD: Rowman and Littlefield, 2016), pp. 59–79.

27. Ibid., p. 93.

28. Brigitte Granville, "Farewell, Ruble Zone," in Anders Åslund, ed., *Russian Economic Reform at Risk* (London: Pinter, 1995), pp. 66–70.

29. Ibid., pp. 77–79.

30. See: Steve LeVine, *The Oil and the Glory: The Pursuit of Empire and Fortune on the Caspian Sea* (NY: Random House, 2007); and S. Frederick Starr and

Svante E. Cornell, eds., *The Baku-Tbilisi-Ceyhan Pipeline: Oil Window to the West* (Washington, DC: Johns Hopkins University SAIS-Central Asia-Caucus Institute and Silk Road Studies Program, 2005).

31. John B. Dunlop, "How Many Soldiers and Civilians Died during the Russo-Chechen War of 1994–1996?" *Central Asian Survey*, 19, no. 3–4 (2000), pp. 329–339; see also "Russia: Chechen Official Puts War Death Toll at 160,000," *Radio Free Europe-Radio Liberty*, August 16, 2005.

32. Carlotta Gall and Thomas de Waal, *Chechnya: Calamity in the Caucasus* (NY: New York University Press, 1998), pp. 360–370.

33. See: Mark Galeotti, *Russia's Wars in Chechnya 1994–2009* (Oxford, UK: Osprey Publishing, 2014); and U.S. Congress, Senate. Committee on Foreign Relations, *The War in Chechnya: Russia's Conduct, The Humanitarian Crisis, and United States Policy* (Washington, DC: War College Series, 2015).

34. See: Catherine Baker, *The Yugoslav Wars of the 1990s* (London: Macmillan, 2015); William Joseph Buckley, ed. *Kosovo: Contending Voices on Balkan Interventions* (Grand Rapids, MI: Eerdmans Publishing Co., 2000); Nader Mousavizadeh, *The Black Book of Bosnia: The Consequences of Appeasement* (NY: Basic Books, 1996); and Michael Parenti, *To Kill A Nation: The Attack on Yugoslavia* (London: Verso, 2000).

35. For example, see Anders Åslund, *Building Capitalism: The Transformation of the Former Soviet Bloc* (UK: Cambridge University Press, 2002); Anders Åslund, *How Capitalism Was Built: The Transformation of Central and Eastern Europe, Russia, and Central Asia* (Cambridge, UK: Cambridge University Press, 2007); Anders Åslund, *Russia's Capitalist Revolution: Why Market Reform Succeeded and Democracy Failed* (Washington, DC: Peterson Institute for International Economics, 2007); Anders Åslund, *Russia's Crony Capitalism: The Path from Market Economy to Kleptocracy* (New Haven, CT: Yale University Press, 2019); Braguinsky, Serguey and Grigory Yavlinsky. *Incentives and Institutions: The Transition to a Market Economy in Russia* (Princeton, NJ: Princeton University Press, 2000); Stephen F. Cohen, *Failed Crusade: America and the Tragedy of Post-Communist Russia* (NY: W.W. Norton, 2000); Marshall I. Goldman, *Lost Opportunity: Why Economic Reforms in Russia Have not Worked* (NY: W.W. Norton, 1996); Marshall I. Goldman, *The Piratization of Russia: Russian Reform Goes Awry* (NY: Routledge, 2003); Marie Lavigne, *The Economics of Transition: From Socialist Economy to Market Economy*. Second edition (NY: St. Martin's Press, 1999); and Lilia Shevtsova, *Lost in Transition: The Yeltsin and Putin Legacies* (Washington, DC: Carnegie Endowment for International Peace, 2007).

36. See: Åslund, *Building Capitalism*; and Anders Åslund, *How Capitalism was Built*.

37. Marshall Goldman, *Lost Opportunity: Why Economic Reforms in Russia Have Not Worked* (NY: W.W. Norton, 1996), Chapter 1.

38. Gregory Yavlinsky, et al., *500 Days: Transition to the Market* (NY: St. Marin's Press, 1991).

39. Serguey Braguinsky and Grigory Yavlinsky, *Incentives and Institutions: The Transition to a Market Economy in Russia* (Princeton, NJ: Princeton University Press, 2000). See also: Shevtsova, *Lost in Transition*; World Bank, *Making Transition Work*

for Everyone: Poverty and Inequality in Europe and Central Asia (Washington, DC, 2000); World Bank, *Poverty in Russia: An Assessment.* Report No. 14110-RU. June 13, 1995; and World Bank, *Russian Federation: Reducing Poverty through Growth and Social Policy Reform.* Report No. 289232-RU. February 24, 2005.

40. See: Laszlo Andor and Martin Summers. *Market Failure: Eastern Europe's 'Economic Miracle'* (London: Pluto Press, 1998).

41. See: Janine R. Wedel. *Collision and Collusion: The Strange Case of Western Aid to Eastern Europe, 1989–1998* (NY: St. Martin's Press, 1998).

42. Stephen F. Cohen, *Failed Crusade: America and the Tragedy of Post-Communist Russia* (NY: W.W. Norton, 2000), pp. 37, and 237–238.

43. Carol Scott Leonard and Eugenia Serova, "The Reform of Agriculture," in Brigitte Granville and Peter Oppenheimer, eds., *Russia's Post-Communist Economy* (NY: Oxford University Press, 2001), p. 371.

44. Ibid., p. 368.

45. David Hoffman, *The Oligarchs: Wealth and Power in the New Russia* (NY: Public Affairs, 2011), Chapters 1 and 2.

46. See: David Satter, *Darkness at Dawn: The Rise of the Russian Criminal State* (New Haven, CT: Yale University Press, 2008), p. 46. See also: Vadim Volkov, *Violent Entrepreneurs: The Use of Force in the Making of Russian Capitalism* (Ithaca, NY: Cornell University Press, 2002).

47. Richard Sakwa, *Putin and the Oligarch: The Khodorkovsky-Yukos Affair* (London: I.B. Tauris, 2014); and Martin Sixsmith, *Putin's Oil: the Yukos Affair and the Struggle for Russia* (NY: Continuum, 2010).

48. See: Stephen Fortescue, *Russia's Oil Barons and Metal Magnates: Oligarchs and the State in Transition* (NY: Palgrave Macmillan, 2006); Hoffman, *The Oligarchs*; and David Satter, *Darkness at Dawn.*

49. Stephen Fortescue, *Russia's Oil Barons and Metal Magnates*, p. 22.

50. Hoffman, *The Oligarchs*, p. 498.

51. Sergei Guriev and Andrei Rachinski, "The Role of Oligarchs in Russian Capitalism," *Journal of Economic Perspectives*, 19, no. 1 (Winter 2005), pp. 131–150. See also Åslund, *How Capitalism Was Built*, Chapter 10.

52. Joseph E. Stiglitz, *Globalization and Its Discontents Revisited: Anti-Globalization in the Era of Trump* (NY: W.W. Norton & Co., 2018), pp. 225–256, 434.

53. Ibid., pp. 225–256.

54. Ibid., p. 237.

55. Ibid., p. 239. John Odling-Smee provides a partial defense of the IMF role in Russia in "The IMF and Russia in the 1990s." *IMF Staff Papers*, 53, no. 1 (2006).

56. Lee Kuan Yew, *From Third World to First: The Singapore Story, 1965–2000* (NY: Harper Collins, 2000).

57. World Bank, 1995, pp. i, ii, 8, 12, 19, 24–30 and 34–36.

58. Ibid., p. 30.

59. World Bank, 2005, pp. i–xiii, 22–25 and Chapters 7 and 11.

60. Larry Diamond, "Toward Democratic Consolidation," in Larry Diamond and Marc F. Plattner, eds., *The Global Resurgence of Democracy*. Second edition (Baltimore, MD: Johns Hopkins University Press, 1996), pp. 238–239.

61. Åslund, *Russia's Capitalist Revolution*, pp. 1–9.

62. Ibid., p. 8.

63. Ibid., p. 6.

64. Bartlett, *The Political Economy of Dual Transformations*, p. 282.

65. Anders Åslund, *Russia's Crony Capitalism: The Path from Market Economy to Kleptocracy* (New Haven, CT: Yale University Press, 2019).

Chapter 4

Putin

Making Russia Great Again through Foreign Adventurism and Authoritarian Political Power

RESTORING STABILITY AND STATE AUTHORITY IN THE RUSSIAN FEDERATION AND LIMITING COMPETITIVE AUTHORITARIANISM

Reviewing the Putin–Medvedev–Putin phase of Russian political history, it is clear that there has been a growing centralization of power in the hands of the president and a corresponding reduction in the role of independent media and political opposition. Shortly after being named acting president upon the resignation of Boris Yeltsin, Vladimir Putin began to strengthen the Russian state. Interviewed in 2000 for his "self-portrait," *First Person*, he noted: "from the very beginning, Russia was created as a supercentralized state. That's practically laid down in its genetic code, its traditions, and the mentality of its people."[1]

A government website: "Russia at Turn of the Millennium" cautioned against a return to ideology but decried the lack of social cohesion that characterized the 1990s and argued that it was necessary to build a strong state again. It stated that it was necessary to respect civil and human rights, but one must not overlook the rights of state institutions and society as a whole. The only people who can bring order to the state are state people.[2]

While preparing for the March presidential elections, Putin issued an "Open Letter to the Voters" that outlined his platform (while holding himself above the campaign, refusing to debate or participate in election activities). His "Open Letter" listed several of the maladies facing Russia in 2000, and stressed, among other things, the need for a rigorous state with a respected tax system (but not a dictatorship), an economy in which "honest work would be more profitable than stealing," a strong state that can "guarantee freedom:

Table 4.1   March 26, 2000 Presidential Election Results, Russian Federation

Candidate	Party	Votes	%
Vladimir Putin	Independent	39,740,467	53.4
Gennady Zyuganov	Communist Party	21,928,468	29.5
Grigory Yavlinsky	Yabloko	4,351,450	5.9
Aman Tuleyev	Independent	2,217,364	3.0
Vladimir Zhirinovsky	Liberal Democratic Party	2,026,509	2.7
Konstantin Titov	Independent[a]	1,107,269	1.5
Ella Pamgilova	For Civic Dignity	758,967	1.0
Stanislav Govorukhin	Independent	328,723	0.4
Yury Skuratov	Independent	319,189	0.4
Alexey Podberezkin	Spiritual Heritage	98,177	0.1
Umar Dzhabrailov	Independent	78,498	0.1

Source: Central Election Commission of the Russian Federation.

freedom of enterprise, personal freedom, public freedom," the rule of law to protect property rights, and an end to poverty.[3]

The "pitch" and strategy worked well, given a Russian population that was fed up with the chaos of much of the 1990s and had bought into the narrative that the West was to blame in important respects.[4] As table 4.1 indicates, Putin won a convincing majority of the votes cast on March 26.

President Putin gained credit at home and abroad early on for apparent improvement in the rule of law, especially in business dealings, and for re-establishing a measure of state control over several natural resource enterprises from oligarchs who had gained ownership of these firms in the questionable voucher privatization programs of the early 1990s.[5] However, some critics argued that this simply amounted to transfer in ownership and economic benefit to his own group of oligarchs, who had been with him since at least his days in St. Petersburg after returning to Russia from Dresden.[6]

On May 13 of 2000, President Putin issued an executive order creating seven new superfederal regions that would supervise the work of the eighty-nine federal units. This could be seen as follow-through on his pledge to regain central state control with a more hierarchical command structure. At the same time, he began a campaign to centralize control over the media and to harass and curtail political opposition.

Putin's centralization laws were passed overwhelmingly by the Duma in July, making it impossible for an override by the upper chamber. This negated the initial veto by the Federation Council (and effort by Boris Berezovskiy to rally regional governors to resist). In Berezovskiy's words: "Only the Federation Council is a guarantee that there will be no usurpation of power in Russia. If the Federation Council is destroyed, we will have one branch of power—authoritarian, a very rough totalitarian regime."[7]

A weakened opposition and the increase in his personal popularity enabled an easy re-election in 2004, with 71.9 percent of the vote. The closest opponent again came from the Communist Party—this time Nikolay Kharitonov with 13.8 percent of the vote. Putin's presidential victory had followed December 7, 2003 elections to the Duma in which Putin's party —United Russia—won a landslide victory.

Putin's prime minister, Dmitry Medvedev, won the 2008 presidential elections convincingly with 71.2 percent of the vote; Zyuganov and Zhirinovsky received 18 percent and 9.5 percent of the vote, respectively. Putin was named prime minister, formally respecting the constitutional limitations on consecutive terms in office, while maintaining substantial influence.

Putin then returned to the presidency in 2012 with 63.6 percent of the vote in the first round. This election campaign was not without controversy, and some spirited opposition in the form of public protests occurred, but the vote was still convincing.

Key media outlets were purchased by state enterprises or otherwise brought under state control after the 2000 election. These included Vladimir Potanin, a principal in the privatization of Norilsk Nickel, and co-owner of *Izvestiya* with Vagit Alekperov, owner of Lukoil, both of whom were charged with tax evasion. This seemed to be part of Putin's effort to limit the autonomy of all the oligarchs, not just those who had media holdings, whom he sought to destroy and drive from the country.[8]

In February of 2001, the Russian government took control of Russia's largest TV network, ORT. On April 3, Gazprom took control of the independent Russian TV station NTV.[9] On January 22 of 2002, Russia's last independent national TV station, TV-6, was forced by the authorities to stop broadcasting, sparking fresh concerns about free speech. It was later awarded a new license after journalists teamed up with Kremlin-backed managers. It was back on air in June with the new name TVS, but it was closed down again (for "financial reasons") in June of 2003. In June of 2005, Gazprom bought the prominent independent daily newspaper, *Izvestiya*. In June of 2006, a law was adopted by the Duma with the stated goal of fighting political extremism. It placed limits on freedoms of speech and assembly. Writing in 2012, Masha Gessen, a prominent journalist and author noted:

> . . . working as a journalist in Russia had become virtually impossible: my colleagues had been killed, maimed, and threatened; the government worked in mysterious ways, behind closed doors, turning the job of describing Russian politics into guesswork at best; reporting had become dangerous and pointless at the same time.[10]

Indeed, there is a long list of political opponents and journalists arrested, exiled, or murdered:

Anatoliy Levin-Utkin, a journalist critical of Sobchak and Putin, is beaten to death outside of his apartment on August 24, 1998. Documents and photos are reported stolen;

Galina Starovoitova, activist for democracy and human rights, murdered at her St Petersburg apartment, November 20, 1998;

Artyom Borovik, died in a plane crash, March 9, 2000;

Vladimir Gusinsky, head of Media-Most, is arrested on charges of swindling and grand larceny on June 28, 2000, after his campaign critical of Putin and the Yeltsin insiders that helped to engineer Putin's succession to the presidency. He subsequently must liquidate his media empire and take up residence in exile in Andalusia, Spain.

Vladimir Kanevsky, Russian media mogul, is killed by a suspected contract killer on February 5, 2002;

Sergei Yushenkov, former army colonel and leader of the Liberal Russia movement, was shot and killed near his Moscow home on April 17, 2003. He was reported to have been collecting evidence that Putin was connected to the 1999 apartment buildings bombings;

Yuri Shchekochihin, Duma Deputy and member of Yabloko, died on July 3, 2003, from a mysterious poisoning. He had been involved in investigations on corruption and the FSB's role in the terrorist attacks on Russian cities in 1999;[11]

Paul Klebnikov, American editor of Forbes Russia murdered by multiple assailants in a suspected contract killing on July 9, 2004. Connection to his criticism of Berezovsky and publishing a list of Russia's 100 richest was suspected, but his track record of investigative journalism also included uncovering memo by KGB First Chief Directorate, Leonid Veselovskiy, on use of party funds to purchase companies and banks in response to the USSR collapse;[12]

Mikhail Khodorkovsky, former Yukos oil oligarch, is sentenced to nine years in prison over charges including tax evasion and fraud on May 31, 2005. He appeals but succeeds only in having sentence cut by a year. He is later sent to serve it in a Siberian penal colony. He had been in custody over investigations into tax evasion and fraud. Mr Khodorkovsky had supported liberal opposition to President Putin. His accounts and shares of YUKOS were frozen;

Anna Politkovskaya, a prominent journalist (*Novaya Gazeta*) investigating the Chechnya war, was shot and killed in the elevator of her apartment building on October 7, 2006; she had been poisoned previously during a trip from Chechnya to investigate the Beslan terrorist attack.

Aleksandr Litvinenko, former Russian security service officer and an outspoken critic of the Kremlin living in exile in London, dies there after being poisoned by a radioactive substance on November 23, 2006. Litvinenko accused Putin of organizing his death;

Ivan Safronov (journalist) mysteriously dies from falling out of his window on March 2, 2007;

Anastasia Baburova, journalist for Novaya Gazeta is shot to death along with human rights lawyer Stanislav Markelov in Sevastopol, Ukraine, January 26, 2009. Both had been engaged in legal proceedings for criticism of Putin and Chechnya;

Natalia Estemirova, human rights activist, is abducted and murdered on July 15, 2009 in Chechnya;

Sergei Magnitsky, a lawyer working with William Browder to investigate large-scale tax fraud in Russia dies in police custody in November 2009. Browder, an American and U.K. citizen subsequently pushed for U.S. sanctions legislation (the Magnitsky Act) to punish Russians linked to Sergei's death and subsequent crimes;

Boris Berezovsky, granted political asylum in the UK; found dead in his home (suicide?) March 23, 2013;

Boris Nemtsov, former deputy prime minister under Yeltsin and opposition leader against Putin, is shot and killed near the Kremlin on February 27, 2015;

Vladimir Kara-Murza, dissident and democracy campaigner, suffers apparent poison attack for second time in January 2017. He was a close friend and political ally of Boris Nemtsov and campaigned in the U.S. for the passage of the Magnitsky act;

Pyotr Verzilov, activist and member of the protest-art group Pussy Riot, suffers poison attack on September 11, 2018, likely in connection with his investigation of Three Russian journalists shot to death in the Central African Republic in July, 2018;

Alexei Navalny, prominent Russian opposition leader, falls ill on flight from Tomsk, Siberia to Moscow on August 20, 2020. Initially treated in Omsk, he is transported to a Berlin hospital where German doctors conclude he was poisoned with Soviet-developed nerve agent Novichok. Upon release from the hospital, Navalny charges Putin in connection with the poisoning.

Several of these died just before they were expected to release some new, politically damaging testimony (e.g., Borovik—possibly implicating the FSB in apartment bombings, Nemtsov—promised information on Russia's involvement in Ukraine), or indeed just after they had done so (e.g., Politkovskaya—criticizing the war in Chechnya; Yushenkov—investigating the "Chechen" bombings of Aug/Sept. 1999).

The gradual destruction of independent media outlets and the intimidation or elimination of critical journalists made it possible for the authoritarian state in Putin's Russia to control the "information war."[13] One only needs to watch the narrative of RT (*Russia Today*) and *Sputnik* English and *ProRussia .tv* French telecasts, not to mention the three main Russian language national television networks, interpreting world events and justifying Russian political decisions, to perceive the bias and occasional "big lie."[14]

Returning to the ingredients of "Totalitarianism"—primarily defined from observation of the Hitler and Stalin regimes—it is clear that this ingredient is well established in centralized state hands. A rather successful effort to rein in the freedom of information and communication provided by the Internet has been an emerging element of this war. Contact with Western or at least non-Russian sources of independent information and opinion is possible (in comparison with much of the Soviet period), but it is expensive and challenging.[15]

Reporters Without Borders ranked Russia 149th out of 180 countries in press freedom in 2019, deteriorating from 121st in 2002, albeit out of a smaller total list of 134. It also issued a troubling evaluation of new anti-terrorism legislation adopted by the Duma on June 24, 2016 which "reinforces government control over communications" with new penalties for telecom operators, blog platforms, and social media suspected of contributing to unauthorized demonstrations.[16] This seems a continuation of the Putin "war" on civil society and political opposition which was ramped up after the large-scale protests following the 2011 Duma elections and the subsequent decision for Medvedev and Putin to simply switch places for the 2012 presidential elections.[17]

Lilia Shevtsova pointed to these events as crucial:

> Things changed, however, when the election-related protests of late 2011 and early 2012 forced the Kremlin to adopt a new survival strategy. The "Putin Doctrine" legitimates a harsher rule at home and a more assertive stance abroad . . . . For the first time in Russian history, representatives of the security services, professionally trained to employ coercion, are not just working for the Kremlin—they are running the Kremlin.[18]

A less authoritarian rule, based on corruption, public indifference, the lack of viable alternatives, and high oil prices had previously looked quite stable, according to Shevtsova. She concluded in 2015 that the Russian system will only continue to degenerate and argued: "Russia can escape the civilizational trap only by means of a revolution that would dismantle the system and create a new chance to build a rule-of-law state."[19]

So what drives the steps toward increased authoritarianism? Is it just a common process where a normal leader simply pursues the path of least resistance. As Lee Kuan Yew famously noted:

Repression, Sir is a habit that grows, I am told it is like making love—it is always easier the second time! The first time there may be pangs of conscience, a sense of guilt. But once embarked on the course with constant repetition you get more and more brazen in the attack. All you have to do is to dissolve organizations and societies and banish and detail the key political workers in these societies. Then miraculously everything is tranquil on the surface. Then an intimidated press and the government-controlled radio together can regularly sing your praises, and slowly and steadily the people are made to forget the evil things that have already been done, or if these things are referred to again they're conveniently distorted and distorted with impunity, because there will be no opposition to contradict.[20]

It is obviously expedient to be able to get on with one's business of development and governance if one does not need to face an independent (and potentially recalcitrant) legislature, a critical press, or significant (more general) political opposition. There are clear advantages to liberal democracy for individual freedom and prosperity that will be discussed below, but there is also a common argument that a deeply divided political system finds it hard to pursue a coherent and efficient development project, particularly if there are important sacrifices to be made.

But there is also something abnormal and perhaps pathological about the drive for power and control or simply personal wealth that seems to be evident in some authoritarian leaders. Much of the literature on Putin's rise to power reflects this perspective. For example, Hill and Gaddy while emphasizing that Putin, the *Operative in the Kremlin,* is pursuing a strategy to maneuver Russia effectively versus the West, also offers a psychological perspective on his drive. Dawisha is systematic in her detailed portrayal of the rise of *Putin's Kleptocracy*, as is Steven Myers detailing the creation of *The New Tsar*.[21] But there may be more to the leadership qualities and drive for absolute power and control that characterizes and sets apart some tyrants from the run-of-the-mill authoritarian.[22]

Based on his own personal political experience and his studies of the Russian political system, Vladimir Gel'man argues in *Russian Authoritarianism* that:

... the ultimate goal of politicians is the maximization of power—in other words, they aspire to stay in power by any means for as long as possible and to acquire as much power as possible, regardless of their democratic rhetoric and public image; this is the essence of politics.[23]

Gel'man is a realist but not so pessimistic to think that Russia could never be democratic, only that the challenge is very steep.

Is there something cultural about the prevalence of authoritarian rule in Russia? Stefan Hedlund raised the question of whether there has been path dependency in Tsarist, Soviet, and Russian Authoritarianism. Success has less to do with applying well-understood Western models of economic reform measures to the Russian historical and cultural context.[24] Indeed, he argued that the reasons for the warped outcomes can actually be traced back through the long sweep of Russian history. Decisions made in the distant past can fully influence policy-making in the present. Hedlund's thesis can be seen as influenced by the "path dependency" theories of Paul David among others. Culture and history really do matter.[25]

Karen Dawisha, in *Putin's Kleptocracy: Who Owns Russia?*, provided rich detail on the rise of Vladimir Putin to develop full control of the Russian political and economic system after his election to the presidency in 2000. She argues that he did this through a system of rewarding those loyal to him and punishing the disloyal (including powerful oligarchs who had seemed to rule much of the wealth of Russia until that point). As noted earlier, it often appeared that he was simply replacing independent-minded oligarchs with those who had been with him closely since his days in the KGB. In Dawisha's words:

> And for those left behind, the gap between rich and poor has become the greatest in the world . . . . the midpoint of wealth for Russians is only $871—as compared to the other BRIC countries—$5,117 for Brazil, $8,023 for China, and $1,040 for India, all energy importers. And on the other side, 35 percent of the total wealth in the country is owned by one hundred ten billionaires. Russia has become the country where the super-rich receive the greatest protection from the state. None of this would be possible without the personal involvement of Putin.
>
> Nor has this come about by historical accident. The book has shown that the group now in power started out with Putin from the beginning. They are committed to a life of looting without parallel. This kleptocracy is abhorrent not just because of the gap between rich and poor that it has created, but because in order to achieve success this cabal has had to destroy any possibility of freedom. They have fed ordinary Russians pabulum of "unique culture" and "Russian values" to camouflage their throttling of civil society and the rule of law.[26]

Henry E. Hale took this further in his book *Patronal Politics*. He argued that

> What is hidden, or "the way things really work," is usually what will be called here the patronalistic dimension of politics. *Patronal politics* refers to politics in societies where individuals organize their political and economic pursuits primarily around the personalized exchange of concrete rewards and punishments through chains of actual acquaintance, and not primarily around abstract,

impersonal principles such as ideological belief or categorizations like economic class that include many people one has not actually met in person. In this politics of individual reward and punishment, power goes to those who can meet these out, those who can position themselves as *patrons* with a large and dependent base of *clients*.

> ... in post-Soviet Eurasia, networks rooted in three broad sets of collective actors typically constitute the most important building blocks of the political system, the moving parts in its regime dynamics: (1) local political machines that emerged from reforms of the early 1990s, (2) giant politicized corporate conglomerates, (3) various branches of the state that are rich either in cash or in coercive capacity. Whoever controls these bosses, "oligarchs," and officials controls the country.[27]

He notes the key importance of expectations:

> Power, then, is an odd self-fulfilling prophecy illuminated by a logic of collective action: So long as elites *expect* the formal chief executive to continue to be in charge in the future, few will dare even initiate an organized attempt to oust him or her because the risk of getting caught is too high and the perceived likelihood of success too low. This is the great power of expectations.
>
> The recent political history of almost every post-Soviet country, therefore, has included the creation of a single pyramid of authority, a giant political machine based on selectively applied coercion and reward, on individualized favor and punishment.[28]
>
> There is a *Pyramida* of power, a *vertical* of authority: "When presidents were ousted, . . . mostly what changed was the patron at the top."[29]

There is some circular reasoning here: "The Patron is able to secure the loyalty of the clients when the clients loyally carry out the will of the patron." But Hale stresses:

> The way out of this circular reasoning, as counterintuitive as it may initially sound, is to recast the tautology as a self-fulfilling prophecy. Specifically: Clients obey patrons when they expect other clients to do so. This is far from a trivial statement because it shifts the focus from clients' organization to clients' expectations.[30]

In the spirit of the powerful logic of collective action that is a "bank run" leading to failure even if there is no shortage of capital of normal operations, Hale cites Mancur Olson's development of collective action theory to explain the collapse of communist Eastern Europe in 1989. Resources and organization did not change but expectations did. "Their own regimes were doomed;"[31]

When clients *believe* their network is strong, therefore, it *is* strong . . . . There is a crucial problem of coordination at the heart of power in patronalistic societies, and how people coordinate depends on what they *expect* other people to do.[32]

Networks are sticky, but switching to other networks occur—how and why?

Organization and resources are thus not independent explanations for network coherence, but themselves result from expectations and in turn influence network coherence *primarily by influencing expectations.*"[33]
   . . . changes in expectations can come from exogenous reasons and can do so without directly affecting organization or resources, but expectations.[34]

Various analysts described the Russian economy since its recovery from the 1998 Russian financial crisis as still severely challenged—one beset with elements of the oil/natural resource curse, with rampant corruption (137th out of 180 on perceived corruption by Transparency International in 2019), minimal industrial diversification (see Goldman's discussion of the "Dutch/ Russian disease"),[35] unreliable legal recourse for enforcing property rights and contract law, strong tendencies toward a kleptocracy and "piratization,"[36] and continued weakness in health, poverty, and human welfare (e.g., ranking still no better than 49th in the UNDP Human Development Index in 2019— though up from 55 in 2012, 62 in 2005, and 72 in 1998). Specific UNDP evaluations of the Russian economy in 1998 and 2005 did reflect some optimism on the impact of proposed reform and recovery from the crisis. But the latter report was framed in terms of progress toward meeting the Millennium Development Goals, and noted:

Poverty alleviation in Russia has been recognized as a state policy priority, but regions have tended to be more successful in reducing the depth of poverty than in bringing people out of poverty. The obstacle is not only slow growth in incomes of the poor or persistence of a considerable inequality in income, but the inefficient social protection system. Available budget revenues are not always used for target[ed] support of the poor, . . . reinforcing an inefficient social aid concept. Substantial poverty growth risks are emerging due to price rises for housing and utilities and planned reform of the housing sector.[37]

The Russian economy both prospered and sputtered under Putin and Medvedev, largely in response to the rise and fall of global oil and gas prices. Marshall Goldman captured this most effectively in Petrostate, especially in chapter 7. See also, Michael Klare and his 2007–2008 argument that Russia was best characterized as an "energy juggernaut."[38] The impact of the 2008 global financial crisis curtailed the enthusiasm of most descriptions of Russia as an energy export-fueled global power. Global oil and gas prices have remained low for several years now, and there are reasons to believe that a return to the $100+ per barrel of oil price is unlikely anytime soon. Indeed, Lester Brown made a convincing argument that we are in the midst of a "Great Transition" from fossil fuels to renewable wind and solar energy that may well ensure an excess of oil and gas supply for the long term.[39] Dieter Helm made a related argument quite persuasively in *Burn Out: The Endgame for Fossil Fuels* (2017).

At this point, we might ask whether the combination of economic sanctions and long-term low global oil prices can have an impact on expectations in the sense that Hale suggests? Clearly the Russian economy is already weak, given the overdependence on natural resource exports and the lack of substantial progress or even commitment to industrial and economic diversification? Putin seems to remain very popular, given his apparent successful appeal to nationalism, but if his "pyramida" cannot deliver to meet the basic needs, let alone ambitions and desires, of most of the population, will expectations about his centrality to Russian governance weaken?

There are clearly some good examples of countries using their natural resource riches to strengthen and diversify their economies. Norway is often cited as the best example, where oil income was used to support investment in other parts of the economy and as contributions to a large Government Pension Fund to cover non-oil government deficits through interest earned. But Pauline Jones Luong and Erika Weinthal also pointed to some post-Soviet resource-rich countries as examples where "oil is not a curse." The key variable they argued is in the structure of the ownership and management of the oil industry. Pointing to the change in ownership under Putin in Russia, from private control by oligarchs to increased state ownership and control of key firms, they noted a corresponding shift in priorities to some social expenditures:

> . . . sustained calls within the administration for Putin to ramp up social spending commensurate with Russia's massive petroleum wealth began to manifest themselves only in mid-2005. And, not coincidentally, this pressure came directly from the *siloviki*, who had been not only opposed to the oligarchs' influence over the development of what they considered a "strategic state asset" but also much less committed to fiscal reform during the first Putin administration . . . . While not the original intention of Putin's assault on Khodorkovsky, it was they who seized this opportunity to expand state ownership over the entire oil sector.[40]

Whether this has had a serious impact on the lives of most Russians was still in question as of 2020. Marshall Goldman summarized the key (continuing) problem quite effectively, writing at the height of the boom in Russian oil and gas profits:

> . . . Russian manufacturers rarely were able to succeed on a purely competitive basis. Russian energy resources were used more as a lifeboat to support a non-market-oriented economy and the country's industrial dinosaurs rather than as a stimulant to growth and the development of a world-class competitive manufacturing complex.[41]

Intent on rebuilding military power and committed to a very expensive construction program for the Winter Olympics in Sochi, the Russian state was not very responsive to mass public needs, and there is little reason to expect that a more responsive political system is on the way. The most constructive, forward-looking public expenditure one can uncover in recent years is the apparent commitment to consolidating and upgrading the major research universities and the higher educational system more generally. But real expenditures to this end have fluctuated annually along with the variation in oil and gas prices. A science and technology powerhouse is not in the making or so it seems as of 2020.

The March 2018 presidential election results did confirm that Putin remained popular and well established as Russia's political leader. He received 76.7 percent of the vote according to the official results of the Central Election Commission. Pavel Grudinin represented the Communist Party with 11.8 percent of the vote, and Zhirinovsky again came in third with 5.7 percent.

DEMOCRACY, AUTOCRACY, AND
THE RUSSIAN ECONOMY

How should we assess the progress of development and governance in Russia on the ability to provide prosperity for a large(r) segment of the population, not just the kleptoelite? Is broad-based development and middle class expansion less likely now, given changes in the world economy? There clearly is more competition for manufacturing exports globally, due to increases in productivity generally, and especially in emerging economies; as a consequence, there is less opportunity for unskilled workers, beyond extractive industries, given the impact of robotics and the continuing rise of the "new" economy. Is Russia under Putin up to meeting the need for innovation and entrepreneurship in a changing global economy? Joshua Kurlantzick argued that development-minded dictators were able to pass economic reforms that set the stage for sustained growth.[42] Democracies can create rule-based economies that encourage foreign investors.[43] But, Kurlantzick also connects economic stagnation, especially after the global financial crisis in 2008, to growing impatience with democratic political systems:

> The failure of growth fell hardest on working class men and women, who often were barely getting by under the old authoritarian regime, and who did not have the skills, education, and capital to take advantage of international trade and economic liberalization . . . . These working class men and women began associating economic failures with democracy, even though economic globalization, changing terms of international trade, or many other factors also could explain weak growth in the developing world.[44]

The rise of populism in Europe and the United States is often connected to a similar argument about who has been left behind in an increasingly globalized world economy that shifts manufacturing opportunities to other countries. Is there in effect a "race to the bottom" through competition for lower wage workers and less restrictive labor and environmental impact standards.[45]

Why some economies prosper and others do not is a very complicated and contested story. Sweeping comparative historical treatments, like *The Wealth and Poverty of Nations* by David Landes, point to the importance of cultural predispositions such as the Protestant ethic and Confucianism, as well as Western policy choices that led to the industrial revolution and the adoption of free trade policies based on comparative advantage, and Japanese state-led industrialization strategies, begun with the Meiji restoration and resumed after World War II.[46]

Daron Acemoglu and James A. Robinson, in *Why Nations Fail*, stress the importance of inclusive versus extractive political and economic institutions as key. Inclusive institutions make the prospect for economic take-off and broad-based prosperity possible, while extractive ones may foster some industrial development (as in the case of Stalinist Russia) but generally do not produce sustained prosperity beyond a narrow elite.[47]

There are, of course, numerous arguments for and against globalization as the blessing or culprit in global economic trends.[48] The real culprit in the 2007–2008 global financial crisis may be less the overall strategy of globalization per se than the excessive financial deregulation (in the pursuit of unfettered movement of capital). This was then complemented by a strategy of "market fundamentalism" (stemming from short-sighted triumphalism by some in leadership in the West after the collapse of the Soviet Union).[49] George Soros warned of market fundamentalism in his 1998 book, *The Crisis of Global Capitalism*, as did Joseph Stiglitz in his Nobel Prize acceptance speech in 2001. Stiglitz extended his critique in 2018 with *Globalization and Its Discontents: Revisited* and offered "An Agenda for Equitable Globalization with Shared Prosperity."[50]

More recently, much attention has been focused on increased global inequality, between and within nations. Some of the leading scholars in this effort, of course, include: Thomas Piketty, *Capital in the Twenty-First Century* (2014); Joseph Stiglitz, *The Great Divide: Unequal Societies and What We Can Do About Them* (2015), and Francois Bourguignon, *The Globalization of Inequality* (2015). Some argue that this was allowed to happen not just by kleptocratic authoritarian regimes but also by rigged (oligarchic?) democratic systems; to many analysts, inequality is the key problem we face—not so much lack of growth. Data from the UN Human Development Report do indicate that for the most part "democracies have higher rates of literacy, greater access to basic health care and safe drinking water, greater enrollment in primary school, and less malnutrition than autocracies with similar per capita incomes."[51] But democratic governments vary substantially in their ability to generate and maintain broad-based prosperity.

Robert Reich developed a series of reform proposals for the growing inequality, particularly in the United States, under the title *Saving Capitalism* in 2016.[52] An interesting element of his argument is the way in which U.S. corporate leadership changed its posture from the post–World War II "deal" which had formed the basis of a growing middle class and a vibrant and innovative economy. There had been some balance in salary scales. Corporate CEOs earned twenty times than the average worker in the 1950s and 1960s; now they earn over 200 times the average worker. The richest 1 percent took home 9–10 percent of total income initially, but now they have more than 20 percent. Globalization and technological change explains part of this rising inequality, but corporate lobbying and the general influence of the "1%" on tax cuts restrain access to quality public education and industrial development and infrastructure investment. The concentration of political power in a corporate and financial elite has influenced the rules by which the economy runs for narrow benefit. This complements the arguments Stiglitz makes in his criticism of the way globalization has been implemented, including influence on the policies of the IMF to promote capital movement liberalization. In the views of both Reich and Stiglitz, there needs to be a return to the countervailing power that was the key to the growth and broadening of prosperity in the early decades after World War II.[53]

Ruchir Sharma has provided a refreshing, and perhaps more practical guide to *The Rise and Fall of Nations* (2016), in an effort to uncover the key rules or "Forces of Change in the Post-Crisis World." Much of these focus on the proper role of the state: Is it investing more or less, engaged in or at least ready to reform, controlling inflation effectively, limiting debt growth, acting strategically with investment in manufacturing and industrial diversification, tackling or hastening inequality, and encouraging a growing pool of work-force talent?[54]

The Russian Federation comes off poorly in most, if not all, of these dimensions:

- there is no evidence of reform to improve governance, especially in terms of accountability/legitimacy and economic development; even initial efforts to reform and rationalize the higher education system have stalled due to funding cutbacks;
- there has been little or no productive investment, especially of the sort that can be reasonably expected to promote industrial diversification, and much of the country's infrastructure is crumbling; strategy 2010 was only partially implemented, and strategy 2020, adopted in 2011, seems to have disappeared into a bureaucratic holding pattern; continued reliance on oil and gas exports is troubling, especially as alternative energy sources and suppliers multiply and global demand stagnates with predictable impact on historically low prices;
- various measures and analyses rate Russia as among the worst in the world now in economic inequality and corruption;
- demographic indicators continue to suggest stagnancy, indeed decline in the potential pool of workers and efforts to develop a modern and techno-logically adept workforce are modest at best;
- internal debt is growing, and access to foreign investment and borrowing is miniscule, as political and economic strategies backfire with previously close economic partners;
- inflation continues to depress the living standards of most of the population.

And yet, President Putin still remains popular through aggressive foreign policy initiatives and nationalist rhetoric.

Jochen Bittner's argument on the rise of "Orderism" is not dissimilar from points made by Chantal Delsol and Ryszard Legutko, as discussed later. In other respects, however, Bittner's argument has a stronger economic fla-vor. The proper role for the state (and of leaders) in "national" economies remains relevant here. This debate has long been intense and includes those who argued for a more coherent industrial policy and a focus on educational reform to meet the needs of twenty-first century capitalism as discussed in detail by Robert Reich in 1991, versus those who, like Kenichi Ohmae in 1995, argued that the state has largely become obsolete as an effective instru-ment of economic prosperity.[55]

Linda Weiss, in *The Myth of the Powerless State* (1998), pointed to the evolving nature of the state's role in the economy, drawing on the cases of Germany, Japan, and Sweden, to suggest that proclamations of "the end of the nation state" were premature at best.[56] Lee Kuan Yew's emphasis on the need for discipline and centralized state power for effective economic development had proved effective in Singapore (and subsequently in the Republic of Korea and perhaps Taiwan and Chile).[57]

Alternatively, there was the approach advocated by Nobel laureate Amartya Sen, who stressed the "instrumental" and "constructive" values of democracy in the economic development process. Sen wrote in 1999 that democracy played a crucial role in avoiding famine because "a responsive government intervenes to help alleviate hunger."[58] He went on to stress that the economies worst hit by the 1997 Asian financial crisis, particularly South Korea, Thailand, and Indonesia suffered, "the penalties of undemocratic governance." Here he pointed to the "lack of transparency in business, in particular the lack of public participation in reviewing financial arrangements." Finally, Sen argued that the data did not support any particular negative or positive connection between economic development and democracy.[59]

The challenges of simultaneous democratization and economic liberalization are daunting. Aside from the common argument that economic reform should be the initial focus, transition in Russia and several of the successor states to the FSU, was criticized mainly because the social safety net of the state socialist system was dismantled too quickly and completely without a viable alternative in place. Privatization was pushed for its own sake in some cases, not for reasons of constructive reform. That is, private ownership, not competitiveness, was seen as the key goal. There was a one-size-fits-all approach when in fact diverse models were available with considerable variance in timing and scale. Privatization dominated by insider deals was all too frequent, with disastrous results for average citizens. The rule of law—especially relating to property rights—was absent.

Anders Åslund's case for a strategy of shock therapy or big bang reform as opposed to gradualism was not heeded in Russia. His stress on the importance of minimizing the role of the old state institutions and pushing for speed and comprehensiveness to avoid the "scourge of rent seeking" would prove to be prescient. The rise of the "oligarchs" would demonstrate that those that favored gradual reform most were those who saw ways of making money on the transition to a market economy. Profits in excess of the prevailing competition level were in effect rents.[60] President Putin regained some control over the economy after 2000 with his campaign to reassert state power, but the legacy of industrial weakness, poverty, and inequality would be endemic well into his subsequent terms of office.

This brings us to the direct question: Why do some authoritarian leaders last and others do not? Mary Gallagher and Jonathan K. Hanson explore this in relation to "the selectorate theory," examining "The Logic of Political Survival" (LPS) by Bruce Bueno de Mesquita and Alastair Smith in the

Russian context. It is particularly interesting on why some Eurasian authoritarian leaders survive and are resilient and others not. It is all about whether there are real incentives to defect from the ruler's coalition or remain loyal.[61]

This is similar to Henry Hale's arguments in *Patronal Politics*, as he discusses the dynamics of when supporters perceive it is time to withdraw support because the leader appears vulnerable. What determines this? An economy that is not generally prosperous enough to provide modest economic benefits to mollify a suffering population would seem to be an important ingredient but only when the other ingredients of popularity and patronal support or repression are constrained or disrupted.

Acemoglu and Robinson in *Economic Origins of Dictatorship and Democracy* provide an interesting discussion of the revolutionary threat from the unenfranchised, noting the tradeoff between the costs of repression versus the costs of providing public goods.[62] See also Atul Kohli's discussion of cohesive-capitalist states (especially Asian tiger economies) in *State-Directed Development.*[63]

China can be seen as a case of autocratic survival—using a complicated balancing act between measures that make opposing the ruler more costly and measures that reduce the expected gains of a successful overthrow. The LPS does not account for these trade-offs, according to Gallagher and Hanson.[64]

One factor that distinguishes resilient regimes from those that merely survive is the preferences of the ruling coalition. There exists an alignment between the personal interests of the members of the ruling coalition and the more encompassing interests of the society. Regime resilience or survival appears to be predicated on the ability, given certain conditions, to maintain an optimal mixture of carrots and sticks. Perhaps Lee Kuan Yew's strategic success in Singapore can be viewed in these terms?

But other China watchers argue that the PRC is increasingly "Trapped in Transition" and may be unable to keep up with population growth and continuing rural to urban migration, with developmental autocracy, according to Minxin Pei.[65] Indeed, he argues more recently that this constitutes an increasingly corrupt society that is best described as "crony capitalism."[66] China has an increased need for broad-based entrepreneurial development and prosperity, as export-led growth reaches its limits, especially in a global trading system that seems now to be constrained by threats of economic nationalism/protectionism. Can it be demonstrated that freedom and democracy is necessary for broad-based prosperity?

Where does Russia fit into this argument? Putin's excessive spending and widely reported corruption in connection with the Sochi Olympics, and his growing focus on military spending, beyond concrete national interests or realistic security concerns, is noteworthy. The fact that much of this seems to come in place of expenditures to improve infrastructure, agricultural productivity, industrial diversification, and human capital development would seem to be problematic.

There are numerous analyses that capture the enormous extent of corruption in Putin's Russia. Indeed, anyone who has traveled to Russia since 2000 has undoubtedly noticed the extent to which extra fees and payoffs are required to perform even basic commercial or personal operations. If one looks at the Transparency International Corruption Perceptions Index (CPI) comparatively, it is clear that the Russian Federation is scored as more corrupt than nearly any other transition state in Eastern Europe and the Former Soviet Union; indeed, only Tajikistan, Turkmenistan, and Uzbekistan were ranked as more corrupt in 2019.

There are of course important methodological considerations in these kinds of expert surveys. One can point to concerns about survey sampling and choice of experts for the review panels, as well as a range of potential definitional and coding biases. Fredrik Galtung also notes quite simply:

> Significant corruption transactions are hidden from public view and the parties to a successful agreement seldom have an incentive to be open about their dealings. Until the mid-1990s, most of the empirical findings on corruption in the academic literature were of an incidental or anecdotal nature.[67]

Galtung goes on to review several alternative macro corruption indices that have evolved and discusses "seven failings" that he attributes to the CPI ranking and scoring in particular. The relationship between authoritarianism and corruption, nonetheless, is commonly articulated as a strong connection.

It should also be noted that Johann Graf Lambsdorff, a key framer of the original CPI approach to measuring corruption, offers an interesting response to Galtung's criticism in the same volume, while detailing the steps in the construction of the index. Lambsdorff is not blind to the limitations, but he is rather persuasive on the value of cross-national comparison efforts in this "complex and controversial" area.[68]

PUTIN'S FOREIGN AND SECURITY POLICY: THE SEARCH FOR LOST EMPIRE

As with President Yeltsin, concern about maintaining the territorial integrity of the Russian Federation was a primary concern for President Putin. Indeed, one can see that his role in the Second Chechen War was an important ingredient in his rising popularity toward the end of 1999. Subsequent initiatives beyond the borders of the Federation were calculated to both restore Russian autonomy and international standing, while appealing to the traditionally strong vein of Russian nationalism.[69]

Toward the end of Yeltsin's second term as president, there was considerable maneuvering among his supporters and adversaries. Yeltsin sacked Primakov, replacing him with Sergey Stepashin; this left Primakov free to join the Fatherland-All Russia (OVR) faction. If successful in the Duma and presidential elections, this faction might then pose a threat to Yeltsin's vulnerability on corruption charges. Yeltsin then replaced Stepashin as prime minister with Putin (who had been serving as secretary of the Security Council and head of the FSB, or Federal Security Service—successor to the KGB) on August 9, 1999. Putin began to strengthen the administration's posture both in Moscow and in relation to the emerging renewed "threat" from Chechnya. This included Chechen Wahhabite rebel attacks in neighboring Dagestan and bombings in other parts of the Federation. Putin's tough stance in response increased his popularity and paved the way for Yeltsin's surprise resignation announcement on December 31 that also named Putin as acting president. The Communist Party had gained the most seats in the December 19 Duma elections, but Putin's elevation to presidential power seemed not under any serious challenge. Putin promptly issued an order declaring that Yeltsin would be immune from prosecution after his resignation.[70]

There were critics of Putin's handling of Chechnya, of course. For example, in *A Dirty War,* Anna Politikovskaya was particularly riveting in her interviews and accounts of the violence. She offered penetrating questions of the official strategy and its justification:

> To begin with, I thought how senseless everything happening here was. If you look at it from the State's point of view, why scatter a vast number of mines around the city and receive in return an astronomic growth in the number of disabled people, who require tons of medicine, artificial limbs and so on? And then scatter more mines. And again ferry in medicine, etc. Now it's clear what the State is up to. Its concern for the situation is purely virtual; the only reality is the scattering of mines. No matter how much we want to believe the reverse, or attribute everything to our chronic disorder or thieving, the reality is that the inhabitants of Grozny have been sentenced to this fate. Evidently, the ultimate aim is to ensure that as many people in the city as possible are either left without legs— or dead. Perhaps this is a new stage in the "anti-terrorist operation," an unhurried punitive mission directed against one ethnic community, which now requires hardly any more ammunition, just the patience to wait for the inevitable outcome.[71]

Masha Gessen was also critical of Putin's prosecution of the Second Chechnyan War. She visited Grozny and reported on the devastation and civilian suffering. Gessen also provided detail on Politkovskaya's treatment during and after her journalistic service in Grozny and its environs—subjected to a mock execution, poisoned on a flight to Beslan to observe the vicious and bungled school attack purportedly by Muslim extremists, and ultimately murdered on her Moscow doorstep.[72]

Putin, for his side, was unrelenting in his efforts to pacify the Chechens. Suspicions about whether the precipitatory bombings of Russian apartment buildings in Buynaksk, Moscow, and Volgodonsk in September 1999 were in fact orchestrated by FSB agents were reinforced subsequently by the discovery of an explosive device in the city of Ryazan.[73] This was later passed off as a security training exercise, and Putin ordered air strikes on Grozny on September 24.

Alexander Litvinenko and Yuri Felshtinsky amassed considerable evidence against the view that the attacks were by Chechens and argued in *Blowing Up Russia* that this was a "Plot to Bring Back KGB Terror"—and foment war in Chechnya, presumably as a way to raise Putin's popularity in the eyes of nationalistic Russians.[74] Litvinenko was later poisoned with Polonium and died in London on November 23, 2006. The Fourth Edition of his book with Felshtinsky not only trumpeted that the book was banned in Russia but declared it was "The Bestseller that got Litvinenko Assassinated"!

The Putin administration forcefully denied any connection to the death of Litvinenko. The question of how Litvinenko would have come into contact with this unusual and normally unavailable substance without some FSB or related complicity seems puzzling to most observers, including UK authorities.[75] British Journalist Luke Harding explored this and "Putin's War with the West" in great detail in *A Very Expensive Poison.*[76] Harding was expelled from Russia where he was serving as *The Guardian*'s bureau chief in Moscow (2007–2011), apparently in response to his reporting on Litvinenko's murder.

Western reaction to Putin's campaigns in the Second Chechen War was somewhat divided, at least initially. In part, this reflected the legacy of concern about the global threat of terrorism, especially that perceived as growing from Wahabbist Islamic fundamentalism, but there was also sentiment in support of the Russian government's effort to maintain the territorial integrity of the Russian Federation. Part of this legacy undoubtedly harkened back to sentiments that led President Clinton to compliment Boris Yeltsin's own campaign against the Chechen drive for national self-determination as akin to Abraham Lincoln's posture during the Civil War: "that no state had a right to withdraw from our union. And so, the United States has taken the position that Chechnya is a part of Russia." Presidents Clinton and Yeltsin faced serious electoral tests in 1996 and saw advantage in playing down differences.[77]

President Putin's support of President Bush after the Osama Bin Laden inspired attacks on the United States on September 11, 2001 also helped to downplay sentiment against his Chechnyan campaign. President Bush famously claimed that during his meeting with Putin at the Slovenia Summit, June 16, 2001: "We had a very good dialogue. I was able to get a sense of his soul. He's a man deeply committed to his country and the best interests of his country and I appreciate very much the frank dialogue and that's the beginning of a very constructive relationship."[78] Part of this dialogue included discussion of NATO enlargement and the prospect of strategic cooperation between the United States and Russia. The NATO–Russia Council was established at the NATO–Russia Summit in Rome on May 28, 2002, with a declaration on "NATO–Russia Relations: A New Quality." The groundwork for this had been established in the 1997 NATO–Russia Founding Act on Mutual Relations.[79]

Putin reportedly was the first head of state to telephone President Bush after the 9-11 attacks. Maybe this was a reflection of the president's initial judgment of Putin in Slovenia, but it did seem to be the beginning of serious cooperation between the two countries during the U.S. actions to bring down the Taliban regime in Afghanistan and the search for Bin Laden. Rare and valuable overflight and logistics support was granted by Russia, enabling more efficient supply of the United States and allied forces on the ground in the region. The Russians did not stand in the way of U.S. military bases established in Kyrgyzstan and Uzbekistan as part of the logistics effort.

What then happened to this budding relationship that seemed to be an initial "reset" of relations that had deteriorated toward the end of the Clinton and Yeltsin relationship? Much has been written on both U.S. neglect of the relationship and the negative impact of NATO enlargement and the NATO military operations in Serbia and Kosovo. But was Putin really interested in a strong U.S.–Russia strategic partnership? Did subsequent actions by the George W. Bush and Obama administrations change any inclinations he may have had in this direction?

Or did Putin's subsequent international posture derive from other motivations? This is an unsettled area of controversy and debate. Stephen F. Cohen and Michael McFaul, for example, see this very differently. In *War with Russia?: From Putin and Ukraine to Trump and Russiagate*, Cohen places primary blame for the deterioration in U.S.–Russian relations under President Obama and since on a vicious and biased media and U.S. foreign policy establishment that demonized Putin and neglected U.S. missteps and provocations. Cohen is not blameless in his selective reporting of the facts, for example, on whether NATO enlargement really amounted to a betrayal of promises/agreements made by President George H. W. Bush to Gorbachev. Neither Bush nor Gorbachev admit to such an agreement in any of their writings on the period. Nonetheless, Cohen's worries that "The new US–Russian Cold War is more dangerous than was its 40-year predecessor, which the world survived." This should be a matter of concern, especially if the deterioration in relations does not reflect objective conflicts of national interest.[80] Are we sleepwalking into a potential shooting war, as in World War I, and indeed as the history of misperceptions in U.S.–Russian/Soviet relations might suggest?[81] Cohen goes on to argue that Western demonization of Putin has in fact sanctified him and that the post-Crimean annexation sanctions were both mindless and ineffective.[82]

Michael McFaul wrote from his vantage point as a longtime scholar of Russian democratization efforts and as a White House special assistant and then U.S. ambassador to Russia during the Obama administration. McFaul is eloquent in recounting the evolution of Putin's changing posture toward the West, placing reasonable emphasis on the changing environment that Russia faced by the mid-to-late 2000s. He argued that "By the end of his second term in 2008, Putin had redefined Russia's role in the world largely, but not completely, in opposition to the United States and the West."[83] The Russian invasion of Georgia was an important illustration of this. Putin had reacted quite negatively to President George W. Bush's justification for invading Iraq. He felt that U.S. unilateralism needed to be resisted. McFaul argued that Putin was irked in part by Bush's unwillingness to allow him to take a strong role on the world stage especially regarding Iraq.[84]

Putin's strong words at the 2007 Munich Security Conference reflected his attitude:

> Today we are witnessing an almost uncontained hyper use of force—military force—in international relations, force that is plunging the world into an abyss of permanent conflicts. As a result we do not have sufficient strength to find a comprehensive solution to any one of these conflicts. Finding a political settlement also becomes impossible.
>
> We are seeing a greater and greater disdain for the basic principles of international law. And independent legal norms are, as a matter of fact, coming increasingly closer to one state's legal system. One state and, of course, first and foremost the United States, has overstepped its national borders in every way. This is visible in the economic, political, cultural and educational policies it imposes on other nations. Well, who likes this? Who is happy about this?[85]

There was a sincere effort by the Obama administration to "reset" U.S.–Russian relations again. This reflected clear recognition that Russia's cooperation was needed for meeting major objectives, and that the Bush administration had allowed the relationship to stagnate, mostly through neglect. As McFaul described it, the Obama administration posture for the reset was to determine and pursue shared interests, develop a multidimensional relationship, avoid any temptation to try to isolate or coerce Russia, increase engagement with Russian society, and display respect for Putin and his accomplishments in revitalizing Russia. However, U.S. values would not be down played, and U.S. relations with Russia's neighbors, most notably Georgia and Ukraine, would not be sacrificed. A "benign" regional environment was necessary if there was to be a chance for Russian democratization.[86] The timing of the reset was optimal given that Medvedev was president. Putin had stepped aside in line with the constitutional prohibition against more than two consecutive terms. He was certainly not out of the picture, however, as prime minister (and president-in-waiting, as it turned out), but Medvedev seemed more accommodating to U.S. initiatives and seemed to have a more globalist perspective on the best path to a prosperous future for Russia. Isolation from the world economy, beyond oil and gas exports, seemed not viable to him, as he announced at various venues that Russia was open for foreign direct investment and commercial partnerships. His "Go Russia!" initiative stressed this as well as the need to improve quality of the institutions and self-government.[87]

Obama and Medvedev worked together on a number of important initiatives, including overflight support for the war in Afghanistan and concerns about the threat from a potential nuclear-armed Iran.[88] Looking back on it, Putin was remarkably tolerant of Medvedev's posture on close relations with the United States and Europe (at least publicly), but his time to return to the presidency was approaching; and Putin saw personal motivations for establishing his control and his plan for reclaiming lost empire that did not envision subordination to the United States. Accordingly, McFaul regarded 2010 as the high point of the reset progress. It was all downhill from there.

McFaul stressed the impact of the Arab Spring revolts on a clear change in Putin's attitude toward the reset, ultimately chastising Medvedev's modest support for Western action in Libya. The revolts against conservative authoritarian regimes in the Middle East essentially began with the public response in Tunisia to a street vendor's self-immolation in December 2010. The anti-government movements, based largely on economic privation and lack of opportunity perceived for the growing youth populations, spread to Egypt, Libya, Syria, Yemen, and Bahrain, among others. Ben Ali in Tunisia, Gaddafi in Libya, and Mubarak in Egypt were deposed; a vicious civil war erupted to challenge Bashar al-Assad in Syria. Notable in all of this was the extent to which "social media" seemed to play a critical role in motivating and constituting the movements. "Digital democracy" became a thing in the minds of many observers.

Putin responded with some alarm to what appeared to him as a similar episode of rising opposition surrounding the Duma election on December 4, 2011. Concern for his own future may have been accentuated by the commentary of Secretary of State Hillary Clinton. Her speech to the ministerial meeting of the Organization for Security and Cooperation in Europe, two days after the election, openly criticized the fairness of the election and the treatment of opposition candidates and protestors, and clearly riled Putin and his advisors.[89] Indeed, Putin subsequently blamed the United States for actually fomenting the Arab Spring revolts. There is little evidence of this, since the risings clearly caught U.S. politicians by surprise. One could point to part of President Bush's justification for the U.S. intervention in Iraq—to remake the Middle East with regime change and democratization—as a factor. Putin also charged Clinton with interfering in Russian elections.[90] In 2009, President Obama did make a strong case for democratization in a speech in Accra, Ghana: "No person wants to live in a society where the rule of law gives way to the rule of brutality and bribery. That is not democracy; that is tyranny, even if occasionally you sprinkle an election in there."[91]

McFaul was clear that Obama was not going to finance partisan activities in Russia, but opined that free and fair elections should be a goal for all in Russia, even Putin, since he was very unlikely to lose.[92] His popularity seemed to rise, even as the economy declined after 2008, and his international adventurism increased. Indeed, the "wag the dog" formula seemed to be working for him with both his invasion of Georgia and his intervention in Ukraine, including the annexation of Crimea in March, 2014. These were popular interventions to a nationalist Russia—perhaps not so different from the concept of the 1997 movie starring Robert De Niro and Dustin Hoffman, in which a crisis in Albania was manufactured to distract U.S. voters from scandal in Washington. But it is an open question as to whether this was what was in Putin's thinking. Was he seeking distraction for an increasingly disgruntled but nationalistic population, to avoid a "Russian Spring?" Or was this simply part of his overall strategy to "Make Russia Great Again" by increasing its international standing and indispensability? Catherine Belton argues that Putin was intentional in his efforts to challenge the West from the outset, returning Russia to great power status.[93] Joshua Yaffa captures the impact eloquently, noting that Crimea's "return" "hit the right notes for the Russian national psyche, a measure of revenge for all the slights and insults of the post-Soviet era."[94]

David Shiner stresses that efforts by both the United States and USSR/Russia to influence elections and politics have been long standing and intense—an important element in the generalized Cold War competition. The KGB was central to this, as former KGB general Oleg Kalugin (stationed in the United States from 1958 to 1970) admitted to Shiner: "That was part of the job," he said, "to promote those who would make less damage to the Soviet Union in the election."[95] Shiner presents considerable detail on how Russia under Putin continued this "job," noting the greatly enhanced sophistication of social media manipulation and remote electronic hacking. He lists ten historical lessons from one hundred years of interference that should inform a more comprehensive U.S. response to this authoritarian threat.[96] The well-studied operations of the Internet Research Agency (IRA) in St. Petersburg in the 2016 U.S. presidential election is perhaps the most startling episode of the threat.[97] The IRA was led by Russian oligarch Yevgeny Prigozhin, the "chef of the Kremlin" who has long been a close associate of Putin. The Mueller Report assessed the activities of the IRA in some detail, along with Concord Management and Consulting, LLC.[98]

Is there a doctrine or ideology at work here—perhaps one that would justify sacrifice and hardship? Was a unilateralist United States (e.g., the Iraq invasion) in need of restraint? Certainly, the Obama administration was less so inclined than was the one he succeeded.

With these questions in mind, we might explore whether one can detect the pursuit of an ideological project in Putin's authoritarianism? Is Russian nationalism enough? Writing in 2016, Charles Clover traced the rise of Russia's new nationalism, in the context of Eurasianism, in *Black Wind, White Snow*.[99] In Clover's account, a central figure in this was Alexander Dugin who built a case for a new nationalist orientation first in *The Foundations of Geopolitics* in 1997.[100] Dugin's books added a strong inclination to turn back the tide of Western liberalism. The argument flows from a long-term geopolitical struggle between the civilization of the Sea (especially the United States), and the civilization of the Land (especially Russia), and leads to an irresistible goal that Russia must at minimum dominate the north shore of the Black Sea. With Ukraine in the way of this ambition, one can see the impending geopolitical conflict between Russia and the West.

Dugin became a close advisor to President Putin and subsequently developed his geopolitical ideology in several more books. The clearest statement of his view of Russian Geopolitics is in *Last War of the World-Island: The Geopolitics of Contemporary Russia*.[101] Here he delineates the fundamental features of the civilization of the Land: (1) conservatism; (2) holism; (3) collective anthropology (the *narod* is more important than the individual); (4) sacrifice; (5) an idealistic orientation; and (6) the values of faithfulness, asceticism, honor, and loyalty. "Beyond ideological preferences, Russia is doomed to conflict with the civilization of the Sea."[102]

In *Eurasian Mission: An Introduction to Neo-Eurasianism*, Dugin pointed to globalization (which comes from the West), as a challenge to the nations and civilizations of the Eurasian continent. He argued that there is a need for a multilateral dialogue for sovereign subjects and that the Eurasian Movement is an appropriate venue; it stresses the need for "an intensive dialogue of cultures, civilizations, confessions, states, social groups both large and small, and ethnicities of the European continent in this historical age."[103] The movement is "strongly against globalization as a form of ideological, economic, political, and value-based imperialism . . . . The nations of Eurasia must be free and independent."[104] In important respects, Dugin sees liberalism with its focus on individualism as the key threat. The principles of Eurasianism in his view are:

- differentialism: a plurality of value systems versus the conventional and obligatory domination of a single ideology (American liberal democracy first and foremost);
- tradition versus the suppression of cultures, their dogmas, and the wisdom of traditional society;
- the rights of nations versus the "golden billion" and the neocolonial hegemony of the "rich North";
- ethnicities as the primary value and the subjects of history versus the homogenization of peoples, which are to be imprisoned within artificial social constructions;
- social fairness and human solidarity versus exploitation and the humiliation of man by man.[105]

Dugin subsequently argued for a Fourth Political Theory, superseding the first (liberalism), the second (Communism/socialism), and the third (fascism/National Socialism). In his words: "The 4PT considers itself non-modern or counter-modern." It emphasizes the importance of history and tradition, as well as the centrality of the problem of identity.[106] From the point of view of the 4PT, totalitarianism is connected with liberal ideology—the third totalitarianism:

> Liberalism is a totalitarian ideology that insists, through the classical methods of totalitarian propaganda, that the individual has the highest value . . . .
>
> Liberal society, which puts itself in opposition to the collective societies of socialism and fascism, has itself become a collective—a standardized and stereotypical one. The more an individual aspires to be unique within the context of the liberal paradigm, the more he becomes similar to everyone else. Liberalism brings with itself the stereotyping and homogenization of the world, which destroys all forms of diversity and differentiation.[107]

The United States is simply a "conceptual society" that lacks a real tradition. Dugin identified the United States then as a "Country of Absolute Evil."[108] The twenty-first century will be defined by the conflict between Eurasianists and Atlanticists.[109] Indeed, his view is that the Atlanticists want "to impose a single model of economic order on all peoples in the world, elevating the experience of the economic development of the Western part of world civilization in the nineteenth and twentieth centuries to the status of a universal standard."[110] Dugin's animosity toward the United States and the West in general led him to embrace extreme right nationalist groups in Europe and the United States as potential allies. For example, he shockingly admits:

> I consider the "white nationalists" allies when they refuse modernity, the global oligarchy and liberal-capitalism. In other words everything that is killing all ethnic cultures and traditions. The modern political order is essentially global-ist and based entirely on the primacy of individual identity in opposition to community. It is the worst order that has ever existed and it should be totally destroyed. When "White nationalists" reaffirm Tradition and the ancient culture of the European peoples, they are right.[111]

Dugin seems not to have a positive economic strategy, beyond curtailing globalization—nothing that would promote broad-based prosperity in Russia and the Eurasian successors to the Soviet Union. He makes no effort to defend the old Soviet system's centrally planned economy, or indeed any sort of stat-ist recipe. Indeed, he is preoccupied with defending Eurasia from the West and preserving traditions and "differentialism." He is not sanguine about the current state of the Russian economy, however; in *Putin vs Putin*, he stresses the need to develop a "real economy" in Russia, but he provides no details on what must be done to match or surpass the diversified manufacturing and high technology economies of the West and East Asia.[112] His only verdict on the challenges and prospect of developing high technology industries is to denigrate Medvedev and his support for the Skolkovo Innovation Centre project (which had been developed with MIT participation and became the Skolkovo Institute of Science and Technology).[113]

While Dugin served as an advisor to Putin, especially in the early years of his presidency (when there appeared to be a clear search for a justifying ide-ology), he became disenchanted with Putin's indecisiveness and his apparent willingness to accept the liberal globalizing paradigm. Commentary on this view is offered in an interview format at the end of his *Putin vs. Putin* book.[114]

Writing in 2008, Marlene Laruelle offered an interesting and detailed exposition of the Eurasianist arguments in *Russian Eurasianism*, noting:

> . . . the strength of (Neo-) Eurasianism lies not in its impact on the electoral scene but in the ability to cater to the needs of a regime that seems to be looking for a new ideology.
>
> The (Neo-) Eurasianists' desire to become the Kremlin's (or the new states') ideological gray eminences is linked to their search for scientific legitimacy.[115]

Dugin owes a debt for his Eurasianist perspective to the writings of Lev Gumilev, often regarded as the true father of Neo-Eurasianism. Mark

Bassin offers an excellent delineation of these ideas and their impact in *The Gumilev Mystique*. Gumilev is honored in Russia and Central Asia, especially Kazakhstan. His influence in the late 1980s and 1990s placed emphasis on socio-biological explanations of nationality and ethnicity (ethnos and ethnogenesis) and on the deterministic historical development of Russia. His early writings on the Gokturk Khaganates and on the Rus and the Golden Horde established his scholarly reputation and have been drawn upon to help construct notions of Russian geopolitical connections to Central Asia. He has been criticized for Anti-Semitism and for writings that others use for exclusionary arguments against foreign ethnic groups; he was bitterly anti-Western in his assessment of the collapse of the USSR and his rejection of the West's "so-called universal human values,"[116] but as Bassin concludes:

> . . . .Gumilev spoke and speaks today to a diverse variety of constituencies— from the Russian president to fundamentalist insurgents—and offers a diverse (and contradictory) array of explanations for the most important social and national issues . . . . It is not too much to say that Lev Gumilev has become a universal point of reference and metadiscourse in his own right: a venerable and apparently inexhaustible wellspring of ideas and inspiration for pretty much anyone seeking to make sense of the Russian past, present, and future.[117]

The ideology of Eurasianism is of course less attractive, beyond Russia and Central Asia—at least less attractive than was/is Marxism. This is also likely true of the argument that "orderism" is the new ideology of authoritarian leaders, as described by Jochen Bittner in 2016:

> The ideology's basic political premise is that liberal democracy and international law have not lived up to their promise. Instead of creating stability, they have produced inequality and chaos. The secular religion worshiped in the Western parliaments was globalization (or, in the European Union's case, Europeanization). These beliefs, according to the orderists, overlooked the downsides. The most obvious downside, according to orderism, is that open borders and global trade have led to vanishing jobs and mass migration. At the same time, a mental borderlessness has shaken liberal societies: With potentially every traditional value now up for negotiation, no habit, custom or institution is sacred.[118]

This has some resonance with the precept, often attributed to Islamic and/or Chinese roots: "Better Sixty Years of Tyranny than One Night of Anarchy."[119] Preserving order is a key value; freedom is less important than order.

In the Russian context, it can also be connected with the arguments of Ivan Alexandrovich Ilyin, the early twentieth-century Russian religious philosopher who, in the context of the Russian Civil War, called for "Resistance to Evil by Force" and warned against chaotic doctrines and movements. He stressed concern about (democratic?) doctrines that "were legitimizing weakness, exalting egocentrism, indulging a lack of will, robbing the soul of its social and civic duties . . . prone to simplifying a naively idyllic world outlook." The common argument that Russians largely desire a strong leader of a strong state, especially since the chaotic experiment with democracy under Yeltsin, is relevant. Indeed, Putin has made this claim in speeches, quoting Ilyin's anti-democratic arguments (especially in defense of the Russian Orthodox Faith).[120]

Can these notions drive the long-term project of committed authoritarian leaders or are they simply another "passing illusion"? Is legitimacy important to a leader like Putin? Does it matter from where or how it is derived?

Both Eurasianism and orderism put some blame on the impact of Western-inspired globalization for the ills besetting post-Communist Russia. What is interesting, however, is the extent to which this argument ignores what happened in Yeltsin's faulty transition Russia, and indeed what is really happening globally. As Richard Baldwin argues in *The Great Convergence*, while globalization was indeed Western inspired, the losers were the G7, at least in terms of lost manufacturing capacity and jobs, and the real beneficiaries were what he terms the industrializing 6: China, Korea, India, Poland, Indonesia, and Thailand.[121] See also Steven Radelet's *The Great Surge*, 2015, which points to the reduction in poverty that has occurred in many developing countries in recent decades, at least in part due to some of the liberal economic policies that undergird globalization.[122] Russia is nowhere to be found on either list, of course, since it did not manufacture much in the way of competitive products under the old Soviet system and makes little beyond weapons and software now that has a global trade impact. Russia's troubles are much more indigenous than Western sourced. (Neo-) Eurasianism is simply a fig leaf for authoritarian rule and imperialism. But it seems to have some staying power, at least in the minds/imaginations of much of the Russian political leadership.

That being said, it may be that President Putin is not fully committed to Eurasianism, as Dugin's criticism seems to suggest. Eurasianism offers a convenient justification for aggressive actions in Georgia, Ukraine, and the Baltics, but it is possible that Putin is not ready to pursue it fully, given domestic economic constraints and the prospect for further alarming Western countries in a counterproductive reaffirming of NATO commitments and national rearmament steps.

James J. Sheehan's argument in *Where Have All the Soldiers Gone* that Europe was already transforming into a "Civilian Super-State" had a certain reality through much of the post–World War II rise of the European

Community and Union. Some European governments were especially eager to take advantage of the expected "peace dividend" after the end of the Cold War and essentially disarm after the collapse of the Soviet Union. This added to the objective reality that NATO was, at best, a paper defensive alliance and posed no real offensive threat to Russia. NATO enlarged, but offensive force projection capacity was minimal, and there were clear reductions in NATO member defense expenditure and readiness.[123] This began to change with Putin's military build-up and naval and air operations in the Baltic Sea and Black Sea regions, and of course the interventions in Georgia and Ukraine. Putin's fixation on the threat from the West while ignoring (at least in public pronouncements) the growth of China as a rival to the East, especially in the "near abroad" regions of Central Eurasia, seemed puzzling and counterproductive. One could argue with some confidence that Russia's security has in fact declined as a result of Putin's post-2007 initiatives, now Russia facing challenge from the East, West, and South.[124] Putin in effect has stimulated a reluctant European rearmament and encouraged a better prepared alliance to its West while ignoring a potentially rising power to the East and Southeast. Was this an unintended consequence or the result of a calculation that the domestic payoffs from a more assertive and interventionist Russia outweighed the potential security drawbacks? Catherine Belton paints a darker more aggressive picture of Russian Foreign Policy under Putin, citing the influence of the former KGB cronies that protect and promote Putin's posture of challenging the liberal world order.[125] Russia's engagement in Syria since September 2015, at the request of President Assad, has been expensive in lives and treasure, but the payoff in gaining a foothold in the Middle East, helping to counter ISIS terrorism, and confronting the United States, and perhaps Turkey geopolitically may be worth the expense to Putin. As the United States seemingly retreats, is this re-enacting the old struggle for the region between the Russian and Ottoman empires?[126]

CAN AN AUTHORITARIAN RUSSIA PROVIDE BROAD-BASED PROSPERITY?

By 2020, it seemed clear that Russia's heavy dependence on oil and gas export income had become less and less viable as a long-term strategy for broad-based prosperity. Oil and gas still account for nearly 60 percent of Russian exports. But the growth in competition from new exporters, including the United States, reduced demand in Europe (alarmed by imprudent dependence on Russia and committed to increased use of renewable energy sources), and the revolution in technology and pricing for wind and solar sources and energy transmission and storage systems, all present an increasingly bleak future for the Russian economy as currently structured.

Sanctions imposed on the Russian financial, energy, and defense sectors have been significant. Curiously, one of Putin's counterpoints to the sanctions was to place restrictions on imports of food and luxury items from Europe. One of his motivations seems to have been to encourage domestic production and self-sufficiency. To date, it is not clear that domestic production has increased in quantity, not to mention quality. Russian cheese, for example, is still a very poor substitute for almost any cheese available from Europe. Vodka production is still an important source of exports, but there is little production of fine wine and spirits. Putin's strategy of import substitution seems to punish Russian wealthier consumers more than Europeans. However, agricultural production in Russia seems to have improved, with some growth in exports of wheat, for example.[127] If this is calculated as a more general strategy for Russia to become more self-sufficient and less subject to the vagaries of globalization, some would argue it has some merit. The critiques of "globalization over-reach" seem to be gathering steam.

Nonetheless, the poverty rate in Russia remains high for an industrialized economy, declining to 10.7 percent in 2012 but rising to 13–14 percent between 2015 and 2018.[128] Large numbers of households lack formal employment. Informal employment is still rising, and there is negligible net job creation by medium and large enterprises. Overall economic growth has been stagnant at 1.5 percent for several years.[129]

There is some evidence that the Russians have adapted to the sanctions moderately, though unevenly. Economic growth remains slow in 2020, but some analysts argue that it is no longer "teetering on the brink," as it was in response to Western sanctions after the March 2014 invasion and annexation of Crimea. The Russian response of prudent fiscal policy and self-sufficiency has strengthened the currency and stabilized the macroeconomy.[130] Western capital movement controls on the international deposits of Russian oligarchs (and the "Russian 1%") were somewhat effective, and not surprisingly, led Putin and his close associates to rail against the tyranny of the U.S. dollar as the global reserve currency, which enables control by the U.S. Federal Reserve Bank. Efforts to find an alternative to the dollar remain unsatisfactory, however, despite substantial Russian and Chinese cooperation in the search. Moreover, the economy has not diversified into effective new product development and quality manufacturing. Russia remains eclipsed in this respect by neighboring China, which started its development in a much weaker position (in the late 1970s) and has much less natural resource base to support its efforts!

Russian dependence on energy exports is the key challenge. Lester Brown and his colleagues at the Earth Policy Institute argued strongly in 2015 that

The Great Transition was clearly underway, suggesting a dramatic shift from fossil fuels to renewable sources of energy, especially solar panel arrays and wind turbines. They stressed that heavily subsidized fossil fuels are no longer an enviable economic option, particularly when the costs of climate change and healthcare expenditures (traced to carbon emissions) are taken into account.[131]

Similarly, Dieter Helm argued that we are reaching the *Endgame for Fossil Fuels*. While noting recent volatility in the price of oil, which was $147 per barrel in 2008 and then $27 in early 2016, he stressed that the days of sustained high oil prices are over in his medium- to long-term calculations. He criticized the concept of "peak oil," with a complicated argument for: (1) the "end of the commodity super cycle"; (2) more effective policies in response to climate change realities and air pollution sensitivity in key fossil fuel consumer countries; and (3) the impact of the growing revolution in technology that will change the nature of the world economy and end the reliance on energy-intensive manufacturing. In his view, OPEC countries and Russia face a future of severe budgetary constraint if they continue to fail to diversify their economies. EU member states have made some notable efforts to diversify their energy supply sources, but Helm argued that some of the European investment in renewable energy was premature, given the current weakness of energy storage and transmission network technology.[132]

By 2012, the degree of European natural gas dependence on imports from Russia was substantial. The three Baltic countries, Latvia, Lithuania, and Estonia along with Finland were at the maximum 100 percent dependence on Russia for their natural gas consumption, while the United Kingdom, Sweden, Spain, Portugal, Ireland, Denmark, and Croatia were at the other end of the spectrum with basically no dependence on Russian natural gas imports. Turkey was 59 percent dependent; Germany came in at 37 percent, while France was at 16 percent. Table 4.2 indicates some initial stability in this dependence as of 2014. EU programs and directives to reduce dependence and fossil fuel use generally have been important, but not wildly successful.[133]

Table 4.3 depicts Russia's overall oil and gas export performance in light of global competition and the emerging reduction in the demand, especially for oil, in many countries. The percentage of global exports accounted for by Russian oil and gas exporters has declined significantly since 2008. If one adds to this the impact of reduced prices (e.g., per barrel of oil) in recent years—generally to the famous Saudi "goldilocks" price of around $60, the financial hit to Russian economic well-being is serious.[134] Indeed, in early 2020, the price dipped to below $50 per barrel. Surprisingly, Russian negotiators in March 2020 OPEC+ meetings argued that $50 was OK—no need for production cuts. This is not the usual Russian position, but if one is not looking for contribution to broad-based development plans, crony capitalists

Table 4.2   Natural Gas Supplies to Europe from Russia 2014

	Indigenous Production*	Imports from Russia*	Russian % of Total	Total Consumption*
Country				
Austria	14	42.2	44	96.1
Belgium	0	0	0	172.6
Bulgaria	1	24	96	25
Croatia	18.7	0	0	26.2
Cyprus	0	0	0	0
Czech Republic	1.8	51.6	65	78.8
Denmark	53.6	0	0	53.6
Estonia	0	5.5	100	5.5
Finland	0	32.4	100	32.4
France	0.2	62.3	14	436.8
Germany	98	402.9	49	830.4
Greece	0	18.4	58	31.9
Hungary	19.7	101.4	84	121.1
Ireland	1.6	0	0	48
Italy	75.7	255.4	39	663.2
Latvia	0	13.4	100	13.4
Lithuania	0	26.4	100	26.4
Luxembourg	0	2.8	25	11
Malta	0	0	0	0
Netherlands	648.5	32	5	648.5
Poland	48.1	95.1	55	172.8
Portugal	0	0	0	47.5
Romania	118.1	9.5	7	127.6
Slovakia	0.9	46.9	96	49.1
Slovenia	0	4.8	67	7.2
Spain	0.4	0	0	320.3
Sweden	0	0	0	9.7
United Kingdom	425.5	0	0	774.8
EU-28	1525.8	1227	27	4536.3
%Change 2014/2013	-10.40%	-7.60%		
Switzerland	0	0	0	34.7
Turkey	5.4	287	46	622.9

Source: Eurogas, *Statistical Report*, 2015.
*Terawatt hour (gross calorific value).

may be satisfied as long as sales continue. Clearly, Putin did not want to agree to production cuts initially, but a Saudi–Russian deal on deep cuts was finally reached on April 12.[135]

Fearing a downturn in oil and gas exports to Europe in response to European sanctions and renewable energy program development, Putin hurriedly completed decade-long negotiations for expanded exports to China in May 2014. Reportedly agreeing suddenly to unfavorable terms that he could have had years earlier, the total value of the trade package was estimated to be

Table 4.3   Exports of Oil and Natural Gas by the Russian Federation, 2008–2018

Year	(unit: Thousand Oil Barrels Daily)			(unit: Billion Cubic Meters of Gas)		
	Russian Exports	Total World Exports	Russian % of Total	Russian Exports	Total World Exports	Russian % of Total
2008	7,540	56,561	13.3	251.7	762.4	33.0
2009	7,257	54,320	13.4	196.5	670.3	29.3
2010	7,397	55,346	13.4	207.5	738.0	28.1
2011	7,448	56,072	13.3	224.9	795.2	28.3
2012	7,457	56,706	13.2	215.8	785.2	27.5
2013	7,948	58,776	13.5	225.2	786.4	28.6
2014	7,792	59,328	13.1	203.2	769.7	26.4
2015	8,313	62,515	13.3	208.8	782.7	26.7
2016	8,814	66,526	13.2	216.7	838.0	25.9
2017	8,979	69,633	12.9	235.2	904.4	26.0
2018	9,159	71,344	12.8	247.9	943.4	26.3

Source: BP Statistical Review of World Energy 2019.

worth 400 billion dollars.[136] The fruits from this deal will not be realized for some time, given the need to expand the Russian pipeline network dramatically to meet Chinese demands for supply to the Eastern regions of China, but the agreement does seem to provide a stable market for Russian energy exports in the face of concern about European energy markets. An initial gas pipeline from Siberia to Northern China became operational in December 2019.[137]

Was the die cast by the Western push for privatization at all costs to the transition countries of Eurasia? Would modest social democracy and maintenance of a basic social safety net rather than market fundamentalism and corrupt privatization have led to a more sustainable political economic system; is it too late to go back, even for regimes that find exploitation of nature resource reserves so irresistible that broad-based economic diversification efforts seem too onerous or at least burdensome? Will it take a different regime?

As noted earlier, the oil curse phenomenon in Eurasia has been explored in some depth by Pauline Jones Luong and Erika Weinthal in *Oil Is Not a Curse*, but the dynamics of the challenging processes of industrial diversification are not well understood or studied thoroughly as yet. First, how sustainable is the Russian political economy as now configured? This obviously raises immediate questions of the size of oil and gas reserves, the volatility of oil pricing, and the security of transportation networks—all of which are potentially constrained. There is no immediate crisis in each area as yet, but analysts suggest that oil prices may remain well under $100 a barrel for some time. Global production continues to increase, as new technology is applied (hydraulic fracturing in the United States, Europe, and even China) and political decisions make continued production levels high (despite Russian and OPEC attempts at coordinated cuts) and expand it elsewhere (Iran?). The possibility of transportation network disruptions is not out of the question, particularly given the aging energy infrastructure in the Russian Federation.

With these potential constraints in mind, the incentive to look for economic development and prosperity from other sectors is high. Successful natural resource countries have marshaled resources from previous energy exports for investments to this end (in contrast to kleptocratic systems that simply steal the profits or make wasteful or otherwise unproductive expenditures). A preliminary review of Russian investments indicates considerable infrastructure development and ancillary enterprise development in the energy sector but little exemplary economic development in non-energy sectors. There is commitment to diversify the industrial and commercial base, but like many oil- and/or gas-rich countries—especially those with authoritarian regimes—the result is modest at best. Certainly, there is no evidence of an economic take-off in manufacturing, high technology innovation, and commercialization; increases in agricultural productivity and even the development of indigenous service industries, despite the added motivation of Western economic sanctions in response to the annexation of Crimea in early 2014, remain modest. What explains this?

The first part of the answer to this challenging question is that there is something critical missing in all post-Soviet states that have not liberalized economically and politically. As Linda Weiss reminded us, state-led industrialization can work under certain circumstances (e.g., in Germany, Japan, Korea); one might add China to her sample. But more often than not, it seems that states make poor investment decisions and waste resources on industrial and commercial dead ends. This is particularly true if the system is beset with corruption, as is the tradition in most of Eurasia (see Henry Hale's analysis of this in *Patronal Politics* and Karen Dawisha's elaborate focus on Russia in *Putin's Kleptocracy*). Anders Åslund has recently demonstrated that this corruption may in fact be worsening in Russia in his sobering treatment of *Russia's Crony Capitalism*. Åslund concludes in part:

> . . . This system can deliver macroeconomic stability but only minimal economic growth; it is so petrified that it is more likely to collapse than reform . . . .
>
> The Putin economic system is based on monopolies and cartels. The most important economic sectors are divided among a few companies, which in turn are each dominated by one person. Oil and gas production belongs to five companies—Gazprom, Rosneft, Novatek, Surgut, and Lukoil. Pipelines are built by the companies belonging to either the Rotenbergs or Timchenko. The crony company Sogaz is the leading insurance company. Rotenberg's Mostotrest is responsible for big road construction projects. Mergers are allowed, but antitrust is not. Creative destruction appears to be declining, as is new enterprise

formation. Competition is dissuaded or worse, allowing the incumbent companies to reap monopoly rents. Outstanding new entrepreneurs tend to emigrate.[138]

Lillia Shevtsova discusses some elements of this with respect to Russia in
Lonely Power. She notes the impact of the West's involvement in the Balkan
crisis, the bombing of Belgrade, recognition of Kosovo's independence, and
the American invasion in Iraq, as impetus for the "patriotic consolidation"
which derailed liberalization and modernization reforms. In her words:

> Putin and Medvedev couldn't offer the elite and Russian society a moderniza-
> tion agenda that could realistically become the foundation for a constructive
> consolidation . . . . if the West did not exist as a scapegoat, the regime would
> have to invent it . . . . How can we hope for modernization if investors are too
> afraid to invest in a country where the prime minister can crash the market with
> just a few words spoken in public? How can there be modernization if there are
> no rules?[139]

Speaking directly to a Russian audience, she asks:

> Where is the actual program of this modernization? Where is Putin's plan,
> which was in the [United Russia] party's election platform? And generally, how
> can you modernize a country and defeat corruption while rejecting the political
> competition, rule of law, and independent institutions? If there is a recipe for
> this innovation, it would be good to show it at last.[140]

Shevtsova argues pointedly: "It may happen only if the Russian elite stops fak-
ing modernization and does it for real, and the West decides to support it."[141]

Russia finally acceded to formal WTO membership toward the end of
2012, after considerable ambivalence in its political leadership—and eighteen
years of negotiation. But the pervasive corruption that was evident in the
early years of transition had only deepened and remains the most startling
characteristic of a political economy, with concomitant weakness in the rule
of law, which still fails to meet the basic needs of large segments of the
population.

The heat in Russia's relationship with the West is obviously back now
(especially since the annexation of Crimea), as is reinforcement of the decline
in the myth of Russian invincibility. Russia is not back, given the sustained
decline in oil prices and the apparent impact of sanctions. Shevtsova's notion
of fake modernization includes a fake or at least halting effort to modernize
its university and technology development system. Promised new investment
was curtailed or withdrawn as the amount of money available after endemic
graft and payoffs was much reduced in a low oil price world.

There were various attempts by the United States, Germany, and France (esp. Sarkozy in 2009) to offer partnership for modernization, but as Shevtsova argues:

> They were bound to fail. The Kremlin sees modernization as a tool to strengthen the status quo, so it expects the West to infuse Russia with money and technology without any conditions or talk of values. But how could one expect any high-tech modernization program to succeed if the Russian leadership is not ready to allow competition or to guarantee property rights, or if it intends the state to keep a tight grip on "innovations"? . . . it (the EU) must try to persuade the Russian leadership that their concept of modernization is a non-starter."[142]

Stefan Hedlund notes that the global financial crisis in 2008 forced a change in the calculus of relations between Europe and Russia. He describes Russian energy policy (and its impact on the Russian economy) as in disarray.[143] Russia did make some investments aimed directly at enhancing its participation in high technology industries. For example, there was the ill-fated plan for Miracle/Innovation City—Russia's Silicon Valley. Marlene Laruelle and Jean Radvanyi are skeptical about Putin's investments in this regard, and his reassertion of "national sovereignty" for industrial development but suggest that this "national champions" strategy, perhaps patterned after similar efforts in France in response to "Le Defi Americain" (largely unsuccessful), but in this case "placed in the care of individuals close to the President."[144]

In February 2010, Vladislav Surkov, announced the plan to build an "innovative city" concentrating 30,000–40,000 of the brightest and most talented people from all corners of the world in a new high technology center. According to Surkov, by 2015, this Miracle City would generate up to $7 billion of annual income.[145] Vladimir Ryzhkov countered: "The real attraction of the Kremlin's Innovation City lies not in what it will accomplish for innovation but in how it *will line the pockets of Russia's corrupt officials.*"[146]

This kind of effort at industrial diversification and economic liberalization was promoted by President Medvedev, as he made clear in his article entitled "Go Russia!" which appeared in September 10, 2009. Shevtsova quoted Vladimir Putin's response to the failure of innovation city, as he put himself in charge of the Russian government's high-tech commission: "Two years and billions of dollars have been spent to promote innovation and no results. It's my turn to get things done!"[147] James Appell provided a detailed assessment of the shortcomings of innovation city in 2015.[148]

Loren Graham, perhaps the foremost Western authority on Russian and Soviet science and technology successes and failures, puts his finger on the nub of the problem facing Russia and other post-Soviet states that restrict freedom. In 2015, he reported on the partnership of his university, MIT, with

Russia to establish the Skolkovol Institute of Science and Technology in Skolkovol Oblast on the outskirts of Moscow. A project begun in 2011 and estimated to involve payment of at least $300 million to MIT, it was slated to graduate its first students in 2015.[149]

Graham also analyses RUSNANO, a foundation established by the Russian government at President Dmitry Medvedev's urging and patterned somewhat after the U.S. National Nanotechnology Initiative (NNI). The aim of RUSNANO was to fund nanotechnology business ventures, and many have been supported since the first round of applications in 2011–2012.

The level of investment made in these two ventures is impressive, but Graham points out some flaws in both the "SkolTech" and RUSNANO efforts. Quite simply, the technological research promotion and entrepreneurial training are not accompanied by a larger political and economic environment that supports freedom of idea exchange and productive commercial development investment. In his words:

> The stated goal of the Russian government's spending so much money on Skolkovo is to elevate the Russian economy from one dependent largely on extractive industries to one boosted by knowledge, by high technology . . . so much of the success of commercial technology depends on factors outside the laboratory (politics, social barriers, investment climate, corruption, etc.) a micro-technical center like Skolkovo, however talented its researchers and students, is likely to have limited commercial success in Russian society at large. . . .
>
> The greatest flaw of the Skolkovo and Rusnano projects is that both are attempts to improve technology without basically changing the society in which technology must develop. This is the same defect that has plagued modernization efforts in Russia for three hundred years.[150]

This digression into some of the features of the Russian failed industrial and technological diversification effort is offered here for two reasons. First, it may be seen as a contrast to the more successful innovation and entrepreneurial development efforts underway in the last 10–15 years in other countries, particularly in East and Southeast Asia, but also India and Turkey (see chapter 6).

Second is the Russian trap of authoritarianism, crony capitalism, and restrictions on economic choice. One can see broad-based impacts of the fossil fuel wealth in social programs and infrastructure development, especially when world oil and gas prices are high. The focus on educational reform and modernization seems sincere, despite the effect of low energy prices. Industrial and technological partnerships with Turkish and Western companies are priority goals for the government, but the regulatory environment and ease of doing business ratings are not yet promising. Keith Crane and Artur Usanov argue that the Russian computer software industry is perhaps the one bright spot in their review of high technology industries.[151]

The positive role that the state can play in broad-based economic development is obviously dependent on the quality of the relevant state agencies and the personnel directing and staffing them. The long tradition of *blat* (corrupt favor) appointments in Russia, perhaps raised to the status of a science or indeed specially adapted to modern technologies and practices under the Putin administration, is captured quite thoroughly as a critical continuing weakness by Alena Ledeneva in *Can Russia Modernise? Sistema, Power Networks and Informal Governance* (2013). Ledeneva stresses that the Russian economy, and what she calls the *sistema*:

> . . . functions in a dysfunctional way: the economic growth and stability of Putin's Russia is detrimental to Russia's development in the long term. Understanding *sistema's* paradoxes is essential for shifting the analytical frame beyond dualities, binaries and dichotomies. I document the tensions that exist between conflicting or interacting power networks, explain how key players cope with the "doublethink" emerging from the clash of their formal and informal capacities and show how subversive practices can support *Sistema* . . . .Though formally defined by the law and institutions, the operations of power networks are equally dependent on the unwritten rules, social networks and informal norms widespread in society.[152]

There was an effort under President Medvedev to reform the *blat* appointments which undergird this system:

> Medvedev raised concerns over appointments through personal contacts or by payment—"*blat* appointments"—shortly after his inauguration in July 2008. Medvedev called for an integrated system for the reproduction and renovation of the professional elite and suggested the creation of a national reserve of cadres . . . . Yet the initiative remained unpopular . . . . the leader of the Liberal Democratic Party of Russia (LDPR) faction in the Duma, Vladimir Zhirinovskii, claimed in an interview with *Komsomolskaya pravda* that the trade in appointments is a national practice and volunteered a price list. With the notable exception of the price for a place on a party list for election to the Duma, his list included the following tariffs: from 5 to 7 million euros for the position of governor, from 5 to 7 million euros for a seat in the Federation Council and between 3 and 4 million euros for the position of head of the Federal Service or head of department . . . .[153]

Ledeneva then quotes Mikhail Gorbachev's 2010 article *"Perestroika, 25 years later"*:

> I sense alarm in the words of President Dmitri Medvedev when he wonders, as he has in recent public remarks: 'Should a primitive economy based on raw materials and endemic corruption accompany us into the future?' Can we be complacent when 'the government apparatus in our country is the biggest employer, the biggest publisher, the best producer, its own judiciary, a party in its own right, and ultimately a nation unto itself'? You cannot say it any more strongly. I agree with the President. I agree with his goal of modernization.[154]

On the challenges of developing an independent judiciary, Ledeneva describes Medvedev's effort to combat "Telephone justice," a large hold-over from the Soviet period where Party officials regularly called judges to explain the Party Line on what needed to happen in a pertinent court case.[155] Ledeneva argues that it still denotes "inequality before the law, selectivity in law enforcement and the consequent gap between law and justice."[156]

The sum total of Ledeneva's position on the prospects for reform and modernization in Russia is unavoidably negative/pessimistic, as she speaks of the "modernization trap of informality" continuing to plague effective governance. In this respect, she joins Dawisha, Dimitrov, Gel'man, Hale, Petrov, Shevtsova, and so on. in a view that while substantial change is possible, democratization and broad-based economic prosperity certainly may not be the most likely alternative to the current characteristics of the Putin regime.

Writing on *The Politics of Economic Reform in the Soviet* Union back in 1972, Abraham Katz stressed:

> The main problem from the point of view of the leadership is that the Soviet economy is not keeping pace in the technological race, is not producing the variety of goods that much smaller economies are producing, and is producing many goods of inferior quality. Indeed, it is hard to name a single manufactured item for which the Soviets could find a ready commercial market in the free world. It is a shocking commentary that the country that is the first socialist country in the world, dedicated to the proposition that its economic system is the highest form of social organization and represents the way of the future, continues to rely on buying, borrowing, and stealing technology in almost every "progressive" field. It cannot sell a piece of equipment or a bolt of cloth outside the socialist camp, except under compensation deals, at meaninglessly low prices, or as part of aid programs in underdeveloped countries. The factors of technological backwardness and poor quality are among the most powerful motivations for reform. Yet, these are the factors that the Soviets admit have been least affected and are least

likely to be affected by the reform in the short term. Judgments as to the degree of success of the reform as it affects levels of technological advancement, degree of innovation, and quality of product will be even less amenable to statistical quantification.[157]

Interestingly, one can argue that Russia's lack of success in modern industrial manufacturing and agricultural productivity since 1991 parallels earlier reform failures, particularly if one examines the period since 2000 under the Putin/Medvedev administrations. Substantial resources from oil and gas exports were available, especially during the high global oil price years, for investment in industrial diversification and higher education modernization. As noted above, there were some efforts and expenditures along these lines, but they were relatively modest and were negated in important respects by the overall repressive environment that failed to nurture innovation and entrepreneurial development. Instead, entrepreneurs and technologists seem to be emigrating from Russia at a rapid pace, especially since 2014.

Breaking or reducing the imperatives of the network of "Patronal Politics," so evident in the region according to Henry Hale, may be the key step for broad-based diversification and prosperity. Many in the West assumed that Russians (and Azerbaijanis, Kazakhs, Uzbeks, etc.) would welcome and continue to fight for freedom after the collapse of the Soviet Union. Indeed, some naively believed Russia would want to join the West as a normal democratic and liberal economic member. There clearly were some missed opportunities and perhaps some humiliating decisions by arrogant and short-sighted Western leaders, but the naiveté that discounted the pull of Russian nationalism (and fear of encirclement) and the tradition of authoritarianism (see, for example: Gel'man [2015] and Hedlund [2005]) must be added to the calculus. One must also allow for the fact that "values" seem to be held and ranked differently in some Eurasian cultures than they might be in most Western countries. The processes by which values change are complex and difficult to assess.[158]

Is there reason to believe Vladimir Putin can turn an economically declining Russia around? Does he even have a serious interest in doing so? Garry Kasparov, writing on *Winter is Coming* in 2015 was both devastatingly critical of Putin but guardedly optimistic about the future of Russia. Quoting Andrei Piontkovsky, he argued that there should have been no surprise that Putin would move decidedly away from the liberal democratic (but corrupt) system led by Boris Yeltsin:

This is a man who has shown a complete disregard for human life . . . and a willingness to use war and the deaths of thousands of Russian soldiers and innocent civilians as a PR instrument in his election campaign. This is a man who raised a toast on the anniversary of Stalin's birth, had the plaque commemorating former KGB head Yury Andropov restored to its place on the wall of the Lubyanka—Federal Security Service headquarters—and dreams of seeing the statue of butcher Felix Dzerzhinsky, founder of the Soviet secret police, stand once again in the center of Moscow.[159]

Kasparov generalized the concern by stressing:

The world's dictators are very aware of the power wielded by the free world today. This is why nearly all of them role-play at democracy with sham elections and perform other acts of theater to stay in the good graces of the world's largest economies and militaries. Unfortunately, the free world is too uninformed, callous, or apathetic to use this influence. They enjoy the benefits of engagement with dictatorships—oil from the Middle East, gas from Russia, everything else from China—while the dictators use the money to fund repression. But not all dictatorships are the same.[160]

His specific assessment of Putin in this context followed:

Putin's instinct was to align himself with power and to bring power to himself. Anything he didn't control was something he couldn't trust. His solution was to try to control everything. Unlike the totalitarianism of the Soviet Union, which handed all control to the system, Putin aimed for the totalitarianism of one person: himself.[161]

Media outlets were taken over by forces friendly to Putin and his closest associates. This "takeover censorship" was accompanied by the more conventional kind, with its lists of non grata names and verboten topics. Media power was centralized in the same fashion as political power and with the same purpose: looting the country without causing a popular revolt.[162]

Indeed, there is a long list of critical analyses of Putin as leader and what might be called "Putinism," characterizing a drive for power and personal wealth that is self-serving, cynical, and what Steven Kotkin recently described as an example of "fascism without commitment."[163]

THE WAY FORWARD: PRESIDENT FOR LIFE OR SERIOUS REFORM TOWARD BROADER PROSPERITY?

Anders Åslund's recipe for what we would categorize as the *dim prospect* of broad-based prosperity in Russia is sweeping and probably unrealistic, (but likely correct):

1. Elect a new political elite
2. Abolish the secret police
3. Build a new judicial system

"After these three critical political and judicial tasks, the ordinary slog of economic reforms could start."[164]

In response to significant constitutional initiatives by Vladimir Putin, Dmitri Medvedev's cabinet resigned in January 2020; Mikhail Mishutin, former director of the Federal Tax Service was nominated and confirmed as the new prime minister of Russia. His new cabinet replaced former ministers but retained a few long-serving ministers, including Minister of Defense Sergei Shoigu, Minister of Finance Anton Siluanov, and Minister of Foreign Affairs Sergei Lavrov. This was a significant change, but it remains unclear what the long-term intent was and impact will be. The cabinet reshuffling occurred during the rise of the Coronavirus (COVID-19) to a global pandemic, as well as during the dramatic decline in world oil prices that led to serious strategic conflict between Russia and Saudi Arabia. Accordingly, the Russian government found itself in some turmoil.

At this writing, President Putin's dramatic reorganization of the Russian government is not well understood. Changes to the constitution were approved.[165] Speculation on the implications of the changes and the subsequent referendum includes the optimistic view that it is the beginning of a constructive effort to revitalize governance and economic reform—though certainly not as far-reaching as Åslund proposes. Alternatively, it may be simply a not very imaginative step in the direction of setting Putin up to be president for Life, retaining power after his second (actually 4th) term is up in 2024. He would not be alone in this inclination.[166]

An interesting variant on this option would be for Putin eventually to take leadership of a strengthened State Council of the Union State, the supranational agreement between Belarus and Russia that has been in place in various forms for many years. In order to strengthen the State Council, further integration between the two countries is necessary. Putin pressured Belarusian president Alexander Lukashenko to accept more integration in 2019 by effectively cutting crude oil exports to Belarus which had been a substantial source of Belarus income in a strategy of re-exporting at a higher price level.[167] Lukashenko found himself in a weakened position entering the presidential election in 2020, as his domestic opposition, and indeed Belarusian nationalism grew substantially. His past skill in playing off Russia against the West while maintaining a soft authoritarian system seemed rather less effective, and at the same time seemed to frustrate Putin's goal of Eurasian economic integration.[168]

Lukashenko's subsequent declaration of a landslide victory with a tally of more than 80 percent of the vote on August 9, 2020 was unbelievable. The election was widely reported to be fraudulent in the face of unusual mobilization of the opposition and a generally fed-up population, stressed by the pandemic and Lukashenko's cavalier attitude toward it. The key opposition candidate Sviatlana Tsikhanouskaya (wife of a jailed, or at least disqualified candidate) protested the results and called for them to be declared invalid. She later backtracked unconvincingly, under pressure, and fled to Lithuania with her children in fear for their security. Intense protests against Lukashenko continued for weeks. Lukashenko's response was to consult more closely with President Putin and authorize increasingly violent means for dissuading the protests.

To what extent did this present an opportunity for Putin to intervene and pursue his dream of Russia–Belarus union? Lithuanian president Gitanas Nauseda argued that this was indeed quite possible, opining that Putin had probably learned from his bold but somewhat dysfunctional intervention in Ukraine and could make this union a practical reality, if he was more subtle and gradual in his pressure and presentation of opportunity. Nauseda expected Lukashenko would not finally save his rule in Belarus. He called for a strong Western response to support the opposition, noting his confidence in Lithuania's growing support from its NATO membership, but he was not overly optimistic that Belarus could remain independent if Putin was clever and the West, especially the EU remained overly cautious.[169] This would be a key step in Putin's campaign to regain "lost empire."

The "frozen conflict" over Nagorno-Karabakh between Armenia and Azerbaijan thawed a bit as Azerbaijan seemed finally to lose patience in the mediating role of France, Russia, and the United States with renewed fighting on September 27, 2020. Serious attacks on Armenian separatist positions by Azerbaijan along the line of contact were apparent. The self-proclaimed Republic of Artsakh (by ethnic Armenians) in Nagorno-Karabakh suggested that forces of Azerbaijan initiated the conflict. Russia joined France and the United States in calling for a cease fire after a few days but was rather restrained in its role.[170] Normally a close ally of Armenia, Russia was not overtly supportive, while Turkey was unusually public in its support for the Azerbaijani position.[171] The prospect for serious political conflict between Russia and Turkey over the dispute was not out of the question, but Russian authorities seemed less interested in defending Armenia this time than on previous iterations of the conflict. Some speculate that Russian enthusiasm for Armenia had been dampened by the closer relationship that seemed to be building between Armenia and France. The possibility of a long-term stable resolution of the dispute remains remote. Russian foreign minister Sergey Lavrov did succeed in Moscow meetings to broker a cease fire set to take effect on October 10, but it soon collapsed, and the casualties continued to mount.

After substantial Azerbaijani successes in battle, the Armenians agreed to a settlement brokered by Russia early in November. Armenia recognized the lands reconquered by Azerbaijan, much to the protest of many Armenians in Yerevan who cursed the prime minister, Nikol Pashinyan. Pashinyan simply argued he had no choice, given the facts on the ground and the Russian posture; the protestors were not satisfied and attacked his office. Azerbaijani president Aliyev did not get all he wanted, but there was considerable celebration in Baku. Putin seems to have punished Armenia for its recent pro-Western leaning, particularly its closer relations with France. Turkey was pleased with the result and committed to providing troops to help supervise the peace. Kremlin spokesman Dmitry Peskov, however, argued that only Russian troops would be in place. The peace may be marginally more durable, given Russian and Turkish support, and current Armenian weakness. But Nagorno-Karabakh remains a frozen conflict that clearly does not satisfy either adversary.[172]

In late 2020, Putin found himself with instability and conflict in much of the former Soviet empire: economic stagnation in the Eurasian Economic Community, war in the Caucasus, unstable authoritarian rule in Belarus, and unexpected regime change in Kyrgyzstan. Staving off Chinese and Turkish influence in Eurasia continue to preoccupy him, and domestic economic and pandemic health concerns threaten his popularity.

Putin's constitutional changes have been the source of considerable commentary in the Russian media, notably because they seem to strip some powers from the presidency and give them to the Duma. Instead, Duma deputy Valentina Tereshkova proposed an amendment to simply "reset" Putin's presidency, allowing him to run again in 2024. She claimed that resetting Putin's presidency "would be a stabilizing factor for our society."[173] Polling from the Levada organization suggested a different story, however. To a question asking whether or not Putin should leave in 2024, 45 percent said that he should step down, while 45 percent said that he should stay. This presents a problem for Putin as his usual solid support among Russians seems to be cracking. In May of 2019, state-run pollster VTsIOM revealed that the public's trust in Putin had fallen to 31.7 percent.[174] His performance in response to the COVID-19 pandemic, which grew in the Russian Federation at an alarming rate (indeed infecting Prime Minister Mishutin) did not inspire broad confidence, but his celebration of Russia's development of the world's first COVID-19 vaccine on August 11, labeled *Sputnik V* (a not to subtle reference to the great Soviet successes in the space race of the 1950s and 1960s), did seem to deflect some of the criticism. Nonetheless, there was widespread doubt on the achievement expressed in the global scientific community, given that vaccine was not widely tested in the normal human trial regimen to ensure it was both safe and effective.

Protests in Khabarovsk after the arrest of the popular governor, Sergei Furgal, reputedly for organizing contract killings fifteen years ago, were extensive and continued for weeks; Russian analysts suggested that the unrest was connected to broader concerns about Putin's administration.[175]

Furthermore, international outrage erupted when Alexei Navalny, an outspoken and long-term Putin critic, was taken off his Siberian flight to Moscow in Omsk, after a sudden critical illness. He reportedly had a cup of tea before boarding in Tomsk, but ingested nothing on the plane. Navalny's campaigns against corruption in the Putin regime were clearly uncomfortable for Putin's "crony capitalism." Germany offered to treat Navalny, as it had for a similar (apparent) poison victim. There was some delay in the subsequent Kremlin approval, raising speculation that this was a strategy similar to that employed with Kremlin critic Pyotr Verzilov, where the intent seemed to be to prolong his time in Russia so that all traces of the possible poison had disappeared. The German doctors subsequently concluded that Navalny had been poisoned with the nerve agent Novichok. Chancellor Merkel expressed alarm and seemed to indicate that European sanctions were possible in response, including some prospect that the controversial Nordstream 2 natural gas pipeline from Russia to Germany completion might be threatened. The EU did levy financial sanctions on six key associates of Putin in mid-October, 2020. This seemed to be recognition of Navalny's clear argument that the means of the esoteric poisoning could not have been provided to the attackers without Kremlin authorization.

These events did seem to cast a shadow over Putin's rule in Russia. But the referendum on the constitutional changes was convincing (77.2% in favor with a 67.9% turnout of eligible voters), and there is little evidence that a powerful opposition leader is rising to challenge him.

As noted earlier, the authoritarian inclinations of Putin fit well with the sentiments of Ivan Ilyan and the Eurasianist arguments of Gumilev and Dugin which are marshaled to support Eurasian economic integration against Western economic and political liberalism. One must keep this in mind as we continue to assess the persistence of authoritarianism and the fragility of democracy.

Anne Applebaum is eloquent on "The Seductive Lure of Authoritarianism" which in her view extends well beyond Russia and the Former Soviet Union: "Given the right conditions, any society can turn against democracy. Indeed, if history is anything to go by, all of our societies eventually will."[176] Putin does not need luring, nor perhaps does Russia. As Applebaum stresses: "The liberalism of John Stewart Mill, Thomas Jefferson, or Vaclav Havel never promised anything permanent."[177] Putin never had the inclination to try seriously the liberal project. Indeed, his KGB roots and supporting cast have led him to disrupt other democracies whenever possible.[178]

NOTES

1. Vladimir Putin, *First Person: An Astonishingly Frank Self-Portrait by Russia's President* (NY: Public Affairs/Perseus, 2000), p. 186.

2. Putin gave this as a New Year address on December 31, 1999. It is available at https://www.sott.net/article/310072 and is included as an Appendix to later additions of *First Person.*

3. *Izvestia*, February 25, 2000; also available at http://www.putin2000.ru/07/05.html. See: the detailed analysis of this strategy by Dawisha, 2014, Chapter 5.

4. Arkady Ostrovsky, *The Invention of Russia: From Gorbachev's Freedom to Putin's War* (NY: Viking/Penguin/Random House, 2015). See also: Ostrovsky, "For Putin, Disinformation Is Power," *The New York Times*, August 8, 2016.

5. Ben Mezrich, *Once Upon a Time in Russia: The Rise of the Oligarchs* (NY: Atria Books, 2015), p. 7.

6. Karen Dawisha, *Putin's Kleptocracy: Who Owns Russia* (NY: Simon and Schuster, 2014), p. 164; See also: David E. Hoffman, *The Oligarchs: Wealth and Power in the New Russia* (NY: Public Affairs/Perseus, 2011); and Richard Sakwa, *Putin and the Oligarch: The Khodorkovsky—Yukos Affair* (NY: I.B. Tauris and Co., 2014).

7. Dawisha, *Putin's Kleptocracy*, p. 271.

8. Ibid., p. 277; Masha Gessen, *The Man Without a Face: The Unlikely Rise of Vladimir Putin* (NY: Riverhead Books/Penguin, 2012), Chapter 7; and Ostrovsky, *The Invention of Russia.*

9. Fiona Hill and Clifford G. Gaddy. *Mr. Putin: Operative in the Kremlin*. Rev. edition (Washington, DC: The Brookings Institution Press, 2015), p. 403.

10. Gessen, *The Man Without a Face*, p. 292.

11. See: Yuriy Felshtinsky and Vladimir Pribylovskiy, *The Age of Assassins: The Rise and Rise of Vladimir Putin* (London: Gibson Square, 2008); and Felshtinskiy and Pribylovskiy, Glava 11. Vremya naemnyh ubiyc, 2010.

12. Dawisha, *Putin's Kleptocracy*, p. 22; Mezrich, *Once Upon a Time in Russia*, pp. 254–255.

13. See: Peter Pomerantsev, "The Kremlin's Information War," *Journal of Democracy*, 26, no. 4 (October 2015), pp. 40–50; and Ostrovsky, 2015.

14. See Ostrovsky, 2015 on the critical role that the dominance of television broadcasts plays in *The Invention of Russia.*

15. See: Ron Deibert, "Cyberspace Under Siege," *Journal of Democracy*, 26, no. 3 (July 2015), pp. 64–78.

16. "2020 World Press Freedom Index," *Reporters Without Borders*. See also: https://rsf.org/en/news.

17. See: Leon Aron, "The Long Struggle for Freedom," *Journal of Democracy*, 24, no. 3 (July, 2013), pp. 62–74.

18. Lilia Shevtsova, "Forward to the Past in Russia," *Journal of Democracy*, 26, no. 2 (November, 2015), p. 23.

19. Ibid., p. 34.

20. Lee Kuan Yew, speaking as an opposition member in the Singapore Legislative Assembly, 4 October, 1956.

21. Fiona Hill and Clifford G. Gaddy, *Mr. Putin: Operative in the Kremlin* (Washington, DC: Brookings Institution Press, 2015); Karin Dawisha, *Putin's Kleptocracy*; and Steve Myers, *The New Tsar: The Rise and Reign of Vladimir Putin* (NY: Alfred A. Knopf, 2015).

22. See: Anna Arutunyan, *The Putin Mystique: Inside Russia's Power Cult* (Northampton, MA: Interlink Publishing Group/Olive Branch Press, 2015); Anne Garrels, *Putin Country: A Journey Into the Real Russia* (NY: Picador/Rarrar, Straus and Giroux, 2019); Samuel A. Greene and Graeme B. Robertson, *Putin v. the People: The Perilous Politics of a Divided Russia* (New Haven, CT: Yale University Press, 2019); Andrew Jack, *Inside Putin's Russia* (UK: Oxford University Press, 2004); Walter Laqueur, *Putinism: Russia and Its Future with the West* (NY: Thomas Dunne Books/St. Martin's Press, 2015); Steve LeVine, *Putin's Labyrinth: Spies, Murder, and the Dark Heart of the New Russia* (NY: Random House, 2008); Richard Lourie, *Putin: His Downfall and Russia's Coming Crash* (NY: Thomas Dunne Books/St. Martin's Press, 2017); and Brian D. Taylor, *The Code of Putinism* (UK: Oxford University Press, 2018).

23. Vladimir Gel'man, *Russian Authoritarianism: Analyzing Post-Soviet Regime Changes* (Pittsburgh, PA: University of Pittsburgh Press, 2015), p. xii.

24. Stefan Hedlund, *Russian Path Dependence* (London: Routledge, 2005), pp. 7–11.

25. Ibid., pp. 24–26.

26. Dawisha, *Putin's Kleptocracy*, p. 350.

27. Henry Hale, *Patronal Politics: Eurasian Regime Dynamics in Comparative Perspective* (UK: Cambridge University Press, 2015), pp. 9–10.

28. Ibid., p. 11.

29. Ibid., p. 13.

30. Ibid., p. 34.

31. Ibid., pp. 34–35.

32. Ibid., p. 36.

33. Ibid., p. 37.

34. Ibid., pp. 37–38.

35. Marshall Goldman, *Petrostate: Putin, Power and the New Russia* (NY: Oxford University Press, 2008), pp. 12–14.

36. See: Marshall Goldman, *The Piratization of Russia: Russian Reform Goes Awry* (NY: Routledge, 2003), esp. chapters 6–9.

37. United Nations Development Programme, *Human Development Report 2005: Russian Federation—Russia in 2015: Development Goals and Policy Priorities* (Moscow, 2005), p. 157.

38. Michael Klare, *Rising Powers, Shrinking Planet: the New Geopolitics of Energy* (NY: Metropolitan Books, 2008).

39. Brown, Lester, *The Great Transition: Shifting from Fossil Fuels to Solar and Wind Energy* (NY: W.W. Norton, 2015). See also: Dieter Helm's *Burn Out: The Endgame for Fossil Fuels* (New Haven, CT: Yale University Press, 2017).

40. Pauline Jones Luong and Erika Weinfall, *Oil is Not a Curse: Ownership Structure and Institutions in Soviet Successor States* (Cambridge, UK: Cambridge University Press, 2010), p. 179.

41. Goldman, *Petrostate*, pp. 13–14.

42. Joshua Kurlantzick, *Democracy in Retreat: The Revolt of the Middle Class and the Worldwide Decline of Representative Government* (New Haven, CT: Yale University Press, 2013), pp. 55–56.

43. Ibid., p. 66.

44. Ibid., p. 74. See also his comments on the corresponding middle class revolt on p. 77.

45. See: Robert Eatwell and Matthew Goodwin, *National Populism: The Revolt Against Liberal Democracy* (UK: Penguin Books/Random House, 2018); Jan-Werner Muller, *What Is Populism?* (Philadelphia, PA: University of Pennsylvania Press, 2016); Ian Bremmer, *US vs. Them: The Failure of Globalism* (UK: Penguin/Random House, 2018); and Joan C. Williams, *White Working Class: Overcoming Class Cluelessness in America* (Boston: Harvard Business Review Press, 2018).

46. David Landes, *The Wealth and Poverty of Nations: Why Some are so Rich and Some so Poor* (NY: W.W.Norton, 1998).

47. Daron Acemoglu and James A. Robinson, *Why Nations Fail: The Origins of Power, Prosperity, and Poverty* (NY: Crown/Random House, 2012).

48. Peter Dicken, *Global Shift: Reshaping the Global Economic Map in the 21st Century* (NY: The Guilford Press, 2003); Jagdish Bhagwati, *In Defense of Globalization* (NY: Oxford University Press, 2004); Joseph Stiglitz, *Globalization and Its Discontents* (NY: W.W. Norton, 2002); Joseph Stiglitz, *Globalization and Its Discontents—Revisited* (NY: W.W. Norton, 2018); Steven C. Radelet, *The Great Surge: The Ascent of the Developing World* (NY: Simon and Schuster, 2015).

49. For interesting arguments to this effect, see chapter 3 in *The Collapse of Western Civilization* by Oreskes and Conway (2014); *Zombie Capitalism: How Dead Ideas Still Walk Among Us*, by John Quiggin (2010).

50. George Soros, *The Crisis of Global Capitalism: Open Society Endangered* (NY: Public Affairs, 1998); and Joseph E. Stiglitz, "Information and the Change in the Paradigm of Economics," *Prize Lecture*, December 8, 2001.

51. Kurlantzick, *Democracy in Retreat*, p. 206.

52. Robert B. Reich, *Saving Capitalism: For the Many, Not the Few* (NY: Vintage Books, 2016), Chapter 1.

53. Stiglitz, *Globalization and Its Discontents—Revisited*, especially pp. 30–40 and 94–97.

54. Ruchir Sharma, *The Rise and Fall of Nations: Forces of Change in the Post-Crisis World* (NY: W.W. Norton, 2016).

55. Robert B. Reich, *The Work of Nations: Preparing Ourselves for the 21ˢᵗ Century* (NY: Random House/Vintage Books, 1991); and Kenichi Ohmae, *The End of the Nation State: The Rise of Regional Economies* (NY: The Free Press, 1995).

56. Linda Weiss, *The Myth of the Powerless State* (Ithaca, NY: Cornell University Press, 1998).

57. Lee Kuan Yew, *From Third World to First: The Singapore Story, 1965–2000* (NY: Harper Collins, 2000).

58. Amartya Sen, *Journal of Democracy*, July 1999.

59. Ibid.

60. Anders Åslund, *How Capitalism Was Built: The Transformation of Central and Eastern Europe, Russia and Central Asia* (Cambridge, UK: Cambridge University Press 2007), esp. Chapter 2.

61. Mary Gallagher and Johnathan K. Hanson, "Authoritarian Survival, Resilience and the Selectorate Theory," in Dimitrov, Martin K., ed., *Why Communism Did Not Collapse: Understanding Authoritarian Regime Resilience in Asia and Europe* (Cambridge, UK: Cambridge University Press, 2013), pp. 187–189. See also: Bruce Bueno de Mesquita and Alastair Smith, *The Logic of Political Survival* (Cambridge, MA: The MIT Press, 2003).

62. Daron Acemoglu and James A. Robinson, *Economic Origins of Dictatorship and Democracy* (Cambridge, UK: Cambridge University Press, 2006).

63. Atuhl Kohli, *State-Directed Development: Political Power and Industrialization in the Global Periphery* (Cambridge, UK: Cambridge University Press, 2004).

64. Gallagher and Hanson, "Authoritarian Survival," p. 202.

65. Minxin Pei, *China's Trapped Transition: The Limits of Developmental Autocracy* (Cambridge, MA: Harvard University Press. Pei, Minxin. 2006).

66. Minxin Pei, *China's Crony Capitalism: The Dynamics of Regime Decay* (Cambridge, MA: Harvard University Press, 2016).

67. Fredrik Galtung, "Measuring the Immeasurable: Boundaries and Functions of (Macro) Corruption Indices," in Charles Sampford, Arthur Shacklock, Carmel Connors and Fredrik Galtung, eds., *Measuring Corruption* (Aldershot, UK: Ashgate Publishing, 2006). pp. 101–130.

68. Johann Graf Lambsdorff, "Measuring Corruption—The Validity and Precision of Subjective Indicators (CPI)," *Measuring Corruption*, pp. 81–99.

69. A more systematic assessment of these factors, among others, is available in: Norman A. Graham, "Russian Foreign Policy toward Central Asia and the Caucasus since the End of the Cold War: A Search for Identity with Geopolitical Characteristics," in Mohammed Ayoob and Murad Ismayilov, eds., *Identity and Politics in Central Eurasia and the Caucasus* (Routledge, 2015).

70. Gessen, *The Man Without a Face*, p. 153.

71. Anna Politkovskaya, *A Dirty War: A Russian Reporter in Chechnya* (London: The Harvill Press, 2001), pp. 218–219.

72. Gessen, *The Man Without a Face*, pp. 145–154; and 212–218.

73. Ibid., pp. 216–217. See also: Alexander Litvinenko and Yuri Felshtinsky, *Blowing Up Russia: The Secret Plot to Bring Back KGB Terror* (NY: Encounter Books, 2007).

74. Litvinenko and Felshtinsky, *Blowing Up Russia*, pp. 3–30.

75. Sir Robert Owen, *The Litvinenko Inquiry: Report into the Death of Alexander Litvinenko*. Presented to Parliament pursuant to Section 26 of the Inquiries Act 2005. 21 January 2016, especially, pp. 183–226.

76. Luke Harding, *A Very Expensive Poison: The Assassination of Alexander Litvinenko and Putin's War with the West* (NY: Vintage Books, 2016).

77. Terrence Hunt, "Clinton, Yeltsin Trade Compliments, Play Down Differences," *Associated Press News*, April 21, 1996.

78. http://www.ljubljana-summit.gov.si/en/index.html.

79. https://nato.int/cps/en/natohq/topics_50091.htm.

80. Stephen F. Cohen, *War with Russia? From Putin and Ukraine to Trump and Russiagate* (NY: Skyhorse Publishing, 2019), p. 207.

81. See: Marshall Shulman, *Beyond the Cold War* (New Haven, CT: Yale University Press, 1966), pp. 2–3.

82. Cohen, *War with Russia?*, p. 212.

83. Michael McFaul, *From Cold War to Hot Peace: An American Ambassador in Putin's Russia* (Boston, MA: Houghton Mifflin Harcourt, 2018), p. 58.

84. Ibid., p. 67.

85. Vladimir Putin, *Speech to the Munich Conference on Security Policy*, February 10, 2007, http://en.kremlin.ru/events/president/transcripts/24034.

86. McFaul, *From Cold War to Hot Peace*, chapters 6 and 7.

87. Ibid., p. 116.

88. Ibid., pp. 102–106.

89. McFaul, *From Cold War to Hot Peace*, pp. 244–245. See also: https://www.cnn.com/2011/12/06/world/europe/russia-elections-clinton/.

90. For example, see: Michael Crowley and Julia Ioffe, "Why Putin Hates Hillary," *Politico*, July 25, 2016.

91. McFaul, *From Cold War to Hot Peace*, p. 111.

92. Ibid., pp. 288–292.

93. Catherine Belton, *Putin's People: How the KGB Took Back Russia and Then Took on the West* (NY: Farrar, Straus and Giroux, 2020).

94. Joshua Yaffa, *Between Two Fires: Truth, Ambition, and Compromise in Putin's Russia* (NY: Tim Duggan Books, 2020), p. 209.

95. David Shimer, *Rigged: America, Russia, and One Hundred Years of Covert Electoral Interference* (NY: Alfred A. Knopf, 2020), p. 84.

96. Ibid., pp. 242–243.

97. Ibid., pp. 209–226.

98. U.S. Department of Justice, *Report on the Investigation into Russian Interference in the 2016 Presidential Election*. Robert S. Mueller, III, Special Counsel, Washington, DC, March 2019, Volume I, Section V, A.

99. Charles Clover, *Black Wind, White Snow: The Rise of Russia's New Nationalism* (New Haven, CT: Yale University Press, 2016).

100. Alexander Dugin, *The Foundations of Geopolitics*. Russian edition (Moscow: Arktogia, 1997).

101. Alexander Dugin, *Last War of the World-Island: The Geopolitics of Contemporary Russia* (London: Arktos, 2015).

102. Ibid., pp. 7–11.

103. Alexander Dugin, *Eurasian Mission: An Introduction to Neo-Eurasianism* (London: Arktos, 2014).

104. Ibid., p. 39.

105. Ibid., p. 54.

106. Ibid., pp. 115–116.

107. Ibid., p. 107.

108. Ibid., p. 145.

109. Ibid., see pp. 110–126.

110. Ibid., p. 64.

111. Ibid., p. 168.

112. Alexander Dugin, *Putin vs. Putin: Vladimir Putin Viewed from the Right* (London: Arktos, 2014), p. 226.

113. Ibid., p. 192.

114. Ibid., pp. 178–179.

115. Marlene Laruelle, *Russian Eurasianism: An Ideology of Empire* (Baltimore, MD: The Johns Hopkins University Press, 2008), p. 216.

116. Mark Bassin, *The Gumilev Mystique: Biopolitics, Eurasianism, and the Construction of Community in Modern Russia* (Ithaca, NY: Cornell University Press, 2016), pp. 211–214.

117. Ibid., p. 316.

118. Jochen Bittner, "The New Ideology of the New Cold War," *The New York Times*, August 1, 2016.

119. Noah Feldman, "Better Sixty Years of Tyranny than One Night of Anarchy," Luncheon Speech delivered to Loyola Law School and published in *Loyola of Los Angeles International and Comparative Law Review*, 143 (2009), p. 143.

120. Ivan Alexandrovich Ilyin, *On Resistance to Evil by Force* (London: Taxiarch Press, 2018) (originally published privately in 1925, Berlin), p. 6. See also: *Our Tasks*. Volume 1 (a collection of his articles 1948–1951 published together in Russian in 2014, Pubmix.com); and Snyder, Timothy. "Putin's Philosopher of Russian Fascism," *The New York Review*, April 5, 2018, https://www.nybooks.com/daily/2018/03/16 /ivan-ilyin-putins-philosopher-of-russian-fascism/ A discussion of the impact of Ilyin's writings on Putin in Catherine Belton, *Putin's People*, pp. 259 and 272.

121. Richard Baldwin, *The Great Convergence: Information Technology and the New Globalization* (Cambridge, MA: Harvard University Press, 2016), Chapter 1.

122. Steven C. Radelet, *The Great Surge: The Ascent of the Developing World* (NY: Simon and Schuster, 2015).

123. James J. Sheehan, *Where Have All the Soldiers Gone: The Transformation of Modern Europe* (NY: Houghton Mifflin Harcourt, 2008). See also: U.S. Congress. Office of Technology Assessment. *After the Cold War: Living with Lower Defense Spending*. OTA-ITE-524. February 1992.

124. On the prospect for Russian rivalry and partnership with China, see: Paul J. Bolt and Sharyl N. Cross, *China, Russia and Twenty-First Century Global Geopolitics* (UK: Oxford University Press, 2018); and Michal Lubina, *Russia and China: A Political Marriage of Convenience—Stable and Successful* (Opladen, Germany: Barbara Budrich Publishers, 2017).

125. Belton, *Putin's People*, especially Parts Two and Three.

126. See: Henry Foy, Laura Pitel an Chloe Cornish, "Erdoğan and Putin Announce Ceasefire in Idlib," *Financial Times*, March 5, 2020.

127. U.S. Department of Agriculture, *Russian Agricultural Policy and Situation Bi-Weekly Update –5*. Global Agricultural Information Network. Gain Report RS1725 (April 13, 2017); and U.S. Department of Agriculture, Foreign Agricultural Service. *Grain: World Markets and Trade*. February 2020.

128. World Bank, "Modest Growth: Focus on Informality," *Russia Economic Report*, No. 41 (June 2019), p. 5.

129. Ibid., pp. iii, 5 and 28–38.

130. Henry Foy, "Russia: Adapting to Sanctions Leaves Economy in Robust Health," *Financial Times*, January 29, 2020.

131. Lester Brown, et al. *The Great Transition: Shifting from Fossil Fuels to Solar and Wind Energy* (NY: W.W. Norton, Earth Policy Institute, 2015), pp. xxii–xiv.

132. Dieter Helm, *Burn Out: The Endgame for Fossil Fuels* (New Haven, CT: Yale University Press, 2017), Chapters 1–3 and 8.

133. *The Economist*, April 5, 2014.

134. This refers to the reputed Saudi objective of keeping the price of oil (through OPEC cartel operations on production levels, etc.) high enough that it is profitable, but not so high that it stimulates the search for alternative (non-OPEC) suppliers and alternative (perhaps renewable) sources of energy. For Russia, this is somewhat problematic because the cost of production and transportation in Russia is so much higher than in Saudi Arabia that a much higher price is desirable.

135. *Financial Times*, April 12, 2020. See also: Anders Åslund, *Russia's Crony Capitalism: The Path from Market Economy to Kleptocracy* (New Haven, CT: Yale University Press, 2019).

136. Bolt and Cross, *China, Russia and Twenty-First Century Global Geopolitics*, pp. 92–93.

137. *The Wall Street Journal*, December 1, 2019.

138. Åslund, *Russia's Crony Capitalism*, pp. 226–228.

139. Lilia Shevtsova, *Lonely Power: Why Russia has Failed to Become the West and the West is Weary of Russia* (Washington, DC: Carnegie Endowment for International Peace, 2010), pp. 134–135.

140. *Vedomosti*, October 23, 2008.

141. Shevtsova, *Lonely Power*, p. 94.

142. Ibid., p. 222.

143. Stefan Hedlund, *Putin's Energy Agenda: The Contradictions of Russia's Resource Wealth* (Boulder, CO: Lynne Rienner, 2014, pp. 167–173. See also the comments of Arkady Moses on this issue as reported in the *Russian Gazette*, November 12, 2008, http://www.gazeta.ru/comments/2008/11/11_x_2879867 .shtml.

144. Marlene Laruelle and Jean Radvanyi, *Understanding Russia: The Challenges of Transformation* (Lanham, MD: Rowman & Littlefield, 2019), p. 79. See: Jean-Jacques Servan-Schreiber, *Le Défi Américain (The American Challenge)* (Paris: Versilio, 1969).

145. Vladislav Surkov, February 2010.

146. Vladimir Ryzhkov, "Build Innovation City and They Won't Come," *The Moscow Times*, February 25, 2010.

147. Shevtsova, *Lonely Power*, pp. 324–325.

148. James Appell, "The Short Life and Speedy Death of Russia's Silicon Valley," *Foreign Policy*, May 6, 2015.

149. Loren Graham, *Lonely Ideas: Can Russia Compete?* (Cambridge, MA: MIT Press, 2013).

150. Ibid., pp. 158–159.

151. Keith Crane and Artur Usanov, "Role of High-Technology Industries," in Åslund, Anders, Sergei Guriev, and Andrew C. Kuchins, eds., *Russia After the Global Economic Crisis* (Washington, DC: Peterson Institute for International Economics, 2010), pp. 95–124.

152. Alena Ledeneva, *Can Russia Modernise? Sistema, Power Networks and Informal Governance* (Cambridge, UK: Cambridge University Press, 2013), pp. 21–22.

153. Ibid.

154. Ibid., p. 110.

155. Alena Ledeneva, "Can Russia Modernise? Sistema, Power Networks and Informal Governance," in Kononenko, Vadim and Arkady Moshes, eds., *Russia As A Network State: What Works in Russia When State Institutions Do Not?* (NY: Palgrave MacMillan, 2011), pp. 52–56.

156. Ledeneva, *Can Russia Modernise?*, p. 232. See also her earlier books: *Russia's Economy of Favors* (1998), for a detailed description of the evolution of "blat" appointments and favors in the Soviet system and beyond; and *How Russia Really Works (2006)*.

157. Abraham Katz, *The Politics of Economic Reform in the Soviet Union* (NY: Praeger, 1972), p. 189.

158. Vladimir Gel'man, *Russian Authoritarianism: Analyzing Post-Soviet Regime Changes* (Pittsburgh, PA: University of Pittsburgh Press, 2015); and Stefan Hedlund, *Russian Path Dependence* (London: Routledge, 2005).

159. Garry Kasparov, *Winter is Coming : Why Vladimir Putin and the Enemies of the Free World Must Be Stopped* (London: Atlantic Books, 2015), p. 94.

160. Ibid., p. 59.

161. Ibid., p. 91.

162. Ibid., pp. 96–97.

163. Steven Kotkin, Delivering Keynote Address at the 17th Annual Conference of the Central Eurasian Studies Society, November 5, 2016, Princeton University.

164. Åslund, *Russia's Crony Capitalism*, pp. 252–253.

165. "Russian Lawmakers Approve Final Bill on Amendments to Constitution," *RT International*, March 11, 2020, www.rt.com/russia/482810-russian-constitution-final-amendments-bill/.

166. See: Tim Horley, Anne Meng, and Mila Versteeg, "The World Is Experiencing a New Form of Autocracy," *The Atlantic*, March 1, 2020.

167. Artyom Shraibman, "Oatmeal and Water: The Thinning Belarus-Russia Relationship," *The Moscow Times*, March 12, 2020, www.themoscowtimes.com/20 20/02/12/oatmeal-and-water-the-thinning-belarus-russia-relationship-a69266.

168. See: Tomasz Grzywaczewski, "The Birth of Belarusian Nationalism," *Foreign Policy*, January 30, 2020; and Max Seddon and James Shotter, "Lukashenko Rhetoric Shows Fallout between Minsk and Moscow," *Financial Times*, August 5, 2020. See also: Slawomir Sierakowski, "Inside the Belarus Uprising: The Making of a Revolution," *Journal of Democracy*, 31, no. 4 (October 2020), pp. 5–16; and Lucan Ahmad Way, "Inside the Belarus Uprising: How a Dictator Became Vulnerable," *Journal of Democracy*, 31, no. 4 (October 2020), pp. 17–27.

169. Gitanas Nauseda, interviewed on "Hard Talk" program, *BBC World News*, September 11, 2020.

170. Henry Foy, Laura Pitel, and Michael Peel, "Russia, France and US demand Nagorno-Karabakh Ceasefire," *Financial Times*, October 1, 2020.

171. Suzan Fraser, "What Lies Behind Turkish Support for Azerbaijan," *Associated Press*, October 2, 2020.

172. Henry Foy and Laura Pitel, "Russia Open to Return of Occupied Azeri Land by Armenia," *Financial Times*, October 29, 2020; and Henry Foy, "Azerbaijan and Armenia Agree Full Ceasefire in Nagorno-Karabakh," *Financial Times*, November 9, 2020. See also, statement by Kremlin spokesman Dmitry Peskov, as quoted in *Reuters*, November 10, 2020.

173. Evan Gershkovich, "'President for Life': Putin Opens Door to Extending Rule until 2036," *The Moscow Times*, March 10, 2020, www.themoscowtimes.c om/2020/03/10/president-for-life-putin-opens-door-to-extending-rule-until-2036-a 69576.

174. "Putin's Trust Rating Hits Historic Low—State Poll," *The Moscow Times*, May 25, 2019, www.themoscowtimes.com/2019/05/25/putins-trust-rating-hits-histor ic-low-state-poll-a65744.

175. See: Lucian Kim, "Protesters In Russia's Far East Challenge Putin's Authority, Demand His Resignation," *NPR*, July 24, 2020.

176. Anne Applebaum, *The Twilight of Democracy: The Seductive Lure of Authoritarianism* (NY: Doubleday, 2020), p. 14.

177. Ibid., p. 189.

178. See: Catherine Belton, *Putin's People*, especially Part III. See also: United Kingdom, House of Commons, Intelligence and Security Committee. *Russia (Influence on British Politics and Elections)*, July 21, 2020; and U.S., Special Counsel Robert S. Mueller, *Report On The Investigation Into Russian Interference In The 2016 Presidential Election*. Volumes I and II (Washington, DC, March 2019).

Part II

FROM THE FOUNDING OF THE REPUBLIC OF TURKEY TO THE AUTHORITARIAN PRESIDENT

Chapter 5

The Collapse of the Ottoman Empire and the Emergence of Atatürk's Republic

Turkey's slow, erratic, but on occasion, impressive evolution toward democracy, and then regression, is merely one possible scenario; but it is a unique and interesting case, however fragile, that illustrates the productive tension between long-term continuities and sudden discontinuities in the unpredictable and unfinished struggle toward or away from some form of democracy, liberal or not. (As we will see, the liberal dimension in democracy remains the Achilles' heel in Turkey's long authoritarian road toward democracy. Liberal ideals and sentiments do not sit well with authoritarianism.)[1]

Turkey is also a case which can, if not prove, at least suggest that with the right and strong leadership, and with favorable and fortunate historical circumstances, it is possible to argue that a certain type of authoritarian political culture can indeed foster democracy, but with the wrong leadership, it can also move away from democracy toward a hardened authoritarianism. If plausible, the significance of this argument—and what makes it different from the typical European unintended long-term transitions from feudal and monarchical authoritarianism toward liberal democracy, mentioned earlier— lies in the fact that we can trace a sustained and willful political trajectory from authoritarianism to democracy, and then possibly a reversal back again; that there are tendencies and convictions present in the authoritarian regime structure itself that prepare for, or aim at the establishment of democracy, but then, depending on leadership and circumstances—public sentiments and mores—can also reverse itself. There is no historical necessity here in either direction. At the very least, for democracy to have a chance, the leader and a powerful segment of the authoritarian elite have to seriously embrace an ideology that is somehow linked to, or compatible with, a democratic evolution. Or, from a more Machiavellian perspective: the leader and the elite (the one, and the few) have to understand the democratization process as being in their own self-interest. But, it is of course important that the ideology or the mores of the elite are not merely a cynical tool for staying in power. Arguably, these criteria set the Turkish democratization process apart from most other transitions from authoritarianism.[2] The downside of this scenario is the risk, especially in crises, of reversal and a return to more rigid authoritarian patterns. Democracy remains relatively thinly anchored in both elites and people in general, and democratic consolidation is fragile and remains superficial and often more rhetorical than actual.

By targeting Turkey and Russia as rather special cases, the approach taken here also deviates from much of the recent democratization literature on authoritarianism which tends to treat Turkey, if not Russia, as one of a host of authoritarian countries that over time has evolved in the direction of democracy, often ending up with a discussion on whether or not this or that country can be considered a consolidated democracy; and, if not, what should be done about it. By necessity, this is a general approach that paints with a huge brush and one which is not concerned with the more subtle regional and local hues and nuances. Both long-term historical continuities and particular discontinuities have to be sacrificed in the name of commonalities and generalities. Needless to say, this does not imply that the global, regional, or comparative approaches to democratization have not contributed to our understanding of the various processes of democratization; on the contrary, thanks to this immense literature, we now have much better knowledge of democracy both as a regime type and as a trend—whether in terms of conditions for democracy, its institutionalization, or its consolidation—than we did just a generation back.

For example, Juan Linz's general typology of authoritarianism characterizes one type as "mobilizational authoritarian regimes." He describes this category as a regime that attempts

> to mobilize the citizens to participate in well-defined, more or less monopolistic channels created by the political leadership, most characteristically through a mobilization of single or dominant party and its dependent mass and functional organizations. Insofar as such a single party is not conceived to exclude other organizations and institutions from a limited political pluralism and does not thoroughly penetrate them, we are dealing with an authoritarian regime.[3]

It is the "limited political pluralism" that distinguishes this type of authoritarianism from more extreme forms of totalitarianism. Once the single party feels confident enough in power, it might extend political freedom, and even encourage a limited competitive democracy which eventually evolves into a full-fledged democratic regime. Also, built into the "mobilizational authoritarian regime" is an ideological commitment to citizen participation;

a commitment which holds out a promise of further democratization. Not surprisingly, Linz locates the early Turkish Republic within this categorical frame: "In view of this we can understand that the Turkey of Atatürk, in which a bureaucratic-military regime had become a single-party, moderately mobilizational authoritarian regime, could transform itself after World War II into a competitive democracy."[4,5] However, even in the Turkish case, we need to add a caveat to this description: "competitive democracy" can continue to harbor strong authoritarian tendencies without necessarily disqualifing the label itself. What the persistent authoritarian streak in Turkish politics does reveal, however, is the stubbornness of certain illiberal and anti-democratic legacies to survive simultaneously with progress in terms of democratization. These traditions or patterns disappear from view in certain circumstances and periods, just to resurface and become dominant in others.

Linz's analysis certainly explicitly confirms the possibility that certain forms of authoritarianism can foster and encourage democracy. And undoubtedly, there are other cases, in addition to Turkey, that can be seen as having traveled a similar trajectory in the direction of consolidated democracy. More common, arguably, is the authoritarian scenario which either failed to transition toward democracy or did so inadvertently; that is, authoritarian regimes became democracies, but for reasons that cannot be described as being in the category of encouraging democracy. Revolutions, international pressure, internal upheavals and social, economic, and political failures are more apt descriptions of why these regimes changed from authoritarianism toward democratic rule. From the perspective of our investigation, one of the significant features of the broad and comparative studies is that they clearly show the relative uniqueness but also, it should be emphasized here, ambivalence regarding the deliberate "fostering" of democracy in the Russian and Turkish cases.

Four continuous large themes of Turkish politics will be introduced below, and then discussed in more concrete details through forays into some significant political events in modern Turkey. The four themes can be characterized as follows: (1) nationalism/sovereignty/independence; (2) the guardian state, and the role of the military; (3) secularism versus Islam; and (4) top-down leadership reformism/centralization/social engineering/modernization. It is of some importance, of course, that none of these cluster topics contains the word democracy or democratization. Throughout modern Turkish history, sometimes each of these categories seems to encourage democracy; at other times, they hinder or weaken further democratization. All, however, contribute in different ways to the maintenance of the authoritarian streak, and all have their roots or origins in eighteenth-century Ottoman Empire, if not earlier. (There is nothing arbitrary about this categorization since these are themes that are highlighted and addressed in virtually all scholarly histories of Turkey.)

Turkey's peculiar history, as the rump state of the Ottoman Empire, with no direct experience of having been colonized, is often emphasized as a contrast to most emerging and developing countries, especially in the Middle East and the Muslim world. For example, in a comparative study of the role of the military in Egypt, Algeria, and Turkey, Steven Cook considers this one of the distinct aspect of Turkish politics and society:

> The nationalist Turks under the leadership of Mustafa Kemal successfully resisted British, French, Italian, and Greek efforts to dismember the Anatolian rectangle in the aftermath of World War I and forced the European powers to recognize the Republic of Turkey in the Treaty of Lausanne (1923). In contrast, both Egypt and Algeria have long histories of European domination.[6]

The political consequences of this relative independence are deep and significant, to say the least:

> As a result, despite ideological battles between different groups of elites, first-order questions about the nature of the republic and the Turkish nation are largely settled. In contrast, although Egypt and Algeria reached the stage of radical nationalism and the military dominates both political systems, fierce competition among the forces representing each moment of national consciousness continues.[7]

It is difficult to exaggerate the impact of this national experience on the Turkish psyche.[8] It constitutes one crucial layer of the national consciousness within the leadership, the elites and the population, in general—the one, the few, and the many. For one thing, the strong sense of Turkish nationalism, including a patriotic and sensitive pride in Turkish independence, is grounded in this "non-colonized" experience. And given the close call in the War of Independence—it could easily have been lost and thereby destroyed the formation of the Turkish Republic—the issue of national *sovereignty*, whether Turkish nationalism a la Atatürk and CHP or neo-Ottomanism *a la* Erdoğan and AKP, is deeply emotional and a central part of Turkish patriotism. (This should be kept in mind when we discuss the possibility of Turkey joining EU.) That this intense nationalism contains an authoritarian element is not surprising, and, to this day, it plays a role in the persistence of authoritarianism in Turkey (and Russia). However understood, the interests of the nation and its sovereignty have emotionally intense popular and elite appeal, and they trump virtually any other overarching pleas.

A different structural and authoritarian pattern that puts its stamp on Turkish politics and that reoccurs in all general treatments of Turkish political history is the role of a guardian state—or, better, an independent organization, part of the state, but semi-independent from government and everyday politics. This has been characterized recently as the *deep state*.[9] It can take the form of a closely knit segment of the state bureaucracy, a highly politicized judiciary, or an independent, but politically inclined military. In the post–World War II period, we associate this with the role of the military, and its tendency to exercise its power through temporary military coups, but it has deep roots in history and goes back to the Ottoman Empire. It came to the forefront during the late nineteenth century and solidified itself in the actions of the Young Turks and the Committee of Union and Progress (CUP) in the beginning of the twentieth century. As Findley perceptively formulates the issue through a telling comparison:

> How much the Young Turks' constitutionalism might differ from the liberal paradigm became apparent from a lesson they drew from other revolutions: that the survival of the parliament depended on an external organization capable of protecting it. The Ottoman parliament of 1876 had been dissolved for want of such a shield; the Russian duma survived an attempt at counterrevolution in 1906 because of the revolutionary secret organizations. The CUP assumed the stance of a secret body, monitoring the constitutional politics from behind the scenes and not seizing control openly until 1913. The same civil and military elites who made the revolution of 1908 governed Turkey until 1950. The guardian role assumed by the CUP, and later by the Turkish high command, became a lasting fact of Turkish politics.[10]

This guardian rule by committee or by the military has haunted Turkish politics throughout the Republic and remains an important element of the contemporary power struggle in Turkey. In recent decades, until Erdoğan's AKP began to "reform" the judiciary by replacing secularist judges with more pro-AKP personnel in the past fifteen years or so, the court system took on an increasingly important role as a civilian guardian of the Kemalist and Republican ideology.[11] We have here another authoritarian legacy that is a double-edged sword: it hinders the democratization process as we have come to understand it in liberal democracies, while it has, at the same time, arguably protected the stability of the Turkish Republic in times of deep crisis. This is, to put it mildly, a delicate and controversial issue which has to be soberly treated. In contemporary Turkish politics, and beyond, it congers up the pervasive "fear" of the Turkish Deep State.[12]

Just to provide one example of the Ottoman foundation of this tendency, we can turn to the role of the Janissary corps for centuries until it was destroyed and abolished in the 1820s. The Janissaries were the military part of the institution of child levy (*devsirme*) through which the state recruited and raised "a family of elite military and bureaucratic leaders whose only attachment in theory was to the state and the objective fulfillment of its purpose."[13] The state took upon itself to educate and train its future elite solely for the aim of maintaining the state. "A military career was one of the most prestigious professions in the state, and the Janissary tradition of being a force unto itself, above society and even above the direct control of the state's bureaucratic apparatus, was a tradition that continued into the Republican period."[14] After the abolition of the Janissaries, the military remained powerful and influential but somewhat outside of the formulation of specific policies. It was the Young Turk Revolution and the paramilitary CUP that in 1908 moved to consolidate the power of the military in a more comprehensive and authoritarian manner. The by-now-fragile empire moved, under the guidance and influence of the German military theorist Colmar von der Goltz, in the direction of "a militarized nation guided by army officers."[15] Goltz was responsible for restructuring the Ottoman Royal Military Academy along German lines, and his book *Das Volk in Waffen* (The Nation in Arms) had an enormous impact on the Ottoman officer corps. "By 1908, virtually the entire senior Ottoman officer corps had come around to the opinion that it was their duty to transform the empire into a nation in arms."[16]

Mustafa Kemal (henceforth Atatürk) inherited this legacy and, to some extent and unsurprisingly, intensified it. Two obvious reasons for the intensification stand out: Atatürk was a military man, and he was the architect, leader, and hero of the War of Independence. He can be said to both have ruled by guardian committee, and simultaneously enhanced the status and role of the military and prepared the way for the independent power of the military in the later Republic. The scholarly community is intensely divided on the pros and cons of this Kemalist strategy. Was the strategy developed in the interest of the nation or for the purpose of Kemal's own power? Can we separate the two? Parla and Davison hold the most critical position:

> The party documents and Kemal described an army that was "loyal to the principles of Kemalism." Consequently, in Kemalist discourse, the army is ideologically constituted as the servant and indeed the embodiment of Kemalist goals. It becomes not only a department of the Kemalist state, but an arena that manifests the highest goals of Kemalism and serves as an exemplary vehicle through which Kemalist ideological ends are achieved. In its glorification and exaltation of the values of military life and learning, the hegemonic ideology evinces a militaristic tone and creates a new political and ideological relation between politics and the military, not no relation as the common account posits.[17]

The two authors lift Atatürk's argument out of its historical context and treat it in an ahistorical principled manner. They do not ask questions regarding necessity or what alternatives were realistically available. This distorts the picture, but it also highlights how authoritarianism was an integral part of Kemalism. Atatürk didn't invent it, but he did enhance it, and he strengthened its legacy for the future of Turkey. It remains an open question whether this legacy has been broken recently or whether this typical Turkish (and Ottoman) form of politics remains a subterranean but dominant streak to this day. The guardian state phenomenon is obviously linked to the strong Turkish statist tradition, but it needs to be separated out from the latter, in our opinion. Statism, as part of Kemal's "Six Arrows" does not explicitly include the guardian role as articulated by Findley and others. It is a unique feature in having an authority almost above and separate from the state. Hence, it deserves its own category, like perhaps *the deep state*.

The third major political controversy or long-term conflict structuring Ottoman–Turkish politics is the battle between secularism and Islam. At several conjunctures during the past two centuries (if not longer), these two elements clash and structure the political conflicts in Turkish society. Findley defines them as "a comparatively radical, secularizing current and a more conservative, Islamically committed current." This is how he more specifically characterizes the struggle:

Like political parties or other large sociocultural formations, both currents also included divergent tendencies or movements. Moreover, many Ottomans and Turks identified with both currents and resisted choosing between them. At critical moments, however, the choices embodied by the two currents became unavoidable and polarized opinion. At such moments, binary opposition between radical and conservatives approaches organized the field of contestation in the same way that binary opposition of parties or teams optimizes contests in politics or sports. At such moments, the opposition between the two currents could become starkly antagonistic. Still, exponents of both shared common interest. . . . As time went by, both currents interacted dialectically, alternately clashing and converging, transforming themselves and flowing toward a future whose imagined contours shifted as global modernity continued to evolve.[18]

This is arguably the most central and most long-term controversy in Turkish politics in both the twentieth and twenty-first centuries. And, obviously, this conflict, too, has its origins in Ottoman times. The first decisive secular impulse in the Ottoman Empire is usually said to begin with the indirect impact of the French Revolution and the subsequent reforms during the so-called *Tanzimat* period (1839–1876). The former had mostly a negative effect, from the Ottomans' perspective.

It instilled a longing for national independence in the Christian communities in the empire, and thus began the growth of nationalism among the
various territories in the Balkans which ultimately was one of the major reasons for the decline and fall of the Ottoman regime itself.[19] But the ideas of
the French Revolution also impacted a limited number of Ottoman officials
who had spent time in France and had become enamored of the intellectual
ideas of the Enlightenment in general. These ideas were slowly disseminated
among a handful of intellectuals and elite bureaucrats and influenced the
intellectual climate surrounding the *Tanzimat* reforms in the mid-nineteenth
century. It particularly impressed and stimulated the thoughts of the group of
intellectuals that we have come to refer to as "the Young Ottomans" in the
latter part of the *Tanzimat* era in the 1860s and 1870s.

The Young Ottomans are important for all our main themes, but their relevance for the secularism vs. Islam controversy is especially pertinent. Serif
Mardin, the most authoritative scholar of the Young Ottoman thought, summarized this significance in his classic 1962 study:

> . . . there is hardly a single area of modernization in Turkey today, from the
> simplification of the written language to the idea of fundamental civil liber-
> ties, that does not take its roots in the pioneering work of the Young Ottomans.
> Paradoxically, any serious attempt to reinject Islam into the foundations of the
> Turkish state, were it to appear today, would also have to look back to their time.
> This is so because the Young Ottomans were at one and the same time the first
> men to make the ideas of the Enlightenment part of the intellectual equipment
> of the Turkish reading public and the first thinkers to try to work out a synthesis
> between these ideas and Islam.[20]

One needs to add that this heroic attempt at a synthesis between the
Enlightenment and Islam failed, and that maybe it had to fail. To implement
such a synthesis would demand a restructuring of both the state apparatus and
the institution of the Sultan. Virtually all of the Young Ottomans were rebel-
lious bureaucrats who wanted to reform the state apparatus, but they were not
revolutionaries, and their theories did not contain an argument for resistance
or revolt. Their primary goal was to preserve the state, and thus argued for
reforms that would strengthen the empire at the center. However, there were
also explicit signs of a liberal temperament among the Young Ottomans.

Namik Kemal (1840–1888)—the most intellectually impressive and
famous writer in the group—argued in his earlier writings in favor of both
representative government with power derived from the people and natural
rights. He studied the English, the French, and the American political systems in order to assess which one was most suitable for Turkey and decided
(unsurprisingly, but perhaps unfortunately) on the French model. (Typically

for the Young Ottomans, and the subsequent generation, it was Paris, the French Revolution, and French Enlightenment thinkers that had the greatest impact on the intellectuals. And Rousseau and Voltaire loom larger than the liberal tradition, even though Montesquieu also appears to have had an extensive readership within this educated group.) In any case, Namik Kemal was certainly attracted to and influenced by liberal thought, and, according to Berkes, "was the first Muslim to understand the real essence of liberalism and the meaning of the sovereignty of the people."[21] His early support for constitutional separation of powers, consent of the people, and guaranteed natural rights for the citizens were clearly in line with European liberal thought. But when confronted with the need to square them with the Seriat (Sharia), these liberal tenets had to be rethought and modified. This (perennial) attempt at a difficult compromise could not be worked out, and the failure made Namik Kemal revise his theory in the direction of the idea of Islamic nationalism. He ended up defending a "romantic ideology of patriotism." As Berkes formulates it: "The one-time disciple of Locke, Rousseau, and Montesquieu became, in time, a thoroughgoing romantic."[22]

The larger context for the debate regarding Islam and the Enlightenment was the awareness that the empire was losing power both militarily and administratively, and that the West had surpassed the Ottomans in both respects. The tension between Islam and Western philosophy was located inside this larger preoccupation, and it was a debate by and for the elite only. There was no "public" with which to communicate, and no "intermediary bodies" *a la* Montesquieu, and no Tocquevillian civil associations, or concerns for the people's mores or "habits of the heart"; there was little or nothing in between the state and the mass of people. According to Mardin, this doomed the project of trying to move from a government for the people to a government by the people. The concept of consultation between ruler and ruled for the purpose of responsible government did not quite come together for the Young Ottomans.

Yet in Islam this consultation was limited to the "weightier part" of the community. Furthermore, it was a feature of government *for* the people. This was also a feature of medieval Western theories, but since then the idea had arisen in the West of government *by* the people. The Islamic theory was not a theory of this nature. The real point at issue was that the Young Ottomans did not realize that the modern Western theory of representation depended on a belief in the intrinsic worth of the subjective will of the individual. Neither Islamic nor Ottoman consultative practices rested on such a basis.[23]

In spite of these apparent shortcomings in the theories of the Young Ottomans, they both initiated and contributed to a discussion that was to become one of the characteristic elements in virtually all intellectual and political debates throughout the decades left for the Ottoman Empire, and subsequently continued during the founding of the Turkish Republic, and even became the focal point for politics after the creation of a multiparty system after World War II. It remains the central political and intellectual theme today, even with AKP electoral success. It is not an exaggeration to claim that the Young Ottomans initiated a "culture war" that has lasted for close to two centuries, and that has, during certain periods been highly politically polarizing, and at other times, more dormant and less intense. But even during times of relative calm, it has never been far from the surface of politics, and potentially always a divisive and controversial subject matter.

From the Young Ottomans through the Young Turks to Atatürk himself there is a tenuous but clear link in terms of intellectual affinities, and Namik Kemal is sometimes viewed as "the intellectual mentor" of Atatürk. Mardin concurs in this judgment, but with an important qualification: "It is often forgotten, however, that Young Ottoman theories were partly of Islamic origin. In the ideas of the Young Turks this substratum is weaker and it disappears completely in Atatürk. The significant strand to follow, then, in establishing the link between the Young Ottomans, the Young Turks, and Atatürk is the weakening of Islamic content."[24] When we follow this strand in some detail below with an emphasis on the connection between authoritarianism and democratization, we will also see how, after the 1950 elections and the beginning of the multiparty system, the "Islamic content" makes its return. From then on, this content will slowly increase and eventually become the most salient theme in Turkish politics culminating in the victory of AKP in the 2002 elections. If it was off the political radar screen during Atatürk's reign, it was only because it had not been allowed to manifest itself in the public arena and had to survive underground so to speak. But it was always there, ready to emerge when the political climate improved and became more permissive toward Islamic concerns. The mores of the vast majority of the people never really accepted or internalized the radical secularism of Kemalism.

The intellectual debate reflects a similar trajectory: the Kemalist perspective, dominant for decades, has become more defensive and less confident, and a growing number of scholars and intellectuals have ratcheted up their criticism of Kemalism and become more positively inclined toward the AKP regime, and show a greater acceptance of the new Islamic content in Turkish politics. Often, this positive treatment is framed in terms of strengthening the Turkish democratization process and enhancing what has traditionally been a weak or feeble civil society. In other words, the rise and victory of Islamic politics have contributed to a weakening of the authoritarian streak in Turkish society and political system. And, certainly, AKP's recurrent victories at the polls suggest that the Islamist emphasis is more in line with the popular mores than a hard secular doctrine. We will shortly return to these claims and critically assess their strengths and weaknesses.

The fourth and final theme is the cluster of issues relating to statism and top-down reformism in the name of modernization, Westernization, scientism, and social engineering. This is the area in which the strong authoritarian tradition in Turkish politics is most prominent, and that is also most persistent. In addition, it is the one feature that clashes most obviously with efforts to democratize society and politics. At the same time, many proponents of statism and modernization have often insisted that the goals and policies embedded in these methods are compatible with democracy, and even necessary prerequisites for further democratization. But, it is the opposite critical voice that is most often heard. As with the previous themes, we discover the origins of the statism/modernization approach in the Ottoman Empire. From the perspective of authoritarianism and the weakness of democracy, it might in fact be the longest, strongest, and deepest current of our categories and the one which confirms most visibly the path dependency argument. In their critical work on the legacies of the Ottoman past, Jung and Piccoli captures the centrality and continuity of this issue:

> It is true that, spurred on by the increasingly disadvantageous position of the Ottoman Empire in the European power game, the Ottoman reforms were aiming at safeguarding the territorial integrity and political sovereignty of the Ottoman State in an international environment of competitive nation-states. Yet, irrespective of the fact that the reforms failed to reach this primary goal, they triggered a major process of internal social change that provided the social, institutional and intellectual ground for the evolution of a Turkish national movement. Furthermore, most aspects of the reforms undertaken by Mustafa Kemal Atatürk and his associates were already visible during the period of Ottoman reforms. With regard to this internal modernisation of Ottoman and Turkish society, in the course of the last 150 years a clear continuity in social, political and ideological terms can be discerned. These continuities contradict the myth of the Kemalist revolution and therefore the official reading of Turkish history.[25]

As with the case of the guardian state, Atatürk didn't invent the top-down modernization process, but he was firmly convinced of its necessity and used it for his own nationalist purposes, and he made it a corner stone in his own Kemalist ideology. As with our other main themes, given the long history of this path dependency, we need to understand the nature of its persistence, as well as assess its presence within today's Turkish politics. Even if it has been transformed, and arguably even weakened in recent decades (top-down reformism remains relevant, while modernization is no longer a salient concept in today's Turkey), we should not rule out the possibility that it exists as a strong undercurrent in a more democratized situation. Without sounding too fatalistic or deterministic, in light of the long-term reliance on top-down reforms throughout both the late Ottoman Empire and the early to middle Turkish Republican era, we should *expect* this legacy to persist in various subterranean forms, even in today's somewhat liberalized and globalized Turkey.

Regarding the contested concept of modernization, two points need to be flagged in this context. Most importantly, modernization (Westernization) will largely be used here as the actors themselves understood it; they argued over its meaning and necessity, but they used the term, and they often gave it central stage in solving the political, administrative, and economic problems they faced, both in the Ottoman and the early Republican eras. Some equated modernization with Westernization; others wanted to promote modernization without Westernization which in turn became a debate between those who favored a national or Ottoman modernization and those who desired an Islamic form of modernization. These conflicts are an integral part of both the intellectual debate and the actual political practice, arguably to this day. Second, we need to distinguish between modernization as a general historical process that occurs regardless of a specific government's actions, and modernization as a political strategy for development and reform. The latter is often a response to the former.[26] Both are inherently vague and open-ended, but they have significantly structured the theory and practice of Ottoman and Turkish politics for over two centuries. The uniform response in terms of political practice and specific policies, however, has always been some form of social engineering from the top-down; in short, statism—or *etatism*, as Kemalism called it. The entire project has consistently been viewed from an elitist perspective—the few rather than the many—with little or no regard for the bottom-up approach.

The huge and unwieldy modernization issue was precipitated by two slowly discernible processes that reinforced each other. On the one hand, the eighteenth and nineteenth century increased Ottoman interaction and communication with the European world, primarily France, but diplomatic and commercial contacts (however sporadic) extended to all the European and Russian empires.[27] As a result, the elites became aware of the European advancements in science, administration, education, printing, publishing, etc., and they began to discuss and demand reforms of what they often perceived as the backwardness of the Ottoman state and society. The Tanzimat reform period (1839–1878), and the intellectual debate among the Young Ottomans should be seen as the first serious Ottoman modernization responses to this process and perception. On the other hand, a related, but more desperate challenge to the regime came in the form of a string of military losses on the battlefield. Modernization of the military became an imperative, and, after some half-hearted efforts at modernizing in the late eighteenth century, plus the elimination of the Janissaries in 1826, the reform efforts took on an increasing urgency.

The Young Ottomans not only struggled with the conflict between Islam and Western Enlightenment, they were at the forefront of a broad range of reform issues.

> They can be considered as the Ottoman pioneers of a modern discourse of con-
> stitutionalism, a representational system of government, the modern division of
> power, and national language reform. This discourse, which grew out of both
> the societal changes of the Tanzimat period and the legal spirit of the reform
> edicts, was later incorporated into the Turkish Republic.[28]

The Tanzimat reforms culminated in the formation of a constitution and the creation of a parliament. Although this first constitutional period only lasted for a year and three months, most scholars agree that this is something of a turning point in Ottoman politics and history. Findley, for example, views this constitutional and parliamentary moment as a decisive step in the direction of a "modern" regime that recognizes a separation of politics from administration. "In an empire where there had been no institutionalized site for 'politics' outside of the bureaucracy and the Tanzimat councils, the first parliamentary elections implied a differentiation between politics and admin-istration, a characteristic of modern government."[29] Sultan Abdulhamid's decision to close the parliament and suspend the constitution in 1878 cut this moment short. It was one of many power struggles throughout the nineteenth century between the palace, the bureaucracy, and a weak political sphere. Although the palace managed to maintain strict control for some time, it was in retrospect the beginning of the end of the power of the sultan and his court. This was the long-lasting legacy of the Tanzimat reforms. "A deep rift had developed within the hegemonic bloc that had dominated the reform process since the destruction of the Janissaries. The genuinely modern forces of the bureaucracy, the army and the intelligentsia were breaking away from the traditional claim to power of the Ottoman dynasty."[30] But, predictably, the new elites repeated the top-down approach with its implicit contempt for the mores and the customs of the general population. Modernization remained an elite project perceived as an issue for the correct social engineering policies.

As under Abdulhamid, again predictably, the new elites ruled as benevo-lent autocrats with no concern for either democracy or liberalism. The Young Ottomans had talked both liberty and equality on occasion, but it was purely theoretical and a debate among the very few. In the same spirit, the Young Turks and CUP, once they took power in 1908, and once they defeated the counterrevolution and deposed Abdulhamid in 1909, they too ruled in the familiar top-down authoritarian fashion. The continuity is palpable: reminiscent of Tocqueville's earlier comment regarding the French Revolution, there was no viable alternative available under the circumstances. The old order had to be overthrown, but the new rulers only knew the ancient regime and recreated it in a new but all-too familiar form. The empire was in crisis, the people miserable, and the Ottoman economy in shambles; hence, the new elites repeated the pattern from the past. As Jung and Piccoli succinctly summarize the long-term problem:

> The social habitus of the modern reforming elite still carried the aristocratic dualism of Ottoman society, with its contempt for the mass of ordinary people. Although the Young Ottomans and later the Young Turks criticized the neglect of "the people," the stark dichotomy between the rulers and the ruled, which over time acquired an ever stronger notion of cultural superiority, they later adopted this attitude of the bureaucratic elite of the Tanzimat.[31]

In so far as there was a hint of democracy in the CUP mentality, it was that of democracy *for* the people by benevolent social engineers who were also young military officers with the backing of most of the army. Although the army, including the officers, were divided in terms of both imperial loyalty and ideological commitments, it was CUP which won out in this struggle.

The Young Turks and CUP operated from the outset as a kind of secret society, and although CUP presented itself as a political party and even won an election, it maintained the conspiratorial secrecy even in power. In the overthrow of the Hamidian regime, the Young Turk Revolution had used the slogan "Liberty, Fraternity, and Justice" and agitated in favor of a constitutional monarchy based on the rule of law. This supposedly entailed a parliamentary democracy, responsible government, and an elite bureaucracy recruited on merit. Hanioglu also includes political parties, a fraternal Ottoman identity, a free press, and individual liberties, in the list of the goals of the movement. But, as he laconically concludes: "Very little of this came to pass."[32] Changes took place, but not the ones intended or explicitly articulated in the manifestos. Three different aspects of the 1908 Revolution are highlighted as "unprecedented" by Hanioglu: first, the leaders were conservatives who wanted to preserve the Ottoman Empire, not undermine it; hence, second, they wanted to restore the constitutional sultanate, not eliminate the ancient regime, as the French Revolution did; and third, this nevertheless resulted in a new form of regime characterized by one-party rule that was to become a common feature of many governments in the twentieth century.[33] The latter was of course also the type of rule that Turkey experienced for close to three decades after independence when the Republican People's

Party (RPP) was firmly in power under the leadership of Atatürk himself, and, after his death, his successor Ismet İnönü. Seen from the Ottoman nineteenth-century top-down reformism perspective, the one-party state made some sense. Given the goals of preserving the empire under pressure from abroad, modernizing the military and the state along more or less Western lines, and overcoming a serious economic and fiscal crisis, there was no alternative to some kind of elite-driven and centralized reform effort.

Not to be ignored, elections to parliament were held in 1908, 1912, and 1914, and (male) tax-payers over twenty-five could vote. In the aftermath of the CUP revolution, its popularity was never in doubt, but there were also both liberal and independent challenges, and the elections were taken seriously and should not be seen as mere rubber stamps. A limited pluralism, in other words, made itself felt in electoral politics during this period, but it was closely monitored by the CUP, and most likely contributed to strengthening the hard-line response by the latter. "Whatever liberal affinities the CUP leaders harbored prior to and immediately following the revolution quickly gave way to authoritarian tendencies."[34] The different political parties that did emerge over these few years were diverse but never capable of a genuine challenge to the CUP's domination. Power was never transferred peacefully, and due to the violent challenges to the power of the CUP, including two putsches (1909 and 1912) by opposing military factions, martial law was imposed after 1909 and remained in force throughout the CUP rule.

Most significantly, from the perspective of our theme of top-down statism and persistence of authoritarian rule, the CUP government was characterized by secrecy and conspiratorial suspicions. This intensified a legacy from the Hamidian period and earlier but took on new characteristics which continue to haunt Turkish politics to this day.

The Committee chose to rule initially from behind the scenes. The conspiratorial mind-set of the CUP leaders, their conservative predilections and reluctance to confront tradition, the protection afforded by the continuity of time-honored institutions, and a disinclination to expose their young, unknown, and inexperienced cadre to the risks of public scrutiny—all these considerations may have played a role in their decision to stay in the shadows. Whatever the reasoning behind it, the decision not to publicize the names of the central committee members shrouded the CUP in mystery, laying the foundations for an institutional cult that would replace the personality cult that had surrounded Sultan Abduhamid II. The Committee regarded itself—and wanted to be seen by others—as the sacred agent of imperial redemption and the guarantor of the empire's future security. The veil was lifted somewhat during the first open congress of the CUP in 1909, but the aura of secrecy remained till the end of the empire. In any event, the decision meant that the very fact of CUP power—its physical hold on the reins of government—was hidden from the public view at the outset.[35]

This perceptive description captures a sentiment which is not far from the surface throughout Turkey's political history as an independent Republic and expresses an undercurrent of conspiracy and secrecy that can permeate, at critical moments, any or all of the three major players of Turkish politics, whether the military, the state bureaucracy, or the government in power. It should come as no surprise that eventually these characteristics even work their way into public opinion, for example, references to the deep state. That this legacy poses an obstacle for the development of a full-fledged liberal democracy is obvious.

In any case, restoration and preservation of the empire via radical reformism was the main goal of the Young Turks and the CUP. The deep political and military crisis demanded drastic and far-reaching measures if the empire was to survive. What were the ideas and ideologies that guided them in this endeavor? To answer this question is also to begin to understand the core of the intellectual influences that shaped Atatürk's own mind, in his Herculean task to lay the foundation for the independent Republic of Turkey in the 1920s, after the heroic victory over the Greeks in the aftermath of World War I. In addition, the answer will also give us the core mindset and political mores of the elites who would rule Turkey after World War II, and who would frame and guide the long, tortuous, and ambivalent democratization process from the late 1940s to today. Through the continuities and discontinuities, through the breaks, reversals, and crises of this process run undercurrents that are strikingly familiar and consistent. Finally, the ideological commitments of the CUP will also help us to better comprehend the persistence of authoritarianism in Turkish modern politics.

The first significant aspect of the entire CUP modernization and reformist project was its radical nature: the economy had to change in a fundamental way; the military had to be restructured, upgraded, and the old officer corps replaced; foreign policy revamped; and the top echelons of the state bureaucracy replaced. The Unionists (CUP members) saw themselves as the vehicle for this giant project and naturally perceived the method as a radical centralized statism. Under the circumstances, there was really no alternative. To repeat Tocqueville's earlier argument regarding the French revolutionaries, the Unionists had only the historical experience and tradition that Tanzimat and the Young Ottomans had provided, and this left no other option than statism. "The emphasis on *etatisme* was merely a reflection of the traditional role of the state in the Ottoman Empire and in Islamic society generally."[36] Like their Young Ottomans predecessors, the Unionists combined their commitment to statism with the Rousseauean myth of the general will. They saw themselves as the embodiment of this popular will, and they envisioned it to be maintained in this consensual form until the reform project was fully realized and implemented. "While the CUP would permit other interests to exist, the latter must recognize their obligations to this single purpose and to society at large."[37] These long-running legacies carry over to Atatürk's reign, and he included both statism and populism in his "Six Arrows"[38] that set the political agenda and framework for the Turkish Republic. And they continue to form a central part of the present political culture of Turkey. "The Kemalists were very firmly in the statist tradition of the Young Turks, seeing the interest of the (republican) State as something of transcendent value. That is also a legacy that is still very much with us today."[39] Neither statism nor populism are unique for Turkey and are not *necessarily* authoritarian, but as they were interpreted practically in Turkish politics, they took on a strong authoritarian bend.

More theoretically, but closely linked to both statism and populism is the adoption by the Young Turks (and Atatürk) of a late nineteenth-century European form of scientism which had also influenced the Young Ottomans. The conviction that there could be a science of society, and that this science could be the foundation for radical social and political reforms which would equal modernization was widespread throughout the periods we have discussed. Whether we focus on the Tanzimat, the Young Ottomans, or the Young Turks (including Atatürk) we find the same fascination with science as the tool for ambitious social engineering projects. The sources for these ideas were a hodge-podge of European, especially French eighteenth and nineteenth-century social science and political theory. Rousseau is prominently present— especially his argument regarding the general will and the unity of the people—as is Saint-Simon, Durkheim, and August Comte. The latter's positivism seems to have been particularly influential with the Young Turks, including Atatürk himself. Likewise, and perhaps most telling, Gustave Le Bon's theories of the crowd and the evolution of races impacted greatly on the Unionists and their politics. It pointed to the need for controlling the masses, it implied a rather unified "people" that could and should be controlled but also ruled in their interest by an enlightened and scientific elite. In line with this, social Darwinism in various forms was also popular with this elite. Science appears to have replaced religion for these reformers. Hanioglu sums up this attitude in the late Ottoman maxim: "Religion is the science of the masses, whereas science is the religion of the elite."[40] He also stresses the unsystematic character of the intellectual influences and highlights the importance of an odd German mid-nineteenth philosophy known as *Vulgarmaterialismus*, especially through the physiologist Ludwig Buchner's main work, *Kraft und Stoff* (Force and Matter). Although not particularly notable or influential in the German context, it created a following among the

Young Turks. "It was thus a bizarre twist of fate that the German doctrine of Vulgarmaterialismus came to bear its most significant fruits in a context entirely alien to its original environment, and that a further vulgarized version of its central tenets would in time form one of the ideological pillars of the modern Turkish nation-state."[41]

Whatever branch of positivism, or whatever type of materialism—vulgar or not—the attraction manifested itself, among the Young Turks, in a firm belief in scientism and social engineering directed by the state as the answers to many of the problems facing the empire. "They shared with this broad church of positivism some basic attitudes: anti-clericalism, scientism, biological materialism, authoritarianism, intellectual elitism, a deep distrust of the masses and a belief in a peculiar kind of social Darwinism projected on nations and societies as a whole."[42] (Absent from this list, it should be noted, is anything that could be associated with democracy, let alone liberal democracy.) That this melange of ideas, dominant in the midst of the most serious set of crises of the empire on the eve of World War I, but deeply rooted in the Ottoman past, would also set the tone for the equally crisis-ridden early Turkish Republic under Atatürk's leadership should be expected. Atatürk was, after all part of the younger segment of the Young Turks, and he was educated in an atmosphere in which all these intellectual and not-so-intellectual currents were pervasive. The difference between him and the early generation of Young Turks was, of course, that the latter only wished for them and discussed them, while Atatürk and his friends, once in power, had the opportunity, through Atatürk's strong leadership, to implement them and turn them into practical politics.

Chapter 6 will continue some of the main themes and issues raised thus far for Turkey, but with a focus on the functioning of the Republic, its modernization and efforts at democratization. Both the theoretical and empirical discussion will focus on the impact of Atatürk's radical secular reforms and subsequent attempts to modernize the Turkish economy through a highly centralized statist mercantilism and the creation of a secular national bourgeoisie. Atatürk's reign was both authoritarian and Machiavellian, and he ruled forcefully as a dictator, however benevolent, through a one-party state, albeit with strong popular support—a kind of authoritarian populism.

Atatürk ruled Turkey from 1923 to 1938. Chapter 6 will evaluate Atatürk's gigantic overall social engineering project from the perspective of subsequent regimes. Did he overreach in his attempts at establishing a secular republic? Did he underestimate the strength and depth of Islam as part of the people's mores, customs, and culture? Was he too enamored by the French Enlightenment and Auguste Comte's positivistic scientism? Was he, in spite of his Machiavellian prudence, too utopian in his convictions that the human being could be remade in the name of reason and science? Did he overemphasize "Westernization" in his desire to modernize the Turkish Republic of which he was by far the most important Founder? The answer to all of these questions is in our view an unqualified yes, but they all play into the challenges facing democratization and the rise of Erdoğan's subsequent authoritarian inclination.

NOTES

1. It is again important in this context to remind ourselves, again, of the illiberal past of most Western European democracies. "It is instructive to remember that modern liberal nationalism has been built on illiberalism, a lineage that most current advocates of liberal democracy try their best to ignore." Mohammed Ayoob, *The Many Faces of Political Islam: Religion and Politics in the Muslim World* (Ann Arbor: The University of Michigan Press, 2008), p. 92.

2. We are well aware that arguments based on ideological commitment are not necessarily the same as those based on self-interest. In fact, they are, if not opposites, certainly in tension with each other. As we will see, both are at work in the Turkish case, and need to be distinguished depending on circumstances and historical contingencies.

3. Juan J. Linz, *Totalitarian and Authoritarian Regimes* (Boulder, CO: Lynne Reinner Publishers, 2000), p. 176.

4. Ibid., pp. 180–181.

5. Ibid.

6. Steven A. Cook, *Ruling But Not Governing: The Military and Political Development in Egypt, Algeria, and Turkey* (Baltimore: The Johns Hopkins University Press, 2007), p. 10.

7. Ibid.

8. Although to claim that the first-order questions are "largely settled" in Turkey might be premature.

9. Mehtap Soyler, *The Turkish Deep State: State Consolidation, Civil-Military Relations and Democracy* (London: Routledge, 2015).

10. Carter Vaughn Findley, *Turkey, Islam, Nationalism, and Modernity: A History, 1789–2007* (New Haven and London: Yale University Press, 2010), p. 165.

11. See for example, M. Hakan Yavuz, *Secularism and Muslim Democracy in Turkey* (Cambridge and New York: Cambridge University Press, 2009), pp. 163–169.

12. See: Soyler, *The Turkish Deep State.*

13. M. Hakan Yavuz, *Islamic Political Identity in Turkey* (Oxford and New York: Oxford University Press, 2003), p. 39.

14. Ibid., p. 40.

15. M. Sukru Hanioglu, *Atatürk: An Intellectual Biography* (Princeton and Oxford: Princeton University Press, 2011), p. 35.

16. Ibid.

17. Taha Parla and Andrew Davison, *Corporatist Ideology in Kemalist Turkey: Progress or Order?* (Syracuse: Syracuse University Press, 2004), p. 235.

18. Findley, *Turkey, Islam, Nationalism, and Modernity*, pp. 18–19.

19. Erik J. Zurcher, *Turkey: A Modern History* (London and New York: I.B. Tauris & Co Ltd, 1997), pp. 28–29.

20. Serif Mardin, *The Genesis of Young Ottoman Thought* (Syracuse, NY: Syracuse University Press, 2000), pp. 3–4. See also Niyazi Berkes, *The Development of Secularism in Turkey* (London: Hurst & Company, 1998), pp. 208–214.

21. Berkes, *The Development of Secularism in Turkey*, p. 211.

22. Ibid., p. 218.

23. Mardin, *The Genesis of Young Ottoman Thought*, p. 399.

24. Ibid., p. 404.

25. Dietrich Jung with Wolfango Piccoli, *Turkey at the Crossroads: Ottoman Legacies and a Greater Middle East* (London and New York: Zed Books, 2001), p. 5. See also: Selim Deringil, *The Well-Protective Domains* (London: I.B. Tauris, 1999).

26. As Jung and Piccoli formulates this distinction in the Ottoman case: "first, the structural transformation of traditional Ottoman society caused by the general modernisation process; second, the deliberate political action of a reforming state elite." Ibid., 54. The same passive and active distinction can be made with regard to secularization as a general process, and secularism as a specific legal regime policy.

27. By the end of the 18th century, Selim III (1789–1807) had established embassies in a number of important European cities. But they did not last long. It was not until the 1830s under Mahmud II (1808–1839) that permanent embassies were created. See, for example, Donald Quataert, *The Ottoman Empire, 1700–1922*, Second edition (Cambridge and New York: Cambridge University Press, 2005), pp. 80–82.

28. Jung and Piccoli, *Turkey at the Crossroads*, p. 45.

29. Findley, *Turkey, Islam, Nationalism and Modernity*, p. 146.

30. Jung and Piccoli, *Turkey at the Crossroads*, p. 46.

31. Ibid.

32. M. Sukru Hanioglu, *A Brief History of the Late Ottoman Empire* (Princeton and Oxford: Princeton University Press, 2008), p. 150.

33. Ibid., 150–151. For a more (exaggerated) democratic interpretation of the Young Turks and the CUP, see Justin McCarthy, *The Ottoman Turks: An Introductory History to 1923* (London and New York: Longman, 1997), pp. 319–320. For general historical overviews of the movement: Erik J. Zurcher, *The Young Turk Legacy and Nation Building: From the Ottoman Empire to Atatürk's Turkey* (London and New York: I.B. Taurus, 2010), and Feroz Ahmad, *The Young Turks: The Committee of Union and Progress in Turkish Politics, 1908–14* (London: Hurst Company, 1969, 2010).

34. Hanioglu, *Late Ottoman Empire*, p. 153.

35. Ibid., p. 157.

36. Ahmad, *The Young Turks*, p. 147. Mardin goes even further in his claim regarding the long-term presence of statism: "Whether promoting their own interests or not, Ottoman officials, at various stages in the development of the empire, seemed uniformly locked into the preservation of a political principle best translated

as "stateness" or "the priority of the state," a principle known in Turkish as *devlet*." Sherif Mardin, "Projects as Methodology: Some Thoughts on Modern Turkish Social Science," in Sibel Bozdogan and Reset Kasaba, eds., *Rethinking Modernity and National Identity in Turkey* (Seattle and London: University of Washington Press, 1997), p. 67.

37. Ahmad, *The Young Turks*, p. 147.

38. The other four were nationalism, republicanism, secularism, and "transform-ism" (or "reformism" or "revolutionism").

39. Zurcher, *The Young Turk Legacy*, p. 117.

40. Hanioglu, *Atatürk: An Intellectual Biography*, p. 56.

41. Ibid., p. 49.

42. Eric-Jan Zurcher, "Ottoman Sources of Kemalist Thought," in Elizabeth Ozdalga, ed., *Late Ottoman Society: The Intellectual Legacy* (London and New York: Routledge, 2005), p. 25.

Chapter 6

Democratization and Authoritarianism in the Maturing of the Republic

GAINING STATE POWER OVER THE ECONOMY AND THE TRANSITION TO DEMOCRACY

After Atatürk's death on November 10, 1938, executive power was transferred to İsmet İnönü at a time of serious national and international crises. A statesman of the most impressive caliber, İnönü is a pivotal figure in the "narrative" toward democracy in Turkey. He was a contemporary of Atatürk, with roots in the CUP, and a military man who participated next to Atatürk himself in the War of Independence against the Greeks. He served as commander in the two victorious battles of İnönü (hence his family name) and became the chief negotiator at Lausanne when the final peace treaty was signed by the great powers in 1923. He served as prime minister for twelve years, and after Atatürk's death, he became president for another twelve years. He remained active in politics until his own death in 1973 and was responsible for turning post-war Turkey into a multiparty political system.[1]

From the perspective of our concern with the challenges of democratization, İnönü plays, for good and bad, a central role—perhaps the most important one—in the history of modern Turkey. On the surface level of events, breaks with the authoritarian legacies do occur, and they appear to move Turkish politics in both democratic and liberal directions, most notably in terms of opening up politics and society for a limited pluralism, as well as taking the decisive step toward a multiparty political system. However, below these obvious and important reforms, the authoritarian pattern persists, albeit in less overt and more subterranean forms than under Atatürk's reign. As we shall try to show, the most important element in this pattern, in terms of continuity and path dependency, is the persistence in treating democracy as a means for other ends. If democratic processes can serve to promote other

143

(non-democratic) goals, they are temporarily institutionalized and explicitly advocated, but for reasons unrelated to democracy. It is a utilitarian top-down (social engineering) approach to democracy—and therefore only vaguely, if at all, related to liberal democracy as a regime type.

A common argument in the democratization literature is that the intentions and goals are not as significant as the processes themselves and that overtime the latter will influence the former: democratic processes, procedures, and institutions will slowly but surely trump mores, values and intentions. This has arguably been true throughout the twentieth century in multiple cases, but Turkey provides a stubborn exception; and by no means the only one, to this "rule"—if we provisionally accept this argument at face value. (The jury is still out on the empirical verification of this perspective.) The history of modern Turkey reveals an opposite trajectory: when democratic procedures are treated as a means to goals and outcomes unrelated to liberal democracy, the latter remains weak and fragile at best and does not substantially alter the underlying authoritarian political culture. İsmet İnönü's presidential period is an interesting and ambivalent illustration of this pivotal problem. In his overall view of the transition from Atatürk to İnönü, John VanderLippe makes the point that Kemalism had focused on "outcome" rather than "process," and thereby also set the stage for any opposition or alternatives to follow the same framework. The opposition to Atatürk's regime remained within the parameters created by Kemalism, and thus perpetuated the emphasis on outcome while being less concerned with the process. His summary judgment of İnönü's reform period is illuminating:

> Thus, in Turkey, opposition to all or parts of the Kemalist regime did not lead to a democratic process, but rather to the incorporation of new hegemony, with new personnel, imposing their own agenda in the same way as their opponents. Reform during the period of İnönü's presidency has not assured full participation in the economy and politics, confrontation of social differentiation, or freedom to express cultural plurality. In effect, it has resulted in the development of political systems separate from society, fostering politics and society as two separate entities linked by the political domination of experts, career politicians, and the military. In this context, not only do bureaucrats and career politicians control political power, but those who question the dominant ideology or group do so within the confines of a narrow discourse.[2]

This characterization of the legacy of İnönü's rule and democratization reforms might sound too stingy and ungenerous, given the importance of İnönü's role in the creation of a multiparty system and a peaceful transition of power from one dominant political party to another, but his argument has to be evaluated on the basis of the assertions in the latter half of the quotation which emphasize the distance between the state and civil society, the rule by state elites and the military, and the repressive policies against those who did not accept the premises of a rather narrowly defined set of political positions. Three aspects of these claims stand out from the perspective of historical continuity: the gap between the dominant, all-powerful state and the weak civil society; the top-down social engineering rule by bureaucratic and political elites; and the power of an independent military. In short, the authoritarian parameters remained intact not far below the surface of the reformist achievements. But, İnönü's greatest contribution to Turkey has to be emphasized, and that was his skillful and prudent (Machiavellian) maneuvering during World War II to keep Turkey out of the war until it was clear that Hitler's Germany was defeated, as well as his dealings with Stalin and the Soviet Union after the war.[3]

İnönü's prudent diplomacy during World War II and his achievement in establishing a multiparty system and democratic elections will be analyzed both in terms of domestic and international factors contributing to these developments. Then the chapter will evaluate and discuss the strengths and weaknesses of the evolution of democracy in Turkey from 1950 to the rise of AKP and Erdoğan in 2002. This period is a case study of the fragile nature of democracy and the persistent features of authoritarianism. The role of the military and the intermittent military coups are of course an important part of this story. Emphasis will be placed in this chapter on both political elections and the evolution of the party system. The role of the state in controlling the economy will receive special attention, along with the economic factors that contributed to the success and failures of the different governments during this period. Eventually there was a change in the role of the state in the economy and a liberalization took place that had important consequences for politics, economic prosperity, and class alliances.

One thread running through the entire period is of course the slow but steady resurgence of Islam as part of both politics and society. Islam has become a more important factor in Turkey and the separation of state and mosque can no longer be maintained; certainly not in the way most think Atatürk envisioned the Republic. It was not that Atatürk wanted to eliminate Islam from Turkey— he knew that was not possible—but he wanted the government to be in control of how it was to function. His secularism was primarily centered on the elites. He eliminated independent Islamic schools and imposed strict secularist rules for the bureaucracy, the military, and his party. He did not focus on the lower classes, but most likely thought that in the long-run, secularism would reach deeper into the Anatolian majority. His goal was to educate a secular business elite, a highly educated, secular civil servant class, and keep the elite in the military secular and independent. Similarly, he gave women the right to vote in 1934— relatively early, even by Western standards—in the hope that educated secular women would influence and encourage more women to follow their example. He wanted a modern Turkish nationalism. Even though he knew that it would have an Islamic element, but not a dominant one.

But that was not to be. The majority of Turks remained faithful to Islamic values and traditions. The slow but steady return to an Islamic-nationalist synthesis after Atatürk's death is proof of this. The AKP and Erdoğan's dominance in politics since 2002 is just the most recent testimony to the Islamic resurgence. The chapter will end with a thorough analysis and assessment of the rise of AKP and Erdoğan, culminating in the referendum which gave virtually unlimited authoritarian power to the president.

Turkey was established as a parliamentary democracy in 1923, but the country was ruled by a single party (CHP–the Cumhuriyet Halk Partisi–Republican People's Party) until 1946. Multiparty politics in the country began in 1946. The second political party, the Democratic Party (DP), was actually formed by several leaders of the ruling CHP. Over the years, more political parties were formed and entered the political scene. Almost all parties have faced banning and have re-emerged sometimes with new names. Competitive multiparty elections in Turkey have been conducted since 1950. No one could claim that these elections were totally fraud free; nevertheless, there have been many improvements and measures were taken to provide for trustworthiness in the elections, at least in the eyes of the public.

The Democratic Party was formed under the leadership of three leading politicians of the CHP:

1. Celal Bayar, a close associate of Mustafa Kemal Atatürk during the War of Independence in 1919–1923, who later served as the Prime Minister from 1937 to 1939;
2. Fuat Köprülü, an internationally recognized scholar;
3. Adnan Menderes, son of a wealthy landowner of Crimean Tatar origin in the Western province of Aydin.

Menderes also fought against the invading Greek army in the Western part of Turkey and was awarded a Medal of Honor. He organized a branch of the short-lived Liberal Republican Party in Aydin in 1930, but after the party dissolved itself, he was invited by Atatürk to join CHP in 1931.

The multiparty system started in Turkey after the landslide victory of the Democratic Party in the 1950 elections (see table 6.1). Surprising to most people in Turkey, the authoritarian president İsmet İnönü recognized the election results and his ruling party's defeat with great maturity and asked Menderes to form a government. After the endorsement of Menderes as prime minister of Turkey, the parliament elected Celal Bayar as the third president of Turkey.

Table 6.1   1950 Parliamentary General Election Results, Republic of Turkey

Party	Votes Received	Percentage (%)
Democratic Party (DP)	4,391.694	55.2
Republican People's Party (CHP)	3,148.62	39.6
Nation Party (MP)	368.337	4.6
Independent (BAĞIMSIZ)	344.537	0.6

Source: Turkey's Supreme Election Council (T.C. Yüksek Seçim Kurulu: YSK).
Website: https://www.ysk.gov.tr/

Adnan Menderes had liberal ideas and plans for both the economy and political life of Turkey. His ten-year rule between 1950 and 1960, however, showed a pattern that Henry Hale has discovered in many post-Soviet countries: A "temporary opening" with relative democratic governance in the very early years, followed by a "closing of the regime" toward more authoritarianism in the remainder of the rein by almost all governing political parties.[4]

In a review of all parliamentary elections and the subsequent governments from 1950 to the present, one can find an "opening/closing" governance paradigm. Only during the short-lived coalition governments does there seem to be a break from the drift toward authoritarianism. The multiparty system in Turkey is complicated to say the least. There is no space in this volume to analyze each election and the complete details of change in the Turkish political party system since 1950. Fortunately, there are some excellent analyses available to supplement our brief presentation, for example, Barry Rubin and Metin Heper's *Political Parties in Turkey* and F. Michael Wuthrich's *National Elections in Turkey: People, Politics, and the Party System.* We shall, however, provide considerable commentary and analysis on the rise of Recep Tayyip Erdoğan to authoritarian rule beginning in 2002. The complete election results are available from the Republic of Turkey's Supreme Election Council.[5]

What is important to remember when looking at Turkish election results is that many of the smaller parties are short-lived and not significant for the overall picture. Second, Turkey has an unusually high, not to say extreme, threshold in vote percentage for parties to gain representation in parliament after each election: 10 percent! Third, there are ways to get around this rule through electoral alliances. A larger party (for example, either the AKP or CHP) can nominate a certain number of the candidates of a smaller party who cannot achieve the 10 percent as its own candidates in the local and parliamentary elections. After an election coalition, called a "Nation's Coalition" between a larger and smaller one or two parties, the candidate of the smaller party (or parties) would be able to enter the parliament. In the June 24, 2018 Parliamentary elections, the IYI (Good) Party of Meral Akşener was able to have their forty-seven candidates enter the parliament. In the same way the "Republican Coalition" Erdoğan's AKP has used this to favor the MHP (Nationalist Action Party) of Devlet Bahçeli so that forty-nine MHP candidates became members of the parliament.

Table 6.1 shows the rise to governance of the Democratic Party of Menderes, achieving 55.2 percent of the vote in the parliamentary elections of 1950. The DP subsequently tallied 58.4 percent in 1954, but declined to 48.6 percent in 1957. While the opposition party CHP tallied 39.6 percent in 1950, 35.1 percent in 1954, it managed to rise to 41.4 percent in 1957.

In many of the elections since 1950 there was a center-right polling up to 70 percent of the votes and a center-left votes of about 30 percent. When there are at least two strong and rival center-right parties, the 70 percent would be divided depending on their changing popularity. A weaker third center-right party would generally get a smaller portion from the 70 percent. This is true for the 30 percent of center-left votes as well. In both cases, no party could secure more than 50 percent vote; reaching as much as 46 percent of the votes was quite hard to achieve.

Only when the second and the third center-right parties lose popularity, could a single center-right party get 51 percent of the votes or more. The same is applicable to the center-left parties, except that none could reach close to 50 percent; the best attained was 41.09 percent in 1957 and 41.38 percent in 1977. The Democratic Party (DP) of Adnan Menderes was able to get 55.2 percent in 1950 and 58.4 percent in the 1954 elections at the height of its popularity, when there was no second center-right party to challenge it. When the new center-right Republican Nation Party entered the election in 1954, it polled only 5.3 percent; but it did challenge the DP more in the 1957 election, polling 6.5 percent. As a result, the Democratic Party's tally fell from 58.4 percent in the 1954 election to 48.6 percent in 1957.

The first three years of Prime Minister Adnan Menderes' rule were successful in liberal approaches to both political and economic life, while promoting some basic human rights. After this short-lived "opening" in democratization, Menderes started to restrict the press and media, arresting journalists, burning the headquarters of a leading newspaper, forming a quasi "Fatherland Front" (Vatan cephesi) organization that supported his government and policies; harsh measures were levied against the main opposition party CHP, including a physical attack on the chairman of the CHP (İsmet İnönü), along with brutal treatment of anti-government protesters, and the infamous burning and looting of the business offices, stores, and homes of the Christian Greek and Jewish minorities on September 16–17, 1957.

As the DP's Prime Minister, Menderes become more authoritarian; motivation for the 1960 military coup rose. It can be argued that the military calculated that the country had a majority—above 60 percent—which opposed the rule of the DP and that there would not be much resistance to a temporary military takeover of a democratic government.

The military coup of 1960 not only ended the rule of Prime Minister Menderes. It outlawed the Democratic Party, tried all the MP's of the party, and hanged Menderes and two other ministers!

Military rule lasted for a year; parliamentary elections were held in 1961, with the CHP of İnönü gaining 36.7 percent of the vote; two other right and center-right political parties, formed after the banning of the Democratic Party: the Justice Party (of Demirel) and the Republican Domestic Country Party gained 34.7 percent and 13.9 percent of the votes, respectively. The governing CHP party ruled Turkey largely with democratic norms, given this division of electoral support.

Bülent Ecevit, whose political career started when he was elected to the Turkish parliament in 1957 as a CHP member of parliament, rose to be secretary-general of the party and served as the minister of labor (1965–1969) under coalition governments of Prime Minister İnönü. While serving as Minister of Labor, Ecevit legalized strikes by workers for the first time in Turkish history. He initiated the "left-of-centre group" and became its leader within the CHP and more broadly. He opposed İsmet İnönü for the latter's cooperation with the military government. After continued pressure, İnönü resigned voluntarily, and Ecevit became the chairman of the CHP in 1972. Ecevit's popularity rose with a nickname "Karaoğlan" (Black Boy). A Turkish politician describes this nickname as follows:

> In the 1970s, late then-CHP leader Bülent Ecevit was nicknamed "Karaoğlan" (Black Boy) by the masses. Such embracement by the people was widely considered as a reflection of a very strong bond and interaction between the party leadership and the masses, uniquely achieved by Ecevit as a leftist leader who attached importance to mingling with laborers and peasants and visiting the outskirts to be familiar with the daily troubles of the ordinary people.[6]

Being a journalist and poet, Bülent Ecevit can be regarded as the least authoritarian leader in the history of Turkish multiparty democracy from 1946 to the present day. A graduate of the American High School Robert College in Istanbul, while serving in the Turkish Embassy in London as a junior official, he attended the School of Oriental and African Studies at the University of London.

When the next election was held four years later in 1965, the Justice Party came to power with 52.8 percent of the votes, while the CHP's vote fell to 28.7 percent; five other parties got votes ranging from 6.2 percent to 2.2 percent. The 1969 elections also resulted in a big win for the Justice Party with 46.6 percent; the CHP managed 27.3 percent. The Justice Party stayed in power for eight years under Prime Minister Süleyman Demirel. The coalition of groups united in the party later began to split away, and a no-confidence vote in the parliament caused the Demirel government to fall in 1970.

In the Parliamentary General elections of 1965 and 1969, the center-right Justice Party of Süleyman Demirel was able to form a government with votes of 52.87 percent and 46.55 percent, respectively. In the 1965 elections, seven political parties received fewer votes from 6.26 percent to 2.24 percent, so there was no challenge to the center-right Justice Party. CHP was able to get 28.75 percent. When nine political parties ran for parliamentary elections in 1969, the Justice Party's tally lowered to 46.55 percent. The center-left CHP's vote also fell to 27.37 percent. These reductions can be accounted for in part due to the increase in the number of smaller center-right parties in 1969.

A period of intense fighting and bloodshed ensued between leftists (Socialists and Communists) and rightists (nationalists and Islamists) from 1968 to 1971. Turkish politics reflected the intense Cold War era in Europe and Asia. Alarmed at the instability, the military leadership transmitted an insistent memorandum to the government in 1971, which resulted in the resignation of Prime Minister Demirel. As in the past, military rule was somewhat transitory, lasting two years. The subsequent parliamentary elections in 1973 had CHP gaining 33.3 percent of the vote; Demirel's Justice Party received 29.8 percent. The CHP formed a coalition government with an Islamist-leaning party—the National Salvation Party which had gained 11.8 percent of the vote.

During his prime ministership, in a coalition with the National Salvation Party of Necmettin Erbakan, Ecevit ordered the Turkish invasion of Northern Cyprus on July 20, 1974 after reports of a series of massacres against Turkish Cypriots by the Greek junta leaders. In the 1970s, he formed several weak coalition governments lasting a few months or years; he served as Prime Minister of Turkey in 1974, 1977, 1978–79, and then during 1999–2002.

In the 1977 elections, the CHP increased its position to 41.4 percent of the vote; the Justice Party achieved 36.9 percent. The CHP and later the Justice Party formed separate weak coalitions with other partners. The latter coalition, however, fell as a result of the third military coup in 1980. There had been an increase of left-right, secular-Islamic rivalries, and the government was unable to stop the bloodshed on the streets and the fights in the parliament between the center-left and center-right parties.

After the coup, the military allowed elections in 1983 which resulted in the victory of the Motherland Party (ANAP) of Turgut Özal with a vote of 45.14 percent. Since the CHP and the Justice Party were banned from participation in the elections, new center-left and center-right parties were founded and participated in elections in 1987 and 1991: the SHP (Social Democratic

People's Party) and Demirel's DYP (True Path Party). Ecevit's new party, the DSP (Democratic Left Party) and the old CHP were able to participate only in the 1995 elections. With these elections, Turkey was ruled by short-lived governments of a single party or coalition governments. None of the prime ministers could establish clear authoritarian or even authoritative rule.

The newly formed liberal-rightist Motherland Party of Turgut Özal won in 1983, building a broad coalition of groups to form a government. Özal had briefly worked at the World Bank in Washington and had served as an analyst at the Central Planning Department of Turkey. His government marked the beginning of a strategy of economic liberalization, which ushered in a long but gradual period of private sector development and economic growth. He stayed in power for six years, although his party experienced a drop in support to 36.3 percent in the 1987 elections. The parliament elected him the eighth president of Turkey while his party stayed in government. The Justice Party, his former political base, continued to lose support in the elections.

Bülent Ecevit was imprisoned briefly after the military coup of 1980 and was suspended from active politics for life; but by a referendum in 1987, he was able to return to political activities. His wife had served as the chairman of his newly formed Democratic Left Party until his return.

Süleyman Demirel had been banned from politics after the 1980 military coup, and his Justice Party was outlawed; but he made a comeback in the 1987 elections with his new True Path Party getting 19.1 percent, and in the 1991 elections, his party scored 27 percent while President Turgut Özal's former Motherland Party under different leadership got only 24 percent. The Social Democratic People's Party got 20.7 percent of the vote, followed by the Welfare Party with 16.8 percent, and the Democratic Left Party with 10.7 percent. Demirel formed a coalition government with the Social Democratic People's Party. Following the sudden death of the President Turgut Özal in 1993, the parliament elected Demirel the ninth president of Turkey. Demirel served as president until 2000. His True Path Party under the leadership of Tansu Çiller kept losing votes in the subsequent elections, after forming a short-lived coalition government with the Welfare Party in 1995.

President Özal's surprising death in 1993 was a serious loss for Turkish politics and economy. He had contributed greatly to the international opening up and liberalization of business and enterprises in Turkey. He remains a pivotal figure for this period in Turkey. His background in the World Bank as an economist gave him an independent perspective. He was brought back by the military during the coup of 1980 in order to create some stability in the Turkish economy and society. By 1983, he had formed center-right Motherland Party and won the parliamentary election that year. He became prime minister until the end of 1989 after which he became president. As a relatively moderate Muslim, he was able to further strengthen the Islamic drift in society and in the economy. He increased the number of Imam Hatip schools and mosques and introduced banking according to sharia laws. In all these endeavors, he was quite successful.[7]

Barry Rubin and Metin Heper edited a valuable collection of assessments of the seven main political parties that operated from the 1950s through the 1990s. Among other things, they argued:

> On the one hand, Turkey has retained its democracy and overcome extremist threats to its unity and stability. However, at the same time, the party system has driven voters to more militant parties through frustration and unresponsiveness. Its leaders allowed an Islamist party to take power due to their own venality and readiness to battle for personal partisan gain even at the risk of the country's future . . . . it is hard to dispute the fact that the party system is in bad shape, more often endangering rather than producing effective government.
>
> In general, the parties have no significant internal democracy. Leaders who make bad mistakes in government or elections survive. Corruption does not lead to a political fall. Ideas are not generated within parties where debate is discouraged. Obedience rather than competition governs the parties' political culture. The centrist parties have done especially badly in these categories, encouraging activists and voters to migrate to the fringes of the system.[8]

Although written twenty years ago, this sounds somewhat familiar to the current situation, even in the West. It is a reminder of the arguments made by Jan Pakulski and Andras Korosenyi in *Toward Leader Democracy*[9] and many current works on populism and the rise of authoritarianism in many Western democratic countries. We shall discuss some of these arguments and interpretations in chapter 7.

As we shall see, Erdoğan and the rule of his AKP have taken this tendency to a new level, more akin to Putin's Russia than to the problems facing Europe and the United States. Still, there are serious trends in this direction in many parts of the world. One is inclined to argue that these tendencies have gone global.

On the other hand, Bülent Ecevit was a staunch secularist and Kemalist and had pledged to curb the growing influence of Islam in Turkish politics as much as he could; however, his popularity was declining. During his last coalition government in 1999, Ecevit initiated a number of reforms to stabilize the Turkish economy, but he was unable to stop a financial crash, and his government was dissolved. Before the fall of his government, Ecevit appointed Turkish economist Kemal Derviş as Minister of Economic Affairs. Derviş launched a very successful economic program which was later followed by the Erdoğan government for some time. Because of his poor health, Ecevit resigned as DSP leader in 2004; he died after a long illness in 2006.

Ecevit is remembered for his brave service as a less authoritarian politician, a composer of sentimental poems, and a translator of the Indian poet of Rabindranath Tagore's poems and T. S. Eliot's play *The Cocktail Party*. Ecevit's political leadership thus can be seen as in great contrast with that subsequently represented by Erdoğan.

THE RISE OF THE AKP AND RECEP TAYYIP ERDOĞAN

Turkish politics changed dramatically with the 2002 elections when Erdoğan's AKP tallied 34.3 percent of the vote, and the CHP managed only 19.4 percent (see table 6.2). Subsequently, the AKP continued to rise in popularity steadily in all national and local elections with votes of 46.6 percent in 2007, 49.8 percent in 2011, 40.9 percent in June 2015, 49.5 percent in November 2015. After the July 15, 2016 failed Gülenist coup attempt, Erdoğan was able to get the help of Devlet Bahçeli's MHP to reach 51 percent in the 2017 referendum on the new constitution—replacing the Parliamentary system with a Presidential system. The AKP and MHP election cooperation continued into the Presidential Elections of June 2018, where Erdoğan received 52.59 against five other presidential candidates. This was in part due to loss of support for two center-right parties: the Justice Party and the Motherland Party.

The new presidential system brought several serious problems to Turkey. The most important is that a future president needs to secure 50.1 percent of the votes. This may prove to be a challenge for any candidate, including Erdoğan, who now faces continued political division and dissent arising from serious economic problems and destabilizing foreign policy. The rise of additional opposition parties which in effect have splintered from the AKP, may

Table 6.2   2002 Parliamentary General Election Results, Republic of Turkey

Party	Votes Received	Percentage (%)
Justice and Development Party (AKP)	10,808,229	34.3
Republican People's Party (CHP)	6,113,352	19.4
Independents	314,251	1.0
True Path Party (DYP)	3,008,942	9.5
Nationalist Action Party (MHP)	2,635,787	8.4
Young Party (GP)	2,285,598	7.2
Democratic People's Party (DEHAP)	1,960,660	6.2
Motherland Party (ANAP)	1,618,465	5.1
Independent (BAĞIMSIZ)	1,614,001	5.1
Felicity Party (SP)	785,489	2.5
Democratic Left Party (DSP)	384,009	1.2

Source: Turkey's Supreme Election Council (T.C. Yüksek Seçim Kurulu: YSK).
Website: https://www.ysk.gov.tr/

threaten his prospects in the presidential election. This is currently planned for 2023, but could be held as early as Spring or Summer of 2021.

The failed coup attempt on July 15, 2016 more than anything else reveals the fragility of democracy and the persistence of authoritarianism in Turkey since the foundation of the Republic in 1923. One may find various degrees of authoritarianism in the rules of almost all of the past prime ministers and presidents of Turkey from its first president, Mustafa Kemal Atatürk, through Recep Tayyip Erdoğan. The main argument of this chapter, however, is that Erdoğan, as both prime minister (from March 14, 2003 to August 28, 2014) and president (since August 28 2014), differs substantially in the degree of authoritarianism exercised to date. Erdoğan has used his election as president not by the parliament, but at the presidential elections in July 2014 as justification for his use of extraordinary powers, beyond what is stipulated in the Turkish constitution. Subsequently, he led a campaign to change the governance system of Turkey from a parliamentary democracy to a presidential democracy. Erdoğan also took advantage of the July 15, 2016 coup attempt to support his argument for a strengthened presidential rule. In his words, "[A] Presidential system has been my personal project since I was the mayor of Istanbul."[10]

All of the single party and coalition government changes together with the military coups (essentially once every ten years) have not given a chance to any politician to stay long enough as prime minister to exercise full authoritarian rule. The ambitions of both Özal and Demirel to serve as president while leaving their parties to other politicians, made them give up the powers of the prime minister's office in order to contend with more symbolic powers of the presidency. Their decisions not only limited them from becoming more politically dominant leaders but also weakened their political parties. They disappeared from the political scene of the country after the 2002 elections; this left an opening for the new Justice and Development Party under the leadership of Erdoğan. Erdoğan also followed the path of both Özal and Demirel to become President in 2014 with the only difference from his predecessors being that he never gave up his strong control of his former party even after he became president.

During his presidency, Erdoğan first chose his former Minister of Foreign Affairs Ahmet Davutoğlu as a caretaker prime minister who would take orders directly from him. He replaced Davutoğlu with Prime Minister Binali Yıldırım on May 24, 2016 just less than two months before the July 16, 2016 failed coup. The most common theory is that the coup attempt was inspired, if not personally directed, by Fetullah Gülen and was manned by Gülenist followers who had penetrated the Turkish military, police, and judiciary, as well as universities and media outlets.[11]

When Erdoğan came to power, he depended on the Gülenist functionaries already in the organs of the Turkish state. His good relations with the Gülenists began to decline because of their aggressive demands to gain more positions in the parliament. Erdoğan turned down their request. Under approval of the Erdoğan government, the Gülenists in the judiciary (judges and prosecutors) forged documents against several high-ranking generals as if they were plotting against the government and were jailed after unjust trials. As a result, those generals also lost their army ranks. The Gülenists were quick to fill those high-ranking military posts with their followers among low-ranking officers through promotions signed by the Erdoğan government. Subsequently, relations between Erdoğan and the Gülenists deteriorated sharply, reaching an apex with the attempted coup on July 15, 2016.

Since the failed coup attempt, Erdoğan benefited from both the State of Emergency and the continued purges of so-called Gülenists in various influential positions to increase his authoritarian rule. He was successful in convincing the fourth largest party in parliament, the National Movement Party of Devlet Bahçeli, in endorsing the Presidential Constitution in the parliament, although the main opposition party CHP largely voted "no," and the Kurdish People's Democratic Party boycotted the motion on the ground that its leader, Selahattin Demirtaş, was in jail.

With a constitutional presidential system, many in Turkey claimed that Erdoğan sought to diminish the role of the parliament and eliminate the office of prime minister, so that he could collect the entire executive power of the country in his hands. The pre-referendum public opinion polls conducted daily by different organizations indicated a very close contest, with a substantial percentage of 8–10 percent undecided.

The referendum to change the constitution on April 16, 2017 resulted in 51 percent yes votes against 49 percent no votes. This result, however, was rejected by two of the opposition parties. Turkey's main opposition party and scores of citizens appealed to the election watchdog, the Supreme Election Board (YSK), for the annulment of the critical referendum, arguing that unsealed ballot papers and envelopes were counted in open violation of the law. Bülent Tezcan, the deputy leader of the Republican People's Party (CHP), told reporters that he officially submitted a petition for the annulment to the Supreme Election Board on April 18. He informed the public at a press conference: "This referendum will be recalled as the 'unsealed election.' The only thing that needs to be done with regard to this referendum, which has lost its legitimacy, is its annulment." Prime Minister Binali Yıldırım, however, expressed his belief in the accuracy of the referendum results in an address to his AKP group on April 18, saying: "We as politicians must be able to say new things. It's time to update ourselves. Everybody, particularly the main opposition party, has to respect the results."[12]

Controversy over the Turkish referendum results on April 16 escalated, as thousands of voters rushed to the courts on April 18 in big cities to submit their claims of irregularity regarding the individual ballot boxes in which they had cast their votes. There were also small-scale and sporadic street rallies in some districts of big cities like Istanbul and Ankara on the evenings of April 17 and 18 to protest the referendum procedures, resulting in detentions by the police. In addition to the internal objections, international monitors from the OSCE and the Council of Europe criticized both the uneven pre-referendum campaign where the ruling party AKP ministers and spokespersons dominated the airtime in television programming, while limitations were placed on the meetings and media coverage of "no" campaigners. There were also irregularities in counting unstamped voting envelopes as valid.

Despite this, president Erdoğan, long before the announcement of the official results, appeared on the balcony of the AKP's headquarters and greeted the cheering crowd with victory. According to Erdoğan, "We won the referendum whether the result is 1.0 or 5.0 it doesn't make a difference!" (It appears he was making a reference to the typical margin of soccer scores.)

At least two points are evident from Erdoğan's narrow referendum victory: first, the referendum shows an obvious regional divide: The Western regions of Turkey—from the entire European part of Turkey with the city of Istanbul, the Sea of Marmara (both European and Asian shores), the Aegean coast of Turkey with the big cities from Izmir to Mugla, the Mediterranean coast of Turkey from Antalya in the West to Adana and Mersin to the East, as well as the capital city Ankara with Dıyarbakir in South Eastern Anatolia—cast a majority no vote against the presidential constitution. These include the most developed industrial regions of Turkey. This is the first time the AKP has not prevailed in Erdoğan's former political base in Istanbul and in Ankara.[13]

Second, the slim victory for the AKP and Erdoğan actually reinforced the position of the main opposition party (CHP). Erdoğan and his AKP were expected to face a strong and confident opposition in the parliament and public arena until 2019 when the presidential elections were held for a new president who will implement the executive presidency officially. Accordingly, the referendum was interpreted by some analysts as in fact a defeat for Erdoğan. Erdoğan could not have achieved endorsement of the presidential system without the backing of his close ally Bahçeli since the failed coup of 2016. But the association between Erdoğan and Bahçeli continued to be solid according to the results of the presidential election in 2018 and later 2019 local elections.

The presidential election was originally scheduled for November 2019. However, it took place on June 24, 2018 as part of the 2018 general election,

Table 6.3   June 24, 2018 Presidential Election Results, Republic of Turkey

Candidate	Political Party	Votes #	Votes %
Recep Tayyip Erdoğan	Justice and Development Party (AKP)	26,330,823	52.59
Muharrem İnce	Republican People's Party (CHP)	15,340,321	30.64
Selahattin Demirtaş	Peoples' Democratic Party (HDP)	4,205,794	8.40
Meral Akşener	Good Party (IYI)	3,649,030	7.29
Temel Karamollaoğlu	Felicity Party (SP)	443,704	0.89
Doğu Perinçek	Patriotic Party (VP)	98,955	0.20
Invalid votes		1,129,332	–
Total votes casted		51,197,959	86.24
Registered voters		59,354,840	100.00

Source: Turkey's Supreme Election Council (T.C. Yüksek Seçim Kurulu: YSK).
Website: https://www.ysk.gov.tr/

alongside parliamentary elections on the same day. The speculation over an early vote continued from the 2017 referendum. After calls from Nationalist Movement Party (MHP) leader Devlet Bahçeli for a snap election, President Erdoğan announced on April 18, 2018 that it would take place on 24 June. He managed 52.59 percent of the vote; Muharrem Ince of the CHP tallied 30.64 percent of the vote. See Table 6.3.

Erdoğan was able to mobilize nationalist support both from putting down the attempted coup and in restricting criticism and political opposition afterward. The campaign to "search for conspirators" in the media, universities, police, and armed forces was systematic and relentless. Large numbers of courageous journalists and academics have been fired and/or imprisoned. The riveting tale of Can Dundar in *We Are Arrested* about this period is emblematic of the larger story of the extended period of "National Emergency."[14]

Four main political parties AKP, CHP, IYI, and HDP contested the presidential election. The MHP, however, announced several months before the election that it would not have a presidential candidate, throwing its support to Erdoğan. The AKP also prevailed in the coinciding parliamentary elections, achieving 290 seats and 43.3 percent of the vote. The CHP managed 146 seats with 22.8 percent of the vote.

It seems clear that without MHP's backing, Erdoğan could not pass the first round with the required 50.1 percent. The CHP's candidate, Muharrem Ince, might have had a better change in the second round because both the IYI, Felicity and HDP had earlier declared that they would vote for Ince in the second round.

There was clear concern that Turkey would slide into full authoritarianism after the referendum. Critics in the main opposition party, CHP, feared that the proposed changes would usher in an era of authoritarian one-man rule not just under Erdoğan but with subsequent presidents. Promises made that the new system would cure many of Turkey's economic problems turned out to be unrealistic. Erdoğan's centralized leadership proved even less effective.

After the referendum, the office of the prime minister and the cabinet of ministers were abolished; this and gave the president the power to select his own administration. The president also retained the ability to serve as the head of his own political party. With few checks and balances and a loyalist parliament, Erdoğan had considerable power to shape the judiciary. The minimum age of parliamentarians was lowered to 18, and the number of the seats in the parliament increased. The opposition regarded these provisions as an effort to raise the influence of the president in the parliament, while reducing the traditional role that the parliamentary opposition had played.

Turkish political scientist, Burak Bilgehan Özpek, described this as creating a democracy without opposition in Turkey:

> The AKP regime has from the very beginning of its rule successfully deployed the tactic of defaming and delegitimizing opposition. The seculars were "White Turks" who had supposedly oppressed the popular masses, and their defense of secularism was nothing but an expression of their desire to maintain their material interests by reinstating an unjust system. The liberals and the left, who had supported the AKP but had become critical after peaceful protesters were brutalized by the police in 2013, were held to be conspiring with foreign powers that are scheming to sabotage Turkey's political and economic rise.[15]

Özpek also noted that the real threat to the AKP regime actually came from its former ally, the Gülenists who "used to defame anyone who objects to the authoritarian drift of the country." According to the author, the failed coup attempt in 2016 was allegedly organized by a Gülenist faction in the Turkish military which then gave a free hand to the AKP "to arbitrarily stigmatize opposition groups, and journalists, academics and civil society organizations" that are critical of the government.

Turkish authority on constitutional law, Ergun Özbudun, argued in 1996 that he had great optimism for the future of democracy in Turkey:

> Turkey today seems to occupy a secure place among the delegative democracies of the world. There is little reason to fear that authoritarianism will return, but equally little reason to hope that democracy will soon become consolidated. Like many other delegative democracies, Turkish democracy may endure, but in a state of "inherent vulnerability."[16]

In 2016, however, he argued that "Turkey seems to be even further away from democratic consolidation. On the contrary, many legitimately ask whether it is drifting toward some kind of competitive authoritarianism."[17]

Progress to full authoritarianism was apparent, however, as Erdoğan and the AKP government managed 51 percent yes in the April 16, 2017 constitutional referendum.

Several books recently published in Turkey try to explain both Erdoğan's personal and political character. One of the most interesting of them is *Potent: Turkish Right Tradition and Recep Tayyip Erdoğan,* by H. Bahadir Türk. The book is divided into two parts with each part consisting of four chapters. The first part, entitled "The Road to Erdoğan", examines four former politicians Adnan Menderes (prime minister from 1950 to 1960), Süleyman Demirel (seven times prime minister from 1965 to 1993 and president from 1993 to 2000), Turgut Özal (prime minister from 1989 to 1993 and president between 1983 to 1989), and Necmettin Erbakan (prime minister from 1996 to 1997). The second part of the book, entitled "Understanding R. Tayyip Erdoğan" is devoted entirely to Erdoğan with the following chapter titles: "Erdoğan's Political Perception", "The Turkish Right's Three Ideologies of Erdoğan", "The Masculine Codes in Erdoğan's speech", and "Erdoğan's Cult." Bahadir Türk argues that all these five leaders of the Turkish Right from Menderes to Erdoğan have possessed what the author calls a "fetishism of national will" concept that has been idealized and worshipped by all Turkish Right-leaning political leaders since at least the 1950s.

According to H. Bahadir Türk, this concept of the fetishism of national will provided political leaders with the following functions: (1) The *national will* offers them an ontological ground. Therefore, it is being exalted as their reason for existence; (2) It supplies them with an argument to get even with the single-party period (more precisely with the rival RPP[18]) of Turkey (1923–1950); 3) It furnishes them a means to distract attention of the public from their political and economic crisis, corruption, and scandals, by stating that they are being targeted; (4) It renders a metaphysical power that is sprung from the ballot box; (5) It becomes the engine of a plebiscitary autocracy in which the leader's will is presented as the will of the people; and (6) The mechanism of the election takes precedence over the pluralist principal of democracy. Whenever the leaders are constrained to account for fundamental rights and freedoms, transparency, and accountability, they refer to the nation's will and the ballot box. He concludes as follows:

> In short, the *fetishism of national will* confronts us as an escape line rising from a strong autocracy that inclines to reduce democracy to a procedural and election oriented dimension and keeps alive the perception of enemy (adversary). There is another partnership which binds these leaders: in the road of the Great Turkish Right up to Erdoğan, democracy has been used to its real substance until the state apparatus and its powers were attained, but afterwards democracy has been reduced to majoritarianism.[19]

Critics also point to the extensive use of populism by Turkish rightist politicians.

Barış Yetkin in *Populism and Özal-Erdoğan* (in Turkish) concludes that Erdoğan's use of populism is more developed and vehement than the former prime minister and later president Özal.[20] According to Yetkin's analysis, there is a precipice between the two leaders even in the rough template of populism. After explaining various theoretical definitions of populism, he treats populism as a tool of effective political communication used by the political parties and leaders in Turkey. He observes the following characteristics in the general use of populism by politicians in Turkey:

1) They see the public as a homogenous category (class) that share similar self-interests and benefits;
2) They present themselves frequently as opposing the privileged groups in the country who are purported to be against the masses;
3) They employ anti-state rhetoric in their speeches;
4) They criticize and attack either government or a particular opposition party;
5) They express a discomfort toward certain media organization(s) and complain to the public.[21]

Yetkin follows the well-known Turkish economic historian Zafer Toprak, who divides Turkish populism into two periods: The first period is between 1923 and 1947 and is labeled *Intellectual Populism* when Turkey had a single-party system. The second period is the multiparty system since 1947, which he depicts as *"real* and political" *Populism.*[22] After comparing the speeches of Erdoğan with that of all previous Turkish leaders, his study concludes that Erdoğan has used more effectively the language of populism directed against the elites. In his speeches to the public, Erdoğan utilizes words and terms that not only make fun of the elite but also designates a class difference as "we and those others" as follows:

> *Monsher* (from the French phrase: *mon cher* *"My Dear"*): as a term ridiculing those traditional Turkish diplomats who are the most Westernized elites. Erdoğan is quoted as using this term in several different speeches criticizing certain Turkish diplomats: "The old *monshers* haven't understood this. They've come as Monshers and they've left as Monshers!"
>
> *Beyaz Türkler – Zenci Türkler* (White Turks and Black Turks): a term pointing to class differences between the elite (rich and highly educated) as White and the ordinary people (poor and less educated) as black. Erdoğan said: "We have a distinction between the White Turks and the Black Turks. I as your brother belong to the Black Turks."

Yeni Türkiye (New Turkey): Erdoğan has been using this slogan widely referring to the de facto existence of a different Turkey under the rule of his party
and himself. He depicts the "Old Turkey" as bad and defective as opposed to the
emerging prosperous "New Turkey" with more freedoms.[23]

Several works deal with the creation of a cult followship of Erdoğan in the
pro-government media organs and the state TV and radio stations. Many
terms are utilized to denote the popularity of Erdoğan such as *Reis* (Chief),
Büyük Usta (Great Master), *Uzun Adam* (long man), *Sultan* (Sultan), *Dünya
Lideri* (World Leader), *Davos Fatihi* (The conqueror of Davos)[24], *Aşk Adamı*
(Man of Love).

Cemal Dindar published a psychobiography of Erdoğan using two terms:
allegiance/homage (biat) and fury (öfke) that he claims are key words to
understand Erdoğan's political character through his personal psyche. Dindar
narrates the events based on Erdoğan's own words that in childhood he had
experienced torture and dominance by his father; subsequently, he became a
member of a religious fraternity.[25] Fury when he does not receive due hom-
age seems to be a continuing feature of his personality. Fatma Sibel Yüksek
also mentions the role of anger in Erdoğan's character in her book, the *Art of
Reading Tayyip Erdoğan*.[26]

The enormous number of Turkish political parties, both emerging and
largely defunct (but sporadically important to the politics of the Republic),
makes for a confusing picture. Of particular note to contemporary Turkish
politics is the formation of two splinter parties from the AKP formed by former supporters of Erdoğan: The Development Party, a Center-Liberal party
established in December, 2019 under the leadership of Ahmet Davutoğlu; and
the Democracy and Progress Party/DEVA—also Centrist-Liberal, established
in March 2020 under the leadership of Ali Babacan.

ERDOĞAN AND FETHULLAH GÜLEN

While mayor of Istanbul, Erdoğan made the following (in)famous statement:

"'Democracy is like a streetcar. You ride it until you arrive at your destination,
and then you step off' and, "We believe that democracy can never be the objective, it's only a tool." On sharia: "The statement that sovereignty unconditionally belongs to the people is a huge lie. Sovereignty unconditionally belongs to
Allah." He added: "Praise to God; we are all for sharia. One cannot be secular
and a Muslim at the same time. You will either be a Muslim or a secularist."[27]

In 1997 at a rally in Siirt, he read from a poem: "The mosques are our bar-
racks, the domes are our helmets, the minarets are our bayonets, and the

faithful are our soldiers." This landed Erdoğan in jail for four months in 1999, and he was banned from politics. The Welfare Party was also banned in 1998. This series of events led to the creation of the AKP, a break with Erbakan's radical approach, and a change among younger Islamist leaders. AKP presented itself as a moderate Islamist party with an interest to promote membership in the European Union. Once established, the party defined itself as a conservative democratic party along the lines of European Christian parties.[28]

Similarly, Gülen, in a 1999 televised video, spoke along lines similar to Erdoğan's pronouncements. This is directed as advice to his followers:

> You must move in the arteries of the system without anyone noticing your existence until you reach all the power centers . . . . Until the conditions are ripe, they [the followers] must continue like this. If they do something prematurely, the world will crush our heads, and Muslims will suffer everywhere, like in the tragedies in Algeria, like in 1982 [in] Syria . . . like in the yearly disasters and tragedies in Egypt . . . . The time is not yet right. You must wait for the time when you are complete and conditions are ripe, until we can shoulder the entire world and carry it . . . . You must wait until such time as you have gotten all the state power, until you have brought to your side all the power of the constitutional institutions in Turkey . . . Now, I have expressed my feelings and thoughts to you all—in confidence . . . Trusting your loyalty and secrecy. I know that when you leave here, [just] as you discard your empty juice boxes, you must discard the thoughts and the feelings that I have expressed here.[29]

It is difficult to know how to interpret this in retrospect. Gülen's position is somewhat clearer since he seems to have been consistent over time in pursuing this strategy, while Erdoğan, as a skillful and charismatic politician, has been more Machiavellian over time. But, he might have calculated that the path he took by creating a "moderate" Muslim nationalist party would be the method to reach his goal of firm, authoritarian control of Turkey. He certainly enamored himself to the West, including both the EU and the United States.

But, one also has to take into consideration the possibility that in both cases power and ambition are the dominant factors, in which case their cooperation (until 2012–2013) served the interest of both contestants. In that case, they were bound to come to a power struggle eventually. There is only room for one "sultan." It is most visible with Erdoğan, partly because he is a public top politician who has to be sure he stays in power. That requires both flexibility and careful maneuvering. He has certainly showed that this is part of his strength and success. One might compare this with Putin in Russia.

Given Gülen's overall strategy presented in the 1999 video, he was committed to a gigantic "noble lie" which demanded he and his followers to remain as invisible as possible as they infiltrated the Turkish bureaucracy, military, and police. The Gülen Movement also created a huge global network creating schools, universities, banks, and foundations, including in the United States. But, it came to an end with the break with Erdoğan around 2012. Once Erdoğan ended his support of Gülen and his associations, the crisis for the latter increased, and the years between 2013 and 2016 escalated the conflict, and most likely necessitated the failed coup attempt.

What is remarkable is Gülen's ability to maintain his innocence and ecumenical status outside of Turkey, even after the coup. Joshua Hendricks formulates it this way:

> If Gülen helped orchestrate the coup, tens of thousands of affiliates and sympathizers, as well as those of us who have tried to more objectively study this man and his movement, will need to come to terms with one of the most fantastic frauds in modern history.[30]

Several analysts have argued that the Gülen–Erdoğan cooperation and later conflict was a battle between two Islamic groups to acquire and dominate the state. After the elimination of the Gülen group in 2016–2017, Erdoğan turned his attention to the remaining secularists in Turkey, as Zeyno Baran suggests.[31] The extent to which the State of Emergency purges since July 15, 2016 were prosecuted, with human rights violations, censorship, and state vs. media relations are indications of the virulence of the motivation. This was a serious challenge to the Turkish political culture and the political parties operating at the time: the governing AKP (JDP), the main opposition party CHP (RPP), the nationalist MHP (NMP), and the Kurdish HDP (RDP).

A recent study conducted on the possible anomalies and potential fraud in the legislative elections of June and November 2015 by Walter R. Mebane, Jr. found that most of the districts in eastern Turkey were very likely affected by substantial fraud, and this occurred more extensively in November than in the June elections. He concludes that the "AKP is the party that by some measures benefited from the most extensive 'fraud,' but other parties appear occasionally to have benefited as well."[32]

The academic studies analyzing the Turkish elections are multiple and very rich, but the most extensive recent study is by F. Michael Wuhtrich of the Center for Global and International Studies at the University of Kansas, who received his PhD from Bilkent University in Ankara. His 2015 book, *National Elections in Turkey: People, Politics, and the Party System*, disputes many old assumptions and assertions on the elections and voting behavior in Turkey, such as the left/right ideological positioning, the role of religion, center/periphery, and other social cleavages.

After an analysis of recent Turkish elections, he found that "framing politics and electoral behavior in Turkey as primarily a struggle between secularist and religious voters is similarly unhelpful, especially to the extent that such an assertion is made to describe elections during their long history in Turkey."[33] He argued that:

> Although the role of religion in elections was greater or less from election to election, a precise understanding of Turkish electoral behavior requires us to look at these trends within their contexts and the other factors of that period. Religion most frequently played a role as one of the various domains of identification that secondarily determine the shape of elections. Such domains are often trumped by the dimensions through which the existing political actors and their political parties are competing. During the periods in which appeals to religion entered the political arena as a strategy to mobilize one's voting base, the election outcomes suggest that Turkish voters have often found this strategy to be unwelcome.[34]

In his view, the simple dichotomies of "left/right" and "secular/religious" conceal far more than they explain. On the question of center/periphery cleavages, Wuthrich rejects it by saying there are important logical objections to applying this framework to the Turkish case. He explains this as follows:

> Within Turkey, the concept of central elites pitted against the peripheral masses seems to be a ready-made ideological tool appropriated both by those who identify with the Turkish "center-left" and by those who oppose it. Thus, in the current ideological battle, it is not the existence of a center/periphery divide that is in question, but rather the substance of the attributes used to define one's own position and that of the other, thereby contributing to a binary political polemic within the Turkish landscape.[35]

He draws attention to the fact that something much more complex was and is occurring. He argues first that economic context and material concerns strongly factor into the decision-making of Turkish voters. Then, he notes that campaign discourse often impacts party-to-party interaction far more than it affects outcomes among the electorate. According to Wuthrich, Turkish politics is centered upon charismatic leaders because of the organizational structure of the parties. He argues: "Parties that have made changes in leadership while in government have fared poorly in subsequent elections, usually because the change in leadership suggests weakness in the party."[36]

Wuthrich provides two striking examples. One occurred in 1989 after the ANAP Party's leader Özal resigned from premiership to become president, his party dropped more than 12 percent in the subsequent national election. The second was in 1993, when the leader of the DYP Süleyman Demirel became president leaving his political party's leadership and premiership, the seat was taken by Tansu Çiller, and the party lost 8 percent in the polls subsequently.

Wuthrich and other analysts point to the excessive central control over the nomination of parliamentary candidates. Turkish scholar of constitutional law, Ergun Özbudun notes:

> The present system of nominations has been criticized as leading to excessive control over the process and, consequently, to hierarchical party structure and strict party discipline in party voting. Although such critics contain a great deal of truth, it would be a mistake to hold only the electoral and the nomination systems responsible for such an outcome. Strong leadership and hierarchical party structures are also the result of certain deep-rooted characteristics of Turkish political culture, and they have remained an almost constant feature of Turkish party politics under different electoral and nomination systems.[37]

Özbudun believes that strong party leadership and strict discipline are likely to remain major features of Turkish political parties in the foreseeable future.

The April 16, 2017 referendum provided a narrow victory for President Erdoğan. Does this mean now that Turkey will slide toward a single patronal pyramid under a president with clear powers to dominate his political party, the parliament, the judiciary—indeed all of the key institutions in the country from police and military forces to media and universities? Much will depend on the strength of the opposition together with the half of Turkey's population which rejected a one-man rule. The ability of Erdoğan to deliver on broad-based economic prosperity may well be a determining factor in his support beyond his current well-entrenched political base. Turkey has become an electoral democracy at best, with the evident decline in political liberalism in recent years. Will the push to liberalize the economy, begun well under Prime Minister Özal and strengthened with subsequent administrations as the serious campaign toward EU accession grew, also dissipate?

IS ERDOĞAN'S RULE SUSTAINABLE?

After having analyzed how Erdoğan's imperial foreign policy left Turkey with broken allied relations in the West, namely the United States and the EU, as well as in the Middle East, Soner Cagaptay asks this question at the conclusion of his most recent book, entitled *Erdoğan's Empire*: "Can Erdoğan embrace a different strategy at home and in his foreign policy going forward?"[38] Cagaptay answers this question in the last sentence of his book with some optimism:

> I am not holding my breath that he will make all the choices suggested above, which I believe are all good for Turkey, but if he does, I know that he would then make Turkey great again and leave the lasting legacy that he desires to be written into history.[39]

This may be wishful thinking. Erdoğan's last seventeen years do not suggest that he might change his hardline authoritarian rule domestically and repair the damages that he has inflicted on Turkey's foreign relations. Over the years, he has transformed the AKP political party into a one-man party from a party ruled by a group of Erdoğan's political friends like former President Abdullah Gül, former Prime Minister Ahmet Davutoğlu, former Minister of Finance Ali Babacan, and others. Several of these close colleagues have resigned from AKP and have announced their decision to establish or join two separate political parties. Davutoğlu and Babacan criticize Erdoğan for having betrayed the values and principles that they had agreed upon initially by founding the AKP in 2001. This was after they had resigned from the Welfare Party which was under the leadership of Necmettin Erbakan.

By moving Turkey from a parliamentary constitution to a presidential system, Erdoğan has increased one-man rule. He is now both president and the chairman of the AKP. He alone appoints all the ministers in his government. In the past, he had several well-known and talented economists in his cabinet, but in the new presidential system, he promoted his son-in-law Berat Albayrak, who is not an economist, to become minister of economy and treasury. In sharp contrast to his early years of rule, between 2001 and 2006, when Erdoğan was very popular both inside and outside of Turkey, his turn to more authoritarian rule coincided with a serious economic decline.

There does seem to be discontent within the ranks of Erdoğan's AKP. There is a song which Erdoğan used to sing with his close associates from time to time and especially after an election victory: "We walked together on these roads/We got wet together in this rain." At present, however, there are fewer people left on the side of Erdoğan to sing this song together with great joy.

Davutoğlu and Babacan have criticized Erdoğan for betraying the founding principles of the AKP on economic prosperity, openness in governing, and democracy; he has repressed expressions of free opinion and criticism within the party; and he has begun to interfere with the duties of ministers, given his new found authority under the presidential system. Ministers have become functionaries in place to implement the decisions ordered by the president.

When Davutoğlu and Babacan decided to found two different political parties in late 2019 and early 2020, Erdoğan started to label them as traitors.

Davutoğlu replied in a statement saying "I've served as this country's prime minister. I was elected to the position. No one can call me a traitor."[40]

It appears that the two new parties will not be joining forces. Each leader offers a different approach and focus. But they seem to agree that Erdoğan has abandoned key founding principles of the AKP: rule of law, democracy, and respect for human rights. Whether they will emerge as strong political opponents in the current authoritarian and media constrained political environment remains to be seen.

Former Prime Minister Davutoğlu attended the annual meeting of the Ankara Industrialists and Businessmen Association (ASIAD) and gave an opening speech along with the opposition leaders Kılıçdaroğlu of CHP and Temel Karamollaoğlu of the Felicity Party. In his speech, Davutoğlu criticized President Erdoğan for a lack of foresight when he said "There is no crisis." Davutoğlu continued:

". . . they are unable to manage the crisis at this point and condemn the critics as foreign power groups. They have constructed so many buildings that it ruined the economy. Building does not produce . . . You will manage the process by analyzing and preventing the crisis. If you prevent the crisis from being discussed beyond the resolution, you cannot expect a solution through the generation of ideas. Unfortunately, freedom of thought is restricted in our country today. The first principle that should not be compromised should be the restriction of freedom of thought. We need four things today in Turkey: freedom, openness, democracy, and entrepreneurship.[41]

In his own speech at the ASIAD meeting, the CHP leader Kılıçdaroğlu noted that former Prime Minister Ahmet Davutoğlu had promoted "political morality" in the parliament during his time in office. Davutoğlu registered his "Future Party" on December 13, 2019. Davutoğlu chose the Conference Hall of the Bilkent Hotel in Ankara to launch the new party, as a symbolic reference to the 2001 meeting when the main principles of the AKP were made public for the first time. Former Minister of Finance, Ali Babacan, established his new party formally on March 11, 2020 as the Democracy and Progress Party (DEVA).

Establishment of two new parties by two prominent politicians who were long time close allies of Erdoğan is very crucial for the future of the presidential system. Most of the opposition parties except for the Nationalist Movement Party of Bahçeli and of course the AKP are seeking to change Turkey's system back to the previous parliamentary system. Both Davutoğlu and Babacan acknowledged that they prefer a parliamentary system. Ali Babacan, in particular, warned of the dangers of "one-man rule" and told reporters "We have seen that Turkey has entered a dark tunnel, with its problems on every issue growing by the day."[42]

"Babacan has enormous capacity," said Onur Nezih Kuru, a political scientist at Koc University in Istanbul. According to Kuru, "His party can be an address for large numbers of the electorate, and he can easily reach 10 per cent of the total votes." Kuru, however, warned that Babacan's success would depend on how he positions himself vis-à-vis Erdoğan and the political alliances he might form in the future.[43] In Kuru's opinion, Ali Babacan is a statesman respected in Turkish and international circles. He offers a young, modern, and more importantly a Western face—a desire to put Turkey back in its traditional Western alliances.

On the other hand, President Erdoğan and the pro-Erdoğan media underrated Babacan's new party, as they had done with Davutoğlu's party. The pro-Erdoğan *Daily Sabah* related President Erdoğan's words as follows:

Following Babacan's resignation, the AK Party's leader, President Recep Tayyip Erdoğan, highlighted similar things had occurred in the past when deputies left the AK Party to form splinter parties. "However," he added, "these attempts eventually failed." Turkish politics have witnessed the forming of new political parties that fail to attract supporters or leave a mark on politics. There are several instances of newly formed parties failing just after a year. For instance, Emine Ülker Tarhan founded a new party named the Anatolia Party in 2014 after she resigned from the CHP. Tarhan's discourse was to "raise Turkey to its feet with the Anatolia Party." However, the party only survived a year. An additional example is former Foreign Minister İsmail Cem, who resigned from the Democratic Left Party (DSP) in 2002 and formed the New Turkey Party (YTP), which was closed after failing in its first elections.[44]

At a press conference, Babacan stated that his party would try to bring parliamentary democracy back to Turkey. He argued that President Erdoğan's new executive presidential system has proven to not be suitable for the country, due to the absence of necessary checks and balances. Babacan's new party DEVA (Remedy) is already represented in the current Turkish parliament, because former AKP MP Mustafa Yeneroglu is among the DEVA founders. Yeneroglu was ousted from the AKP in 2019 over disagreements on violations of human rights. Erdoğan had assumed new powers under a constitutional overhaul at the expense of parliament and the government.[45]

FROM PROMISING ECONOMIC LIBERALIZATION TO AUTHORITARIAN ATROPHY?

Beginning under Prime Minister Turgut Özal in the late 1980s, one can point to rather effective implementation of an economic liberalization strategy in Turkey. In some respects, this can be seen in the context of the Western advice given consistently to developing and transition country governments during this period and since on how best to establish a prosperous market economy. Chapters 3 and 4 review the elements of this advice, in the context of "the Washington Consensus" conditionality for IMF and World Bank lending and assistance to Russia. Debate over policy pace and sequencing were an important part of Turkish government debates and struggle, as much as they were for the Russian Federation, though perhaps with better results. There is some evidence of the success of the initial Turkish strategy. One can see a substantial rise in GDP per capita, as measured by Purchasing Power Parity and GDP growth rates, as well as declines in inflation and unemployment rates (see table 6.4).

Nonetheless, there were fits and starts in this process, and the Turkish financial crises of 2000 and 2001 are reminiscent of ineffective, indeed destructive to IMF guidance on financial liberalization offered to the Russian Federation a few years earlier (see chapter 3). But E. Fuat Keyman and Ziya Öniş provide a detailed analysis of this period that suggests there is a general success story beginning in 1980 and continuing to the point that Turkey's relationship with the EC/EU was becoming a "permanent external anchor" for Turkey.[46] Öniş joined Barry Rubin in editing a book *The Turkish Economy in Crisis* that dissects the 2000–2001 period in systematic detail, pointing to the negative impact of IMF policies as well as the government missteps. Öniş concludes the volume with the following indictment:

> There is no doubt that an excessive push towards rapid capital account liberalization represents the weakest element in . . . the so-called "Washington consensus." Clearly, a number of countries have been exposed in a rather premature fashion to the forces of financial globalization without attaining sufficient macroeconomic stability and before developing the appropriate regulatory institutions in the first place . . . .
>
> The IMF is also open to criticism on the grounds that the organization pushed countries too rapidly in the direction of financial and capital account liberalization while underestimating the problem of establishing appropriate regulatory institutions during the process. Admittedly, though, the decision to open up fully Turkey's capital account in August 1989 was a domestic rather than an IMF-induced decision. Turkey was also unique in experiencing financial crises at a time when an IMF program was actually being implemented. . . . Given the fragile environment—that is, the presence of highly volatile and reversible capital flows and the massive economic and social costs of speculative attacks resulting in massive outflows of capital—that countries like Turkey find themselves in, various commentators in the present volume clearly favor at least temporary capital controls as a necessary part of an overall stabilization package. They are also well aware of the difficulties involved, as the IMF is not very sympathetic towards such arrangements.[47]

Table 6.4   The Rise and Decline of the Turkish Economy: Basic Indicators, 1980–2019

Year	GDP (in bn US$PPP)	GDP per Capita (in US$PPP)	GDP Growth (real) (%)	Inflation Rate (%)	Unemployment (%)
1980	155.8	3,443	-0.8	110.6	7.2
1981	178.1	3,844	4.4	36.4	7.2
1982	195.5	4,127	3.4	31.1	7.6
1983	212.8	4,393	0.3	31.3	7.5
1984	235.6	4,756	6.8	48.4	7.4
1985	253.4	5,009	4.3	44.5	7.0
1986	276.4	5,356	6.9	34.6	7.7
1987	311.7	5,924	10.0	38.9	8.1
1988	329.5	6,149	2.1	73.7	8.7
1989	343.3	6,293	0.3	63.3	8.6
1990	389.1	7,009	9.3	60.3	8.0
1991	406.0	7,191	0.9	66.0	7.7
1992	440.1	7,668	6.3	70.1	7.9
1993	486.7	8,345	8.0	66.1	8.4
1994	470.0	7,931	-5.5	104.5	8.0
1995	514.4	8,546	7.2	89.6	7.1
1996	560.5	9,172	7.0	80.2	6.1
1997	613.1	9,884	7.5	85.7	6.3
1998	639.1	10,159	3.1	84.7	6.4
1999	626.4	9,815	-3.4	64.9	7.2
2000	682.9	10,550	6.6	55.0	6.0
2001	656.3	10,004	-6.0	54.2	7.8
2002	709.5	10,685	6.4	45.1	9.8
2003	763.2	11,360	5.6	25.3	9.9
2004	859.4	12,634	9.6	8.6	9.7
2005	966.0	14,028	9.0	8.2	9.5
2006	1,066.0	15,287	7.1	9.6	9.0
2007	1,149.7	16,288	5.0	8.8	9.2
2008	1,181.9	16,527	0.8	10.4	10.0
2009	1,134.9	15,641	-4.7	6.3	13.1
2010	1,245.6	16,896	8.5	8.6	11.1
2011	1,412.9	18,909	11.1	6.5	9.1
2012	1,509.0	19,953	4.8	8.9	8.4
2013	1,665.9	21,729	8.5	7.5	9.0
2014	1,784.4	22,966	5.2	8.9	9.9
2015	1,912.7	24,291	6.1	7.7	10.3
2016	1,994.0	24,983	3.2	7.8	10.9
2017	2,183.3	27,018	7.4	11.1	10.9
2018	2,299.8	28,044	2.8	16.3	11.0
2019	2,346.6	28,264	.9*	15.7	13.8
2020	2,464.6	29,327		12.6	13.7

Source: International Monetary Fund, *Report for Selected Countries and Subjects*, October 2019; and the Turkish Statistical Institute (TÜİK), February, 2020*.

Keyman and Öniş describe the Turkish government's efforts to "reform" out of the crisis, highlighting some the details of the strong role that Economy Minister Kemal Derviş played in the recovery, indeed in the larger process of Turkey's successful liberalization when he joined the government after years of work for the World Bank. They also point to the conflict that developed between Derviş and AKP policy makers, with the latter trying to emphasize a "communitarian-liberal synthesis" which turned out to be a program designed to meet the needs of the disadvantaged and rural poor more directly. The AKP's success in conveying this posture was regarded as an important element in its subsequent electoral success.[48]

The goal of full membership in the European Union was seen by many as the solution to Turkey's drive for export development and increased foreign direct investment. Accession to the EU would require substantial reforms to meet the various "chapters" of harmonization with EU policies and practices. In important respects, this was valuable for the liberalization reform process that Turkey needed to take anyway in order to prosper in the increasingly globalized world economy, even if the prospect of membership was dim due to probable opposition ultimately from Austria, Cyprus, France, Greece, and perhaps others. It now seems clear that when Erdoğan became Prime Minister in 2003, he saw the EU accession process as a means to dismantling the hold that the Turkish military and police had on ensuring the secular state—at least as much as a means to a closer economic relationship with Europe.[49]

European leaders were slow to appreciate this, convinced by statements from Erdoğan and Davutoğlu that Turkey was indeed a viable "bridge" between Europe and the Islamic cultures of the Middle East. A democratic Muslim-dominated state that embraced economic liberalism was highly prized, and the common wishful thinking was that Erdoğan had in fact moderated from his earlier Islamist commitment and had embraced liberal democracy. In reality, as noted earlier, his view was much more instrumental.

European political leaders and commentators may well have been naive in believing that he had abandoned his pre-prison Islamist beliefs. Clearly, Turks on the political left and committed secularists were not so easily deceived, but they no longer held enough votes to derail his path toward authoritarian rule.[50]

On the domestic side, the Turkish development strategy subsequently included steps along with strategic investments in universities and university–industrial collaboration. TUBITAK, the Scientific and Technological Research Council of Turkey, encourages research partnerships with a wide range of grant programs, including the relatively new "Mevlana" program to promote faculty and student exchanges and research collaboration with North American and Asian universities. This is an ancillary effort to the European

Union's Erasmus Program of which Turkey has made good use from its Association Agreement with the EU, still working through the "accession" process of its long-time candidacy for full membership. Major Turkish universities like METU, ITU, Gazi University, Istanbul University, Koc University, Sabanci University, Haciteppi University, and Ankara University have developed high-quality science and ABET accredited engineering degree programs and "Technoparks" for incubating new companies and promoting industrial partnerships. Turkey's industrial and technological sectors have not fully matured, but in contrast to Russia, Turkey makes and grows things that other countries want to buy—beyond oil, gas, and timber (and weapons). Singapore offers a somewhat different example, but along with Germany, Japan, and the Republic of Korea, as Linda Weiss argues, state investment together with some freedom in information exchange and independent entrepreneurial activity can produce broad-based prosperity.[51] Unfortunately, Turkey has suffered a severe downturn over the past several years, as much of the "liberalization" and stimulation of entrepreneurial independence has dissipated. Table 6.4 provides some evidence for this, as inflation and unemployment rates have risen and growth has stagnated in the past few years.

On January 24, 2020, Turkey's Treasury and Finance Minister, Berat Albayrak, claimed that the worst is over for Turkey's economy, and its financial system, although bruised and battered, is now more resilient to internal and external shocks. According to Albayrak, son in-law of President Erdoğan, Turkey is emerging from around a year-and-a-half of economic hardship punctuated by a brief, but steep recession and currency shock that saw the lira lose nearly 30 percent of its value in a single year in 2018. At that time, he argued Turkey was showing signs of economic recovery as it recorded positive quarterly growth rates in the second half of 2019. Economic conditions deteriorated substantially in 2020, however, leading Erdoğan finally to replace Albayrak with Lutfi Elvan on November 10.[52]

Recent World Bank reports suggest some promise in the prospects for corporate development, productivity, and economic growth. However, they are cautious and contingent in stressing that a more consistent and diversified approach to human capital development is indicated—precisely at the time when Erdoğan has weakened the universities in his effort to root out potential political opponents in the frenzy of his post-attempted coup repression.[53]

A return to the diversification into higher technology sectors, away from construction and low-technology manufacturing is recommended in order to boost manufacturing exports and earnings. Sporadic and constrained expenditure on university research and development projects and technoparks are lamented in this environment.[54]

The World Bank notes:

> Turkey maintains a liberal FDI regime when compared to countries such as Brazil, Poland and Mexico. Turkey has decreased FDI restrictions in virtually all sectors and, consequently, FDI stocks have increased across almost all sectors . . . . The largest increase has been experienced by far by the electronic sector.[55]

Unfortunately, while the results of this liberal regulatory regime are potentially positive, especially in comparison with the Russian Federation, signs of growing corruption and executive favoritism to what occurs in Russia are evident, as Erdoğan has tightened his authoritarian political control over the economy since 2016.

On perceived corruption, Turkey was ranked 91st out of 180 countries rated by Transparency International in 2019, worse than China, all former members of COMECON in Eastern Europe and several post-Soviet transition countries, such as the Republic of Georgia, Armenia, and the three Baltic countries: Estonia, Latvia, and Lithuania.[56] Corruption clearly has been seen to worsen in Turkey since 2015.

A troubling brain drain has occurred, as scientists and entrepreneurs seek more freedom and opportunity, and there is evidence that key industrial groups are seeking to outsource their manufacturing and R&D efforts, citing mounting political tensions, uncertainties, and declining rule of law.[57] Important foreign investors have in fact closed down their operations in Turkey.[58]

Independent Turkish economists and commentators remain skeptical about the potential comeback. For example, Hakan Gulseven of the Turkish version of *The Independent* feared a major collapse in the economy over the next year. In his column on Oct 8, 2019, he wrote:

> . . . it can be said that an entire society, especially workers and the poor, will pay a serious bill and a qualitative decline in the standard of living. Let us emphasize once again, the external debt burden that is rapidly progressing towards 60 percent of the national income is a case; the bankruptcy of the concrete-based growth strategy is another case.[59]

The dependence of the economy on AKP government-sponsored construction projects is misleading. The once thriving industrial development and exports of the Turkish private manufacturing sector is stagnating, while foreign debt has grown to more than $500 billion, and corruption seems less than in Russia, but nonetheless substantial and growing.

Gulseven points to a kind of crony capitalism not so dissimilar from Putin's Russia in the connections between government-funded projects and sections of the construction industry in AKP supporter hands.[60]

Gulseven was joined by Peter Kenen, NPR correspondent based in Istanbul, stressing that Erdoğan must loosen his personalistic authoritarian control of the economy if it is to return to broad-based prosperity. The system must be based on rules and independent institutions (especially the Central Bank) free from executive interference.[61] Foreign investors are increasingly reluctant to contemplate new projects in this environment. The fiscal and inflation control reforms announced by the Erdoğan government in 2019 were characterized as empty in content.[62]

The Turkish Statistical Institute (TÜİK) was similarly negative, reporting that in 2019 the country fell below the 2007 level in per capita income.[63] The per capita national income, which rose to $ 12,480 in 2013, declined to $ 9,127 in 2019, below the $ 9,665 level in 2007. Turkey's economy grew by only 0.9 percent in 2019. The 0.9 percent growth was the lowest in ten years after the 4.7 percent contraction in 2009 during the global financial crisis.

A basic challenge that Turkey faces economically, in great contrast to the Russian Federation, is that it is largely dependent on foreign energy sources. The government through successive administrations has sought to diversify its energy trading partners and expand its pursuit of hydroelectric, solar, wind, geothermal, and nuclear energy systems. Table 6.5 is instructive in this respect, noting in effect the impact of the Baku Tbilisi Ceyhan pipeline from Azerbaijan, which supplied 7.2 billion cubic meters to Turkey in 2018, as well as pipeline deliveries of natural gas from Iran (7.6 billion cubic meters) and the Russian Federation (22.8 billion cubic meters).[64] Turkish

Table 6.5   Turkish Liquefied Natural Gas Imports, 2008–2018

Year	LNG Imports (Billion Cubic Meters)
2008	5.6
2009	6.0
2010	7.8
2011	5.9
2012	7.6
2013	5.9
2014	7.1
2015	7.5
2016	7.6
2017	10.9
2018	11.5

Source: BP Statistical Review of World Energy 2019.

imports of Liquefied Natural Gas have grown substantially since 2008, and the sources have diversified. Key suppliers are Algeria, Qatar, Nigeria, the United States, and Trinidad & Tobago.[65] Turkey's consumption of domestic coal has increased substantially since 2008 but plans for expanding renewable sources of energy have begun to pay off. In 2018, electricity generation by wind turbines grew by 10.7 percent, solar systems grew by 173.1 percent, and other renewable sources grew by 21 percent.[66] There are also preliminary arrangements in play for development of electricity from Turkey's first nuclear energy plants. These include negotiations with Russia and China as suppliers and construction contractors.[67]

ERDOĞAN'S FOREIGN AND SECURITY POLICY: FROM ZERO PROBLEMS TO NOTHING BUT PROBLEMS

Also promising, initially, was Turkish foreign policy under Erdoğan and his advisor and eventual Foreign Minister, Ahmet Davutoğlu, with an effort to profess "Zero Problems with Neighbors." Davutoğlu also pushed a strategy of "Strategic Depth" which seemed to offer a more independent posture in the region, not necessarily in tune with NATO/Western aims.[68] This fit nicely with Erdoğan's inclination, as noted in a special report published by *The Economist*:

> . . . the man largely responsible for engineering this dramatic shift is Ahmet Davutoğlu, Turkey's foreign minister since 2009. Before that he was an international-relations adviser to Mr Erdoğan. In 2001, before the AK government came to power, Mr Davutoğlu published a book, *Strategic Depth*, that set out a new policy of engagement with the region. He rejects accusations that he is "neo-Ottoman", yet his doctrine certainly involves rebuilding ties round the former Ottoman empire.
>
> . . . he is convinced that its new strategy of asserting its interests, both in the region and in the world, makes his country more, not less, attractive to the West. Nothing infuriates him more than articles in Western publications suggesting that Turkey has tilted east, or even claiming that "we have lost Turkey." "Who is we?" he asks. After all, Turkey maintains NATO's biggest army after America's; it is committed in Afghanistan and other trouble spots; and it is negotiating to join the EU. As Mr Davutoğlu puts it, "Turkey is not an issue; it is an actor." His country now matters more than ever to Europe and the West, he claims.[69]

The Turkish Ministry of Foreign Affairs' webpage still (as of December 2020) displays a long statement, entitled "Policy of Zero Problems with our Neighbors" (without reference to Ahmet Davutoğlu) as follows:

Aware that development and progress in real terms can only be achieved in a lasting peace and stability environment, Turkey places this objective at the very center of her foreign policy vision. This approach is a natural reflection of the "Peace at Home, Peace in the World" policy laid down by Great Leader Atatürk, founder of the Republic of Turkey. Besides, it is a natural consequence of a contemporary responsibility and a humanistic foreign policy vision.

. . . . we believe that our policy of zero problems with neighbors has gained additional meaning and importance as the Middle East stands at the brink of a historical transformation. We hope that the current dynamic for reform advances in way that will meet the expectations of the people while also contributing to peace and security in the region.[70]

It is interesting that the Turkish Ministry of Foreign Affairs still keeps this "zero problems with neighbors" statement on its website despite Turkey's worsening relations starting with Syria, Greece, and the EU more generally, Armenia, the United States, and Russia—from zero problems to nothing but problems? The criticism of Turkey's involvement in Syria's crisis and the mistakes in Turkey's Syrian foreign policy increased by the news of significant numbers of deaths of Turkish forces in Idlib, northern Syria, in early 2020. This criticism does not come only from Turkey's opposition parties, but Turkish academicians, journalists, as well as retired diplomats.

They point to Erdoğan's radical change of Syrian policy from "excessive sincerity" of Turkish–Syrian relations in 2009, when both Erdoğan and Assad were posing for the cameras, as two brothers to the current stage of not engaging in diplomatic relations but pointing guns toward each other. Ersin Kalaycioglu, professor of political sciences at Sabanci University, was particularly critical of Erdoğan's Syrian policy. In 2012, Kalaycioglu had warned that the risks would be high for Turkey, when Erdoğan reversed his government's friendly policy toward "brother" Assad to cheerlead for the opposition—figuring that Assad would in short order go the way of removed Arab Spring dictators in Tunisia, Egypt, and Libya. Kalaycioglu said:

The Turkish government "assumed this would be a very fast process [and] wanted to have some stake," so began a "proactive involvement in this process. Actually, this calculation turned out to be wrong. Now, we are into this mess up to our waists, probably, if not our neck. [Turkish leaders] don't want to get out of it very easily and they are afraid of losing face. Poor relations, combined with "a few accidents," and a few [incorrect] assumptions and decisions, could go all the way to a greater escalation and perhaps even war, and therefore it's a very unnerving process, The Erdoğan government has been making one error after another, as far as Syria is concerned.[71]

Sedat Ergin, an experienced journalist of the Turkish daily *Hurriyet* newspaper, cautioned on Feb. 12, 2020 that Turkey was moving toward the most dangerous phase in Syria: "Unfortunately, this dangerous escalation could not be brought under control despite talks with Russia during the weekend and even gained a stronger momentum, leading to a sorrowful incident: The martyrdom of our five soldiers, who were targeted by an artillery fire launched by Assad's army."[72]

Gonul Tol, professor at George Washington University's Institute for Middle East Studies, in her article "Turkey's Endgame in Syria" in *Foreign Affairs*, concluded that

> In fact, Turkey's Syria policy has for years turned on Erdoğan's ambition to consolidate his one-man rule at home. Turkey supported Islamist insurgents against Damascus when doing so strengthened Erdoğan's religious credentials at home. After flagging electoral support forced Erdoğan to partner with an anti-Kurdish opposition party, his attention shifted to fighting the Kurdish forces operating in Syria. That goal remains today, but it is slowly being overshadowed by an even more pressing concern: getting rid of the millions of Syrian refugees who have made their way to Turkey over the years, where they have now become a burden on Erdoğan. That a major military incursion will solve these problems is far from guaranteed. But Erdoğan is determined to try.[73]

She also pointed to the negative effects of Erdoğan's failing Syrian policy on his rule in Turkey:

> His party lost control of almost all major cities in the 2019 municipal elections—an immense blow to the city-level patronage system upon which Erdoğan built his power over the last 25 years. The rout owed something to the deepening economic crisis, but it also reflected growing public discontent with the 3.6 million Syrian refugees still in the country.[74]

Another trap that is growing for Erdoğan in Syria concerns Turkey's uncertain and faltering foreign policy direction between the United States and Western Europe, on the one hand, and Russia, on the other. By Erdoğan's swinging policy preferences between the United States and Russia, Turkey has been charting a zigzag course. Turkish columnist Cengiz Aktar writing in a newly formed independent online media, *Ahval*, says that it is not easy to understand the unusual triangular relationship between Russia and the United States, on the one hand, and Turkey, on the other. He argues that:

> All in all, although the U.S.–Turkey partnership is 75 years old, it doesn't look sustainable in the long term due to too many conflicts and controversies in both

ends. This is despite the recent opportunistic move by the U.S. Syria Envoy James Jeffrey trying to exploit the Russo-Turkish feud in Idlib by encouraging Ankara to fight back together with jihadists, prolonging thereby the civil war in Syria. It's noteworthy that the envoy, by doing so, indirectly supports terrorist groups who were behind 9/11 and that Ankara is now nurturing![75]

Aktar concludes that "Erdoğan's brinkmanship is so bankrupted that if he yields to Americans, he will be finished by the Russians, and vice versa."[76]

Two Turkish scholars Muhittin Ataman and Çağatay Özdemir, professors of the University of Ankara's Political Science department, found the shifting policies of Erdoğan toward Syria somewhat productive:

> All in all, in recent years, Turkey's Syria policies have not only been humanitarian but too hard power-based. On the course of the crisis, military assertiveness has become the dominant approach in Ankara. Such a change in foreign policy has increased the role of Turkey in the region, and Ankara has become a decisive actor in the future of Syria.[77]

Prof. Ersin Kalaycioglu counters: "We can no longer leave Idlib even if we want to. Turkey is in deep waters!"[78] According to Kalaycioglu, "Erdoğan's main shortcoming is that he has bypassed the experienced Turkish diplomatic establishment, the staff of the Turkish Foreign Ministry, in his foreign policy decisions."[79]

Turkish stocks and the lira tumbled on Friday, Feb 28, 2020 after the news that thirty-three Turkish soldiers were killed on Feb. 27 in Syria's Idlib province—the result of an air strike of the Syrian air force. Although the official figure of thirty-three killed and many wounded Turkish soldiers in Syria, this number was challenged by many on social media reports claiming a figure between 165 and more than 200. Various social media groups and individual journalists report the slowing down of the internet and social media accesses purposely done by the government. According to the independent TV channel ODATV, Turks began to experience problems with their internet connection while pursuing the developments in Idlib, The ODATV's newspaper also reported this incident with a title "Internet and Social Media Collapsed." [80]

Twitter users were not able to share and refresh the page as of Thursday midnight. The slowdown that started in Istanbul came to a halt after a while. In the following hours on Friday Feb 28, it was seen that all social media had communication problems. There was no government response on this incident. Stocks tumbled 10 percent at the opening, and the Turkish Lira hit a seventeen month low in early trading. "Turkey is facing the perfect storm," said Cristian Maggio, head of emerging markets strategy at TD Securities. "Turkey is between a rock and a hard place in this moment—the rock is the international context risk given the coronavirus emergency, and the hard place is the situation it has put itself into in Syria."[81]

The potential for a traumatic break between Turkey and NATO remains a concern. President Erdoğan's decision to buy anti-aircraft missile systems from Russia sent shockwaves into most NATO member capitals and has stimulated much debate and plans for an adequate political-military response. Turkey took delivery of the initial Russian S-400 equipment in July of 2019. U.S. officials worry that "the S-400 could compromise its Lockheed Martin F-35 stealth fighter jets, an aircraft Turkey is helping build and plans to buy."[82] U.S. President Trump indicated discomfort with the Turkish decision but noted (in Erdoğan's defense) that Turkey took the decision to buy from Russia only after it was denied access to the latest U.S. systems, an apparent dig (not unusual) at the record of his predecessor President Obama. A decision to reverse that policy came too late to stop the procurement effort.[83]

Ziya Öniş and Şuhnaz Yılmaz provide interesting context for the shifts in Turkish foreign policy during the Erdoğan AKP Era. In their view, it can be characterized in some respects as movement from Europeanization to Euro-Asianism. They note that "While Turkey pursued a relatively passive or reactive foreign policy stance during the Cold War era, its post-Cold War foreign policy has been marked by subsequent waves of foreign policy activism."[84] They note some important constructive steps in the initiatives, but also find some of it to be counterproductive.[85]

President Erdoğan dramatically escalated tensions with Greece toward the end of the decade by claiming his "Blue Homeland" doctrine with respect to the Eastern Mediterranean. This can be seen as a clear effort to reclaim "lost empire" as well as an attempt to distract his increasingly suffering population with nationalistic fervor. The complex boundary issues are not new, originally confronted in some detail with the Treaty of Lausanne of 1923; the Lausanne Conference was meant to replace the Treaty of Sevres, which had been repudiated by Atatürk's new Republic.

Turkey was not in a strong negotiating position and perhaps was lucky to hold onto the territorial gains that the Turkish Nationalist Army had made in the war with European occupation forces, especially versus the Greeks, to re-establish control of Anatolia. Many of the Aegean Islands had been part of the Ottoman Empire since 1522. All but two of these became Greek possessions, including the Dodecanese group very close to the Turkish mainland. The Dodecanese were finally ceded to Greece from Italian rule by the 1947 Peace Treaty after World War II. The Dodecanese Island of Kastellorizo has become the focal point of conflict recently, as Erdoğan seeks to claim the right to explore and drill for natural gas on what he argues is essentially part of the Turkish continental shelf. Fellow NATO member Greece, strongly supported by France, rejected this interpretation, arguing that the islands each have their own exclusive economic zones (EEZ). Turkey has not ratified the UN Convention on the Law of the Sea (or indeed the previous Convention on the Continental Shelf), and thus claims not to be bound by the claim by Greece, which is a signatory of UNCLOS. In 2019, Turkey complicated matters by signing an agreement with the UN recognized Libyan Government of National Accord (GNA) providing for expansive maritime rights between the two countries, ignoring the Greek Island EEZs.

Tensions over Turkish ties with the breakaway Northern part of Cyprus have also increased recently, as Erdoğan has pursued drilling for natural gas in the Cyprus EEZ. The Greek–Turkey tension on Cyprus and other long-term disputes have been somewhat under control for most of the period since a dangerous flare up in 1996. This was in part due to the EU efforts to require their resolution as a condition for full Turkish membership. As suggested earlier, however, Erdoğan's interest in the EU accession process was largely instrumental (and temporary)—probably as a means to help him reduce the influence of the military in Turkish politics. Accordingly, the restraints on his regional aggression were removed, particularly when it appeared that such aggression could increase his popularity by fanning bi-partisan feelings of nationalism. As a former Turkish diplomat, Sinan Ulgen, stresses: "This is viewed as an attack on Turkey's national sovereignty."[86]

The dream of exploiting Mediterranean gas reserves for more energy independence remains an important motivation, but one must keep in mind that global oil and gas prices have been at historic lows for some time, and the push for transformation to renewable energy sources in the face of climate change appears to be gaining substantial support. Most major energy companies are reluctant to invest in new large-scale oil and gas development projects, especially expensive ones that require long pipeline infrastructure in difficult, and perhaps politically unstable, conditions. Erdoğan finds himself in the unenviable position of heightened conflict with his NATO allies, especially Greece and France, as well as rising conflict with Egypt (which opposes the boundary agreement with the Libyan GNA) and other Arab states, especially Saudi Arabia, Iraq, and of course Syria, which find his interventions in Syria and against the Kurds destabilizing. In short, there is no way to describe Erdoğan's foreign policy as "Zero Problems with Neighbors."

As noted in chapter 4, President Erdoğan voiced strong support for Azerbaijan in the reopening of hostilities with Armenia over Nagorno-Karabakh in late September, 2020. Indeed, he rejected demands by Russia, France, and the United States for a cease fire, arguing that an end to the Armenian control of internationally recognized Azerbaijani territory should end first.[87] Normally a close ally of Armenia, Russia was not overtly supportive. Turkey's strong public support for the Azerbaijani position may well be related to Erdoğan's increasingly aggressive (and nationally popular) regional policy. But it also reflects a long-standing Turkish affinity for Azerbaijan, often described as a relationship of "One nation, two states."[88] While the Russian brokered settlement reached in early November 2020 has promise, the prospect for serious political conflict between Russia and Turkey over the dispute is not out of the question. Overt and material support for Azerbaijan on Nagorno-Karabakh by Turkey would seem again to cast doubt on "zero problems with neighbors." It is hard to imagine that the Turkish posture contributes to the prospect for a long-term resolution of the dispute. Reports that Turkey provided its own manufactured armed drones to assist the Azerbaijani effort to suppress Armenian air defense installations and attack artillery units and tanks substantiate both Erdoğan's commitment and his tools now available for intervention.[89]

LOOKING AHEAD: TURKEY'S REGIONAL ROLE

The Turkish intellectual and novelist Kaya Genc describes Erdoğan as "the most baffling politician to emerge in the 96-year history of Turkey. He is polarizing and popular, autocratic and fatherly, calculating and listless. Erdoğan's ideology shifts every few years, and he appears to make up his road map as he goes along."[90] Genc gives details on Erdoğan's skills in establishing new alliances with various politicians, groups, and foreign countries; however, he then commonly breaks with the old allies and establishes new ones. On the international scene, his tortured relationship with the EU, NATO, and bilaterally with the United States, Syria, and other Middle Eastern countries are clear examples, as are his flirtations with Russia and post-Soviet Eurasia. Burak Bekdil, Soner Cagaptay, Christopher C. Hull, Asli Kelkitli, and David L. Phillips all have interesting takes on this tendency.[91]

In Turkish domestic politics, Erdoğan successfully allied first with the ethnic Kurdish population, later abandoned them and allied with the Turkish nationalist groups, and made his current alliance with the Nationalist Movement Party of Devlet Bahçeli. Early on, he had tried to win the hearts of the Islamic conservative population and the leftist groups by attacking the Kemalist foundations and the ideology of Kemalist groups; subsequently, he praised Atatürk and his principles.

When he needed the Gülenist groups in the various parts of the bureaucracy in his early years of rule as prime minister and later as president, he had a closed ruling alliance with them, allowing the Gülenist judges and prosecutors to punish, try, and purge the high- and low-ranking Kemalist military generals in the Turkish army. Later, when a struggle between Erdoğan and the leader of the Gülenist group, Fathullah Gülen, started to intensify, Erdoğan purged and arrested the Gülenists. This led to the failed coup in July

2016 by the Gülenists, as their last fight against Erdoğan. He then began to mend his relations with the army by bringing back many purged Kemalist generals and lower level officers to the Turkish army.

On the international stage, Erdoğan showed himself initially as a pro-Western and staunch defender of the EU, but later turned his face to the Middle East, Russia, and China. When he had differences with Russia, he started to appeal to Europe and the United States. However, his continued zigzag politics both internally and internationally have caused him to lose credibility as a leader.

Erdoğan had an ostentatious dream for "The New Turkey"—to sell to the public that it will be a new, strong, prosperous, and big Turkey built during his reign. Now "The New Turkey" story seems to have become an empty shell where more and more people have started to see an economically and politically weak Turkey domestically and regionally. As the results of the latest national and local elections show, Erdoğan has lost much of his popularity in Turkey and his credibility in the world.

Given the emerging domestic and international problems facing Erdoğan's rule, there are perhaps three options that Erdoğan has to rebuild his popularity and win the next election:

1) Return to the path of a democratic leader by diminishing the trend toward an autocratic presidential system. This would be most effective (though also least likely) if it involved steps back to the parliamentary system; an amnesty and release of political prisoners—journalists and public intellectuals; restoring press freedom and re-professionalizing government ministries to engage in serious efforts to repair the domestic economy and international relationships. Expecting this kind of radical change from Erdoğan is a dubious prospect.

2) It also now seems unlikely that Erdoğan can become a fully despotic leader—more like Putin—taking steps perhaps to become President-for-life while cracking down further on political opposition and independent media. This would further distance him from his economic and political life-lines with the EU and United States. At best he could become a decidedly junior partner with Russia or even China. The emerging constellation of opposition political parties and his waning public support also makes this a dubious prospect.

3) A third option seems more likely than the first two—that Erdoğan will mark time, avoiding major (constructive) initiatives, and continue his zigzag politics for the rest of his term as President. He can do this until the 2023 scheduled elections without fear of serious challenge. A possible decision to announce early elections in 2021 might come if the prospects for a stronger economy arise, or the new opposition parties

fizzle. But this does not seem likely, given the current domestic constraints and regional challenges. Erdoğan now seems to stand somewhat isolated, as the AKP appears to disintegrate, or at least diminish in its hold on the imagination of the broad Turkish public. Nevertheless, he has been underestimated before. He is blessed with political skill and guile.

Soner Cagaptay introduces his recent book on *Erdoğan's Empire* by noting:

Erdoğan's quest to seek greatness for Turkey is not unusual, however. It is, in many ways, a continuation of the policies of the country's Turkish leaders, from the late Ottoman sultans to Atatürk, all of whom sought to revive Turkey's great power status. However, Erdoğan's path is different compared to his predecessors. While they folded Turkey under the West to restore its global influence, Erdoğan has picked an unorthodox model: his goal is to make Turkey great as a *stand-alone* power. First, in the Middle East and then globally.[92]

At this point, it appears that Erdoğan's "path" has been frustrated. He has misplayed his hand in a complex game that he perhaps did not fully understand or assess realistically. Domestic weaknesses, fueled by ineffective policies and an enormous refugee burden, will continue to inhibit his regional/ global ambitions. It is unclear whether new opposition challengers like Ahmet Davutoğlu will offer a more effective strategy for broad-based prosperity and regional order, but Davutoğlu's "Action Plan for Regional Order in the Middle East" does seem more deliberative and constructive.[93]

NOTES

1. John M. VanderLippe, *The Politics of Turkish Democracy: İsmet İnönü and the Formation of the Multi-Party System, 1938–1950* (Albany: State University of New York Press, 2005), p. 4. This is the best source in English for this period.

2. VanderLippe's argument is reminiscent of Tocqueville's position on the French Revolution in its relationship to the Ancient Regime. What the French revolutionaries created had an eerie resemblance to the old regime, especially in terms of centralization and top-down authoritarianism.

3. For an excellent treatment of the post-war period, see Jamil Hasanli, *Stalin and the Turkish Crisis of the Cold War, 1945–1953* (Lanham, MD: Lexington Books, 2011).

4. Henry Hale, *Patronal Politics: Eurasian Regime Dynamics in Comparative Perspective* (UK: Cambridge University Press, 2015).

5. Turkey's Supreme Election Council (T.C. Yüksek Seçim Kurulu: YSK) Website: https://www.ysk.gov.tr/. English translations of the Turkish national election results since 1950 and a descriptive compendium of Turkish political parties are available at http://ceres.isp.msu.edu/.

6. Okan Konuralp, "CHP Deputy Regrets His Party's Failure to Attract Workers," *Hurriyet Daily News*, July 31, 2014, https://www.hurriyetdailynews.com/chp-deputy-regrets-his-partys-failure-to-attract-workers-69803.

7. Zeyno Baran, *Torn Country: Turkey Between Secularism and Islam* (Stanford, CA: Hoover Institution Press, 2010), pp. 38–39.

8. Barry Rubin and Metin Heper, eds. *Political Parties in Turkey* (London: Frank Cass, 2002), pp. 2–3.

9. Jan Pakulski and Andras Korosenyi, *Toward Leader Democracy* (London: Anthem Press, 2013).

10. Recep Tayyip Erdoğan, *Hurriyet*, February 17, 2017.

11. See: M. Hakan Yavuz and Bayram Balci, eds. *Turkey's July 15th Coup: What Happened and Why* (Salt Lake City, NM: The University of Utah Press, 2018).

12. *Hurriyet Daily News*, April 18, 2017.

13. An electoral map displaying this remarkable distribution is available at haritalr.web.tr and in English at http://ceres.isp.msu.edu/.

14. Can Dundar, *We Are Arrested: A Journalist's Notes From a Turkish Prison* (London: Biteback Publishing, 2016).

15. Burak Bilgehan Özpek, *The Turkey Analyst*, February 28, 2017.

16. Ergun Özbudun, "Democratization in the Middle East: Turkey-How Far from Consolidation?" *Journal of Democracy*, 7, no. 3 (July 1996), p. 137.

17. Ibid., p. 144.

18. RPP: the Republican People's Party (CHP in Turkish).

19. H. Bahadir Türk, *Muktedir: Türk Sağ Geleneği ve Recep Tayyip Erdoğan (Competent: Turkish Right Tradition and Recep Tayyip Erdoğan)* (Istanbul: İletişim Yayınları, 2014), p. 434.

20. Barış Yetkin, *Popülizm ve Özal-Erdoğan* (Antalya: Y. A. R. Müdafaa-i Hukuk yayınları, 2010), p. 273.

21. Ibid., pp. 51–54

22. Ibid., pp.103–104.

23. Ibid.

24. The conqueror of Davos: Referring to Erdoğan's clash with the Israeli president Peres at the World Economic Forum in Davos in 2009.

25. Cemal Dindar, *Bi'at ve Öfke: Recep Tayyip Erdoğan'ın Psikobiyografisi* (Istanbul: Telos Yayınevi, 2014), p.19.

26. Fatma Sibel Yüksek, *Tayyip Erdoğan'ı Okuma Sanatı (Art of Reading Tayyip Erdoğan)* (Ankara: Tanyeri Kitap, 2013), pp. 15–17.

27. Zeyno Baran, *Torn Country*, p.45.

28. Ibid., pp.45–47.

29. Christopher Holton and Clare Lopez, *Gulen and The Gulenist Movement: Turkey's Islamic Supremacist Cult and its Contributions to the Civilization Jihad* (Washington, DC: Center for Security Policy Press, 2015), pp. 11–12.

30. Ezgi Basaran, *Frontline Turkey: The Heart of the Middle East* (London and New York: I.B. Tauris, 2017), p. 174.

31. Baran, *Torn Country*, pp. 82–103.

32. Walter R. Mebane, Jr., Allen Hicken and Ken Kollman, "Were there İrregularities in Turkey's 2015 Elections? We Used This New Forensic Toolkit to Check," *The Washington Post*, Febuaury 15, 2016.

33. F. Michael Wuhtrich, *National Elections in Turkey: People, Politics, and the Party System* (Syracuse: Syracuse University Press, 2016), p. 51.

34. Ibid.

35. Ibid., pp. 73–74.

36. Ibid., p. 263

37. Ergun Özbudun, *Party Politics and Social Cleavages in Turkey* (London: Lynne Rienner Publishers, 2013), p. 133

38. Soner Cagaptay, *Erdoğan's Empire: Turkey and the Politics of the Middle East* (London: I.B. Tauris, 2020), p. 302.

39. Ibid.

40. *Ahval News*, August 23, 2019.

41. Ahmet Davutoğlu, Speech to the Ankara Industrialists and Businessmen Association ("ASIAD"); "Davutoğlu: Müsteşarlıklar ortadan kaldırıldığı zaman yalvardım," *Cumhuriyet*, November 30, 2019, http://www.cumhuriyet.com.tr/haber/ Davutoğlu-mustesarliklar-ortadan-kaldirildigi-zaman-yalvardim-1705428; see also: "Ahmet Davutoğlu'ndan Bomba Açıklamalar," https://www.youtube.com/watch?v =rfFkY26H95s.

42. "Former Erdoğan ally criticizes 'One Man Rule,' Plans New Party by Yearend," *Turkish Minute*, November 27, 2019, https://www.turkishminute.com/ 2019/11/27/former-Erdoğan-ally-criticizes-one-man-rule-plans-new-party-by -yearend/.

43. "Former Erdoğan Ally Babacan Unveils 'Cure' for Turkey's Ills," *Balkan Inside*, March 11, 2020, https://balkaninsight.com/2020/03/11/former-Erdoğan-all y-babacan-unveils-cure-for-turkeys-ills/.

44. "Former Deputy Prime Minister Babacan Forms New Political Party," *Daily Sabah*, March 9, 2020, https://www.dailysabah.com/politics/legislation/former-deput y-prime-minister-babacan-forms-new-political-party.

45. "Former Erdoğan ally Criticizes 'One Man Rule,' Plans New Party by Yearend," *Turkish Minute*, November 27, 2019, https://www.turkishminute.com/ 2019/11/27/former-Erdoğan-ally-criticizes-one-man-rule-plans-new-party-by-y earend/.

46. E. Fuat Keyman and Ziya Öniş, *Turkish Politics in a Changing World: Global Dynamics and Domestic Transformations* (Istanbul: Istanbul Bilgi University Press, 2007), pp. 107–129.

47. Ziya Öniş and Barry Rubin, eds. *The Turkish Economy in Crisis* (London: Frank Cass, 2003), pp. 188–189.

48. Keyman and Öniş, *Turkish Politics in a Changing World*, pp. 122 and 260–265.

49. Ibid., see pp. 135–158.

50. See for example the collection of critical essays edited by İsmet Akca, Ahmet Bekmen and Baris Alp Ozden in *Turkey Reframed: Constituting Neoliberal Hegemony* (London: Pluto Press, 2014).

51. Linda Weiss, *The Myth of the Powerless State* (Ithaca, NY: Cornell University Pres, 1999).

52. Laura Pitel, "Turkey's New Finance Chief Faces Uphill Task to Turn Economy Round," *Financial Times*, November 10, 2020.

53. World Bank, *Firm Productivity and Economic Growth in Turkey*. Turkey Productivity Report 2019 (Washington, DC: World Bank, 2019). World Bank, *Country Partnership Framework for the Republic of Turkey for the Period FY18-FY21*. Report No. 11096-TR (Washington, DC: World Bank, July 28, 2017).

54. World Bank, *Firm Productivity and Economic Growth in Turkey*, pp. 51–55.

55. Ibid., p. 54.

56. Transparency International, https://www.transparency.org/en/cpi#.

57. Mustafa Sonmez, "Anxious Turkish Investors Eyeing Opportunities Abroad," *al-monitor*, February 16, 2018, https://www.al-monitor.com/pulse/originals/2018/02/turkey-anxious-investors-eye-opportunities-abroad.html; see also Martinne Geller, "Turkey's Arcelik Working on Deals to Expand Abroad," *Reuters*, March 20, 2017, https://de.reuters.com/article/us-arcelik-strategy/turkeys-arcelik-working-on-deals-to-expand-abroad.html; and https://boycott-turkey.net/koc.html.

58. Peter S. Goodman, "Turkey's Long, Painful Economic Crisis Grinds On," *The New York Times*, July 8, 2019.

59. Hakan Gulseven, "Türkiye Ekonomisi Nasıl Battı?" (How Sank Turkey's Economy?) *Independent Türkçe*, October 8, 2019, https://www.independentturkish.com/node/78276/t%C3%BCrkiyeden-sesler/t%C3%BCrkiye-ekonomisi-nas%C4%B1l-batt%C4%B1.

60. Ibid.

61. Peter Kenyon, "To Turn Turkey's Economy Around, Erdoğan May Have To Loosen Control," *NPR*, April 15, 2019, https://www.npr.org/2019/04/15/713387994/to-turn-turkeys-economy-around-Erdoğan-may-have-to-loosen-control; See also: "Turkey's Troubled Economy Needs Another Kemal Derviş," *Ahval News*, November 7, 2018, https://ahvalnews.com/asian-financial-crisis/turkeys-troubled-economy.

62. Güldem Atabay Şanlı, "Bottoming Out in the Turkish Economy? Well Not That Easy!," *PA International*, April 16, 2019, https://www.paraanaliz.com/intelligence/bottoming-out-in-the-turkish-economy-well-not-that-easy/.

63. The TÜİK (Statistics Institute of Turkey)'s report was mentioned in the Turkish daily Sözcü, an independent newspaper on February 28, 2020, https://www.sozcu.com.tr/2020/ekonomi/kisi-basi-gelirde-2007-seviyesinin-altina-geriledik-5651164/?fbclid=IwAR3rmPMK4jn8rdqEx7YSKZh6cCYucecuVOMGnaHVxq37cnJ_MmWJ5PYcVLc.

64. *BP Statistical Review of World Energy 2019* (UK, 2019), pp. 39–41.

65. Ibid.

66. Ibid., p. 52.

67. "Akkuyu NPP to be Completed in 2023," *Nuclear Energy Magazine*, 26 August 2017; Elizabeth Dyck, "Turkey Starts Construction of its First Nuclear Power Plant," *IAEA News*, 5 April 2018; and Sinan Uslu and Huseyin Erdoğan, "Turkey to build 3rd nuclear plant with China," *Anadolu Agency*, 19 June 2018.

68. Ahmet Davutoğlu, *Alternative Paradigms: The Impact of Islamic and Western Weltanshauungs on Political Theory* (Lanham, MD: University Press of America, 1994); and Ahmet Davutoğlu, *Stratejik Derintik: Turkiye'nin Uluslrarasi Konumu (Strategic Depth: Turkey's International Position)* 2014.

69. "The Davutoğlu Effect: All Change for Foreign Policy," *The Economist*, October 23, 2010, https://www.economist.com/special-report/2010/10/23/the-Davutoğlu-effect.

70. For the full text see: http://www.mfa.gov.tr/policy-of-zero-problems-with-our-neighbors.en.mfa.

71. "With Turkey-Syria Escalation, Worries Grow About a Tip Into War," *The Christian Science Monitor*, October 12, 2012, https://www.csmonitor.com/World/Middle-East/2012/1012/With-Turkey-Syria-escalation-worries-grow-about-a-tip-in to-war.

72. Sedat Ergin, "Moving Towards the Most Dangerous Phase in Syria," *Hurriyet Daily News*, February 20, 2020, https://www.hurriyetdailynews.com/opinion/sedat-er gin/moving-towards-the-most-dangerous-phase-in-syria-151949.

73. Gonul Tol, "Turkey's Endgame in Syria," *Foreign Affairs*, October 9, 2019, https://www.foreignaffairs.com/articles/turkey/2019-10-09/turkeys-endgame-syria.

74. Ibid.

75. Cengiz Aktar, "Turkey versus Russia and the U.S.: Decoding the Conundrum," *Ahval*, February 16, 2020, https://ahvalnews.com/turkey-russia-us/turkey-versus-ru ssia-and-us-decoding-conundrum. For historical detail on the U.S.–Turkey relationship, see: Şuhnaz Yılmaz, *Turkish-American Relations, 1800–1952: Between the Stars, Stripes and the Crescent* (London: Routledge, 2015).

76. Ibid.

77. Muhittin Ataman and Çağatay Özdemir, "Turkey's Syria Policy: Constant Objectives, Shifting Priorities," *Turkish Journal of Middle Eastern Studies*, 5, no. 2, pp. 13–35. See: https://dergipark.org.tr/tr/download/article-file/574246.

78. Independent anchorwoman Ruhat Mengi's social media self TV channel "Her Açıdan" interview video with Prof. Ersin Kalaycioglu on February 15, 2020, https://www.youtube.com/watch?v=aVLMaOI_Hyg&t=1771s.

79. Ibid.

80. "İnternet ve sosyal medya çöktü," *ODATV*, February 29, 2020, https://odatv.c om/internet-yavasladi-twitter-coktu-28022018.html.

81. *Reuters*, February 28, 2020, https://www.reuters.com/article/us-syria-security-turkey-military-attack/attack-in-syrias-idlib-killed-33-turkish-soldiers-hatay-govern or-idUSKCN20M030.

82. Alexander Smith and Elena Holodny, "NATO Member Turkey Takes Delivery of Russian S-400 Missile Defense System," *NBC News*, July 12, 2019, https://www.nbcnews.com/news/world/nato-member-turkey-takes-delivery-of-Russian-S-400 -missile-defense-system.html.

83. Interviews with NATO officials, Brussels, July 11, 2019.

84. Ziya Öniş and Şuhnaz Yılmaz, "Between Europeanization and Euro-Asianism: Foreign Policy Activism in Turkey during the AKP Era," *Turkish Studies*, 10, no. 1 (March 2009), p. 7.

85. Ibid., p. 19.

86. As quoted in *The Economist*, August 22, 2020, p. 51.

87. Henry Foy, Laura Pitel, and Michael Peel, "Russia, France and US demand Nagorno-Karabakh ceasefire," *Financial Times*, October 1, 2020.

88. Suzan Fraser, "What lies behind Turkish support for Azerbaijan," *Associated Press*, October 2, 2020. See also, Murad Ismayilov and Norman A. Graham, eds., *Turkish-Azerbaijani Relations: One Nation—Two States?* (London: Routledge, 2016).

89. Laura Pitel, "Turkey's Armed Drones Bolster Erdoğan's Hard Power Tactics," *Financial Times*, October 10, 2020.

90. Kaya Genc, "Erdoğan's Way: The Rise and Rule of Turkey's Islamist Shapeshifter," *Foreign Affairs*, 99, no. 2 (March/April), 2020: the online edition of this article available at https://www.foreignaffairs.com/articles/turkey/2019-08-12/Er doğans-way.

91. Burak Bekdil, "Election 2019: Erdoğan's Existential War," in *Ally No More: Erdoğan's New Turkish Caliphate and the Rising Jihadist Threat to the West* (Washington, DC: Center for Security Policy Press, 2018), pp. 101–120; Soner Cagaptay, *Erdoğan's Empire: Turkey and the Politics of the Middle East* (London: I.B. Tauris, 2020); Christopher C. Hull, "Erdoğan and Europe: The Fox and the Chicken Coop," *Ally No More*, pp. 75–85; Asli Fatma Kelkitli, *Turkish-Russian Relations: Competition and Cooperation in Eurasia* (London: Routledge, 2017); and David L. Phillips, *An Uncertain Ally: Turkey under Erdoğan's Dictatorship* (London: Routledge, 2017).

92. Soner Cagaptay, *Erdoğan's Empire*, p. xvii.

93. Ahmet Davutoğlu, *Systemic Earthquake and the Struggle for World Order: Exclusive Populism versus Inclusive Democracy* (UK: Cambridge University Press, 2020), pp. 220–223.

Conclusion

Must Authoritarianism (and Economic Stagnation) Be the Normal Eurasian Way?

IS THE PERSISTENCE OF AUTHORITARIANISM (AND THE "DECONSOLIDATION" OF DEMOCRACY) GLOBAL?

Writing in 2001, prominent Soviet and, subsequently, American sociologist Vladimir Shlapentokh argued:

> . . .despite all the wishful thinking of Western experts like Francis Fukuyama, only a tiny minority of countries in the world meet the requirements of the liberal model: a competitive market, effective democracy, and the observation of law in society. Countries such as Turkey, Mexico, Pakistan, Belorussia, Uzbekistan, Burma, and Nigeria simply cannot pass these tests. However, these countries functioned and reproduced in the past and will continue to do so in the future, using the same political, economic, and social structures. In some ways, these countries are just as "normal" as was Soviet society. A sober social analysis demands that scholars avoid their personal values as much as possible in their examination of the specific structures of a given society that account for its ability to function and reproduce over a long period of time.[1]

By way of contrast, the *Journal of Democracy* published two essays by Ronald Inglehart and Roberto Foa/Yacha Mounk in July of 2016 on the question of the apparent "Democratic Deconsolidation" underway globally, including in some Western democracies.[2] This trend seemed to be a betrayal of the common argument that wealthy democracies do not deconsolidate.[3] What about less wealthy, emerging, or otherwise fragile democracies— especially those with charismatic/nationalistic leaders, as in Russia and Turkey? Do they have a prayer of democratic consolidation in this environment? What is driving the trend? Why are citizens in democracies less content with their institutions? Are the consequences for prosperity and harmony dire? What is to be done (if anything)?[4]

Inglehart disagreed with Foa and Mounk's conclusion that democracy has reached its peak and is in long-term decline. While admitting the impact of income inequality and dysfunctional governance in the United States, in particular, he stresses:

> Despite the universal desire for freedom and autonomy, when survival is precarious such aspirations may be subordinated to the need for subsistence and order. But as survival becomes more secure, freedom and autonomy become higher priorities, and the basic motivation for democracy—the desire for free choice—becomes more dominant.[5]

This debate in some respects follows upon a set of arguments put forward by Joshua Kurlantzick in 2013 in *Democracy in Retreat: The Revolt of the Middle Class and the Worldwide Decline of Representative Government*. Kurlantzick begins with a discussion of the common assumption that, after the end of the Cold War and the collapse of state socialism in the USSR and Eastern Europe, usual processes of market-driven economic development would produce a growing and increasingly prosperous middle class and democracy. Hold outs were lectured that they were "on the wrong side of history." But in his view, beginning in 2001, it was not so clear that the failures of democracy were exceptions. Kurlantzick proposed that the spate of retreating democracies was a new and disturbing trend: democracy is in worldwide decline. Why has the middle class turned against democracy in some cases? Is the apparent decline in global democratization reversible?[6]

Kurlantzick noted that the early 2000s saw "the height of the antiglobalization movement and the questioning of the Washington consensus regarding economic liberalization, a change that would reverberate through young democracies, as many citizens who had linked economic and political reform would come to question whether democracy was necessarily the best system to produce growth and development."[7]

One could argue that the two (especially broad-based prosperity) are probably still connected, in that freedoms of information exchange and individual entrepreneurial behavior are crucial. Impatience with inappropriate policies and wealth distribution/greed from "market fundamentalism" may be the bigger source of the recent/current anger over failures of democratic political systems. Russia is not working economically, as it tightens authoritarianism and centralizes wealth, but the anger from this either has nowhere to be expressed or is displaced by nationalism and "wag the dog" behavior. Turkey may not be markedly different recently, as initial gains from economic liberalization and corporate competitive development seem to have been eclipsed by a dramatic downturn in economic growth and export performance. The Turkish Lira has devalued substantially, and inflation has induced serious dislocation for middle income urban consumers, not to mention the hard hit rural poor.

Kurlantzick points to the challenge of building a sustainable democracy. Quoting Jeanne Kirkpatrick: "In the relatively few places where they exist, democratic governments have come into being slowly, after extended prior experience with more limited forms of participation."[8] Kirkpatrick in fact was somewhat critical of the modernization literature that posits the crucial role of economic development to create the conditions for successful democracy, placing rather more stress on the need for "peoples" to learn and internalize democratic values:

> If Democratic Government is to survive, schools must teach democratic values . . . . Constitutions, Plato emphasized, are not made of sticks and stones, but depend on the character of citizens.[9]

Countries needed to attain a certain level of economic development to create the conditions for successful democracy; once this "modernization" was achieved, a country rarely goes back to authoritarian rule—one places bets on the role of the middle class as a primary moving force behind democratic change.[10] This claim does not fit well with the post-Cold War Russian and Turkish experience, but one could argue that the "middle class" was only modest in size in both cases.

WHAT DRIVES A POLITICAL LEADER
TOWARD AUTHORITARIANISM?

One must keep in mind the real goals of the principal leader. If the focus is on amassing wealth and/or centralized power, as one might argue is the case now in both Russia and Turkey, the middle class may well be anemic or distracted. Is there a cultural component to this—where it works and does not work—or is it a question of *leadership* and is thus more individually determined—compare Nazarbaev, Aliyev, Karimov, Erdoğan, and Putin. Which of these really have had the interests of their people at heart (as Lee Kuan Yew did by most accounts). Some would argue that Nazarbaev and Aliyev pursued broad-based national interests more than the others, but a systematic comparative assessment remains to be done.

What then makes a strong and effective leader? And how does the role of a strong leader relate to the fragility of democracy and the persistence of

authoritarianism? Writing in 2012, Jan Pakulski and Andras Korosenyi examine these questions in *Toward Leader Democracy*:

> . . . leadership is looked upon with suspicion (as a threat to democracy, rather
> than its essential ingredient) . . . . This suspicion seems reinforced by two
> popular confusions: one between democratic and nondemocratic leadership;
> another between "good" or successful leadership, on the one hand, and solely
> prominent or strong leadership, on the other. The first distinction seems more
> obvious: democratic leadership is based on mass trust acquired through open
> electoral competition and victory; nondemocratic leadership is not. Democratic
> leaders are subject to public critiques and electoral "recalls"; nondemocratic
> leaders are not. Consequently, it is hard to confuse Mandela with Mugabe, or
> Sarkozy with Gaddafi. The second distinction is less obvious, and therefore
> more vulnerable to confusion. Prominent leaders—who, as argued here, are
> increasingly appearing in liberal democratic regimes, and who are increasingly
> welcomed by the public—are not necessary (*sic*) "good" or "successful" in the
> sense of devising effective and successful policies and outcomes. They often
> fail to bring good governance (honest, transparent, effective, etc.) and deliver
> the expected mass prosperity, political stability, national pride and individual
> dignity.[11]

Citing recent examples in the United States and Europe, Pakulski and
Korosenyi stress the importance of the quality of leadership in electoral
victories, replacing the importance of ideology and party bureaucracy. In
recent years, some strong candidates have ridden a populist and nationalist tide; the establishment political party structures are challenged, indeed
defeated by charisma and anti-establishment rhetoric. One can see the rise
of Bernie Sanders and Donald Trump in the 2016 U.S. electoral campaign
in this context, as well as nationalist leaders in Europe like France's Marine
Le Pen, Hungary's Victor Orban, and Poland's Andrej Duda, as well as the
Brexit campaign leaders in the United Kingdom like Nigel Farage and Boris
Johnson.[12]
    Capitalizing on security concerns, anti-immigrant and anti-free trade sen-
timents that offer easy and simplistic targets for the apparent growing economic inequality in their respective countries, these leaders have been able
to mobilize large and disaffected groups. Many feel "left behind" by ruling
elites and find little to persuade them in complex economic theories and arguments (on the dangers of protectionism and the need to pursue comparative
advantage, the changing nature of manufacturing and workforce needs, given
increasing automation, etc.) or in appeals to expanded conceptions of human
rights. The party-based democracy developed after World War II in Western
democracies seems under threat, as "Leader Democracy" prevails:

Over the last 30 to 40 years, we have observed and experienced in almost all advanced Western democracies an ever more pronounced centrality of—and focus on—political leaders. This increasing leader-centeredness is detectable in both parliamentary and presidential systems: it is reflected in the centralization of authority in leaders' hands (vis-à-vis other segments of the political elite); in more firm, often unilateral, actions taken by leaders (and applauded by the mass publics); in a widening media exposure given to leaders and their personalities, especially in election campaigns; in the proliferation of "leader parties," and in the mass expectation and approval of "firm" and "decisive" leadership, typically contrasted with "weak leadership," the latter condemned as a serious political affliction. It does not mean that political heads always deliver such expected and applauded firm and decisive leadership. Nor does this mean that decisive leaders, even when emerging in the competition, deliver the desired outcomes: a sense of prosperity, stability, security and dignity-cum-national pride. Even though many leaders have failed to deliver these outcomes, the role of leaders has been enhanced, especially vis-à-vis other segments of political elites, such as party officialdom, factional bosses and the top mandarins. Leaders gain media exposure and public prominence unprecedented in their intensity, and unusual in democratic politics.[13]

Does this mean that there is an accompanying tendency toward authoritarianism, as we see in some Western democracies? Is it that democracy is not just changing in character from the post–World War II "party democracy," but is in clear decline or *deconsolidation*, after years of post-Cold War optimism? Pakulski and Korosenji seem to argue that the answer is no: Leader-centrism and leader-democratic configuration should not be confused with creeping autocracy, technocracy, tutelage, bureaucratic domination, or "despotic democracy." The latter types seldom involve systematic leader-mass "coupling" and do not rely on the open and fair competition for leadership that lies at the heart of responsible democratic government. By contrast, "leader democracy" is compatible with democratic elitism understood as representative and competitive elite rule.[14]

Paul Edward Gottfried pointed to the rise of the "managerial state" in *After Liberalism*, while Sheldon S. Wolin warned of the rise of "inverted totalitarianism" in *Democracy Incorporated*. Both volumes stress the changes evident in liberal democracies with the rise of the modern welfare state and an elite management system that threatens self-government and freedom. Wolin stressed that the United States in particular had morphed into a kind of hybrid state of combined political and corporate/economic power. Indeed, corporate power was no longer harnessed by state controls. This inverted totalitarian state is not morally or politically comparable to the criminal totalitarian Nazi and Stalinist states of the twentieth century, but according to Wolin, it nonetheless was a devastating threat to traditional liberalism. In his words:

> At the critical moment when a volatile economy and widening class disparities require a government responsive to popular needs, government has become increasingly unresponsive; and, conversely, when an aggressive state stands most in need of being restrained, democracy proved an ineffectual check. A public fearful of terrorist attacks and bewildered by a war based on deceit is unable to function as the rational conscience of the American state, capable of checking the impulse to adventurism and the systematic evasion of constitutional constraints. A politics of dumbed-down public discourse and low voter turnout combines with a dynamic economy of stubborn inequalities to produce the paradox of a powerful state and a failing democracy.[15]

These concerns are joined by a chorus of critics of excessive, misguided (capital) globalization policies that have made economic management increasingly beyond the means of national governments.[16] Some of this can be traced simply to Robert Mundell's famous "Trilemma"—the impossible or inconsistent trinity: that a fixed exchange rate, monetary autonomy, and free flow of capital are incompatible. This "triangle" is summarized concisely by *The Economist*:

> Only two of the three are possible. A country that wants to fix the value of its currency and have an interest-rate policy that is free from outside influence (side C of the triangle) cannot allow capital to flow freely across its borders. If the exchange rate is fixed but the country is open to cross-border capital flows, it cannot have an independent monetary policy (side A). And if a country chooses free capital mobility and wants monetary autonomy, it has to allow its currency to float (side B).[17]

Since a key tenant of globalization enthusiasts is not just freer trade, but the free flow of capital (so that foreign investment readily finds its most productive target), national governments often choose to give up autonomy over monetary policy. As the Greece debt crisis illustrates, this leaves national policy makers with limited tools to stabilize a debt-ridden economy.[18]

The conditionality required by the IMF and World Bank for loans and development project funding to countries often included prescriptions on freeing capital movement—part of the list of liberalization measures making up the "Washington Consensus." This often seemed to contribute to financial instability and especially the inability of governments to stem the effects of regional financial crises with capital flight controls.

Calls by Herman Daly and other ecological economists to "re-nationalize" economies are interesting in this respect;[19] at the same time Kenichi Ohmae and global supply chain enthusiasts sought to expand capital movements and make global transactions more efficient and de-regulated.[20]

Growing inequality, economic stagnation and insecurity in the face of rapid immigration impacts on employment and globalization over-reach seem to threaten liberal democratic regimes in Europe and beyond. Is the character of modern democratic regimes in danger of deconsolidation? Can an authoritarian regime offer a more attractive future economically? Russia under Putin and Turkey under Erdoğan increasingly offer little support for this prospect, as chapters 4 and 6 make clear.

DEMOCRACY, AUTHORITARIANISM, AND PROSPERITY

What then does this mean for the economic vitality, dynamism, and prosperity of the societies under authoritarian regimes, especially "Patronal" ones, as opposed to say Singapore under Lee Kuan Yew or the Republic of Korea before it democratized; both of the latter regimes were focused on national development goals (with hard/unpopular political choices/sacrifices) instead of personal wealth and power maximization. President Putin, thus far, would seem not to be operating in the same vein as Lee Kuan Yew, or indeed any authoritarian ruler who has pursued national modernization and broad-based prosperity as key national goals. Indeed, his criticism and reversal of the modest steps toward economic diversification and modernization instituted by President Medvedev would seem to suggest rather more priority to personal power and wealth maximization. So, what determines whether a strong leader takes the path of the "Lee hypothesis" or the path of Putinist patronalism, especially when beginning with an electoral mandate?[21]

Here we may look to a number of leadership studies for insight. For example, the early work on *Individuals in World Politics* by Robert Isaak may be instructive. Stressing an interplay of situational opportunities and psychological "need" drivers, Isaak describes what determined the historical impact of Lenin, Hitler, De Gaulle, Woodrow Wilson, Henry Kissinger, etc. Personal drive, sometimes with deep psychological components, but also including the value system of the leader, is crucial, but the timing of national and global opportunities, given the social and historical situations, are also important. Isaak's chapter on Lenin noted:

... the psychological dogma and arrogance of the belief that Lenin imparted to Soviet elites—that they possess the truth and key to history—will [would] continue to have a profound impact on future Soviet actions. Such self-righteous and rigid ideology reinforces and justifies the Soviet Union in the age-old

Russian practice of insulating the Russian people from Western ideas and currents and maintaining a garrison state at home. Lenin, most of all, represented the need of impoverished people for a comprehensive faith that justified the elites in controlling the masses.[22]

A similar selection of *Innovative Leaders in International Politics* was collected by Gabriel Sheffer in 1993, organized around eight questions on the requisites for innovation: (1) the role of personality versus institutions; (2) accuracy in perceiving the problems/challenges faced; (3) does the international environment present viable opportunity for innovative leadership? (4) Is the national policy-making process capable of responding to innovative leadership? (5) intelligence, energy, will, and determination versus soundness of the specific policies; (6) the impact of domestic constraints; (7) astuteness about timing and maneuverability; and (8) communication and effective incorporation of feedback.[23] Amnon Sella contributed a chapter on Gorbachev in this collection, noting the crucial role that domestic resistance played in constraining his attempted innovations (viz. question no.6).

In *Presidential Command*, Peter W. Rodman describes how character, focus, determination, persuasiveness, and consistency come to determine success and failure among recent U.S. Presidents. The case studies include paranoid Richard Nixon, who dissipated his strength and global knowledge in pursuit of trivial threats which then led to his demise, and George W. Bush, who relied overmuch on misguided bureaucratic consensus leading to a failed Iraq policy.

Eliot Cohen provides a cross-national comparison along similar lines, as he examines the role of four civilian leaders: Abraham Lincoln, Georges Clemenceau, Winston Churchill, and David Ben-Gurion in their management of the military in dire wartime situations. He delineates and confronts the common theories of civilian control of the military, namely that the prosecution of war should be left to the professionals: "To ask too many questions (let alone to give orders) about tactics, particular pieces of hardware, the design of a campaign, measures of success, or to press too closely for the promotion or dismissal of anything other than the most senior offices is meddling and interference, which is inappropriate and downright dangerous."[24] Instead, he argues from the detailed review of these four cases that strong political leadership can be essential to the success of military campaigns. Cohen concludes his assessment with a discussion of President George W. Bush and Secretary of Defense Rumsfeld and their response to the events of September 11, 2001. Here he traces the impact of Presidential determination and dependence on strong civilian advisors as the administration reversed the so-called Weinberger doctrine.

For example, instead of insisting on a guarantee of public support for the use of action, Rumsfeld declared, "If public support is weak at the outset, U.S.

leadership must be willing to invest the political capital to marshal support to sustain the effort for whatever period of time may be required."[25]

Writing in 2003, Cohen was not ready to pronounce a final verdict on this revised posture. Certainly President Obama took a different path in the prudence of maintaining extensive U.S. ground forces in Afghanistan and Iraq or in committing them elsewhere in Eurasia and the Middle East.

Carnes Lord updates the guidance provided in Machiavelli's *Prince* with his 2018 guide to *The New Prince: What Machiavelli Can Teach Us in the Age of Trump*. This includes specific suggestions on how to manage elites and how to structure and take advice and on the role of intelligence, communication, among other things. Chapter 10 on "Autocratic Democracy" offers an interesting discussion of the tendency of many democratically elected leaders to seek constitutional revision toward presidential and hybrid presidential political systems—away from the classic Westminster model of parliamentary democracy. Here, he traces the efforts of Charles DeGaulle in France and Lee Kuan Yew in Singapore to correct the perceived ills of a country's political institutions for the goal of more effective governance and economic policy. But Lord also warns that "the autocratic temptation is difficult to resist, even—indeed, particularly—for leaders of the stature of de Gaulle and Lee."[26] We can see evidence of this in many of the constitutional reforms implemented in Russia, Turkey, and much of Eurasia after the collapse of the Soviet Union.

Bruce Bueno de Mesquita and Alastair Smith distill the common behavioral patterns of authoritarian (and democratic) leaders in *The Dictator's Handbook: Why Bad Behavior Is Almost Always Good Politics*, arguing that similar imperatives are at work in each case:

> . . . a democratic leader does indeed have a tougher time maintaining her position while looting her country and siphoning off funds. She's constrained by the laws of the land, which also determine—through election procedures—the size of the coalition that she needs in order to come to power. The coalition has to be relatively large, and she has to be responsive to it. . . .[27]

Relating this to the U.S. political context, they discuss five key rules of behavior that both dictators and democratic leaders follow, though to different degrees:

> Why, for example, does Congress gerrymander districts? Precisely because of Rule 1: Keep the coalition as small as possible.
>
> Why do some political parties favor immigration? Rule 2: Expand the set of interchangeables.

Why are there so many battles over the tax code? Rule 3: Take control of the sources of revenue.

Why do Democrats spend so much of that tax money on welfare and social programs? Or why on earth do we have earmarks? Rule 4: Reward your essentials at all costs.

Why do Republicans wish the top tax rate were lower, and have so many problems with the idea of national health care? Rule 5: Don't rob your supporters to give to your opposition.

Just like autocrats and tyrants, leaders of democratic nations follow these rules because they, like every other leader, want to get power and keep it.[28]

Indeed, one might argue that these rules are not that different from those spelled out by Henry Hale in *Patronal Politics: Eurasian Regime Dynamics in Comparative Perspective*. Is it simply a matter of the degree to which some leaders will go in order to get power and keep it? Does a sense of altruism or public service to the nation only rarely play a serious role? Rule 5 (Don't take money out of your supporter's pockets to make the people's lives better.) may well provide the key answer to Putin's recent policies in an environment of kleptocracy. On the other hand, as Bueno de Mesquita and Smith argue: "benevolent dictators like Singapore's are hard to find."[29] They go on to argue that Lee is joined by Deng Xiaoping as

. . . the world's greatest icons in the authoritarian's hall of fame. They did not sock fortunes away in secret bank accounts (to the best of our knowledge). They did not live the lavish lifestyles of Mobutu Sese Seko or Saddam Hussein. They used their discretionary power over revenue to institute successful, market-oriented economic reforms that made Singaporeans among the world's wealthiest people and lifted millions of Chinese out of abject poverty.[30]

Some would also lobby for President Park Chung-hee (1963–1979) of the Republic of Korea, as another member of the "constructive" authoritarian list. Despite a sometimes heavy-handed, politically repressive rule, and charges of human rights violations, Park was also not personally (super) corrupt and is often credited with the development of the "Miracle on the Han" with policies of export-led growth and continuation of the rural land reform begun in the early 1950s. One can argue that the economic and subsequent democratization success of the ROK, rising from the ashes of World War II and the Korean War, offered disheartening evidence of the extent to which Soviet policies and structures had failed, providing added motivation for Gorbachev's reform efforts.

An interesting alternative look at what makes authoritarian leaders "tick" is offered by Riccardo Orizio in *Talk of the Devil: Encounters with Seven*

Dictators. In this study, Orizio focused on disgraced dictators who had fallen from power (Idi Amin Dada, Jean-Bedel Bokassa, Wojciech Jaruzelski, Enver Hoxha, Jean-Claude Duvalier, Mengistu Haile-Mariam, Slobadan Milosevic), noting that those still in office or that "land on their feet" upon leaving rule, rarely are reflective and "tend not to examine their own conscience."[31]

Not surprisingly, there is considerable variation in the individual circumstances of the fallen dictators (some in varying degrees of poverty, some in prison), as well as in the narratives expressed on why they have fallen and on what was good or at least common about why they acted as they did. For example, Wojciech Jaruzelski, speaking with respect to his 2006 trial for the 1981 declaration of martial law in Poland (to restrict the solidarity movement), argued:

> The newspapers have already pronounced their verdict, but I remind those armchair historians sitting, comfortably at home in their slippers that it was not I who decreed the historical circumstances. I only had the unenviable task of choosing the lesser of two evils. Whatever my decision, the results would have been negative. Mine were difficult decisions. No one has the right to dismiss me lightly as a murderer. I am a patriot. I saved Poland from grave danger. In December 1981 the Soviets were about to trample all over us. Even Gorbachev said so many times over.[32]

Others that Orizio interviewed took pains to explain that they were not "the cause of all the ills that befell their countries, but only of some. In their own eyes, sometimes not even that."[33]

David Wallechinsky and Clive Foss, both writing separately in 2006 expand the analysis of authoritarian leaders to compare, respectively, the twenty worst living dictators and the fifty greatest tyrants in history. The vignettes offered by Wallechinsky are brief and summary, but they do note some interesting points on how tyrants have generally come to power historically: inheritance, by slowly working their way up the hierarchy on a one-party or military regime or "entrepreneurs" seizing power at their own initiative. Once in power, violence or the threat of it is commonly employed, but an effort to seek support from at least a substantial minority of the citizenry is desirable. But, he stresses: "almost every dictator presents his citizens with a form of this argument: (1) Our nation is being threatened by an outside force. (2) Only I can protect our nation from this force and if you oppose me, you are opposing our nation and supporting the enemy."[34] Historian Clive Foss notes:

> Tyrants usually have large egos. A few even believed they were gods: Caligula demanded worship; al-Hakim still receives it. Bokassa claimed that he was the Thirteenth Apostle. Cromwell, Franco, Pinochet and most emphatically

Khomeini were convinced that they had God on their side. Many more, like Stalin, Mao or Kim Il Sung built extravagant personality cults that raised them to a superhuman level, and Trujillo, Bokassa and Saddam encouraged something similar.[35]

Waller R. Newell offers a thoughtful historical discussion of some of these themes in his 2016 book entitled *Tyrants: A History of Power, Injustice, and Terror*. Newell categorizes tyrants into three main (not entirely mutually exclusive) categories: (1) garden-variety tyrants "who dispose of an entire country and society as if it were their personal property, exploiting it for their own pleasure and profit";[36] (2) the tyrant as reformer—not a mere hedonist or profit-seeker but one who actually tries to improve society and the people; and (3) a millenarian tyrant—one "driven by an impulse to impose a millenarian blueprint that will bring about a society of the future in which the individual will be submerged in the collective and all privilege and alienation will forever be eradicated."[37]

Frank Dikotter examines "the cult of personality in the twentieth century" in his 2019 volume on *How to Be a Dictator*, which includes a detailed chapter on Stalin, as well as others on Mussolini, Hitler, Mao Zedong, Kim Il-sung, Duvalier, Ceausescu, and Mengistu. Dikotter argues:

> A dictator must rely on military forces, a secret police, a praetorian guard, spies, informants, interrogators, torturers. But it is best to pretend that coercion is actually consent. A dictator must instil fear in his people, but if he can compel them to acclaim him he will probably survive longer. The paradox of a modern dictator, in short, is that he must create the illusion of popular support.[38]

Dikotter goes on to describe the various strategies his sample of dictators used to gain power and eliminate rivals. However, he stresses:

> But in the long run the cult of personality was the most efficient. The cult debased allies and rivals alike, forcing them to collaborate through common subordination. Most of all, by compelling them to acclaim him before the others, a dictator turned everyone into a liar. When everyone lied, no one knew who was lying, making it more difficult to find accomplices and organize a coup.[39]

An ideology, like Marxism, can be important, but it can also be divisive, according to Dikotter. Loyalty to an individual dictator is more crucial than loyalty to a creed.[40]

Vladimir Putin and Recep Erdoğan can be discussed in these terms. They rose to power not through inheritance or a coup but rather by a careful progression of loyal support for key political actors and effort to build a patronal network of allies. For Putin, an appeal to threat from terrorism and later from the West was commonly imagined and expressed. A healthy ego and confidence in their abilities to keep domestic and international competitors or opponents guessing and outflanked have been evident in both cases. Neither is really a reformer, at least not beyond their early years. Whether they emerge as "millenarian tyrants" or simply power-hungry kleptocrats is not entirely clear at this stage.

But little concrete development of economic prosperity can be traced in Russia. Indeed, precisely the opposite seems clear. The Russian economy is weak and likely in long-term decline, unless the kleptocratic imperatives can be reversed, and the economy can be diversified away from dramatic dependence on oil and gas exports. Little evidence of movement in either direction is apparent. Certainly, there is no positive comparison to be made with the modernizing and broad-based prosperity raising efforts of Lee, Park, or Deng, all of whom worked with much less in natural resources, manufacturing base, or initial opportunities for trade and investment.

For much of the rule of Erdoğan and the AKP, the growth of a vibrant manufacturing economy in Turkey put Russia to shame, thanks to policies of economic liberalization as part of the campaign for full membership in the European Union. However, some inclination toward a return to economic nationalism in the face of souring relations with the EU and the impact of the global financial crisis, as well as a preoccupation with maximizing personal political power seems to have sidetracked Erdoğan's economic development success. Independent innovation and entrepreneurial behavior are less possible since the arrests and information clamp down ushered in after the attempted coup in 2016.

NATIONALISM, DEMOCRACY, AND AUTHORITARIANISM

What is the appropriate level of integration and community to foster effective and inclusive governance? We can clearly see an upsurge in Russian and Turkish nationalism, on the one hand, along with some effort to regain lost empires. There is also an increased reluctance to accept regional and global authority over key cultural and social priorities, on the other. Hungary, Poland, Italy, Greece, and the United Kingdom come to mind most readily among current European Union members in this sense but concerns are also evident in Austria, the Czech Republic, Slovakia, France, and Eastern Germany from time to time. Is the concern evident in segments of these nation states a sincere defense of national community and democracy or a reaction to promote moral universalism and internationalism versus national freedom and cultural sovereignty?

Yoram Hazony argues for *The Virtue of Nationalism* (2018) in this context, reminding us of why nation states evolved in the first place (especially national self-determination from empires and to safeguard local communities and cultures). He confronts the critics of nationalism and the proponents of liberal internationalism, a form of imperialism in his view that oppresses (authentic) communities and cultures. Hazony discusses the history of the rise of nation states after the Treaty of Westphalia that ended the Thirty Years' War in 1648, which he characterizes as a war that: "pitted the emerging national states of France, the Netherlands, and Sweden (nations that were, respectively, Catholic, Calvinist, and Lutheran) against German and Spanish armies devoted to the idea that universal empire reflected God's will, and that such empire alone could bring true well-being to mankind."[41] He also reminds us of President Woodrow Wilson's argument for national self-determination, realized somewhat with the breakup of the Austro-Hungarian Empire after World War I and the signing of the Treaty of Versailles.[42]

Hazony is not naïve about the requirements for viable independent states and the dangers of illiberal, aggressive nationalism such as that horrifically illustrated by Nazi Germany and somewhat evident today in Russia and Turkey. But the alternative of imperial rule and the federal myth is also a real threat to him. Collective self-determination—an order of independent states resisting imperial rule in the name of universalist ideological claims—is his answer.[43]

Aleksandras Shtromas, writing as concentration camp survivor, former Marxist, and Lithuanian patriot also stressed the importance of national identity and national self-determination, while warning of the persistence of totalitarianism and the continuing prospect for conflict. He remained optimistic about the prospect for world order, however, through the early transition years, until his death in 1999.[44]

William Galston helps to shed light on the "Enduring Vulnerability of Liberal Democracy" in this connection, providing keen insight on what liberal democracy does and does not offer national populations. He argued:

> Liberalism is a form of cultural imperialism that forces the proponents of traditional values to abandon their beliefs and bow to a new orthodoxy. Like every other creed, regrettably, liberalism has its share of zealots who push beyond its appropriate bounds. But liberalism stands or falls with the distinction between the public realm governed by public principles and a private sphere in which beliefs and practices at odds with public norms are protected from them.[45]

Galston draws upon the writings of Isaiah Berlin, David Miller, and Yael Tamir who defend liberal nationalism as a "coherent" alternative to illiberal nationalism and liberal universalism.[46]

Pierre Manent carries forward the realist and anti-Communist tradition of Raymond Aron in providing theoretical challenges to the European Union humanitarian and regional integration project, as suggested in chapter 2. Manent favors a "national community" in the face of what he sees as the unrealistic ambitions of liberal internationalism that leads to arbitrary decisions without sufficient theoretical justification. This is not the same concern reflected in the writings of Alexander Dugin (and more recently by Putin) about the viability (obsolescence?) of Western style liberalism and globalization, but there are interesting complementarities. Writing in 2014, Manent noted:

> It is because experience tends to prove that liberal mores and institutions are con-ducive to better government that we are politically liberal. This has been true over the long term (starting at the end of the seventeenth century with the Glorious Revolution in England), but this experience has not been felt with the same inten-sity in every epoch. There have been times when people have felt that liberal gov-ernment was failing to do its job and that other types of political regimes would allow for better government. The authoritarian, fascist, and totalitarian regimes of the 1920s and 1930s resulted not only from the (dare I say it?) perversity of cer-tain European nations or of the parties that took power there, but also sprang from a feeling that liberal regimes were increasingly incapable of carrying out the func-tions of government. Hence, Raymond Aron, in the first text in which he made his own political voice heard, took a stand against totalitarianism, but underlined at the same time the weakness of liberal regimes and their incapacity to ensure that the tasks of government were being performed with sufficient energy.[47]

Writing in 2016, Ryszard Legutko in *The Demon in Democracy: Totalitarian Temptations in Free Societies* argues that perhaps a different sort of chal-lenge faces liberal democracies in the wake of the true nature of the imperfect transition made from the state socialist regimes of the former Soviet Union and Eastern Europe. With some emphasis on the emergence of the politics of dignity and rights in Europe, under the sponsorship of the EU, he seems to point to a degradation of privacy, diversity, and excellence in favor of a more common pursuit, not unlike the theoretical/ideological goal to create equality in Communist society. In his view, both systems have similar historical roots and reduce human nature to the common man.[48]

Legutko served in the Polish Government and as a Member of the European Parliament, heading the European Conservatives and Reformists group (ECR). In this context, he observed the EU's posture toward postcom-munist regimes in Eastern and Central Europe. In his words:

> No postcommunist government, even the worst, was condemned by the European Union, while the anticommunist governments—the Polish Law and

Justice Party and the Hungarian Fidesz—sparked fury of enormous intensity. To this day, the former and present-day communists are under the protection of the European Union and the political mainstream it represents.[49]

Legutko argued that the opposition to Communism in this region was more focused on regaining national tradition and establishing independence than on creating liberal democracy:

> The crucial fact that has been widely ignored is that what gave the anti-regime movements the strongest impetus to resist the seemingly irresistible communist power, and what the communists had tried to eradicate from the very beginning but, to their doom, failed, had little to do with liberal democracy. These were patriotism, a reawakened eternal desire for truth and justice, loyalty to the imponderables of the national tradition, and—a factor of paramount importance—religion. People rebelled because the regime deprived them of what they held the most precious. Free elections and a multiparty system were mechanisms—very much hoped for, nevertheless simply mechanisms—but the massive resistance was not in the name of the mechanism; it was for the ideas this mechanism could serve to achieve. And those ideas were derived from the experience of the nation and, in some cases, that of a religious community.[50]

Legutko's suggestion that there is something ideological, even totalitarian in the particular way in which the European Union has framed appropriate behavior and national regime standards is striking, especially in light of the strong political resistance that has developed recently in the United Kingdom and several Eastern and Southern European members. Part of this resistance reflects distress from the impact of the Euro debt and refugee crises, but it also seems to reflect a more general view that the EU has "over-reached" in its pursuit of European integration. The need to retain more national control over borders, social policy, and culture was a driving force in the changing political climate in many member states. Some of this was evident in the failure of the effort to adopt a new constitution for the EU in 2005,[51] but the discontent evident in the UK's Brexit referendum vote (and subsequent parliamentary elections) may be a more striking symbol. The "democratic deficit" together with a supranational (nanny state?) governance inclination promoting extended "rights" may well be problematic for the future of the Union and for liberal democracy.

Chantal Delsol is not quoted or formally referenced in Legutko's volume. (Indeed no other authors are, and there is no bibliography or list of references—just casual mentions of the names of prominent theorists in the text.) But she would seem to provide some of the inspiration for Legutko's focus on the expansion of rights. In *The Unlearned Lessons of the 20th Century* and *Unjust Justice: Against the Tyranny of International Law*, she provides a clear set of arguments against this trend. For example, in the first of these two volumes, she argues:

> . . . we wish to escape our demons in order to restore the same human rights of which the past century made a mockery. Yet, in this effort to escape we are in the process of obliterating the very subject who legitimizes those rights . . . . Late modernity has rejected the terrorist aspects of totalitarianism, but it has not abandoned the ideological underpinnings of totalitarianism itself . . . .
>
> The dignity of man as a unique being without substitute is a postulate of faith, not of science. All of history demonstrates its fragility.[52]

In *Unjust Justice*, Delsol offers a broader critique of efforts at international law and world government:

> International justice thus remains steeped in the particularities it so ardently desires to transcend. It is not the rule of international law that it imposes but rather the rule of hidden particularities. International justice is still a matter of human power and authority, which no one can overcome. We can only dissimulate. Justice that wants to free itself from politics is still political. But it operates clandestinely, does not avow itself, and hides under the guise of the universal. It therefore is a politics that is more arbitrary and more dangerous than others. . . .
>
> We cannot truly aim at the universal without also acknowledging the *particular's* place and status. The search for unity should not take place to the detriment of *diversity*, which also possesses its legitimacy. Because it violates both, we should consider world justice and its correlate, world government, as highly undesirable.[53]

She concludes her critique with the sobering warning that:

> . . . the contemporary desire for total justice is doomed not only to failure, but it inhibits the only search for justice that can succeed. The proposed (and pretended) conquest inhibits the reasonable quest. Western arrogance engenders and increases opposition to the West.[54]

One may want to ponder the apparent rise of populism in Europe and the United States with some of these points in mind. For example, John Judis in *The Populist Explosion: How the Great Recession Transformed American and European Politics* traces the evolution of populism from its American roots in the 1890s and describes its recent manifestations in an engaging narrative. Toward the end of this description, he points to "Populism as an Early Warning." Here, he stresses that while charismatic leaders like Trump,

Le Pen, Wilders, and Grillo and the related populist movements spout racist, nativist, or xenophobic views, "their complaints point to genuine problems." Large segments of the populations in the industrialized countries of the West have been left behind by an "establishment" that has outsourced manufacturing jobs to China and Mexico, promoted unfettered capital movement and debt acquisition, and permitted large-scale low-skilled labor immigration that is often viewed as an ingredient of depressed wages. Some neoliberal/market fundamentalist policies have quite simply increased inequality.[55] The response can be seen (as a warning if not an effective cure?) in the unexpected Brexit referendum vote, the rise of Bernie Sanders, strength of populist campaigns in France, Denmark, Germany, the Netherlands, and of course the final Trump victory in November 2016, and the Boris Johnson victories in 2019–2020. Jan-Werner Muller offers a sharper discussion of populism and how to deal with what he regards as evidence of democratic decay. He offers seven theses on the danger of movements and leaders that claim exclusive moral representation of the people, as they reject pluralism. Number 7 is particularly relevant here:

> Populism is not a corrective to liberal democracy in the sense of bringing politics "closer to the People" or even reasserting popular sovereignty, as is sometimes claimed. But it can be useful in making it clear that parts of the population really are unrepresented (the lack of representation might concern interests or identity or both). This does not justify the populist claim that only their supporters are the real people and that they are the sole legitimate representatives. Populism, then, should force defenders of liberal democracy to think harder about what current failures of representation might be.[56]

Roger Eatwell and Matthew Goodwin offer an interesting analysis of this in the United States and Europe in *National Populism: The Revolt Against Liberal Democracy*, stressing the impact of the "Four Ds": distrust (of the "increasingly elitist nature of liberal democracy") destruction (anxieties about the impact "on the nation of rapid immigration and ethnic change"), deprivation ("resulting from shift towards increasingly unequal economic settlement") and de-alignment ("from the traditional parties, which has rendered our political systems more volatile").[57]

Jonathan Haidt, in *The Righteous Mind: Why Good People are Divided by Politics and Religion*, offers a complex analysis of the social psychology that undergirds our divisions and conflicts, as well as the prospects for intermediate human cooperation. His presentation provides some support for the view that a rationally derived universal set of moral standards or principles is likely simplistic and unrealistic. He argues that political and religious positions are much more determined by intuition or gut feelings than by reason and a process of rational analysis and deliberation. Accordingly, he posits:

. . . Beware of anyone who insists that there is one true morality for all people, times, and places—particularly if that morality is founded upon a single moral foundation. Human societies are complex; their needs and challenges are variable. Our minds contain a toolbox of psychological systems, including the six moral foundations, which can be used to meet those challenges and construct effective moral communities. You don't need all six, and there may be certain organizations or subcultures that can thrive with just one. But anyone who tells you that all societies, in all eras, should be using one particular moral matrix, resting on one particular configuration of moral foundations, is a fundamentalist of one sort or another.[58]

. . . We may spend most of our waking hours advancing our own interests, but we all have the capacity to transcend self-interest and become simply a part of a whole. It's not just a capacity; it's the portal to many of life's most cherished experiences.

. . . The answer [to why people are divided by politics and religion] is not, as Manicheans would have it, because some people are good and others are evil. Instead, the explanation is that our minds were designed for groupish righteousness. We are deeply intuitive creatures whose gut feelings drive our strategic reasoning. This makes it difficult —but not impossible—to connect with those who live in other matrices, which are often built on different configurations of the available moral foundations.

. . . We're all stuck here for a while, so let's try to work it out.[59]

The upshot of all this, in the context of the persistence of authoritarianism, is that the justifications that lie behind political commitments and public policies may yet have to do with the search for utopia (though not likely a "communist" one). But, political power maximization for personal edification (cf. Gel'man) or greed (cf. Dawisha and Åslund) may also be determinative.

Some of the EU critiques discussed above may be over the top in their attention to the danger of supranational totalitarianism, albeit in the direction of soft utopia. At least, one must recognize the remarkable economic miracle that followed the early establishment of the ECSC and the EEC, as the original six signatories grew to twenty-eight, and the customs union became a true common market in many respects. Establishing a Eurozone of common currency with a few too many marginal members was likely over-reach, as was the effort to establish an EU Constitution with an increased drive toward regional versus national sovereignty.[60]

Focusing on the national rather than the supranational level, our examination of the rise in authoritarian leadership behavior in Russia and Turkey, provides us some initial conclusions on some troubling questions. To what extent can authoritarian systems effectively pursue broad-based national development? Do they work more effectively than freer, more democratic systems of governance under some circumstances? What is it that determines whether or not an authoritarian leader will use centralized power for broad (popular) societal goals? Is there something necessary about the trends we have observed in the past century?

Francois Furet is striking on this, that is, on whether we are inclined to the *inevitability* of liberal democracy or the persistence of authoritarianism:

> Neither Fascism nor Communism turned out to be the ensign of a providential destiny for humanity. They were merely brief episodes, framed by what they had sought to destroy. Produced by democracy, they were interred by democracy. There was nothing necessary about them, and the history of the twentieth century, like that of the eighteenth and nineteenth, could have taken a different course: we need only imagine it without Lenin, Hitler, or Stalin. A true understanding of our time is possible only when we free ourselves from the illusion of necessity: the only way to explain the twentieth century, to the extent an explanation is possible, is to reassert its unpredictable character, an attribute denied it by those most responsible for its tragedies.[61]

Neither democracy nor autocracy is inevitable or necessary. There are patterns and tendencies, however. Progress toward liberal democracy can seem continuous at times, but we must avoid the trap of the illusion of necessity. Putin may rule Russia until he dies, but he may not if he cannot ensure more broad prosperity or continue to satisfy key elements of his pyramid of power. If he fails, his replacement may not be more of a democrat.

Erdoğan seems to have a more precarious grip on autocracy in Turkey at the moment. But democracy is not inevitable. Wuthrich and Ingleby are instructive on "how to beat a populist" with evidence from the Istanbul Mayoral election victory of Ekrem Imamoglu in 2019, despite Erdoğan's best efforts. Imamoglu employed an inclusive strategy labeled "Radical Love" meant to counter Erdoğan's divisive strategy.[62] Indeed, elections seem still to matter more in Turkey than in Russia, and there is evidently still more prospect for a diversified economy in Turkey than in Russia. But, as Wuthrich and Ingleby stress:

> While "Radical Love" may offer an escape from the populist trap, it creates expectations that responsive and responsible governance will follow. Rebuilding democracy, moreover, will require restoring legitimacy not just for one party, but for the whole system.[63]

President Erdoğan appears to be intent on retaining power with the help of cultural strategies. Given the challenge he faces by defections from the AKP party leadership and the mayoral election defeats noted above, he has sought to reaffirm his strength within his base of Islamist voters. Changing Haghia Sophia from a globally revered museum back to a Mosque on July 24, 2020 was a step toward building stronger commitment from conservative Muslim Turks, that he had earlier resisted. One can argue that he is only now show-ing his true "colors" as a committed Islamist himself, but it is also simply possible that he is seeking cultural support at a time when his political and economic fortunes seem to be weakening. Early on, he appeared to many as a reformed religious moderate when it suited him to appeal to a broader base and to raise his popularity in European capitals, but he is well aware of the strength that Islam has on the hearts and cultural traditions of many Turks. He has chosen to call on this strength. Turkish journalist, Ruşen Çakır, labels this a serious mistake.[64]

As noted convincingly in the papers presented at an important Harvard Symposium and published in 2000, "culture matters"![65] Many of the papers collected in this impressive volume focused on culture and economic devel-opment, but several tried to explore the ingredients of culture and relate them to political development. Are there measureable differences in social capital that have an influence on the viability of alternative political regimes, as Ronald Inglehart, Robert Putnam, and Francis Fukuyama discuss? Are there cultural determinants of the prospects for stable democracy or the persistence of authoritarianism? We see important tendencies in the political histories of Russia and Turkey which suggest that cultural traits do matter and can be called upon by a skilled leader to shore up a political regime that might otherwise appear to falter or underperform. Religious beliefs and the defense thereof are important here, of course. Putin and Erdoğan both have appealed to cultural identities and exceptionalism to move their populations. Thus far it seems to have worked, but there may be limits. Ronald Inglehart raises new questions on the hold of religion globally, as "modernization" and prosperity grow (or rather survival becomes more secure), but he notes that eighteen Muslim-majority countries are at least partial exceptions: "remaining strongly religious and committed to preserving traditional norms concerning gender and fertility. Even controlling for economic development, Muslim-majority countries tend to be somewhat more religious and culturally conservative than average."[66]

Erdoğan tapped into the religiosity of Turks that appeared dormant under Atatürk's secular state. The degree to which the secular state was supported among the Turkish population was overestimated, but the country in fact still includes a significant secular element, especially in the more prosperous urban centers. Accordingly, the religious cultural division in Turkish society is likely to be a substantial focal point for political competition for some time. Erdoğan's future in power may well depend on how well he manipulates cul-tural traditions to his political ends. It should be noted that there is evidence that this effort does not sit so well with Turkish youth—at least the so-called Generation Z—those who will be eligible to vote in the 2023 elections. Erdoğan's campaign to win them over in a virtual engagement on June 26, 2020 fell flat, generating substantial dissent and unwillingness to commit to vote for him.[67] Marlene Laruelle argues that the youth in Russia are similarly problematic for long-term authoritarian rule, joining middle-class urbanites who suffer "Putin fatigue". Unlike the Russian public of earlier years, they do not accept that stability and predictability must be purchased at the expense of modernization.[68]

Nonetheless, Putin has been motivated to draw upon Russian cultural traditions to build support that distract Russians from their economic suffering, sacrifice, and lost political freedom. His initial success in bringing order to the chaos Yeltsin left and presiding over an economic rebound in the early 2000s has proved impermanent, but his ability to rally nationalist sentiment and characterize themes in deep Russian cultural tradition that seemed not to fit well with Western liberalism added to or at least sustained his popularity. Chapter 4 discussed this in some detail in relation to the arguments for "Eurasianism" versus Western liberalism and globalization. G. Doug Davis and Michael O. Slobodchikoff take it a step further in an interesting effort to delineate Russian "soft power," as they describe Russian "cultural imperialism" in Eastern Europe, especially under Putin.[69] Pointing to vulnerability in perceived Western cultural decay, they discuss the impact of Russian (fascist) theorist Ivan Ilyin as justification for Putin's authoritarianism:

> . . . Russia required a strong state with a very powerful leader in order to stave off revolution.
>
> Ilyin's philosophy was quickly adopted by Russian policy makers, especially under Putin, who argued that Western democracy would not work for Moscow because Russia was unique and needed a strong leader to guide its reemergence as a strong state . . . .
>
> Ilyin's philosophy is important as a counter to Western philosophy because he stresses the strength of the state as being the most important factor of survival and that democracy is problematic as it can weaken the state.[70]

Davis and Slobodchikoff then conclude with five possible outcomes from what they see as "a destabilizing contest between the West and Russia that may determine whether small states are able to resist the cultural hegemony originating in the European Union and the United States." The least likely of these in their view is that Russia would embrace Western norms.[71]

Laruelle notes that Russian illiberalism or "sovereignism" was initially developed out of domestic needs but became an export product that curiously attracts support in both the political right and left of many countries.

That being said, she argues that in the end, Russia, especially after Putin, is reduced to serve as a counterweight to U.S. power, "challenging liberal dominance."[72]

THE THREAT OF PERSISTENT AUTHORITARIANISM IN A DISRUPTED INTERNATIONAL SYSTEM

Richard Haass, president of the Council on Foreign Relations and a long-serving bipartisan foreign policy official, warned of *A World in Disarray* even prior to the serious onset of the Trump presidency with its unilateral focus on "America First" and pull back from key international organizations and agreements. Haass compared the world in 2016 to that of the interwar period of the 1920s and 1930s. He argued that the rules, policies, and institutions guiding the world since World War II had largely run their course. Respect for sovereignty alone cannot uphold order in an age defined by dramatic global challenges and the return of great power rivalry. A "World Order 2.0" is required—one that reflects the reality that power is more widely distributed, and borders mean less. What provided relative stability for much of the post–World War II international system was no longer viable.[73]

Writing in 2018, Robert Kagan sounded a similar but even more pessimistic note in *The Jungle Grows Back: America and Our Imperiled World*:

> The liberal world order is fragile and impermanent. Like a garden, it is ever under siege from the natural forces of history, the jungle whose vines and weeds constantly threaten to overwhelm it. . . .
>
> The story of human progress is a myth. . . . If the last century has taught us anything it is that scientific and technological progress and the expansion of knowledge, while capable of improving our lives materially, have brought no lasting improvement in human behavior. Nor is history rightly viewed as a progressive upward march toward enlightenment.[74]

We should recall that Thérèse Delpech captured the essence of this truth in *Savage Century: Back to Barbarism*: "What is most peculiar about our age is the conviction that evil is installed at the core of history and our frenetic rejection of that conviction."[75] This complemented the detailed history of twentieth-century Europe by Mark Mazower in *Dark Continent,* in which he stressed the fragility of newly established democracies emerging from the breakup of empires after World War I, when faced with determined authoritarian aggression and the "Crisis of Capitalism" during the Great Depression.[76]

Writing in 2018, John J. Mearsheimer offered a devastating critique of the U.S. pursuit of "liberal dreams" in *The Great Delusion.* He opened his argument as follows: "Liberal hegemony is an ambitious strategy in which a state aims to turn as many countries as possible into liberal democracies like itself while also promoting an open international economy and building international institutions. In essence, the liberal state seeks to spread its own values far and wide."[77] Following his consistent and strongly held belief that a strategy of balance-of-power politics is much more feasible, less expensive, and indeed less dangerous, Mearsheimer provided detail on why liberal dreams by U.S. administrations, especially George W. Bush in Iraq and the broader Middle East, were doomed to failure and often counterproductive.

Amitav Acharya was among those who welcomed *The End of American World Order*, stressing the reality of an increasingly intricate "Multiplex World" and urging governments to go "Where No One Has Gone Before."[78] He described key changes that have occurred since the end of the Cold War in some detail, but his recipe for moving forward seemed lacking in the kind of realism that Kagan, Delpech, Mazower, and Mearsheimer offer so persuasively. Instead, he proposed two alternatives to the "hegemonic stability" system of the American World Order: a *concert* of great powers or a world of *regionalism*—neither of which seemed to offer much prospect for real stability. The design failure of the UN Security Council—requiring consensus among great powers for action—leaves one skeptical about the former, and the evident, indeed growing weakness of the European Union—our most advanced example of the latter—also suggests the need to keep looking for a recipe.[79] Pierre Manent is interesting on this in *A World beyond Politics?*, noting the impact of the "Wars of the Twentieth Century" and their aftermath, describing the complexity of the reoccurring threats to peace and the constraints on building effective global or even regional solutions.[80]

It clearly will be difficult to restrain aggressive authoritarian nationalism in a disrupted international system, with weakened international institutions and inward-looking major powers. As suggested earlier in our discussions of theorists Aron, Furet, Manent, Delsol, Hazony, Stiglitz, etc., the answer is unlikely to be found in the transfer of sovereignty to global or even regional institutions or in the diminution of the relevance of national borders. An international order that provides security from aggression and yet does not over-reach and weaken the nation state's ability to ensure security and prosperity is essential. Both Putin and Erdoğan had opportunities to remake their political economies to meet the needs of their broad populations, as well as to contribute to regional order; but both squandered them in favor of personal wealth and power gain and the desire to control their own personal political security. Moreover, regional order was disrupted substantially or at least threatened at times. For example, Putin fostered frozen conflicts, threatened former Soviet regions and meddled in domestic politics well beyond the Russian Federation. Curiously, this often led to counterproductive (for Russia?) mobilization by Russia's neighbors, but it did usually serve to rally Russian nationalist fervor. Erdoğan initially seemed to many in the West to be an answer to the need to bridge the gap between the West and the Muslim Middle East. A promising start collapsed as it became clear that he was almost entirely motivated by self-promotion and cultural expansion.

What then is the appropriate response to a disrupted and weakened international system, as authoritarian regimes persist, and indeed seem to grow in numbers? Do we risk another "Savage Century?" John Mearsheimer would argue for a thoughtful balance-of-power strategy: the United States (in the future?) as an offshore balancer when disruptive actors seek to dominate neighbors or threaten stability in an increasingly vulnerable world. Others might prefer Bismarck's alternative national posture (alternative to Britain in the nineteenth century) to seek to engage with all emerging powers—balancing against another state only after it is clearly disrupting order.[81] Continued, indeed strengthened, engagement with NATO can be valuable in this, enticing Turkey back into the fold, and perhaps encouraging Russia back to the Russia–NATO Council. Skilled diplomacy may be able to avoid driving Turkey into an axis of evil with Russia, as well as to avoid a Sino-Russian entente. NATO members in Europe need to take their defense preparedness seriously; Putin's incursions into Ukraine and the Baltic and Black Sea regions have provided incentives for this, but budgets remain tight in much of Europe, especially given the impact of the COVID-19 pandemic. Moreover, the inclination toward continuing to build the "Civilian Super-State" out of the EU, that James J. Sheehan described so eloquently in 2008, remains strong in Brussels, despite the populist fissures in many member states and the outright resistance in the United Kingdom, and parts of Southern and East Central Europe.[82] The replacement of President Trump's "America First" posture, with the more traditional internationalist approach that President Elect Joseph Biden has promised would seem to be a key ingredient in this effort.

On the economic side, national governments should seek to limit the worst effects of globalization. As Joseph Stiglitz argued, globalization of trade is not in theory wrong-headed. But the implementation of it, especially tax incentives to encourage shifting manufacturing overseas and reckless financial deregulation (at the behest of corporate financial institutions and speculating investors), should be rolled back. National governments should claw back control over capital flows into and especially out of their economies so that national economies can be managed more in line with broad national interests.[83]

There is no question that the postwar economic architecture, initially estab-lished with the Bretton Woods Conference of July, 1944—the International Bank for Reconstruction and Development (the predecessor of the World Bank Group) and the International Monetary Fund—was the beginning of recovery from the devastating war in Europe and Asia. These two institutions later transitioned to support the development objectives of much of the decol-onizing world, and more generally the rural populations of the global South, with project loans and currency stabilization funding. The establishment of the General Agreement on Tariffs and Trade (GATT) in October 1947 led to a long series of Multilateral Trade Negotiations (MTNs) which gradually reduced barriers to trade between a growing number of signatories. As Steven Radelet pointed out in 2015, this liberalization and financial assistance, as well as the work of other institutions of the United Nations system, like the Food and Agriculture Organization and the World Health Organization, did much to reduce poverty globally and improve health, food security, and edu-cational development.[84]

The establishment of the World Trade Organization (WTO) in 1995 sub-sumed and strengthened the GATT's commitment to free trade and estab-lished new trade dispute mechanisms, but by the time of the 2001 Doha MTN Round, most of the "easy" global trade liberalization had been achieved by the previous MTNs. Liberalizing trade in agricultural products and services, together with intellectual property protection, proved beyond where key members were willing to go. Agricultural trade was an important conten-tion between North and South, but also between the United States and the EU. This deadlock, together with the inability to find a global solution to the collapse of the stable fixed currency exchange rates of the "Bretton Woods System" in the mid-1970s, after President Nixon closed the gold-dollar exchange window, helped to mark evidence of the systemic "disarray" that Richard Haass spoke of in 2017. This was in large part what Amitav Acharya recognized, indeed welcomed, as the end of the American World Order.

There are obvious signs of economic instability that result in part from excessive globalization—well beyond trade liberalization. The challenge may well be how to retain some of the benefits of trade liberalization without the financial instability of the elimination of capital movement controls. If this cannot be done by democratic market economies, the prospect for authoritar-ian aggression and regional, perhaps global conflict is not small. As Thérèse Delpech, Francois Furet, Pierre Manent all have argued: We are not done with war.[85] At this writing, the Covid-19 global pandemic is weakening scores of economies even further. The recovery time and desperation is likely to threaten democratic governance in many countries and may well encour-age inter-state and civil conflict to levels unheard of since World War II.[86] Russia's incursions into Europe and Syria, and Turkey's push into the Eastern

Mediterranean, along with engagement in Syria and Libya are destabilizing at best.

THE WAY FORWARD?

Anne Applebaum is pessimistic on Western and Eurasian political trends in her 2020 book, *The Twilight of Democracy: The Seductive Lure of Authoritarianism*:

> . . . The checks and balances of Western constitutional democracies never guaranteed stability. Liberal democracies always demanded things from citizens: participation, argument, effort, struggle. They always required some tolerance for cacophony and chaos, as well as some willingness to push back at the people who create cacophony and chaos.[87]

Moreover, Applebaum stresses that dictators do not rule alone; there are scores of enablers in the media, bureaucracies, and political parties who may not share all of the ambitions of the would-be dictator but who find it politically expedient to accept what they see as the bad with the good. Sometimes it is a matter of simply ensuring more order in a chaotic environment. Sometimes it is a simple calculus that the authoritarian leader will provide policy or program gains that the opposition leadership would never consider, including personally advantageous (corrupt?) financial benefits.

Young democracies like Turkey and the successor states to the Soviet Union and the Warsaw Pact are fragile and susceptible to the "lure" of authoritarianism, especially when times are hard and order is threatened by weak economies and serious public health threats. Elections still seem to matter in Turkey, and political dissent is still evident in Russia, albeit stifled by state-controlled media and permit controls on opposition demonstrations; indeed, deadly attacks on journalists and key opposition leaders, like Alexei Navalny, continue despite little real evidence that President Putin's tenure in office is threatened by a precipitous decline in his popularity. Erdoğan's candidates did lose the mayoral elections in major Turkish cities. Turkey is indeed a "torn country," as Zeyno Baran stresses. Nonetheless, Erdoğan remains in firm control of power, at least until 2023. He continues to repress critical journalists and arrest potential "Gülenists" in the bureaucracy, the military, and the police. Social media are also scrutinized and controlled. What he will do if he really feels that his power is seriously undermined remains to be seen.

It is indeed ironic that Gülen and his associations have become the main target of Erdoğan's wrath. It was Gülen and his supporters that helped Erdoğan and the AKP solidify their power. The United States and EU did not see what was coming. On the contrary, they largely endorsed both Gülen followers and Erdoğan and his party. And Gülen certainly had great influence in supporting Erdoğan's regime from 2002 to around 2012–2013. By 2013, however, Erdoğan started an intense campaign to eliminate the Gülenists in all the various state institutions in Turkey, and even abroad. By most accounts, this caused Gülen and his followers to plan and clear the way for the failed coup of 2016. That gave Erdoğan sufficient reasons to eliminate and arrest not only Gülenists but also any perceived enemy to his rule. There is little or no sympathy for the fate of the Gülenists in Turkey. The question, today, is whether Erdoğan is strengthened or weakened by his authoritarian and repressive response which has gone way beyond the Gülenists. According to *The Economist*, "Nearly 600,000 people, most of them suspected Gülenists, have been investigated since the coup; nearly 100,000 have been arrested." And the numbers are still increasing.[88]

Resistance to external pressure from Russia remains evident in Ukraine, as elections continue to matter there, for example, in the peaceful and orderly change in leadership from Petro Poroshenko to Volodomyr Zelensky in 2019. Moreover, a political awakening seems to have emerged in Belarus, as the Presidential election of 2020 was widely condemned as obnoxiously fraudulent. The unbelievable claims that President Lukashenko had been re-elected by a massive majority of more than 80 percent provoked outrage in a population that had remained largely passive during previous political contests. The "last dictator in Europe" had operated somewhat effectively to maintain economic stability and political order and was careful to avoid ostentatious corruption and violent repression. His relationship with Putin has been tense at times, given the Russian desire to make the "union" between the countries closer, but Lukashenko was in contact with Putin on possible assistance. Putin subsequently promised to supply "police forces" if the opposition got out of hand.[89]

So what does this all mean? What kinds of political change do "we" face in the 2020s? We make no serious claim to predict the future of authoritarianism in Russia or Turkey. But there are some conclusions about evident trends and constraints that need to be reinforced.

First, neither country can be designated "Great Again." Domestic weaknesses remain serious, perhaps increasing, and the general failure to improve regional stability, if either leader was really ever so inclined, is clear. Indeed, turmoil and disputes on the Western and Southern borders of both countries seem to have increased in 2020.

Second, both Putin and Erdoğan seem to have the political skill and support to prolong their authoritarian rule for some time. We argue that this is in large part due to their own successful drive for centralized power, wealth, and personal security. Both are personally driven, and they have judged the weaknesses of potential opponents and the fragile democratic institutions with keen insight and patience. Long-term cultural patterns and influences have been important, and in many respects have enabled both Putin and Erdoğan to gain substantial support for their presidencies. Nationalism and religion (especially in Turkey) are clearly important to their relative popularity and have been manipulated skillfully by each, though to different degrees and extent. Erdoğan seems more politically vulnerable than Putin, but one must not underestimate the staying power of either.

Third, probably neither regime should be designated as "totalitarian," at least according to the most common definitions discussed in chapter 2. There is clearly repression of dissent and a certain degree of "searching for internal enemies." Russia and Turkey do not yet seem to compare with the worst abuses of Stalinism or Nazism, as Stephen F. Cohen stressed in his defense of Putin against "surreal demonizing" in Western press and political criticism, while warning us of the prospect for more than just a new Cold War.[90]

But there clearly are some troubling tendencies. Some of Putin's outspoken critics have been silenced permanently. Others have been kept from the political scene quite effectively. Erdoğan's critics seem less likely to suffer liquidation, but many have been imprisoned indefinitely, particularly the suspected Gülenists discussed above, while others have lost any possibility of earning a livelihood within Turkey. Moreover, the surveillance technology widely available and implemented as of 2020 should give us pause that the worst elements of George Orwell's *1984* dystopia may not be out of the question. On the other hand, the mobilization tools widely available today in social media platforms may continue to frustrate the worst instincts of repressive dictators.

NOTES

1. Vladimir Shlapentokh, *A Normal Totalitarian Society: How the Soviet Union Functioned and How It Collapsed* (Armonk, NY: M.E. Sharpe, 2001), p. 218.

2. See: Roberto Stefan Fao and Yacha Mounk, "The Danger of Deconsolidation: The Democratic Disconnect," *Journal of Democracy*, 27, no. 3 (July 2016), pp. 5–17; and Ronald F. Inglehart, "The Danger of Deconsolidation: How Much Should We Worry?" *Journal of Democracy*, 27, no. 3 (July 2016), pp. 18–23.

3. See, for example, Adam Przeworski and Fernando Limongi, "Democracy and Development," in Axel Hadenius, ed., *Democracy's Victory and Crisis* (UK: Cambridge University Press), pp. 163–165, and 178–179; and Juan Linz, "Some Thoughts on the Victory and Future of Democracy," *Democracy's Victory and Crisis*, pp. 418–420.

4. For some interesting suggestions and scenarios about these questions, see: David Runciman, *How Democracy Ends* (NY: Basic Books 2018).

5. Inglehart, "The Danger of Deconsolidation," p. 22.

6. Joshua Kurlantzick, *Democracy in Retreat: The Revolt of the Middle Class and the Worldwide Decline of Representative Government* (New Haven, CT: Yale University Press, 2013), pp. 26 and 170.

7. Ibid., p. 28.

8. Ibid., p. 36.

9. Jeanne J. Kirkpatrick, *Dictatorships and Double Standards—Rationalism and Reason in Politics* (NY: Simon and Schuster/The American Enterprise Institute, 1982), p. 237.

10. Kurlantzick, *Democracy in Retreat*, pp. 36–37.

11. Jan Pakulski and Andras Korosenyi, *Toward Leader Democracy* (London: Anthem Press, 2012), pp. 5–6.

12. For a detailed treatment of the complexity of this apparent trend, see Roger Eatwell and Matthew Goodwin, *National Populism: The Revolt Against Liberal Democracy* (UK: Random House-Penguin, 2018).

13. Pakulski and Korosenyi, pp. 147–148.

14. Ibid., pp. 149–150.

15. Sheldon S. Wolin, *Democracy Incorporated: Managed Democracy and the Specter of Inverted Totalitarianism.* New edition (Princeton, NJ: Princeton University Press, 2017), p. 259.

16. See, for example, Bhagwati, 2000, 2002; Daly, 1996; Held, 2007; Luttwak, 1999; Manolopolous, 2011; Reich, 2016; Sharma, 2016; Stiglitz, 2018; and Stiglitz, 2019.

17. *The Economist*, August 26, 2016.

18. Jason Manolopolous, *Greece's 'Odious' Debt* (London, UK: Anthem Press, 2011).

19. Herman Daly, *Beyond Growth: The Economics of Sustainable Development* (Boston, MA: Beacon Press, 1996), pp. 92–93.

20. Kenichi Ohmae, *The End of the Nation State: The Rise of Regional Economies* (NY: The Free Press, 1995); and George S. Yip and G. Tomas M. Hult, *Total Global Strategy* (Boston, MA: Prentice Hall, 2012). See also: John Odling-Smee, "The IMF and Russia in the 1990s," *IMF Staff Papers*, 53, no. 1 (2006).

21. As noted in previous chapters, patronalism and its corollaries cronyism and kleptocracy in authoritarian Eurasia are detailed quite well in Dawisha (2014), Hale (2015), Pei (2016), and Aslund (2019).

22. Robert A. Isaak, *Individuals and World Politics* (Monterey, CA: Duxbury Press, 1981), p. 75.

23. Gabriel Sheffer, ed., *Innovative Leaders in International Politics* (Albany, NY: State University of New York Press, 1993), pp. xii–xiv.

24. Elliot A. Cohen, *Supreme Command: Soldiers, Statesmen, and Leadership in Wartime* (New York: Anchor Books, 2003), pp. 4–5.

25. Ibid., p. 229.

26. Carnes Lord, *The New Prince: What Machiavelli Can Teach Us in the Age of Trump* (New Haven, CT: Yale University Press, 2018), p. 104.

27. Bruce Bueno de Mesquita and Alastair Smith, *The Dictator's Handbook: Why Bad Behavior Is Almost Always Good Politics* (2011), p. 19.

28. Ibid.

29. Ibid., p. 104.

30. Ibid., p. 158.

31. Riccardo Orizio, *Talk of the Devil: Encounters with Seven Dictators* (NY: Walker & Company, 2004), p. 4.

32. Ibid., p. 67.

33. Ibid., p. 5.

34. David Wallechninsky, *Tyrants: The World's 20 Worst Living Dictators* (NY: Regan/Harper Collins, 2006), p. 7.

35. Ibid., p. 6.

36. Waller R. Newell, *Tyrants: A History of Power, Injustice, and Terror* (UK: Cambridge University Press, 2016), p. 3.

37. Ibid., p. 4.

38. Frank Dikotter, *How to Be a Dictator: The Cult of Personality in the Twentieth Century* (London: Bloomsbury Publishing, 2019), p. x.

39. Ibid., pp. xi–xii.

40. Ibid., p. xiv.

41. Yoram Hazony, *The Virtue of Nationalism* (NY: Basic Books-Hachette Book Group, 2018), p. 23.

42. Ibid., p. 172.

43. Ibid., pp. 9–13 and 141–154.

44. Aleksandras Shtromas, *Totalitarianism and the Prospects for World Order: Closing the Door on the Twentieth Century*, eds. Robert Faulkner and Daniel J. Mahoney (Lanham, MD: Lexington Books, 2003), pp. 367–388.

45. William A. Galston, "The Enduring Vulnerability of Liberal Democracy," *Journal of Democracy*, 31, no. 3 (July 2020), p. 13.

46. Ibid., p. 14.

47. Pierre Manent, "The Crisis of Democracy," *Journal of Democracy*, 25, no. 1 (January 2014), p. 133. See also: Pierre Manent, *Democracy Without Nations? The Fate of Self-Government in Europe* (Wilmington, DE: ISI Books, 2007), pp. 33–46.

48. Ryszard Legutko, *The Demon in Democracy: Totalitarian Temptations in Free Societies* (NY: Encounter Books, 2016), pp. 31–33.

49. Ibid., p. 140.

50. Ibid., p. 142.

51. See: Norman A. Graham, "A Transatlantic Perspective on the European Union's Constitutional Crisis: Back to the 'Broader before Deeper' Strategy?" in O'Neill, Michael and Nicolae Paun, eds., *Europe's Constitutional Crisis: International Perspectives* (Cluj-Napoca, Romania: European Studies Foundation Publishing House, 2007), pp. 209–238.

52. Chantal Delsol, *The Unlearned Lessons of the 20ᵗʰ Century* (Wilmington, DE: ISI Books, 2006), pp. 7–8.

53. Chantal Delsol, *Unjust Justice: Against the Tyranny of International Law* (Wilmington, DE: ISI Books, 2015), p. 57.

54. Ibid., p. 133.

55. John Judis, *The Populist Explosion: How the Great Recession Transformed American and European Politics* (NY: Columbia Global Reports, 2016), pp. 157–160.

56. Jan-Werner Muller, *What is Populism?* (Philadelphia, PA: University of Pennsylvania Press, 2016), pp. 101–103.

57. Eatwell and Goodwin, *National Populism*, pp. 271–272.

58. Jonathan Haidt, *The Righteous Mind: Why Good People are Divided by Politics and Religion* (NY: Random House/Vintage Books, 2013), p. 368.

59. Ibid., pp. 370–371.

60. Norman A. Graham, "A Transatlantic Perspective on the European Union's Constitutional Crisis: Back to the 'Broader before Deeper' Strategy?" in O'Neill, Michael and Nicolae Paun, eds., *Europe's Constitutional Crisis: International Perspectives* (Cluj-Napoca, Romania: European Studies Foundation Publishing House, 2007), pp. 209–238.

61. Francois Furet, *The Passing of an Illusion: The Idea of Communism in the Twentieth Century* (Chicago, IL: The University of Chicago Press, 1999), p. 2.

62. F. Michael Wuthrich and Melvyn Ingleby, "Running on 'Radical Love' in Turkey," *Journal of Democracy*, 31, no. 2 (April 2020), pp. 24–40.

63. Ibid., p. 38.

64. Ruşen Çakır, "Erdoğan'ın en büyük stratejik yanılgısı [The Greatest Strategic Mistake of Erdoğan]," July 24, 2020, https://www.youtube.com/watch?v=Eqw S6zW8pW0.

65. Lawrence E. Harrison and Samuel P. Huntington, eds., *Culture Matters: How Values Shape Human Progress* (NY: Basic Books, 2000).

66. Ronald F. Inglehart, "Giving Up on God: The Global Decline of Religion," *Foreign Affairs*, September/October, 2020, p. 116.

67. "Why Can't Erdoğan Win Over Generation Z?" https://www.al-monitor .com/pulse/originals/2020/07/turkey-can-Erdoğan-social-media-generation-z-supp ort.html; see also, https://foreignpolicy.com/2020/07/15/turkey-youth-education-Erdoğan/.

68. Marlene Laruelle, "Making Sense of Russia's Illiberalism," *Journal of Democracy*, 31, no. 3 (July 2020), p. 127.

69. G. Doug Davis and Michael O. Slobodchikoff, *Cultural Imperialism and the Decline of the Liberal Order: Russian and Western Soft Power in Eastern Europe* (Lanham, MD: Lexington Books, 2019).

70. Ibid., p. 47. See also: Timothy Snyder, "Putin's Philosopher of Russian Fascism," *The New York Review*, April 5, 2018, https://www.nybooks.com/daily/2018/03/16/ivan-ilyin-putins-philosopher-of-russian-fascism/.

71. Ibid., pp. 111–119. See also: Catherine Belton, *Putin's People: How the KGB Took Back Russia and Then Took on the West* (NY: Farrar, Straus and Giroux, 2020).

72. Laruelle, "Making Sense of Russia's Illiberalism," p. 127.

73. Richard Haass, *A World in Disarray: American Foreign Policy and the Crisis of the Old Order* (NY: Penguin Press/Random House, 2017), pp. 11–14.

74. Robert Kagan, *The Jungle Grows Back: America and Our Imperiled World* (NY: Alfred A. Knopf, 2018), pp. 4–5.

75. Thérèse Delpech, *Savage Century: Back to Barbarism* (Washington, DC: Carnegie Endowment for International Peace, 2007), p. 175.

76. Mark Mazower, *Dark Continent: Europe's Twentieth Century* (NY: Alfred A. Knopf, 1998), pp. 17–40 and 104–137.

77. John J. Mearsheimer, *The Great Delusion: Liberal Dreams and International Realities* (New Haven, CT: Yale University Press, 2018), p. 1.

78. Amitav Acharya, *The End of American World Order.* Second edition (Cambridge, UK: Polity Press, 2018). See especially pp. 147–152.

79. The excessive predictions of the EU model as the future of humanity, for example by Mark Leonard in *Why Europe Will Run the 21ˢᵗ Century* (NY: Public Affairs, 2005) and Jeremy Rifkin, *The European Dream: How Europe's Vision of the Future Is Quietly Eclipsing the American Dream* (NY: Penguin Group, 2004) have been replaced by a large literature on its imminent demise. For example, see: Douglas Murray, *The Strange Death of Europe: Immigration, Identity, Islam* (London: Bloomsbury Publishing, 2017), and William Drozdiak, *Fractured Continent: Europe's Crises and the Fate of the West* (NY: W.W. Norton & Co., 2017). The EU's growing debt crises, and the disunity evident in its response to the COVID-19 pandemic serve to accentuate the arguments by Murray and Drozdiak.

80. Pierre Manent, *A World beyond Politics? A Defense of the Nation-State* (Princeton, NJ: Princeton University Press, 2006), pp. 70–85.

81. See the discussion on this option by Fareed Zakaria, *The Post-American World* (NY: W.W. Norton & Co., 2009), pp. 241–242.

82. James J. Sheehan, *Where Have All the Soldiers Gone: The Transformation of Modern Europe* (NY: Houghton Mifflin Harcourt, 2008).

83. See: Joseph E. Stiglitz, *Globalization and Its Discontents Revisited: Anti-Globalization in the Era of Trump* (NY: W.W. Norton & Company, 2018), pp. 75–97. See also: Manent, *A World beyond Politics*, pp. 86–97.

84. Steven Radelet, *The Great Surge: The Ascent of the Developing World* (NY: Simon & Schuster, 2015).

85. See, for example: Delpech, *Savage Century*, pp. 175–181; Furet, *Lies, Passions & Illusions*, pp. 75–81; Manent, *A World beyond Politics?*, p. 85.

86. See: "The World After the Pandemic," special issue of *Foreign Affairs*, 99, no. 4 (July/August 2020).

87. Anne Applebaum, *Twilight of Democracy: The Seductive Lure of Authoritarianism* (NY: Doubleday, 2020), p. 189.

88. *The Economist*, August 15, 2020, p. 48.

89. Henry Foy and James Shotter, *Financial Times*, August 27, 2020.

90. Stephen F. Cohen, *War With Russia? From Putin & Ukraine to Trump & Russiagate* (NY: Skyhorse Publishing, 2019), especially, pp. 108–109 and 205–212.

References

"Coronavirus in Russia: The Latest News." *The Moscow Times*, 15 Mar. 2020. www.t hemoscowtimes.com/2020/03/15/coronavirus-in-russia-the-latest-news-march-15 -a69117.

"Next Stop the Regions: Russian Lawmakers Approve Final Bill on Amendments to Constitution." *RT International*, RT, 11 Mar. 2020, www.rt.com/russia/482810-russian-constitution-final-amendments-bill/.

"Troubled Turn." *The Economist*, 9 Feb. 2012.

Acemoglu, Daron and James A. Robinson. *Economic Origins of Dictatorship and Democracy*. Cambridge, UK: Cambridge University Press, 2006.

Acemoglu, Daron and James A. Robinson. *Why Nations Fail: The Origins of Power, Prosperity and Poverty*. New York: Crown/Random House, 2012.

Acharya, Amitav. *The End of American World Order*. Second Edition. Cambridge, UK: Polity Press, 2018.

Adam, Jan. *Economic Reforms in the Soviet Union and Eastern Europe since the 1960s*. Hong Kong: Macmillan, 1989.

Ahmad, Feroz. *The Young Turks: The Committee of Union and Progress in Turkish Politics, 1908–1914*. London: C. Hurst Company, 2010. [First published in 1969]

Ahmad, Feroz. *Turkey: The Quest for Identity*. Oxford: Oneworld Publications, 2003.

Akca, Ismet, Ahmet Bekmen and Baris Alp Ozden, eds. *Turkey Reframed: Constituting Neoliberal Hegemony*. London: Pluto Press, 2014.

Akcam, Taner. *From Empire to Republic: Turkish Nationalism and the Armenian Genocide*. London and New York: Zed Books, 2004.

Akcapar, Burak. *Turkey's New European Era: Foreign Policy on the Road to EU Membership*. Lanham, MD: Rowman & Littlefield Publishers, 2007.

Aksakal, Mustafa. *The Ottoman Road to War in 1914: The Ottoman Empire and the First World War*. Cambridge and New York: Cambridge University Press, 2010.

Aksan, Virginia H. *Ottoman Wars 1700–1870: An Empire Besieged*. Harlow, England: Pearson Education Limited, 2007.

Aksin, Sina. *Turkey: From Empire to Revolutionary Republic. The Emergence of the Turkish Nation from 1789 to Present.* Translated by Dexter H. Mursaloglu. New York: New York University Press, 2007.

Alexievich, Svetlana. *Second Hand Time: The Last of the Soviets.* New York: Random House, 2016.

Allawi, Ali A. *The Crisis of Islamic Civilization.* New Haven and London: Yale University Press, 2009.

Almond, Gabriel A. "The Politics of German Business." In Hans Speier and W. Phillips Davison, eds., *West German Leadership and Foreign Policy.* Evanston, IL: Row, Peterson, and Co., 1957. pp. 224–240.

Altstadt, Audrey L. *Frustrated Democracy in Post-Soviet Azerbaijan.* New York: Columbia University Press, 2017.

Altunisik, Meliha Benli and Ozlem Tur. *Turkey: Challenges and Change.* London and New York: RoutledgeCurzon, 2005. (ISBN: 0-415-28710-3)

Andor, Laszlo and Martin Summers. *Market Failure: Eastern Europe's 'Economic Miracle'.* London: Pluto Press, 1998.

An-Na'im, Abdullahi Ahmed. *Islam and the Secular State: Negotiating the Future of Shari'a.* Cambridge and London: Harvard University Press, 2008.

Antonov-Ovseyenko, Anton. *The Time of Stalin: Portrait of a Tyranny.* New York: Harper & Row, 1980.

Appell, James. "The Short Life and Speedy Death of Russia's Silicon Valley." *Foreign Policy*, May 6, 2015.

Applebaum, Anne. "The Leninist Roots of Civil Society Repression." *Washington, DC: Journal of Democracy.* Volume 26, No. 4. October, 2015. pp. 21–27.

Applebaum, Anne. *Red Famine: Stalin's War on Ukraine.* New York: Doubleday, 2017.

Applebaum, Anne. *Twilight of Democracy: The Seductive Lure of Authoritarianism.* New York: Doubleday, 2020.

Arendt, Hannah. *The Origins of Totalitarianism.* New York: Harcourt, Inc., 1951, 1985.

Aron, Leon. *Yeltsin: A Revolutionary Life.* New York: St Martin's Press, 2000.

Aron, Leon. "The Long Struggle for Freedom." *Washington, DC: Journal of Democracy.* Volume 24, No. 3. July, 2013. pp. 62–74.

Aron, Raymond. *The Opium of the Intellectuals.* New Brunswick, NJ: Transaction Publishers, 1957, 2004.

Aron, Raymond. *The Industrial Society: Three Essays on Ideology and Development.* New York: Praeger, 1967.

Aron, Raymond. *Democracy and Totalitarianism.* London: Weidenfeld and Nicolson, 1968.

Arutunyan, Anna. *The Putin Mystique: Inside Russia's Power Cult.* Northampton, MA: Olive Branch Press, 2015.

Askerov, Ali. ed. *Contemporary Russo-Turkish Relations: From Crisis to Cooperation.* Lanham, MD: Lexington Books/ Rowman & Littlefield, 2018.

Åslund, Anders. *Gorbachev's Struggle for Economic Reform, 1985–1988*, Ithaca, NY: Cornell University Press, 1989.

Åslund, Anders. *How Russia Became a Market Economy*. Washington, DC: The Brookings Institution, 1995a.

Åslund, Anders. ed. *Russian Economic Reform at Risk*. London: Pinter, 1995b.

Åslund, Anders. *Building Capitalism: The Transformation of the Former Soviet Bloc*. Cambridge, UK: Cambridge University Press, 2002.

Åslund, Anders. *How Capitalism Was Built: The Transformation of Central and Eastern Europe, Russia and Central Asia*. Cambridge, UK: Cambridge University Press, 2007a.

Åslund, Anders. *Russia's Capitalist Revolution: Why Market Reform Succeeded and Democracy Failed*. Washington, DC: Peterson Institute for International Economics, 2007b.

Åslund, Anders. *Russia's Crony Capitalism: The Path from Market Economy to Kleptocracy*. New Haven, CT: Yale University Press, 2019.

Åslund, Anders, Sergei Guriev and Andrew C. Kuchins. eds. *Russia After the Global Economic Crisis*. Washington, DC: Peterson Institute for International Economics, 2010.

Atabaki, Touraj and Erik J. Zurcher, eds. *Men of Order: Authoritarian Modernization under Atatürk and Reza Shah*. London and New York: I.B. Tauris & Co., 2004.

Ataman, Muhittin and Çağatay Özdemir. "Turkey's Syria Policy: Constant Objectives, Shifting Priorities." *Turkish Journal of Middle Eastern Studies*. Volume 5, No. 2, pp. 13–35. https://dergipark.org.tr/tr/download/article-file/574246.

Ayoob, Mohammed. *The Many Faces of Political Islam: Religion and Politics in the Muslim World*. Ann Arbor: The University of Michigan Press, 2008.

Bachrach, Peter. *The Theory of Democratic Elitism: A Critique*. Boston: Little, Brown, 1967.

Bagci, Huseyin. *Zeitgeist: Global Politics and Turkey*. Ankara: Orion Publications, 2008.

Baker, Catherine. *The Yugoslav Wars of the 1990s*. London: Macmillan, 2015.

Baldwin, Richard. *The Great Convergence: Information Technology and the New Globalization*. Cambridge: Harvard University Press, 2016.

Banerjee, Abhijit V. and Esther Duflo. *Good Economics for Hard Times*. New York: Hachette Book Group/Public Affairs, 2019.

Baran, Zeyno. *Torn Country: Turkey between Secularism and Islam*. Herbert and Jane Dwight Working Group on Islamism and the International Order. Stanford University, Stanford, CA: Hoover Institution Press, 2010.

Barber, Benjamin. "Conceptual Foundations of Totalitarianism." In Carl J. Friedrich, M. Curtis and B. Barber, eds., *Totalitarianism in Perspective: Three Views*. New York: Praeger, 1969. pp. 3–52.

Barnes, Andrew. *Owning Russia: The Struggle Over Factories, Farms and Power*. Ithaca, NY: Cornell University Press, 2006.

Bartlett, David L. *The Political Economy of Dual Transformations: Market Reform and Democratization in Hungary*. Ann Arbor: The University of Michigan Press, 1997.

Basaran, Ezgi. *Frontline Turkey: The Heart of the Middle East*. London and New York: I.B. Tauris, 2017.

Bassin, Mark. *The Gumilev Mystique: Biopolitics, Eurasianism, and the Construction of Community in Modern Russia.* Ithaca, NY: Cornell University Press, 2016.

Bassin, Mark, Sergey Glebov and Marlene Laruelle. eds. *Between Europe & Asia: The Origins, Theories, and Legacies of Russian Eurasianism.* Pittsburgh, PA: University of Pittsburgh Press, 2015.

Bekdil, Burak .*Election 2019: Erdoğan's Existential War,* in *Ally No More: Erdoğan's New Turkish Caliphate and the Rising Jihadist Threat to the West.* Washington, DC: Center for Security Policy Press, 2018.

Belton, Catherine. *Putin's People: How the KGB Took Back Russia and Then Took on the West.* New York: Farrar, Straus and Giroux, 2020.

Bergesen, Helge Ole, Arild Moe and Willy Ostreng. *Soviet Oil and Security Interests in the Barents Sea.* New York: St. Martin's Press, 1987.

Bergson, Abram. *The Economics of Soviet Planning.* New Haven, CT: Yale University Press, 1964, 1980.

Berkes, Niyazi. *The Development of Secularism in Turkey.* Introduction by Feroz Ahmad. London: Hurst & Company, 1998. [First published in 1964] (ISBN: 1-85065-349-6)

Bhagwati, Jagdish. *The Wind of the Hundred Days: How Washington Mismanaged Globalization.* Cambridge, MA: The MIT Press, 2002.

Bhagwati, Jagdish. *In Defense of Globalization.* New York: Oxford University Press, 2004.

Birstein, Vadim J. *The Perversion of Knowledge: The True Story of Soviet Science.* Boulder, CO: Westview Press, 2001.

Bittner, Jochen. "The New Ideology of the New Cold War." *The New York Times,* August 1, 2016.

Blondel, Jean. *Comparing Political Systems.* New York: Praeger. Boberach, 1972.

Bolt Paul J. and Sharyl N. Cross. *China, Russia and Twenty-First Century Global Geopolitics.* UK: Oxford University Press, 2018.

Bourguignon, Francois. *The Globalization of Inequality.* Princeton, NJ: Princeton University Press, 2015.

Boyar, Ebru and Kate Fleet. *A Social History of Ottoman Istanbul.* Cambridge and New York: Cambridge University Press, 2010.

Bozdogan, Sibel. *Modernism and Nation Building: Turkish Architectural Culture in the Early Republic.* Seattle and London: University of Washington Press, 2001.

Bozdogan, Sibel and Resat Kasaba, eds. *Rethinking Modernity and National Identity in Turkey.* Seattle and London: University of Washington Press, 1997.

BP. *BP Statistical Review of World Energy.* Annual.

Brady, Rose. *Kapitalizm: Russia's Struggle to Free Its Economy.* New Haven, CT: Yale University Press, 1999.

Braguinsky, Serguey and Grigory Yavlinsky. *Incentives and Institutions: The Transition to a Market Economy in Russia.* Princeton, NJ: Princeton University Press, 2000.

Bremmer, Ian. *US vs. Them: The Failure of Globalism.* UK: Penguin/Random House, 2018.

Brent, Jonathan. *Inside the Stalin Archives: Discovering the New Russia.* New York: Atlas & Co., 2008.

Broekmeyer, Marius. *Stalin, the Russians, and Their War 1941–1945*. Madison, WI: University of Wisconsin Press, 2004.

Brock, Gregory. "Regional Growth in Russia During the 1990s—What Role Did FDI Play?" *London: Post-Communist Economies*. Volume 17, No. 3. 2007. pp. 319–329.

Brown, Archie. *The Gorbachev Factor*. Oxford: Oxford University Press, 1996.

Brown, Archie. *The Rise and Fall of Communism*. London: Vintage Books, 2009.

Brown, L. Carl. *Religion and State: The Muslim Approach to Politics*. New York: Columbia University Press, 2000. (ISBN: 0-231-12039-7)

Brown, Lester, et al. *The Great Transition: Shifting from Fossil Fuels to Solar and Wind Energy*. New York: W.W. Norton/ earth Policy Institute, 2015.

Brownlee, Jason. *Authoritarianism in the Age of Democratization*. UK: Cambridge University Press, 2007.

Brzezinski, Zbigniew. *The Permanent Purge: Politics in Soviet Totalitarianism*. Cambridge, MA: Harvard University Press, 1956.

Brzezinski, Zbigniew. *Ideology and Power in Soviet Politics*. Revised Edition. New York: Praeger, 1967.

Brzezinski, Zbigniew. *The Grand Failure: The Birth and Death of Communism in the Twentieth Century*. New York: Scribner, 1989. London: Macdonald, 1990.

Buchheim, Hans. *Totalitarian Rule: Its Nature and Characteristics*. Middletown, CT: Wesleyan University Press, 1968.

Buckley, William Joseph. ed. *Kosovo: Contending Voices on Balkan Interventions* Grand Rapids, MI: Eerdmans Publishing Co., 2000.

Bueno de Mesquita, Bruce and Alastair Smith. *The Logic of Political Survival*. Cambridge, MA: The MIT Press. 2003.

Bueno de Mesquita, Bruce and Alastair Smith. *The Dictator's Handbook: Why Bad Behavior is Almost Always Good Politics*. New York: Perseus/Public Affairs, 2011.

Bunce, Valerie J. and Sharon L. Wolchik. *Defeating Authoritarian Leaders in Postcommunist Countries*. New York: Cambridge University Press, 2011.

Burns, James McGregor. "Moscow-Bonn Pact: A Historian's Assessment." *The New York Times*, August 13, 1970. p. 3.

Burrowes, Robert. "Totalitarianism: The Revised Standard Version." *World Politics*. Volume 21. 1969. pp. 272–294.

Cagaptay, Soner. *The Rise of Turkey: The Twenty-First Century's First Muslim Power*. N.p.: Potomac Books; The University of Nebraska Press, 2014.

Cagaptay, Soner. *The New Sultan: Erdoğan adn the Crisis o Modern Turkey*. London: I.B. Tauris, 2017.

Cagaptay, Soner. *Erdoğan's Empire: Turkey and the Politics of the Middle East*. London: I.B. Tauris, 2020.

Çarkoğlu, Ali and Ersin Kalaycıoğlu. *Turkish Democracy Today: Elections, Protest and Stability in an Islamic Society*. New York: I.B. Tauris, 2007.

Central Intelligence Agency. "Soviet Economic Problems and Prospects." National Intelligence Estimate. 11. 5. 67. May 25, 1967.

Central Intelligence Agency. *Gross National Product of the USSR, 1950–1982*. Washington, DC: Government Printing Office, 1982.

Central Intelligence Agency. "Measures of Soviet Gross National Product in 1982 Prices." November 1990. Joint Economic Committee. U.S. Congress.

Chapman, Brian. *Police State.* London: Pall Mall, 1970.

Charles River Editors. *Vladimir Putin: The Controversial Life of Russia's President.* San Bernardino, CA, 2015.

Ciddi, Sinan. *Kemalism in Turkish Politics: The Republican People's Party, Secularism and Nationalism.* Routledge Studies in Middle Eastern Politics. London and New York: Routledge, 2009.

Cinar, Alev. *Modernity, Islam, and Secularism in Turkey: Bodies, Places, and Time.* Public Worlds Series, Volume 14. Minneapolis and London: University of Minnesota Press, 2005.

Cizre, Umit. *Secular and Islamic Politics in Turkey: The Making of the Justice and Development Party.* Routledge Studies in Middle Eastern Politics. London and New York: Routledge, 2008.

Clark, Bruce. *Twice a Stranger: The Mass Expulsions that Forged Modern Greece and Turkey.* Cambridge, MA: Harvard University Press, 2006.

Clover, Charles. *Black Wind, White Snow: The Rise of Russia's New Nationalism.* New Haven, CT: Yale University Press, 2016.

Cohen, Elliot A. *Supreme Command: Soldiers, Statesmen, and Leadership in Wartime.* New York: Anchor Books, 2003.

Cohen, Stephen F. *Failed Crusade: America and the Tragedy of Post-Communist Russia.* New York: W.W. Norton, 2000.

Cohen, Stephen F. *War with Russia? From Putin and Ukraine to Trump and Russiagate.* New York: Skyhorse Publishing, 2019.

Cohen, Stephen F. and Katrina Vanden Heuvel. *Voices of Glasnost: Interviews with Gorbachev's Reformers.* New York: W.W. Norton, 1989.

Colton, Timothy J. *The Dilemma of Reform in the Soviet Union.* New York: Council on Foreign Affairs, 1984.

Conquest, Robert. *The Great Terror: A Reassessment.* Oxford, UK: Oxford University Press, 1990.

Cook, Steven A. *Ruling But Not Governing: The Military and Political Development in Egypt, Algeria, and Turkey.* Baltimore: The Johns Hopkins University Press, 2007.

Cooley, Alexander. *Great Game, Local Rules: The New Great Power Contest in Central Asia.* UK: Oxford University Press, 2012.

Cooley, Alexander. "Countering Democratic Tools." *Washington, DC: Journal of Democracy.* Volume 26, No. 3. July, 2015. pp. 48–63.

Cooley, Alexander and John Heathershaw. *Dictators Without Borders: Power and Money in Central Asia.* New Haven, CT: Yale University Press, 2017.

Crane, Keith and Artur Usanov. "Role of High-Technology Industries." In Åslund, Anders, Sergei Guriev and Andrew C. Kuchins, eds., *Russia after the Global Economic Crisis.* Washington, DC: Peterson Institute for International Economics, 2010. pp. 95–124.

Crowley, Michael. "Why Putin Hates Hillary." *Politico,* July 25, 2016.

Crowley, Roger. *Constantinople: The Last Great Siege, 1453.* London: Faber and Faber, 2005.

Dagi, Ihsan. *Turkey: Between Democracy and Militarism. Post Kemalist Perspectives.* Ankara: Orion Kitabevi, 2008.

Dallin, Alexander. "Causes of the Collapse of the USSR." *London: Post-Soviet Affairs.* Volume 8. No. 2. 1992. pp. 279–302.

Dalpino, Cathrin E. *Deferring Democracy: Promoting Openness in Authoritarian Regimes.* Washington, DC: The Brookings Institution, 2000.

Daly, Herman. *Beyond Growth: The Economics of Sustainable Development.* Boston, MA: Beacon Press, 1996.

Davies, R.W. and Stephen G. Wheatcroft. *The Years of Hunger: Soviet Agriculture, 1931–1933.* London: Palgrave/Macmillan, 2009.

Davis, G. Doug and Michael O. Slobodchikoff. *Cultural Imperialism and the Decline of the Liberal Order: Russian and Western Soft Power in Eastern Europe.* Lanham, MD: Lexington Books/Rowman & Littlefield, 2018.

Davison, Andrew. *Secularism and Revivalism in Turkey: A Hermeneutic Reconsideration.* New Haven and London: Yale University Press, 1998.

Davutoglu, Ahmet. *Alternative Paradigms: The Impact of Islamic and Western Weltanshauungs on Political Theory.* Lanham, MD: University Press of America, 1994.

Davutoglu, Ahmet. *Stratejik Derinlik: Turkiye'nin Uluslararasi Konumu (Strategic Depth: Turkey's International Position)* 2014.

Davutoglu, Ahmet. *Systemic earthquake and the Struggle for World Order: Exclusive Populism versus Inclusive Democracy.* UK: Cambridge University Press, 2020.

Dawisha, Karen. *Putin's Kleptocracy: Who Owns Russia?* New York: Simon and Schuster, 2014.

Deibert, Ron. "Cyberspace Under Siege." *Washington, DC: Journal of Democracy.* Volume 26, No. 3. July, 2015. pp. 64–78.

De Jonge, Alex. *Stalin and the Shaping of the Soviet Union.* New York: William Morrow and Co., Inc, 1986.

Dellecker, Adrian and Thomas Gomart, eds. *Russian Energy Security and Foreign Policy.* London: Routledge, 2011.

Delpech, Therese. *Savage Century: Back to Barbarism.* Washington, DC: Carnegie Endowment for International Peace, 2007.

Delsol, Chantal. *The Unlearned Lessons of the 20th Century: An Essay on Late Modernity.* Wilmington, DE: ISI Books, 2006.

Delsol, Chantal. *Unjust Justice: Against the Tyranny of International Law.* Wilmington, DE: ISI Books, 2015.

Demir, Mustafa. *Geopolitics of Turkey-Kurdistan Relations: Cooperation, Security Dilemmas, and Economies.* Lanham, MD: Lexington Books/Rowman & Littlefield, 2019.

Denes, Ivan Zoltan, ed. *Liberty and the Search for Identity: Liberal Nationalisms and the Legacy of Empires.* Budapest and New York: Central European University Press, 2006.

Deringil, Selim. *The Well-Protected Domains: Ideology and the Legitimation of Power in the Ottoman Empire, 1876–1909.* London and New York: I. B. Tauris, 1999.

Diamond, Larry. *Developing Democracy: Toward Consolidation.* Baltimore, MD: Johns Hopkins University Press, 1999.

Diamond, Larry. "Toward Democratic Consolidation." In Larry Diamond and Marc F. Plattner, eds., *The Global Resurgence of Democracy.* Second Edition. Baltimore, MD: Johns Hopkins University Press, 1996. pp. 227–240.

Dicken, Peter. *Global Shift: Reshapint the Global Economic Map in the 21ˢᵗ Century.* New York: The Guilford Press, 2003.

Diamond, Larry, Marc F. Plattner and Daniel Brumberg, eds. *Islam and Democracy in the Middle East.* Baltimore and London: The Johns Hopkins University Press, 2003.

Dikotter, Frank. *How to Be a Dictator: The Cult of Personality in the Twentieth Century.* London: Bloomsbury, 2019.

Dimitrov, Martin K. *Why Communism Did Not Collapse: Understanding Authoritarian Regime Resilience in Asia and Europe.* Cambridge, UK: Cambridge University Press, 2013.

Dindar, Cemal. *Bi'at ve Öfke: Recep Tayyip Erdoğan'ın Psikobiyografisi.* Istanbul: Telos Yayınevi, 2014.

Dismorr, Ann. *Turkey Decoded.* London, San Francisco, and Beirut: SAQI, 2008.

Djilas, Milovan. *The New Class: An Analysis of the Communist System.* New York: Praeger, 1957.

Drozdiak, William. *Fractured Continent: Europe's Crises and the Fate of the West.* New York: W.W. Norton, 2017.

Dugin, Alexander. *The Foundations of Geopolitics.* Russian Edition. Moscow: Arktogia, 1997.

Dugin, Alexander. *Eurasian Mission: An Introduction to Neo-Eurasianism.* London: Arktos, 2014a.

Dugin, Alexander. *Putin vs. Putin: Vladiir Putin Viewed from the Right.* London: Arktos, 2014b.

Dugin, Alexander. *The War of the World-Island: The Geopolitics of Contemporary Russia.* London: Arktos, 2015.

Dundar, Can. *We Are Arrested: A Journalist's Notes From A Turkish Prison.* London: Biteback Publishing, 2016.

Dunlop, John B. "How Many Soldiers and Civilians Died During the Russo-Chechen War of 1994–1996?" *Central Asian Survey.* Volume 19. 2000. pp. 3–4.

Dunn, John . *Democracy: A History.* New York: Atlantic Monthly Press, 2005.

Easter, Gerald M. "The Russian State in the Time of Putin." *London: Post-Soviet Affairs.* Volume 24, No. 3. July–September, 2008. pp. 199–230.

Eatwell, Roger and Matthew Goodwin. *National Populism: The Revolt Against Liberal Democracy.* UK: Random House-Penguin/Pelican Books, 2018.

Ebaugh, Helen Rose. *The Gülen Movement: A Sociological Analysis of a Civic Movement Rooted in Moderate Islam.* Dordrecht, Germany: Springer, 2010.

Eggers, Andrew, Clifford Gaddy and Carol Graham. "Well-Being and Unemployment in Russia in the 1990s: Can Society's Suffering be Individuals' Solace?" *Journal of Socio-Economics.* Volume 35. 2006. pp. 209–242.

Ellman, Michael. *Soviet Planning Today: Proposals for an Optimally Functioning Economic System.* Cambridge, UK: Cambridge University, Department of Applied Economics, Occasional Paper 25. Cambridge University Press, 1972.

El-Shagi, Makram, Jarko Fidrmuc and Steven Yamarik. "Inequality and Credit Growth in Russian Regions," *CFDS Discussion Paper Series.* June 4, 2019. pp. 1–19.

Enayat, Hamid. *Modern Islamic Political Thought.* Foreword by Roy P. Mottahedeh. London and New York: I.B. Tauris, 2005. [First published in 1982] (ISBN: 1-85043-466-2)

European Bank for Reconstruction and Development. *Transition Report 2000: Employment, Skills and Transition,* 2000.

European Bank for Reconstruction and Development. *Life in Transition: A Decade of Measuring Transition,* 2017.

European Bank for Reconstruction and Development. *Regional Economic Prospects in the EBRD Regions: Stalling Engines of Growth.* November, 2019a.

European Bank for Reconstruction and Development. *Transition Report 2019–20: Better Governance, Better Economies,* 2019b.

European Bank for Reconstruction and Development. *Transition Report 2019–20: Russia.* London, 2019c.

European Bank for Reconstruction and Development. *Transition Report 2019–20: Turkey.* London, 2019d.

Fairbanks, Charles H. and Alexi Gugushvili. "A New Chance for Georgian Democracy." *Journal of Democracy.* Volume 24, No. 1. January, 2013. pp. 117–127.

Feiwel, George R. *The Soviet Quest for Economic Efficiency: Issues, Controversies, and Reforms.* New York: Praeger, 1972.

Felshtinsky, Yuriy and Vladimir Pribylovskiy. *The Age of Assassins: The Rise and Rise of Vladimir Putin.* London: Gibson Square, 2008a.

Felshtinsky, Yuriy and Vladimir Pribylovskiy. *The Corporation: Russia and the KGB in the Age of President Putin.* New York: Encounter Books, 2008b.

Findley, Caret Vaughn. *The Turks in World History.* Oxford and New York: Oxford University Press, 2005. (ISBN: 0-19-516770-8)

Findley, Caret Vaughn. *Turkey, Islam, Nationalism, and Modernity: A History, 1789–2007.* New Haven and London: Yale University Press, 2010.

Finkel, Caroline. *Osman's Dream: The Story of the Ottoman Empire 1300–1923.* New York: Basic Books, 2005.

Fitzpatrick, Sheila. *Stalin's Peasants: Resistance and Survival in the Russian Village After Collectivization.* Oxford, UK: Oxford University Press, 1994.

Fitzpatrick, Sheila. *Everyday Stalinism, Ordinary Life in Extraordinary Times; Soviet Russia in the 1930s.* New York: Oxford University Press, 1999.

Foa, Roberto Stefan and Yacha Mounk. "The Danger of Deconsolidation: The Democratic Disconnect." *Washington, DC: Journal of Democracy.* Volume 27, No. 3. July, 2016. pp. 5–17.

Fortescue, Stephen. *Russia's Oil Barons and Metal Magnates: Oligarchs and the State in Transition.* New York: Palgrave Macmillan, 2006.

Foss, Clive. *The Tyrants: 2500 Years of Absolute Power and Corruption.* London: Quercus Publishing, 2006.

Foy, Henry. "Russia: Adapting to Sanctions Leaves Economy in Robust Health." *Financial Times*, January 29, 2020.

Foy, Henry, Laura Pitel and Michael Peel. "Russia, France and US Demand Nagorno-Karabakh Ceasefire." *Financial Times*, October 1, 2020.

Fraser, Suzan. "What Lies Behind Turkish Support for Azerbaijan." *Associated Press*, October 2, 2020.

Freeland, Chrystia. *Sale of the Century: Russia's Wild Ride from Communism to Capitalism*. New York: Crown Business/Random House, 2000.

Freye, Timothy. "Corruption and Rule of Law." In Aslund, Anders, Sergei Guriev and Andrew C. Kuchins, eds., *Russia After the Global Economic Crisis*. Washington, DC: Peterson Institute for International Economics, 2010. pp. 79–94.

Friedrich, Carl J. and Zbigniew K. Brzezinski. *Totalitarian Dictatorship and Autocracy*. Second Edition Revised by Friedrich, 1965. New York: Praeger, 1956, 1965.

Friedrich, Carl J., Michael Curtis and Benjamin R. Barber. *Totalitarianism in Perspective: Three Views*. New York: Praeger, 1969.

Fuller, Graham E. *Turkey and the Arab Spring: Leadership in the Middle East*. Vancouver, BC: Bozorg Press, 2004.

Fuller, Graham E. *The New Turkish Republic: Turkey As a Pivotal State in the Muslim World*. Washington, DC: United States Institute of Peace Press, 2008.

Furet, Francois. *The Passing of an Illusion: The Idea of Communism in the Twentieth Century*. Chicago, IL: The University of Chicago Press, 1999.

Furet, Francois. *Lies, Passions & Illusions: The Democratic Imagination in the Twentieth Century*. Chicago: University of Chicago Press, 2014.

Furet, Francois and Ernst Nolte. *Fascism and Communism*. Lincoln, NE: University of Nebraska Press, 2001.

Gaddy, Clifford G. and Barry W. Ickes. *Russia's Virtual Economy*. Washington, DC: Brookings Institution Press, 2002.

Gaidar, Yegor, ed. *The Economics of Transition*. Cambridge, MA: The MIT Press, 2003.

Gaidar, Yegor. *Collapse of an Empire: Lessons for Modern Russia*. Washington, DC: The Brookings Institution, 2007.

Gaidar, Yegor. *Russia: A Long View*. Cambridge, MA: The MIT Press, 2012.

Galeotti, Mark. *Russia's Wars in Chechnya 1994–2009*. Oxford, UK: Osprey Publishing, 2014.

Gall, Carlotta and Thomas de Waal. *Chechnya: Calamity in the Caucasus*. New York: New York University Press, 1998.

Gallagher, Mary and Jonathan K. Hanson. "Authoritarian Survival, Resilience and the Selectorate Theory." In Dimitrov, Martin K., ed., *Why Communism Did Not Collapse: Understanding Authoritarian Regime Resilience in Asia and Europe*. Cambridge, UK: Cambridge University Press, 2013. pp. 185–204.

Galston, William A. "The Enduring Vulnerability of Liberal Democracy." *Journal of Democracy*. Volume 31, No. 3. July, 2020. pp. 8–24.

Galtung, Fredrick. "Measuring the Immeasurable: Boundaries and Functions of (Macro) Corruption Indices." In Charles Sampford, Arthur Shacklock, Carmel

Connors and Fredrik Galtung, eds., *Measuring Corruption*. Aldershot, UK: Ashgate Publishing, 2006. pp. 101–130.

Garrels, Anne. *Putin Country: A Journey Into the Real Russia*. New York: Picador-Farrar, Straus and Giroux, 2016.

Gawrych, George W. *The Young Atatürk: From Ottoman Soldier to Statesman of Turkey*. London and New York: I.B. Taurus, 2013.

Geller, Martinne. "Turkey's Arcelik Working on Deals to Expand Abroad." *Reuters*, March 20, 2017.

Gel'man, Vladimir. *Russian Authoritarianism: Analyzing Post-Soviet Regime Changes*. Pittsburgh, PA: University of Pittsburgh Press, 2015.

Genç, Kaya. *Under the Shadow: Rage and Revolution in Modern Turkey*. New York: I. B. Tauris, 2016.

Genc, Kaya. "Erdoğan's Way: The Rise and Rule of Turkey's Islamist Shapeshifter." *Foreign Affairs*, Volume 99, No. 2. March/April, 2020. https://www.foreignaffairs.com/articles/turkey/2019-08-12/Erdoğans-way.

Gershkovich, Evan. "'President for Life': Putin Opens Door to Extending Rule until 2036." *The Moscow Times*, 10 Mar. 2020, www.themoscowtimes.com/2020/03/10/president-for-life-putin-opens-door-to-extending-rule-until-2036-a69576.

Gessen, Masha. *The Man Without a Face: The Unlikely Rise of Vladimir Putin*. New York: Riverhead Books/Penguin, 2012.

Gessen, Masha. *Surviving Autocracy*. New York: Riverhead Books, 2020.

Geyer, Michael and Sheila Fitzpatrick. eds. *Beyond Totalitarianism: Stalinism and Nazism Compared*. Cambridge, UK: Cambridge University Press, 2009.

Gleason, Abbott. *Totalitarianism: The Inner History of the Cold War*. New York: Oxford University Press, 1995.

Goldman, Marshall I. *The Soviet Economy: Myth and Reality*. New York: Prentice-Hall, 1968.

Goldman, Marshall I. "The Role of Communist Countries." In David A. Deese and Joseph S. Nye, eds., *Energy and Security*. Cambridge, MA: Ballinger/Harper & Row, 1981. pp. 111–130.

Goldman, Marshall I. *USSR in Crisis: The Failure of an Economic System*. New York: W.W. Norton, 1983.

Goldman, Marshall I. *What Went Wrong with Perestroika*. New York: W.W. Norton, 1991.

Goldman, Marshall I. *Lost Opportunity: Why Economic Reforms in Russia Have Not Worked*. New York: W.W. Norton, 1996.

Goldman, Marshall I. *The Piratization of Russia: Russian Reform Goes Awry*. New York: Routledge, 2003.

Goldman, Marshall I. *Petrostate: Putin, Power and the New Russia*. New York: Oxford University Press, 2008. (also published as Oilopoly by OneWorld Publications, 2008)

Goodman, Peter S. "Turkey's Long, Painful Economic Crisis Grinds On." *The New York Times*, July 8, 2019.

Goodwin, Godfrey. *The Janissaries*. London: Saqi Books, 2006. [First published in 1994]

Goodwin, Jason. *Lords of the Horizons: A History of the Ottoman Empire*. London: Vintage; Random House, 1999.

Gorbachev, Mikhail. *Perestroika: New Thinking for Our Country and the World*. New York: Harper & Row, 1987.

Gorbachev, Mikhail. *The August Coup: The Truth and the Lessons*. New York: Harper Collins, 1991.

Gorbachev, Mikhail. *The New Russia*. Cambridge, UK: The Polity Press, 2016.

Gordievsky, Oleg. *Next Stop Execution: The Autobiography of Oleg Gordievsky*. London: Macmillan, 1985, 2018.

Gordon, Philip H. and Omer Taspinar. *Winning Turkey: How America, Europe, and Turkey Can Revive a Fading Partnership*. Afterword by Soli Ozel. Washington, DC: Brookings Institution Press, 2008.

Gottfried, Paul Edward. *After Liberalism: Mass Democracy in the Managerial State*. Princeton, NJ: Princeton University Press, 2001.

Gottfried, Paul Edward. *The Strange Death of Marxism: The European Left in the New Millennium*. Columbia, MO: University of Missouri Press, 2005, 2018.

Graham, Loren. *Lonely Ideas: Can Russia Compete?* Cambridge, MA: MIT Press, 2013.

Graham, Norman A. "A Transatlantic Perspective on the European Union's Constitutional Crisis: Back to the 'Broader before Deeper' Strategy?" In O'Neill, Michael and Nicolae Paun, eds., *Europe's Constitutional Crisis: International Perspectives*. Cluj-Napoca, Romania: European Studies Foundation Publishing House, 2007, pp. 209–238.

Graham, Norman A. "Russian Foreign Policy toward Central Asia and the Caucasus since the End of the Cold War: A Search for Identity with Geopolitical Characteristics." In Mohammed Ayoob and Murad Ismayilov, eds., *Identity and Politics in Central Eurasia and the Caucasus*. London/Abingdon, UK: Routledge, 2015. pp. 109–132.

Graham, Norman A. and Folke Lindahl, eds. *The Political Economy of Transition in Eurasia: Democratization and Economic Liberalization in a Global Economy*. East Lansing, MI: Michigan State University Press, 2006.

Granville, Brigitte. "Farewell, Ruble Zone." In Anders Åslund, ed., *Russian Economic Reform at Risk*. London: Pinter, 1995, pp. 65–88.

Granville, Brigitte and Peter Oppenheimer, eds. *Russia's Post-Communist Economy*. New York: Oxford University Press, 2001.

Greene, Samuel A. and Graeme B. Robertson. *Putin v. The People: The Perilous Politics of a Divided Russia*. New Haven, CT: Yale University Press, 2019.

Gregory, Paul R. *The Political Economy of Stalinism: Evidence From the Soviet Secret Archives*. Cambridge, UK: Cambridge University Press, 2004.

Grzywaczewski, Tomasz. "The Birth of Belarusian Nationalism." *Foreign Policy*, January 30, 2020.

Gulseven, Hakan. "Türkiye Ekonomisi Nasıl Battı?" (How was the Turkey's economy sunk?) Independent Türkçe, October 8, 2019: https://www.independentturkish .com/node/78276/t%C3%BCrkiyeden-sesler/t%C3%BCrkiye-ekonomisi-nas%C4 %B1l-batt%C4%B1.

Gumilev, L.N. *Ethnogenesis and the Biosphere*. Moscow: Progress Publishers, 1990.

Guriev, Sergei and Andrei Rachinski. "The Role of Oligarchs in Russian Capitalism." *Journal of Economic Perspectives*. Volume 19, No. 1. Winter, 2005. pp. 131–150.

Gustafson, Thane. *Wheel of Fortune: The Battle for Oil and Power in Russia*. Cambridge, MA: Harvard University Press, 2012.

Guvenc, Bozkurt. *The Other: Turks' Quest for Identity & Image*. Istanbul: Alkin Publishing House, 2006.

Gwertzman, Bernard and Michael T. Kaufman, ed., *The Collapse of Communism*. New York: Times Books/Random House, 1990.

Haass, Richard. *A World Disarray: American Foreign Policy and the Crisis of the Old Order*. New York: Penguin Press/Random House, 2017.

Hadenius, Axel. ed. *Democracy's Victory and Crisis*. UK: Cambridge University Press, 1997.

Haidt, Jonathan. *The Righteous Mind: Why Good People are Divided by Politics and Religion*. New York: Random House/Vintage Books, 2013.

Hale, Henry. *Patronal Politics: Eurasian Regime Dynamics in Comparative Perspective*. UK: Cambridge University Press, 2015.

Hale, Henry. "25 Years after the USSR: What's Gone Wrong?" *Washington, DC: Journal of Democracy*. Volume 27, No. 3. July, 2016. pp. 24–35.

Hale, William. *Turkish Foreign Policy 1774–2000*. London and Portland, Oregon: Frank Cass, 2002. (ISBN: 0-7146-8246-2)

Hale, William. *Turkey, the US and Iraq*. SOAS Middle East Series. London: SAQI and London Middle East Institute, 2007.

Hale, William and Ergun Özbudun. *Islamism, Democracy and Liberalism in Turkey: The Case of the AKP*. Routledge Studies in Middle Eastern Politics. London and New York: Routledge, 2011.

Hamid, Shadi. *Temptations of Power: Islamists and Illiberal Democracy in a New Middle East*. Oxford and New York: Oxford University Press, 2014.

Hanioglu, M. Sukru. *A Brief History of the Late Ottoman Empire*. Princeton and Oxford: Princeton University Press, 2008.

Hanioglu, M. Sukru. *Atatürk: An Intellectual Biography*. Princeton and Oxford: Princeton University Press, 2011.

Hanisch, Werner and Joachim Kruger. *On the Dialectics of Home and Foreign Policy in the Strategy and Tactics of the Socialist Unity Party of Germany*. Volume X, 4th Edition. Germany: German Foreign Policy, 1971.

Harding, Luke. *A Very Expensive Poison: The Assassination of Alexander Litvinenko and Putin's War with the West*. New York: Vintage Books, 2016.

Harrison, Lawrence E. and Samuel P. Huntington, editors. *Culture Matters: How Values Shape Human Progress*. New York: Basic Books, 2000.

Harrison, Mark. *Accounting for War: Soviet Production, Employment, and the Defence Burden, 1940–1945*. UK: Cambridge University Press, 1996.

Harrison, Mark. "The Soviet Economy, 1917–1991: Its Life and Afterlife." *Independent Review*. Volume 22, No. 2. 2017. pp. 199–206.

Hasanli, Jamil. *Stalin and the Turkish Crisis of the Cold War, 1945–1953.* Lanham, MD: Lexington Books, 2011.

Haslip, Joan. *The Sultan: The Life of Abdul Hamid II.* New York: Holt, Rinehart and Winston, 1973.

Hauser, Megan. *Electoral Strategies under Authoritarianism: Evidence from the Former Soviet Union.* Lanham, MD: Lexington Books/Rowman & Littlefield, 2019.

Hazony, Yoram. *The Virtue of Nationalism.* New York: Basic Books-Hachette Book Group, 2018.

Hedlund, Stefan. *Russian Path Dependence.* London: Routledge, 2005.

Hedlund, Stefan. *Putin's Energy Agenda: The Contradictions of Russia's Resource Wealth.* Boulder, CO: Lynne Rienner, Publishers, 2014.

Held, David. *Globalization/Anti-Globalization: Beyond the Great Divide.* Second Edition. Cambridge, UK: Polity Press, 2007.

Helm, Dieter. *Burn Out: The Endgame for Fossil Fuels.* New Haven, CT: Yale University Press, 2017.

Hendrick, Joshua D. *Gulen: The Ambiguous Politics of Market Islam in Turkey and the World.* New York: New York University Press, 2013.

Heper, Metin. *The State and Kurds in Turkey: The Question of Assimilation.* Houndsmills, Basingtoke, Hampshire and New York: Palgrave Macmillan, 2007.

Hewett, Ed A. *Reforming the Soviet Economy: Equality versus Efficiency.* Washington, DC: The Brookings Institution, 1988.

Hill, Fiona and Clifford G. Gaddy. *Mr. Putin: Operative in the Kremlin.* Revised Edition. Washington, DC: The Brookings Institution Press, 2015.

Hobsbawm, E.J. *Nations and Nationalism Since 1780: Programme, Myth, Reality.* Second Edition. Cambridge, UK: Cambridge University Press, 1990.

Hoffman, David E. *The Oligarchs: Wealth and Power in the New Russia.* New York: Public Affairs, Inc., 2011.

Holton, Christopher and Clare Lopez. *Gulen and the Gulenist Movement: Turkey's Islamic Supremacist Cult and its Contributions to the Civilization Jihad.* Washington, DC: The Center for Security Policy, 2015.

Horley, Tim, Anne Meng and Mila Versteeg. "The World Is Experiencing a New Form of Autocracy." *The Atlantic*, March 1, 2020.

Hourani, Albert. *Arabic Thought in the Liberal Age 1798–1939.* Cambridge and New York: Cambridge University Press, 2008. [First published in 1962]

Hourani, Albert. *A History of the Arab Peoples.* New York and Boston: Grand Central Publishing, 1992.

Houston, Christopher. *Islam, Kurds and the Turkish Nation State.* Oxford and New York: Berg, 2003.

Howe, Marvine. *Turkey: A Nation Divided over Islam's Revival.* Boulder, CO: Westview Press, 2000.

Huizinga, Todd. *The New Totalitarian Temptation: Global Governance and the Crisis of Democracy.* New York: Encounter Books, 2016.

Hull, Christopher C. "Erdoğan and Europe: The Fox and the Chicken Coop." In Clare M. Lopez, Harold Rhode, et al., eds., *Ally No More: Erdogan's New Turkish*

Caliphate and the Rising Jihadist Threat to the West. Washington, DC: Center for Security Policy, 2018. pp. 75–85.

Hunt, Terrence. "Clinton, Yeltsin Trade Compliments, Play Down Differences." *Associated Press News*, April 21, 1996.

Huntington, Samuel P. *The Third Wave: Democratization in the Late Twentieth Century.* Norman: University of Oklahoma Press, 1991.

Ilyin, Ivan. *The Singing Heart: A Book of Quiet Reflections.* Translated by Alexandra Weber. Memphis, TN: Orthodox Christian Translation Society, 2016.

Ilyin, Ivan. *Our Tasks.* Volume 1 (a collection of his articles 1948–1951 published together in Russian in 2014, Pubmix.com).

Ilyin, Ivan Alexandrovich. *On Resistance to Evil By Force.* Translated by K. Benois. London: TAXIARCH Press, 2018.

Inglehart, Ronald F. "The Danger of Deconsolidation: How Much Should We Worry?" *Washington, DC: Journal of Democracy.* Volume 27, No. 3. July, 2016. pp. 18–23.

Inglehart, Ronald F. "Giving Up on God: The Global Decline of Religion." *Foreign Affairs*, Septermber/October, 2020. pp. 110–118.

International Monetary Fund. *Financial Programming and Policy: The Case of Turkey.* Washington, DC. 2000.

International Monetary Fund. *Report for Selected Countries and Subjects.* Washington, DC: World Economic Outlook Database, October, 2019.

Isaak, Robert A. *Individuals in World Politics.* Monterey, CA: Duxbury Press, 1981.

Ismayilov, Murad and Norman A. Graham. eds. *Turkish-Azerbaijani Relations: One Nation—Two States?* London: Routledge, 2016.

Jack, Andrew. *Inside Putin's Russia.* UK: Oxford University Press, 2004.

Jacoby, Tim. *Social Power and the Turkish State.* Foreword by Michael Mann. London and New York: Frank Cass Publishers, 2004. (ISBN: 0-7146-8466-X)

Jenkins, Gareth H. *Between Fact and Fantasy: Turkey's Ergenekon Investigation.* Silk Road Paper, August 2009. Washington, DC: Central Asia-Caucasus Institute & Silk Road Studies Program, 2009.

Johnson, Chalmers. *Change in Communist Systems.* Palo Alto, CA: Stanford University Press, 1970.

Jones Luong, Pauline and Erika Weinfall. *Oil is Not a Curse: Ownership Structure and Institutions in Soviet Successor States.* Cambridge, UK: Cambridge University Press, 2010.

Jonson, Lena. *Vladimir Putin and Central Asia: The Shaping of Reussian Foreign Policy.* London: I.B. Tauris, 2006.

Judis, John B. *The Populist Explosion: How the Great Recession Transformed American and European Politics.* New York: Columbia Global Reports, 2016.

Jung, Dietrich, with Wolfango Piccoli. *Turkey at the Crossroads: Ottoman Legacies and a Greater Middle East.* London and New York: Zed Books, 2001.

Kagan, Robert. *The Jungle Grows Back: America and Our Imperiled World.* New York: Alfred A. Knopf, 2018.

Kaiser, Robert G. *Why Gorbachev Happened: His Triumphs and His Failure.* New York: Simon and Schuster, 1991.

Kalathil, Shanthi and Taylor C. Boas. *Open Networks, Closed Regimes: The Impact of the Internet on Authoritarian Rule.* Washington, DC: Carnegie Endowment for International Peace, 2002.

Kalaycioglu, Ersin. *Turkish Dynamics: Bridge across Troubled Lands.* New York: Palgrave Macmillan, 2005.

Kandiyoti, Deniz and Ayse Saktenber, eds. *Fragments of Culture: The Every day of Modern Turkey.* London and New York: I. B. Tauris & Co. Publishers, 2002.

Kasparov, Garry. *Winter Is Coming: Why Vladimir Putin and the Enemies of the Free World Must Be Stopped.* London: Atlantic Books, 2015.

Katz, Abraham. *The Politics of Economic Reform in the Soviet Union.* New York: Praeger, 1972.

Katzarova, Elitza. *The Social Construction of Global Corruption: From Utopia to Neoliberalism.* London: Palgrave Macmillan, 2019.

Kaylan, Muammer. *The Kemalists: Islamic Revival and the Fate of Secular Turkey.* New York: Prometheus Books, 2005.

Kazancigil, Ali and Ergun Özbudun, eds. *Atatürk: Founder of a Modern State.* London: C. Hurst & Company, 2006. [First published in 1981]

Kelkitli, Asli Fatma. *Turkish-Russian Relations: Competition and Cooperation in Eurasia.* London: Routledge, 2017.

Kedourie, Sylvia, ed. *Turkey before and after Atatürk: Internal and External Affairs.* Foreword by Andrew Mango. London and Portland, Oregon: Frank Cass, 2005. [First published in 1999]

Kenyon, Peter. "To Turn Turkey's Economy Around, Erdoğan May Have To Loosen Control." *National Public Radio.* April 15, 2019: https://www.npr.org/2019/04/15/713387994/to-turn-turkeys-economy-around-Erdoğan-may-have-to-loosen-control

Keyman, Fuat, ed. *Remaking Turkey: Globalization, Alternative Modernities, and Democracy.* Lanham, MD: Lexington Books, 2007.

Keyman, Fuat E. and Ziya Onis. *Turkish Politics in a Changing World: Global Dynamics and Domestic Transformations.* Istanbul: Istanbul Bilgi University Press, 2007.

Khazanov, Anatoly M. *After the USSR: Ethnicity, Nationalism, and Politics in the Commonwealth of Independent States.* Madison, WI: University of Wisconsin Press, 1995.

Kili, Suna. *The Atatürk Revolution: A Paradigm of Modernization.* Translated by Sylvia Zeybekoglu. Third Edition. Istanbul: Turkiye Is Bankasi Kultur Yayinlari, 2007.

Kim, Lucian. "Protesters in Russia's Far East Challenge Putin's Authority, Demand His Resignation." *National Public Radio*, July 24, 2020.

Kinross, Patrick. *The Ottoman Centuries: The Rise and Fall of the Turkish Empire.* New York: HarperCollins; Perennial, 2002. [First published in 1977]

Kinross, Patrick. *Atatürk: The Rebirth of a Nation.* London: Phoenix Press, 2001.

Kinzer, Stephen. *Crescent and Star: Turkey between Two Worlds.* New York: Farrar, Straus and Giroux, 2002. (ISBN: 0-374-52866-7)

Kinzer, Stephen. *All the Shah's Men: An American Coup and the Roots of the Middle East Terror.* Hoboken, NJ: John Wiley & Sons, 2003.

Kinzer, Stephen. *Reset Middle East: Old Friends and New Alliances. Saudi Arabia, Israel, Turkey, Iran.* London and New York: I. B. Tauris, 2011.

Kirisci, Kemal and Gareth M. Winrow. *The Kurdish Question and Turkey: An Example of a Trans-state Ethnic Conflict.* London and New York: RoutledgeCurzon, 2004. [First published in 1997] (ISBN: 0-7146-4304-1)

Kirkpatrick, Jeane J. *Dictatorships and Double Standards—Rationalism and Reason in Politics.* New York: Simon and Schuster/The American Enterprise Institute, 1982.

Kis, Janos. *Constitutional Democracy.* Budapest, Hungary: Central European University Press, 2003.

Klare, Michel. *Rising Powers, Shrinking Planet: The New Geopolitics of Energy.* New York: Metropolitan Books, 2008.

Klass, Phillip J. "Soviet Microcircuits Found Trailing U.S." *Aviation Week and Space Technology*, December 8, 1980.

Klebnikov, Paul. *Godfather of the Kremlin: The Decline of Russia in the Age of Gangster Capitalism.* New York: Harcourt, 2000.

Kochan, Nick and Robin Goodyear. *Corruption: The New Corporate Challenge.* London: Palgrave Macmillan, 2011.

Kocs, Stephen A. *International Order: A Political History.* Boulder, CO: Lynne Rienner, 2019.

Kohli, Atuhl. *State Directed Development: Political Power and Industrialization in the Global Periphery.* Cambridge UK: Cambridge University Press, 2004.

Kononenko, Vadim and Arkady Moshes. eds. *Russia As A Network State: What Works in Russia When State Institutions Do Not?* New York: Palgrave MacMillan, 2011.

Kotkin, Stephen. *Armageddon Averted: The Soviet Collapse, 1970–2000.* New York: Oxford University Press, 2008.

Kotkin, Stephen. *Uncivil Society: 1989 and the Implosion of the Communist Establishment.* New York: Modern Library, 2009.

Kotkin, Steven. "Keynote Address." *17th Annual Conference of the Central Eurasian Studies Society.* Princeton University. November 5, 2016.

Kotkin, Stephen. *Stalin: Waiting for Hitler, 1929–1941.* New York: Penguin Press, 2017.

Kramer, Andrew E. "More of Kremlin's Opponents are Ending Up Dead." *The New York Times*, August 21, 2016.

Kurlantzick, Joshua. *Democracy in Retreat: The Revolt of the Middle Class and the Worldwide Decline of Representative Government.* New Haven, CT: Yale University Press, 2013.

Kuru, Ahmet T. and Alfred Stepan, eds. *Democracy, Islam, and Secularism in Turkey.* New York: Columbia University Press, 2012.

Lagutina, Maria L. *Russia's Arctic Policy in the Twenty-First Century: National and International Dimensions.* Lanham, MD: Lexington Books/Rowman & Littlefield, 2019.

Lake, Michael, ed. *The EU & Turkey: A Glittering Prize or a Millstone?* London: The Federal Trust for Education and Research, 2005.

Lambsdorff, Johann Graf. "Measuring Corruption—The Validity and Precision of Subjective Indicators (CPI)." In Charles Sampford, Arthur Shacklock, Carmel Connors and Fredrik Galtung, eds., *Measuring Corruption*. Aldershot, UK: Ashgate Publishing, 2006, pp. 81–99.

Landes, David S. *The Wealth and Poverty of Nations: Why Some Are So Rich and Some So Poor*. New York: W.W. Norton, 1998.

Lanskoy, Miriam and Elspeth Suthers. "Outlawing the Opposition." *Washington, DC: Journal of Democracy*. Volume 24, No. 3. July, 2013. pp. 75–87.

Laqueur, Walter. *Putinism: Russia and Its Future with the West*. New York: St. Martin's Press, 2015.

Larrabee, F. Stephen and Ian O. Lesser. *Turkish foreign Policy in an Age of Uncertainty*. RAND's Center for Middle East Public Policy. Santa Monica, California: RAND, 2003.

Laruelle, Marlene. *Russian Eurasianism: An Ideology of Empire*. Baltimore, MD: The Johns Hopkins University Press, 2008.

Laruelle, Marlene. *Understanding Russia: The Challenges of Transformation*. Lanham, MD: Rowman & Littlefield, 2019.

Laruelle, Marlene. "Making Sense of Russia's Illiberalism." *Journal of Democracy*. Volume 31, No. 3. July 2020. pp. 115–129.

Lavigne, Marie. "Problems Facing the Soviet Economy." In Alexander Dallin and Condoleezza Rice, eds., *The Gorbachev Era*. Palo Alto, CA: Stanford Alumni Assoc, 1986. pp. 43–59.

Lavigne, Marie. *The Economics of Transition: From Socialist Economy to Market Economy*. Second Edition. New York: St. Martin's Press, 1999.

Ledeneva, Alena V. *Russia's Economy of Favours*. Cambridge, UK: Cambridge University Press, 1998.

Ledeneva, Alena V. *How Russia Really Works*. Ithaca, NY: Cornell University Press, 2006.

Ledeneva, Alena. "Can Russia Modernise? Sistema, Power Networks and Informal Governance." In Kononenko, Vadim and Arkady Moshes, eds., *Russia As A Network State: What Works in Russia When State Institutions Do Not?* New York: Palgrave MacMillan, 2011. pp. 39–61.

Ledeneva, Alena V. *Can Russia Modernise? Sistema, Power Networks and Informal Governance*. Cambridge, UK: Cambridge University Press, 2013.

Lee, Kuan Yew. *From Third World to First: The Singapore Story, 1965–2000*. New York: Harper Collins, 2000.

Lee, Kuan Yew. "Speech to the Singapore Legislative Assembly." October 4, 1956.

Legutko, Ryszard. *The Demon in Democracy: Totalitarian Temptations in Free Societies*. New York: Encounter Books, 2016, 2018.

Leonard, Carol Scott and Eugenia Serova. "The Reform of Agriculture." In Brigitte Granville and Peter Oppenheimer, eds., *Russia's Post-Communist Economy*. New York: Oxford University Press, 2001, pp. 367–396.

Leonard, Mark. *Why Europe Will Run the 21st Century*. New York: Public Affairs, 2005.

LeVine, Steve. *The Oil and the Glory: The Pursuit of Empire and Fortune on the Caspian Sea*. New York: Random House, 2007.

LeVine, Steve. *Putin's Labyrinth: Spies, Murder, and the Dark Heart of the New Russia.* New York: Random House, 2008.

Levitsky, Steven and Lucan Way. *Competitive Authoritarianism: Hybrid Regimes after the Cold War.* New York: Cambridge University Press, 2010.

Levitsky, Steven and Lucan Way. "The Durability of Revolutionary Regimes." *Washington, DC: Journal of Democracy.* Volume 24, No. 3. July, 2013. pp. 7–17.

Lewis, Bernard. *Istanbul and the Civilization of the Ottoman Empire.* Norman, OK: University of Oklahoma Press, 1963.

Lewis, Bernard. *The Multiple Identities of the Middle East.* London: Phoenix; Orion Books, 1999.

Lewis, Bernard. *The Middle East: 2000 Years of History from the Rise of Christianity to the Present Day.* London: Phoenix Press, 2000.

Lewis, Bernard. *The Emergence of Modern Turkey.* Third Edition. New York and Oxford: Oxford University Press, 2002. [First ed. published in 1961] (ISBN: 0-19-513460-5)

Lewis, Bernard. *From Babel to Dragomans: Interpreting the Middle East.* London: Phoenix, 2005.

Li, Shaomin. *Bribery and Corruption in Weak Institutional Environments: Connecting the Dots from a Comparative Perspective.* Cambridge, UK: Cambridge University Press, 2019.

Linz, Juan J. "Some Thoughts on the Victory and Future of Democracy." In Axel Hadenius, ed., *Democracy's Victory and Crisis.* UK: Cambridge University Press, 1997. pp. 418–420.

Linz, Juan J. *Totalitarian and Authoritarian Regimes.* Boulder, CO: Lynne Reinner Publishers, 2000.

Litvinenko, Alexander and Yuri Felshtinsky. *Blowing Up Russia: The Secret Plot to Bring Back KGB Terror.* New York: Encounter Books, 2007.

Lopez, Clare M., Harold Rhode, et al. *Ally No More: Erdogan's New Turkish Caliphate and the Rising Jihadist Threat to the West.* Washington, DC: Center for Security Policy, 2018.

Lord, Carnes. *The New Prince: What Machiavelli Can Teach Us in the Age of Trump.* New Haven, CT: Yale University Press, 2018.

Lourie, Richard. *Putin: His Downfall and Russia's Coming Crash.* New York: St. Martin's Press, 2017.

Lubina, Michal. *Russia and China: A Political Marriage of Convenience—Stable and Successful.* Opladen, Germany: Barbara Budrich Publishers, 2017.

Luttwak, Edward. *Turbo Capitalism: Winners and Losers in the Global Economy.* New York: Harper Collins, 1999.

Luttwak, Edward N. *Coup d'Etat: A Practical Handbook.* Revised Edition. Cambridge, MA: Harvard University Press, 2016.

MacFie, A. L. *Atatürk.* Profiles in Power. London and New York: Longman; Pearson Education Print on Demand Edition, 2003. [First published in 1994]

Mahoney, Daniel J. *The Solzhenitsyn Reader: New and Essential Writings 1947–2005.* Wilmington, DE: ISI Books, 2007.

Mahoney, Daniel J. *The Conservative Foundations of the Liberal Order: Defending Democracy against Its Modern Enemies and Immoderate Friends*. Wilmington, DE: ISI Books, 2011.

Mahoney, Daniel J. *The Other Solzhenitsyn: Telling the Truth about a Misunderstood Writer and Thinker* South Bend, IN: St Augustine's Press, 2014.

Mahoney, Daniel J. *The Idol of Our Age: How the Religion of Humanity Subverts Christianity*. New York: Encounter Books, 2018.

Mahoney, Daniel J., Aleksandras Shtromas and Robert Faulkner. *Totalitarianism and the Prospects for World Order: Closing the Door on the Twentieth Century*. Lanham, MD: Lexington Books, 2003.

Mak, Geert. *The Bridge: A Journey Between Orient and Occident*. London: Harvill Secker, 2008.

Malia, Martin. *The Soviet Tragedy: A History of Socialism in Russia, 1917–1991*. New York: Simon and Schuster/The Free Press, 1994.

Manent, Pierre. *An Intellectual History of Liberalism*. Translated by Rebecca Balinski. Princeton: Princeton University Press, 1994.

Manent, Pierre. *A World beyond Politics? A Defense of the Nation-State*. Princeton, NJ: Princeton University Press, 2006.

Manent, Pierre. *Democracy Without Nations? The Fate of Self-Government in Europe*. Wilmington, DE: ISI Books, 2007.

Manent, Pierre. "The Crisis of Liberalism." *Journal of Democracy*, Volume 25, No. 1. January, 2014. pp. 131–141.

Manent, Pierre. *Seeing Things Politically: Interviews with Benedicte Delorme-Montini*. South Bend, IN: St. Augustine's Press, 2015.

Mango, Andrew. *Atatürk: The Biography of the Founder of Modern Turkey*. Woodstock and New York: The Overlook Press, 1999.

Mango, Andrew. *The Turks Today*. London: John Murray, 2004. (ISBN: 0-7195-6595-2)

Mango, Andrew. *Turkey and the War on Terror: For Forty Years We Fought Alone*. London and New York: Routledge, 2005.

Mango, Andrew. *From the Sultan to Atatürk: Turkey*. Makers of the Modern World. London: Haus Publishing Ltd, 2009.

Mankoff, Jeffrey. *Russian Foreign Policy: The Return of Great Power Politics*. Lanham, MD: Rowman and Littlefield, 2012.

Mankoff, Jeffrey. "Russia's Latest Land Grab: How Putin Won Crimea and Lost Ukraine." *Foreign Affairs*, May/June, 2014. pp. 60–68.

Manolopolous, Jason. *Greece's 'Odious' Debt*. London, UK: Anthem Press, 2011.

Mansfield, Harvey C. Jr. and Delba Winthrop. "Tocqueville's New Political Science." In Cheryl B. Welch, ed., *The Cambridge Companion to Tocqueville*. Cambridge, UK and New York: Cambridge University Press, 2006. pp. 81–107.

Mardin, Serif. *The Genesis of Young Ottoman Thought: A Study in the Modernization of Turkish Political Ideas*. Syracuse: Syracuse University Press, 2000. [Originally published in 1962]

Mardin, Serif. *Religion and Social Change in Modern Turkey: The Case of Bediuzzaman Said Nursi.* Albany, NY: State University of New York Press, 1989.

Mardin, Serif. *Religion, Society, and Modernity in Turkey.* Syracuse: Syracuse University Press, 2006.

Martin, Lenore G. and Dimitris Keridis, eds. *The Future of Turkish Foreign Policy.* Cambridge, MA and London: The MIT Press, 2004. (ISBN: 0-262-63243-8)

Matthews, Mervyn. *Privilege in the Soviet Union: A Study of Elite Life-Styles under Communism.* London: George Allen & Unwin, 1978.

Mazower, Mark. *Dark Continent: Europe's Twentieth Century.* New York: Alfred A. Knopf, 1998.

McCarthy, Justin. *The Ottoman Turks: An Introductory History to 1923.* London and New York: Longman; Pearson Education Limited, 1997.

McCarthy, Justin. *The Ottoman Peoples and the End of Empire.* Historical Endings Series. London and New York: Hodder Arnold, 2005.

McCauley, Martin. *The Rise and Fall of the Soviet Union.* Harlow, UK: Pearson Longman, 2008.

McFaul, Michael. *From Cold War to Hot Peace: An American Ambassador in Putin's Russia.* Boston, MA: Houghton Mifflin Harcourt, 2018.

McFaul, Michael, Nikolay Petrov and Andrei Ryabov. *Between Dictatorship and Democracy: Russian Post-Communist Political Reform.* Washington, DC: Carnegie Endowment for International Peace, 2004.

McMeekin, Sean. *The Berlin-Baghdad Express: The Ottoman Empire and Germany's Bid for World Power, 1898–1918.* London and New York: Penguin Books, 2011.

Mearsheimer, John J. *The Great Delusion: Liberal Dreams and International Realities.* New Haven, CT: Yale University Press, 2018.

Medvedev, Roy A. *Let History Judge: The Origins and Consequences of Stalinism.* New York: Alfred A. Knopf. Rev. and expanded edition published in 1989. New York: Columbia University Press, 1972.

Medvedev, Roy A. *On Socialist Democracy.* New York: Alfred A. Knopf, 1975.

Medvedev, Zhores A. *Nuclear Disaster in the Urals.* New York: W.W. Norton & Co., 1979.

Medvedev, Roy A. *Nikolai Bukharin: The Last Years.* New York: W.W. Norton & Co., 1980.

Meeker, Michael E. *A Nation of Empire: The Ottoman Legacy of Turkish Modernity.* Berkeley and Los Angeles: University of California Press, 2002.

Melville, Andrei and Gail W. Lapidus, eds. *The Glasnost Papers: Voices on Reform from Moscow.* Boulder, CO: Westview Press, 1990.

Meyer, Alfred G. *The Soviet Political System: An Interpretation.* New York: Random House, 1965.

Mezrich, Ben. *Once Upon a Time in Russia: The Rise of the Oligarchs.* New York: Atria Books, 2015.

Milanovic, Branko. "The Clash of Capitalisms: The Real Fight for the Global Economy's Future." Special Issue on "The Future of Capitalism." *NY: Foreign Affairs.* Volume 99, No. 1. January/February, 2020. pp. 10–21.

Milosz, Czeslaw. *The Captive Mind*. New York: Vintage Books, 1981.

Miller, Chris. *Putinomics: Power and Money in Resurgent Russia*. Chapel Hill, NC: University of North Carolina Press, 2018.

Milton, Giles. *Paradise Lost. Smyrna 1922: The Destruction of Islam's City of Tolerance*. London: Sceptre; Houghton & Stoughton, 2009.

Montefiore, Simon Sebag. *Stalin: The Court of the Red Tsar*. New York: Alfred A. Knopf, 2004.

Morgan, Roger. *West European Politics Since 1945: The Shaping of the European Community*. New York: Capricorn, 1972.

Morris, Chris. *The New Turkey: The Quiet Revolution on the Edge of Europe*. London: Granta Books, 2005.

Morrison, John. *Boris Yeltsin: From Bolshevik to Democrat*. New York: Dutton/ Penguin, 1991.

Morse, Edward L. "Welcome to the Revolution." In Special Segment on Shale and the Future of Energy. *Foreign Affairs*, May/June, 2014, pp. 3–8.

Mousavizadeh, Nader. *The Black Book of Bosnia: The Consequences of Appeasement*. New York: Basic Books, 1996.

Muller, Jan-Werner. *What is Populism?* Philadelphia, PA: University of Pennsylvania Press, 2016.

Murray, Douglas. *The Strange Death of Europe: Immigration, Identity, Islam*. London: Bloomsbury Publishing, 2017.

Myers, Steven Lee. *The New Tsar: The Rise and Reign of Vladimir Putin*. New York: Alfred A. Knopf, 2015.

Nasr, Vali. *Forces of Fortune: The Rise of the New Muslim Middle Class and What It Will Mean for Our World*. New York: Free Press, 2009.

Nauseda, Gitanas. "Interview on "Hard Talk" Program." *BBC World News*, September 11, 2020.

Navaro-Yashin, Yael. *Faces of the State: Secularism and Public Life in Turkey*. Princeton and Oxford: Princeton University Press, 2002.

Nelson, Lynn D. and Irina Y. Kuzes. *Property to the People: The Struggle for Radical Economic Reform in Russia*. Armonk, NY: M.E. Sharpe, Inc., 1994.

Newell, Waller R. *Tyrants: A History of Power, Injustice, and Terror*. UK: Cambridge University Press, 2016, 2019.

Nodia, Ghia. "Freedom and the State." *Journal of Democracy*. Volume 21, No. 1. January, 2010. pp. 136–143.

Nodia, Gia. "About the Love of Peace and Conflict of Liberalism." In Leila Alieva, ed., *The Soviet Legacy 22 Years On: Reversed or Reinforced*. Baku, Azerbaijan: Qanun Publishing, 2013.

Nove, Alec. ed., *The Stalin Phenomenon*. New York: St. Martin's Press, 1992.

Odling-Smee, John. "The IMF and Russia in the 1990s." Washington, DC: IMF Staff Papers. Volume 53, No. 1, 2006.

Offe, Claus. "Capitalism by Democratic Design? Democratic Theory Facing the Triple Transition in East Central Europe." *Social Research*. Volume 58, No. 4. 1991. pp. 865–892.

Ohmae, Kenichi. *The End of the Nation State: The Rise of Regional Economies*. New York: The Free Press, 1995.

Ohmae, Kenichi. *The Borderless World: Power and Strategy in the Interlinked Economy.* New York: Harper Collins, 1999.

Oktem, Kerem. *Turkey since 1989: Angry Nation.* Global History of the Present. London and New York: Zed Books, 2011.

O'Neill, Michael and Nicolae Paun, eds. *Europe's Constitutional Crisis: International Perspectives.* Cluj-Napoca, Romania: European Studies Foundation Publishing House, 2007.

Onis, Ziya and Barry Rubin, eds. *The Turkish Economy in Crisis.* London and Portland, Oregon: Frank Cass, 2003. (ISBN: 0-7146-8397-3)

Onis, Ziya and Suhnaz Yilmaz. "Between Europeanization and Euro-Asianism: Foreign Policy Activism in Turkey during the AKP Era." *Turkish Studies.* Volume 10, No. 1. March, 2009. pp. 7–24.

Oreskes, Naomi and Erik Conway. *The Collapse of Western Civilization: A View from the Future.* New York: Columbia University Press, 2014.

Orga, Irfan. *Portrait of a Turkish Family.* London: Eland, 2004.

Orizio, Riccardo. *Talk of the Devil: Encounters with Seven Dictators.* New York: Walker & Company, 2002.

Osdemir, Adil and Kenneth Frank. *Visible Islam in Modern Turkey.* Library of Philosophy and Religion. New York: St. Martin's Press, 2000.

Ostrovsky, Arkady. *The Invention of Russia: From Gorbachev's Freedom to Putin's War.* New York: Atlantic Books, 2015.

Ostrovsky, Arkady. "For Putin, Disinformation Is Power." *The New York Times,* August 8, 2016.

Ottaway, Marina. *Democracy Challenged: The Rise of Semi-Authoritarianism.* Washington, DC: Carnegie Endowment for International Peace, 2003.

Owen, Sir Robert. *The Litvinenko Inquiry: Report into the death of Alexander Litvinenko.* Presented to Parliament pursuant to Section 26 of the Inquiries Act 2005. 21 January 2016.

Özbudun, Ergun. "Democratization in the Middle East: Turkey-How Far from Consolidation?" *Journal of Democracy.* Volume 7, No. 3. July, 1996. pp. 123–137.

Özbudun, Ergun. *Party Politics and Social Cleavages in Turkey.* London: Lynne Rienner Publishers, 2013.

Özbudun, Ergun. "Problems of Rule of Law and Horizontal Accountability in Turkey: Defective Democracy or Competitive Authoritarianism?" In Cengiz Erisen, Paul Kubicek, eds., *Democratic Consolidation in Turkey: Micro and Macro Challenges.* London: Routledge, 2016. pp. 144–165.

Özbudun, Ergun and Omer Faruk Genckaya. *Democratization and the Politics of Constitution-Making in Turkey.* Budapest and New York: Central European University Press, 2009.

Ozdalga, Elisabeth. *The Veiling Issue, Official Secularism and Popular Islam in Modern Turkey.* Nordic Institute of Asian Studies, NIAS Report Series, No. 33. Surrey, England: Curzon Press, 1998.

Ozdalga, Elisabeth, ed. *Late Ottoman Society: The Intellectual Legacy.* London and New York: Routledge, 2005.

Ozkirimli, Umut and Spyros A. Sofos. *Tormented by History: Nationalism in Greece and Turkey.* London: Hurst & Company, 2008.

Özpek, Burak Bilgehan. *The Turkey Analyst*, February 28, 2017.

Ozyurek, Esra. *Nostalgia for the Modern: State Secularism and Everyday Politics in Turkey*. Durham and London: Duke University Press, 2006.

Pakulski, Jan and Andras Korosenyi. *Toward Leader Democracy*. London: Anthem Press, 2012.

Parenti, Michael. *To Kill A Nation: The Attack on Yugoslavia*. London: Verso, 2000.

Park, Bill. *Turkey's Policy Towards Northern Iraq: Problems and Perspectives*. Adelphi Papers No. 374. Oxford and New York: Routledge, for the International Institute for Strategic Studies, 2005.

Parla, Taha and Andrew Davison. *Corporatist Ideology in Kemalist Turkey: Progress or Order?* Modern Intellectual and Political History of the Middle East. Syracuse, NY: Syracuse University Press, 2004.

Parrott, Bruce. *Politics and Technology in the Soviet Union*. Cambridge, MA: MIT Press, 1983.

Pei, Minxin. *China's Trapped Transition: The Limits of Developmental Autocracy*. Cambridge, MA: Harvard University Press. Pei, Minxin. 2006.

Pei, Minxin. *China's Crony Capitalism: The Dynamics of Regime Decay*. Cambridge, MA: Harvard University Press, 2016.

Perry, William J. and Cynthia A. Roberts. "Winning Through Sophistication: How to Meet the Soviet Military Challenge." *Technology Review*. July, 1982. pp. 27–35.

Petrov, Nikolay. *Putin's Downfall: The Coming Crisis of the Russian Regime*. London: European Council on Foreign Relations, 2016.

Phillips, David L. *An Uncertain Ally: Turkey under Erdoğan's Dictatorship*. London: Routledge, 2017.

Piketty, Thomas. *Capital in the Twenty-First Century*. Cambridge, MA: Harvard University Press, 2014.

Pitel, Laura. "Turkey's Armed Drones Bolster Erdogan's Hard Power Tactics." *Financial Times*, October 10, 2020.

Plattner, Marc F. *Democracy Without Borders? Global Challenges to Liberal Democracy*. Lanham, MD: Rowman & Littlefield Publishers, 2008.

Pleshakov, Constantine. *The Crimean Nexus: Putin's War and the Clash of Civilizations*. New Haven: Yale University Press, 2017.

Politkovskaya, Anna. *A Dirty War: A Russian Reporter in Chechnya*. London: The Harvill Press, 2001.

Politkovskaya, Anna. *Putin's Russia: Life in a Failing Democracy*. New York: Henry Holt and Co., 2004.

Pomerantsev, Peter. "The Kremlin's Information War." *Washington, DC: Journal of Democracy*. Volume 26, No. 4. October, 2015. pp. 40–50.

Pope, Nicole and Hugh Pope. *Turkey Unveiled: A History of Modern Turkey*. Woodstock and New York: The Overlook Press, 2004. (ISBN: 1-58567-581-4)

Popper, Karl R. *The Open Society and Its Enemies*. Princeton, NJ: Princeton University Press, 1945.

Poulton, Hugh. *Top Hat, Grey Wolf and Crescent: Turkish Nationalism and the Turkish Republic*. London: Hurst & Company, 1997.

Przeworski, Adam. ed. *Democracy in a Russian Mirror.* UK: Cambridge University Press, 2015.

Przeworski, Adam and Fernando Limongi. "Democracy and Development." In Axel Hadenius, ed., *Democracy's Victory and Crisis.* UK: Cambridge University Press, 1997. pp. 163–194.

Putin, Vladimir. *First Person: An Astonishingly Prank Self-Portrait by Russia's President.* New York: Public Affairs/Perseus, 2000.

Putin, Vladimir. *Speech to the Munich Conference on Security Policy,* February 10, 2007. http://en.kremlin.ru/events/president/transcripts/24034.

Quataert, Donald. *The Ottoman Empire, 1700–1922.* Second Edition. New Approaches to European History. Cambridge and New York: Cambridge University Press, 2005.

Quiggin, John. *Zombie Capitalism: How Dead Ideas Still Walk Among Us.* Princeton, NJ: Princeton University Press, 2010.

Rabasa, Angel and F. Stephen Larrabee. *The Rise of Political Islam in Turkey.* Santa Monica, CA: The RAND Corporation, 2008.

Radelet, Steven C. *The Great Surge: The Ascent of the Developing World.* New York: Simon and Schuster, 2015.

Reddaway, Peter. *The Dissidents: A Memoir of Working with the Resistance in Russia, 1960-1990.* Washington, DC: The Brookings Institution, 2020.

Reddaway, Peter and Dmitri Glinski. *The Tragedy of Russia's Reforms: Market Bolshevism Against Democracy.* Washington, DC: US Institute of Peace Press, 2001.

Reich, Robert. *Saving Capitalism: For the Many, Not the Few.* New York: Vintage Books/Random House, 2016.

Reich, Robert. *The Common Good.* New York: Vintage Books/Random House, 2018.

Reich, Robert B. *The Work of Nations: Preparing Ourselves for the 21ˢᵗ Century.* New York: Random House/Vintage Books, 1991.

Reiman, Michal. *The Birth of Stalinism: The USSR on the Eve of the "Second Revolution".* Bloomington, IN: Indiana University Press, 1987.

Rhode, Harold, et al., *Ally No More: Erdogan's New Turkish Caliphate and the Rising Jihadist Threat to the West.* Washington, DC: The Center for Security Policy, 2020.

Rifkin, Jeremy. *The European Dream: How Europe's Vision of the Future Is Quietly Eclipsing the American Dream.* New York: Penguin Group, 2004.

Roberts, David D. *The Totalitarian Experiment in Twentieth-Century Europe: Understanding the Poverty of Great Politics.* New York: Routledge, 2006.

Robins, Philip. *Suits and Uniforms: Turkish Foreign Policy since the Cold War.* London: Hurst & Company, 2003. (ISBN: 1-85065-675-4)

Rodman, Peter S. *Presidential Command: Power, Leadership, and the Making of Foreign Policy from Richard Nixon to George W. Bush.* New York: Alfred A. Knopf, 2009.

Rogan, Eugene. *The Fall of the Ottomans: The Great War in the Middle East.* New York: Basic Books, 2015.

Rosanvallon, Pierre. *The Demands of Liberty: Civil Society in France since the Revolution*. Translated by Arthur Goldhammer. Cambridge and London: Harvard University Press, 2007.

Rose, Gideon, ed. "The Future of Capitalism." *Foreign Affairs*, 99, No. 1. January/ February, 2020. Special Issue.

Rosenberg, William G. and Lewis H. Siegelbaum. eds. *Social Dimensions of Soviet Industrialization*. Bloomington, IN: Indiana University Press, 1993.

Roy, Olivier, *The New Central Asia: The Creation of Nations*. New York: New York University Press, 2000.

Roy, Olivier, ed. *Turkey Today—A European Country?* Translated by Monica Sandor. London: Anthem Press, 2005.

Rubin, Barry. *Istanbul Intrigues*. Istanbul: Bogazici University Press, 2002.

Rubin, Barry and Kemal Kirisci, eds. *Turkey in World Politics: An Emerging Multiregional Power*. Istanbul: Bogazici University Press, 2002a.

Rubin, Barry and Metin Heper, eds. *Political Parties in Turkey*. London: Frank Cass, 2002b.

Rubin, Barry and Metin Heper, eds. *Political Parties in Turkey*. London and Portland, Oregon: Frank Cass, 2002c.

Runciman, David. *How Democracy Ends*. New York: Basic Books, 2018.

Russell, David M. "Is there a Soviet Computer Challenge?" *Defense Electronics*, March 1984.

Rutzen, Douglas. "Civil Society Under Assault." *Washington, DC: Journal of Democracy*. Volume 26, No. 4. October, 2015. pp. 28–39.

Ryzhkov , Vladimir. "Build Innovation City and They Won't Come." *The Moscow Times*, February 25, 2010.

Sachs, Jeffrey D. "Why Russia Has Failed to Stabilize." Anders Aslund, *Russian Economic Reform at Risk*. London: Pinter, 1995, pp. 53–65.

Sakwa, Richard. *Putin and the Oligarch: The Khodorkovsky—Yukos Affair*. New York: I.B. Tauris and Co, 2014.

Salame, Ghassan, ed. *Democracy Without Democrats? The Renewal of Politics in the Muslim World*. London and New York: I. B. Tauris Publishers, 2001. [First published in 1994]

Sampford, Charles, Arthur Shacklock, Carmel Connors and Fredrik Galtung, eds. *Measuring Corruption*. Aldershot, UK: Ashgate Publishing, 2006.

Satter, David. *Darkness at Dawn: The Rise of the Russian Criminal State*. New Haven, CT: Yale University Press, 2008.

Schechter, Michael G. ed. *The Revival of Civil Society: Global and Comparative Perspectives*. London: Macmillan. 1999.

Schmitter, Phillippe. "Dangers and Dilemmas of Democracy." In Larry Diamond and Marc F. Plattner, eds., *The Global Resurgence of Democracy*. Second Edition. Baltimore, MD: Johns Hopkins University Press, 1996. pp. 57–74.

Schwartz, Harry. "Comecon: The Wide Gap Between Dream and Reality." *NY: The New York Times*, August 8, 1971, Section 4, p. 4.

Sebestyen, Victor. *Revolution 1989: The Fall of the Soviet Empire*. New York: Pantheon Books, 2009.

Seddon, Max and James Shotter. "Lukashenko rhetoric shows fallout between Minsk and Moscow." *Financial Times*, August 5, 2020.

Sella, Amnon. "Gorbachev: The Devolution of Power." In Sheffer, Gabriel, ed., *Innovative Leaders in International Politics*. Albany, NY: State University of New York Press, 1993. pp. 217–230.

Sen, Amartya. "Democracy as a Universal Value." *Journal of Democracy*. Volume 10, No. 3. July, 1999. pp. 3–17.

Sen, Amartya. *Development As Freedom*. New York: Random House/Anchor Books, 2000.

Servan-Schreiber, Jean-Jacques. *Le Défi Américain (The American Challenge)*. Paris: Versilio, 1969.

Sharma, Ruchir. *The Rise and Fall of Nations: Forces of Change in the Post-Crisis World*. New York: W.W. Norton, 2016.

Shaw, Stanford J. *Reform, Revolution, and Republic: The Rise of Modern Turkey, 1808–1975*. Vol. II of *History of the Ottoman Empire and Modern Turkey*. Cambridge: Cambridge University Press, 1977.

Shaw, Stanford J. and Ezel Kural Shaw. *Empire of the Gazis: The Rise and Decline of the Ottoman Empire, 1280–1808*. Vol. I of *History of the Ottoman Empire and Modern Turkey*. Cambridge: Cambridge University Press, 1976.

Shaxson, Nicholas. *The Finance Curse: How Global Finance is Making Us All Poorer*. New York: Grove Press, 2018.

Sheehan, James J. *Where Have All the Soldiers Gone: The Transformation of Modern Europe*. New York: Houghton Mifflin Harcourt, 2008.

Sheffer, Gabriel, ed. *Innovative Leaders in International Politics*. Albany, NY: State University of New York Press, 1993.

Sheldon, Garrett Ward. *Jefferson & Atatürk: Political Philosophies*. New York: Peter Lang Publishing, 2000.

Shevtsova, Lilia. *Lost in Transition: The Yeltsin and Putin Legacies*. Washington, DC: Carnegie Endowment for International Peace, 2007.

Shevtsova, Lilia. *Lonely Power: Why Russia has Failed to Become the West and the West is Weary of Russia*. Washington, DC: Carnegie Endowment for International Peace, 2010.

Shevtsova, Lilia. *Putin's Russia*. Washington, DC: Carnegie Endowment for International Peace, 2013.

Shevtsova, Lilia. "The Authoritarian Resurgence: Forward to the Past in Russia." *Journal of Democracy*. Volume 26, No. 2. November, 2015. pp. 22–36.

Shevtsova, Lilia. "The Kremlin Emboldened: Paradoxes of Decline." *Journal of Democracy*. Volume 28, No. 4. October, 2017. pp. 101–109.

Shevtsova, Lilia. "Russia's Ukraine Obsession." *Journal of Democracy*. Volume 31, No. 1. January, 2020. pp. 138–147.

Shimer, David. *Rigged: America, Russia, and One Hundred Years of Covert Electoral Interference*. New York: Alfred A. Knopf, 2020.

Shlapentokh, Vladimir. *A Normal Totalitarian Society: How the Soviet Union Functioned and How It Collapsed*. Armonk, NY: M.E. Sharpe, 2001.

Shraibman, Artyom. "Oatmeal and Water: The Thinning Belarus-Russia Relationship." *The Moscow Times*, Mar. 2020. www.themoscowtimes.com/2020/02/12/oatmeal -and-water-the-thinning-belarus-russia-relationship-a69266.

Shulman, Marshall. *Stalin's Foreign Policy Reappraised*. Cambridge, MA: Harvard University Press, 1963.

Shulman, Marshall. *Beyond the Cold War*. New Haven, CT: Yale University Press, 1966.

Siedentop, Larry. *Democracy in Europe*. New York: Columbia University Press, 2001.

Siedentop, Larry. *Inventing the Individual: The Origins of Western Liberalism*. Cambridge: The Belknap Press of Harvard University Press, 2014.

Siegelbaum, Lewis and Andrei Sokolov. *Stalinism as a Way of Life*. New Haven, CT: Yale University Press, 2000.

Sierakowski, Slawomir. "Belarus Uprising: The Making of a Revolution." *Journal of Democracy*. Volume 31, No. 4. October 2020. pp. 5–16.

Simis, Konstantin. *USSR: The Corrupt Society—The Secret World of Soviet Capitalism*. New York: Simon and Schuster, 1982.

Sixsmith, Martin. *Putin's Oil: the Yukos Affair and the Struggle for Russia*. New York: Continuum, 2010.

Smith, Alexander and Elena Holodny. "NATO member Turkey takes delivery of Russian S-400 missile defense system." *NBC News*, July 12, 2019. https://www .nbcnews.com/news/world/nato-member-turkey-takes-delivery-of-Russian-S-400 -missile-defense-system.html.

Smith, Timothy B. *France in Crisis: Welfare, Inequality and Globalization since 1980*. Cambridge, UK and New York: Cambridge University Press, 2004.

Snyder, Timothy. "Putin's Philosopher of Russian Fascism." *The New York Review*, April 5, 2018. https://www.nybooks.com/daily/2018/03/16/ivan-ilyin-putins-p hilosopher-of-russian-fascism/.

Solovyov, Vladimir and Elena Klepikova. *Boris Yeltsin: A Political Biography*. New York: G.P. Putnam's Sons, 1992.

Solzhenitsyn, Aleksandr. *One Day in the Life of Ivan Denisovich*. New York: Dutton, 1963.

Solzhenitsyn, Aleksandr. *The Gulag Archipelago, 1918–1956*. New York: Harper, 1973.

Sonmez, Mustafa. "Anxious Turkish investors eyeing opportunities abroad." *al-monitor*, February 16, 2018. https://www.al-monitor.com/pulse/originals/2018/02 /turkey-anxious-investors-eye-opportunities-abroad.html.

Soros, George. *The Crisis of Global Capitalism: Open Society Endangered*. New York: Public Affairs, 1998.

Soyler, Mehtap. *The Turkish Deep State: State Consolidation, Civil-Military Relations and Democracy*. London: Routledge, 2015.

Starr, S. Frederick and Svante E. Cornell, eds. *The Baku-Tbilisi-Ceyhan Pipeline: Oil Window to the West*. Washington, DC: Johns Hopkins University SAIS-Central Asia-Caucus Institute and Silk Road Studies Program, 2005.

Steel, Nigel and Peter Hart. *Defeat at Gallipoli*. London: Pan Macmillan; Pan Books, 2002.

Stein, Aaron, *Turkey's New Foreign Policy: Davutoglu, the AKP and the Pursuit of Regional Order*. UK: Royal United Services Institute for Defence and Security Studies-Routledge Journals, Whitehall Papers, 2014.

Stent, Angela E. *The Limits of Partnership: U.S.-Russian Relations in the Twenty-First Century*. Princeton, NJ: Princeton University Press, 2014.

Stewart, Susan, et al., eds. *Presidents, Oligarchs and Bureaucrats: Forms of Rule in the Post-Soviet Space*. Burlington, VT: Ashgate, 2012.

Stiglitz, Joseph E. *Whither Socialism?* Cambridge, MA: MIT Press, 1994.

Stiglitz, Joseph E. "Information and the Change in the Paradigm of Economics." *Nobel Prize Lecture*, December 8, 2001.

Stiglitz, Joseph E. *Globalization and Its Discontents*. New York: W.W. Norton, 2002.

Stiglitz, Joseph E. *The Great Divide: Unequal Societies and What We Can Do About Them*. New York: W.W. Norton, 2015.

Stiglitz, Joseph E. *Globalization and Its Discontents Revisited: Anti-Globalizatin in the Era of Trump*. New York: W.W. Norton & Company, 2018.

Stiglitz, Joseph E., Todd N. Tucker and Gabriel Zucman. "The Starving State: Why Capitalism's Salvation Depends on Taxation." Special Issue on "The Future of Capitalism." *NY: Foreign Affairs*. Volume 99, No. 1. January/February, 2020. pp. 30–37.

Strayer, Robert. *Why Did the Soviet Union Collapse? Understanding Historical Change*. Armonk, NY: M.E. Sharpe, Ind. 1998.

Stone, Norman. *Turkey: A Short History*. London: Thames & Hudson, 2010.

Stulberg, Adam N. *Well-Oiled Diplomacy: Strategic Manipulation and Russia's Energy Statecraft in Eurasia*. Albany, NY: SUNY Press, 2007.

Sun, Xin. "Autocrats' Dilemma: The Dual Impacts of Village Elections on Public Opinion in China," *China Journal*. Volume 71. January, 2014. pp. 109–131.

Surovell, Jeffrey. *Capitalist Russia and the West*. Burlington, VT: Ashgate, 2000.

Talmon, J.L. *The Origins of Totalitarian Democracy*. New York: Praeger, 1951 (1960 reprint).

Talmon, J.L. *Political Messianism: The Romantic Phase*. New York: Praeger, 1960.

Taplin, Mark. *Open Lands: Travels Through Russia's Once Forbidden Places*. South Royalton, VT: Steerforth Press, 1997.

Taussig, Torrey. "The Autocrat's Succession Dilemma." *The American Interest*, March 14, 2018.

Taylor, Brian D. *The Code of Putinism*. UK: Oxford University Press, 2018.

Tekin, Ali and Paul Andrew Williams. *Geo-Politics of the Euro-Asia Energy Nexus: The European Union, Russia and Turkey*. New York: Palgrave Macmillan, 2011.

Temelkuran, Ece. *Turkey: The Insane and the Melancholy*. London: Zed Books, 2015.

Tezel, Yahya Sezai. *Transformation of State and Society in Turkey: From the Ottoman Empire to the Turkish Republic*. Ankara: Roma Publications, 2005. (ISBN: 975-6349-15-8)

Therborn, Goran. *The Killing Fields of Inequality*. Cambridge, UK: Polity Press, 2013.

Thurston, Robert W. *Life and Terror in Stalin's Russia, 1934–1941*. New Haven, CT: Yale University Press, 1996.

Tocqueville, Alexis de, *The Old Regime and the French Revolution*. Garden City, NY: Doubleday, 1955.

Tocqueville, Alexis de. *Democracy in America*. Translated and edited by Harvey Mansfield and Delba Winthrop. Chicago, IL: University of Chicago Press, 2000.

Tol, Gonul. "Turkey's Endgame in Syria." *Foreign Affairs*, October 2019. https://www.foreignaffairs.com/articles/turkey/2019-10-09/turkeys-endgame-syria.

Trachtenberg, Marc. "Assessing Soviet Economic Performance During the Cold War: A Failure of Intelligence?" *Texas National Security Review*. Volume 1, No. 2. March, 2018. pp. 94–98.

Trenin, Dmitri. *The End of Eurasia: Russia on the Border Between Geopolitics and Globalization*. Washington, DC: Carnegie Endowment for International Peace, 2002.

Trenin, Dmitri. *Should We Fear Russia?* Cambridge, UK: Polity Press, 2016.

Tsygankov, Andrei P. *Russia's Foreign Policy: Change and Continuity in National Identity*. Fourth Edition. Lanham, MD: Rowman and Littlefield, 2016.

Tucker, Robert C. *Stalin in Power: The Revolution From Above 1928–1941*. New York: W.W. Norton & Co, 1990.

Türk, H. Bahadir. *Muktedir: Türk Sağ Geleneği ve Recep Tayyip Erdoğan (Competent: Turkish Right Tradition and Recep Tayyip Erdoğan)*. Istanbul: İletişim Yayınları, 2014.

Ulam, Adam B. *Stalin: The Man and His Era*. New York: The Viking Press, 1973.

United Kingdom, House of Commons, Intelligence and Security Committee. *Russia (Influence on British Politics and Elections)*, July 21, 2020.

United Nations Development Programme. *Human Development Report*. New York: 1998, 2005 and 2013.

United Nations Development Programme. *Human Development Report 1998-Russian Federation*. Moscow, 1998.

United Nations Development Programme. *Human Development Report 2005: Russian Federation—Russia in 2015: Development Goals and Policy Priorities*. Moscow, 2005.

U.S. Congress. Senate. Committee on Foreign Relations. *The War in Chechnya: Russia's Conduct, The Humanitarian Crisis, and United States Policy*. Washington, DC: War College Series, 2015.

U.S. Congress. Office of Technology Assessment. *After the Cold War: Living with Lower Defense Spending*. OTA-ITE-524. February 1992.

U.S. Department of Agriculture. *Russian Agricultural Policy and Situation Bi-Weekly Update—5*. Global Agricultural Information Network. Gain Report RS1725, April 13, 2017.

U.S. Department of Agriculture, Foreign Agricultural Service. *Grain: World Markets and Trade*. February 2020.

U.S. Special Counsel Robert S. Mueller, *Report On The Investigation Into Russian Interference In The 2016 Presidential Election*. Volumes I and II, Washington, DC, March 2019.

Vahide, Sukran. *Islam in Modern Turkey: An Intellectual Biography of Bediuzzaman Said Nursi.* Edited and with an Introduction by Ibrahim M. Abu-Rabi'. Albany, NY: State University of New York Press, 2005.

Van der Lippe, John M. *The Politics of Turkish Democracy: Ismet İnönü and the Formation of the Multi-Party System, 1938–1950.* Albany, NY: State University of New York Press, 2005.

Van Herpen, Marcel H. *Putin's Wars: The Rise of Russia's New Imperialism.* Second Edition. Lanham, MD: Rowman and Littlefield, 2015.

Vasilyeva, Nataliya and Maria L. Lagutina. *Russian Project of Eurasian Integration: Geopolitical Prospects.* Lanham, MD: Lexington Books/Rowman & Littlefield, 2016.

Vatandaş, Aydoğan. *Hungry for Power: Erdoğan's Witch Hunt and Abuse of State Power.* New York: Blue Dome Press, 2015.

Verney, Susannah and Kostas Ifantis, eds. *Turkey's Road to European Membership: National Identity and Political Change.* London and New York: Routledge, 2009.

Verona, Jack. "The Soviet March Toward Technological Superiority." *Defense.* Volume 80. March 1980.

Viktorova, L. "7 millionov evro—i ty gubernator." *Komsomol'skaia pravda.* Volume 109. July 26, 2008.

Volkogonov, Dmitri. *Stalin: Triumph and Tragedy.* Rocklin, CA: Prima Publishing, 1992.

Volkov, Vadim. *Violent Entrepreneurs: The Use of Force in the Making of Russian Capitalism.* Ithaca, NY: Cornell University Press, 2002.

Wallechninsky, David. *Tyrants: The World's 20 Worst Living Dictators.* New York: Regan/Harper Collins, 2006.

Walter R. Mebane, Jr. "Brief Election Forensics Report on the 2015 Legislative Elections in Turkey." January 20, 2016. https://pdfs.semanticscholar.org/5ddb /01a71e5dd1771cc9058607d01b22c131b430.pdf?_ga=1.187310056.179513981. 1491162419.

Way, Lucian Ahmad. "Belarus Uprising: How a Dictator Became Vulnerable." *Journal of Democracy.* Volume 31, No. 4. October, 2020. pp. 17–27.

Wedel, Janine R. *Collision and Collusion: The Strange Case of Western Aid to Eastern Europe, 1989–1998.* New York: St. Martin's Press, 1998.

Wegren, Stephen K. and Dale R. Herspring. Eds. *After Putin's Russia: Past Imperfect, Future Uncertain.* Lanham, MD: Rowman and Littlefield, 2010.

Weiss, Linda. *The Myth of the Powerless State.* Ithaca, NY: Cornell University Press, 1999.

White, Jenny B. *Islamist Mobilization in Turkey: A Study in Vernacular Politics.* Seattle and London: University of Washington Press, 2002.

White, Jenny B. *Muslim Nationalism and the New Turks.* Princeton and Oxford: Princeton University Press, 2013.

White, Stephen. *Communism and its Collapse.* London: Routledge, 1990.

White, Stephen. *Gorbachev in Power.* Cambridge, UK: Cambridge University Press, 2001.

Williams, Joan C. *Working Class Notes: Overcoming Class Cluelessness in America.* Revised Edition. Cambridge, MA: Harvard Business School Press, 2020.

Wintrobe, Ronald. *The Political Economy of Dictatorship.* UK: Cambridge University Press, 1998.

Wolin, Sheldon S. *Democracy Incorporated: Managed Democracy and the Specter of Inverted Totalitarianism.* New Edition. Princeton, NJ: Princeton University Press, 2017.

World Bank. *Poverty in Russia: An Assessment.* Report No. 14110-RU. June 13, 1995.

World Bank. *Making Transition Work for Everyone: Poverty and Inequality in Europe and Central Asia.* Washington, DC: World Bank, 2000.

World Bank. *Russian Federation: Reducing Poverty through Growth and Social Policy Reform.* Report No. 289232-RU. February 24, 2005.

World Bank. *Country Partnership Framework for the Republic of Turkey for the Period FY18–FY21.* Report No. 11096-TR. Washington, DC: World Bank, July 28, 2017.

World Bank. *Preserving Stability, Doubling Growth, Halving Poverty—How?* Russia Economic Report 40. November 2018.

World Bank. *Firm Productivity and Economic Growth in Turkey.* Turkey Productivity Report 2019. Washington, DC: World Bank, 2019.

World Bank. *Modest Growth; Focus on Informality.* Russia Economic Report 41. June 2019.

World Bank. *World Development Report.* Annual.

Wuthrich, F. Michael. *National Elections in Turkey: People, Politics, and the Party System.* Syracuse: Syracuse University Press, 2016.

Wuthrich, F. Michael and Melvyn Ingleby. "Running on 'Radical Love' in Turkey." *Journal of Democracy.* Volume 31, No. 2. April, 2020. pp. 24–40.

Yaffa, Joshua. *Between Two Fires: Truth, Ambition, and Compromise in Putin's Russia.* New York: Tim Duggan Books/Random House, 2020.

Yakovlev, Alexander N. *A Century of Violence in Soviet Russia.* New Haven, CT: Yale University Press, 2002.

Yavlinsky, Grigory, et al. *500 Days: Transition to the Market.* New York: St. Martin's Press, 1991.

Yavuz, M. Hakan. *Islamic Political Identity in Turkey.* Religion and Global Politics Series. Oxford and New York: Oxford University Press, 2003.

Yavuz, M. Hakan, ed. *The Emergence of a New Turkey: Democracy and the AK Party.* Salt Lake City: The University of Utah Press, 2006.

Yavuz, M. Hakan. *Secularism and Muslim Democracy in Turkey.* Cambridge Middle East Studies 28. Cambridge and New York: Cambridge University Press, 2009.

Yavuz, M. Hakan. *Toward an Islamic Enlightenment: The Gulen Movement.* Oxford and New York: Oxford University Press, 2013.

Yavuz, Hakan and Bayram Balci, eds. *Turkey's July 15th Coup: What Happened and Why.* Salt Lake City, UT: University of Utah Press, 2018.

Yeltsin, Boris. *Against the Grain: Boris Yeltsin, An Autobiography.* New York: Summit Books, 1990.

Yeltsin, Boris, et al. *Putsch: The Diary—Three Days That Collapsed the Empire, August 19–21, 1991.* Oakville, ON: Mosaic Press, 1992.

Yergin, Daniel A. and Joseph Stanislaw, *The Commanding Heights.* New York: Simon & Schuster, 2002.

Yesil, Bilge. *Media in Turkey: The Origins of an Authoritarian Neoliberal State.* Urbana, IL : University of Illinois Press, 2016.

Yetkin, Barış. *Popülizm ve Özal-Erdoğan.* Antalya: Y. A. R. Müdafaa-i Hukuk yayınları, 2010.

Yildirim, Onur. *Diplomacy and Displacement: Reconsidering the Turco-Greek Exchange of Populations, 1922–1934.* Middle East Studies: History, Politics, and Law. New York and London: Routledge, 2006.

Yilmaz, Suhnaz. *Turkish-American Relations, 1800–1952: Between the Stars, Stripes and the Crescent.* London: Routledge, 2015.

Yip, George S. and G. Tomas M. Hult. *Total Global Strategy.* Boston, MA: Prentice Hall, 2012.

Yüksek, Fatma Sibel. *Tayyip Erdoğan'ı Okuma Sanatı* (Art of Reading Tayyip Erdoğan). Ankara: Tanyeri Kitap, 2013.

Zakaria, Fareed. *The Post-American World.* New York: W.W. Norton & Company, 2009.

Zimmerman, William. *Ruling Russia: Authoritarianism From The Revolution to Putin.* Princeton, NJ: Princeton University Press, 2014, 2016.

Zurcher, Eric-Jan. "Ottoman Sources of Kemalist Thought." In Elizabeth Ozdalga, ed., *Late Ottoman Society: The Intellectual Legacy.* London and New York: Routledge, 2005. pp. 14–27.

Zurcher, Erik J. *Turkey: A Modern History.* London and New York: I.B. Tauris & Co Ltd, 2003. [First published in 1993] (ISBN: 1-86064-222-5)

Zurcher, Erik J. *The Young Turk Legacy and Nation Building: From the Ottoman Empire to Atatürk's Turkey.* London and New York: I. B. Tauris, 2010.

Zygar, Mikhail. *All the Kremlin's Men: Inside the Court of Vladimir Putin.* New York: Public Affairs/PBG Publishing, 2016.

Index

About the Authors

Norman A. Graham is professor of international relations at Michigan State University's James Madison College of Public Affairs. He also serves as the director of the Center for European, Russian, and Eurasian Studies at the university. Prof. Graham's long-term research interests include international security and economic relations, environmental challenges and sustainable development, Central and Southeastern Europe, Russia, and Central and South Asia. He has published nine books and numerous articles and reports. Graham has been a visiting professor at the Institute of Political Studies of the University of Lille in France; the Azerbaijan Diplomatic Academy in Baku; Ilya State University in Tbilisi, Georgia; and Kazakh National Agrarian University in Almaty. He has also served as a research associate with the United Nations, the World Health Organization, and The Futures Group. He earned his PhD in international relations and political science from Columbia University.

Timur Kocaoglu is Adjunct Professor at Michigan State University, where he also served as associate director of the Center for European, Russian, and Eurasian Studies (CERES) at Michigan State University. He has previously taught at Koc and Marmara universities in Istanbul and served as the director of the Strategic Studies Center, Koc University. Kocaoglu received his B.A. (1971) at the Department of Turkish Language and Literature of Istanbul University; M.A. (1977) & PhD (1982) at the Department of Middle East Languages and Cultures, Columbia University, New York. He has published books, book chapters, and articles in English, Turkish, Uzbek, Kazakh, and Russian languages on politics, cultural history, literature, and linguistics of the Turkic peoples in various Eurasian countries.

Folke Lindahl is professor emeritus of political theory and constitutional democracy at Michigan State University's James Madison College of Public Affairs. Prof. Lindahl's research and teaching interests include Tocqueville and American political thought, Eastern European politics and history, Turkish politics and history, and Caribbean political thought. He has published articles and edited books in all these fields. He has been visiting professor at the political science department at Uppsala University in Sweden, Babes-Bolyai University in Cluj, Romania, the Institute of Political Studies of the University of Lille in France, and Ilya State University in Tibilisi, Georgia. He earned his PhD in political science from the University of Hawaii. He has received an award for Outstanding Service to Study Abroad at Michigan State University and Outstanding Faculty Award for Excellence in Research, Teaching, and Contribution to Latin American and Caribbean Studies at Michigan State University. He has devoted the past ten years to researching and teaching about Turkish and Eurasian history and politics.

www.ingramcontent.com/pod-product-compliance
Lightning Source LLC
Chambersburg PA
CBHW022304280326
41932CB00010B/981